The Combat History of
GERMAN HEAVY
ANTI-TANK UNIT 653
IN WORLD WAR II

The Combat History of

GERMAN HEAVY ANTI-TANK UNIT 653
IN WORLD WAR II

✛ KARLHEINZ MÜNCH ✛

STACKPOLE
BOOKS

Copyright © 1997 by J. J. Fedorowicz Publishing, Inc.

Published in 2005 by
STACKPOLE BOOKS
5067 Ritter Road
Mechanicsburg, PA 17055
www.stackpolebooks.com

www.jjfpub.mb.ca

Printed in the United States of America

10 9 8 7 6 5 4 3 2 1

FIRST EDITION

Library of Congress Cataloging-in-Publication Data

Münch, Karlheinz.
 [Combat history of Schwere Panzerjager Abteilung 653]
 The combat history of German Heavy Anti-Tank Unit 653 in World War II / Karlheinz Münch ;
translated by Bo H. Friesen.— 1st ed.
  p. cm.
 Originally published : Combat history of Schwere Panzerjäger Abteilung 653. Winnipeg, Man. : J.J.
Fedorowicz, c1997.
 Includes bibliographical references.
 ISBN-13: 978-0-8117-3242-0
 ISBN-10: 0-8117-3242-8
 1. Germany. Heer. Schwere Panzerjäger Abteilung, 653. 2. World War, 1939–1945—Regimental
histories—Germany. 3. World War, 1939–1945—Campaigns—Eastern Front. I. Title.

D757.57653rd .M86 2005
940.54'217—dc22
                                        2005016410

TABLE OF CONTENTS

PREFACE

Schwere Panzerjäger-Abteilung 653 (653rd Heavy Antitank Battalion) was equipped with the heaviest tank destroyers in the German armed forces during its operational period from 1943–1945. These were the Sd.Kfz. 184 Panzerjäger "Ferdinand"—renamed "Elefant" ("Elephant") in February 1944—and, after September 1944, the Sd.Kfz. 186 Panzerjäger "Jagdtiger" ("Hunting Tiger"). Technical literature inside and outside the country contains many descriptions of both types of these tank destroyers, and the technology behind these vehicles is certainly covered adequately. What has been absent until now is a close examination of one of the heavy antitank battalions that fielded these weapons systems. The book before you is an effort to close this gap.

Sturmgeschütz-Abteilung 197 (the 197th Assault Gun Battalion), established in November 1940, was the nucleus of schwere Panzerjäger-Abteilung 653. It is still unclear to this day why this particular assault gun battalion was chosen for the conversion. The material available at the Freiburg Military Archives offers no clues. Perhaps the selection of Sturmgeschütz-Abteilung 197 was due not only to its outstanding military achievements between 1941 and 1942, but also because of good personal relations between its commander, Hauptmann (Captain) Steinwachs, and other officers at the highest level of the armed forces high command.

There existed a rivalry between the artillery, to which the assault gun battalions belonged, and the armor force, which laid claim to the production of the heaviest tracked vehicles. The Inspector General of Armored Forces at that time, Generaloberst Guderian, settled this issue, at least in the case of Sturmgeschütz-Abteilung 197, with an order issued on 28 February 1943. Sturmgeschütz-Abteilung 197 was transferred from the assault-gun branch of the artillery to the antitank branch of the armored forces. Many seasoned assault artillerymen found this change painful, as most of them had volunteered for duty with these elite assault gun formations. The cohesion and camaraderie in this formation had been forged and grown during its two years of combat duty.

ABOUT THE VEHICLES

The Ferdinand/Elefant tank destroyer is usually considered a faulty design by Professor Ferdinand Porsche, whereas the Jagdtiger enjoys the myth of invulnerability to this day. Both judgments are too superficial, of course, and portray a false portrait of the actual performance of these vehicles. It is still debated whether the German tank-destroyer branch lacked a heavy tank destroyer from 1942–1944 that met the criteria for a successful tank-destroyer design: Solid construction; adequate protection for the crew; and a heavy caliber, long-range gun, which could successfully counter the masses of Russian tanks.

All these requirements were finally fulfilled in May 1944 when the "Jagdpanther" tank destroyer (Sd.Kfz. 176) was delivered to the field. According to the experts, this was the optimal tank destroyer of the time. The history of these tank destroyers, as fielded to schwere Panzer-Jäger-Abteilung 654, are covered in the companion volume to this book, which has been published by JJ Fedorowicz Publishing., Inc.

The Porsche Tiger VK 4501 (P) tank chassis was used to bridge the period until the Jagdpanther series was complete. These chassis were available from the originally planned Porsche Tiger production and, after several modifications, were completed by the Alkett Company. The fact that the technology behind the Ferdinand was too complex and its weight too heavy became clear as early as the testing phase. It was the forces in the field, however, who bore the brunt of the logistical problems brought about by the need for repair parts and the incredible efforts required to recover and maintain damaged Ferdinande. Despite the difficulties associated with maintaining this vehicle, the crews were generally very satisfied with it. The enormous armor and the 88 mm 43 L/71 gun made up for many automotive deficiencies. The accuracy and penetrating power of this gun remained unmatched up to the end of the war. Even though Hitler ordered the name of the Ferdinand changed to Elefant in February 1944, the vehicle remained the "good old Ferdinand" among its crews until the end of the war.

Another step in the wrong direction was the production of the "Jagdtiger" tank destroyer. This vehicle, with a combat weight of 75 tons, was also too heavy and completely underpowered with the series of engines available at that time. Jagdtiger, which were often taken out of frontline service by the smallest of mechanical problems, frequently had to be abandoned because there was no means of recovering the gigantic vehicles. The main gun of the Jagdtiger, the 128 mm Pak 80/L55, had enormous penetrating power and range, so that no enemy tank at that time could stand up to it. Its rate of fire, constrained by the separation of projectile and casing, remained far behind the 88 mm Pak, however. Its above-average armor protection, which saved the lives of many crewmembers, was the vehicle's greatest advantage. Its combat value was mediocre.

The book before you describes in word and picture, 60 years after the end of the war, the achievements of the members of schwere Panzerjäger-Abteilung 653 and the combat operations they were employed in. My thanks to all former members of Sturmgeschütz-Abteilung 197 and schwere Panzerjäger-Abteilung 653, and their survivors, who gave me support over the course of many years and helped me in my efforts.

Karlheinz Münch
Schwetzingen, Germany

AUTHOR'S ACKNOWLEDGEMENTS

I would like to take this opportunity to thank the following individuals and institutions:

Mr. John Fedorowicz for agreeing to originally publish this book.

Mr. Jean Restayn for preparing outstanding color prints.

Mr. Hilary L. Doyle for the use of his drawings.

Mr. George Bradford for creating the organizational charts.

Brigadier General (Ret.) of the Austrian Army, Dr. Gerald de la Renotiere. Without his energetic help and personal intercession, my research would not have been possible.

Mr. Heinrich Appel (President of the Association of Former Members of Sturmgeschütz-Abteilung 197 / schwere Panzerjäger-Abteilung 653) for his cheerful support of my endeavors.

Mr. Reinhold Schlabs, Mr. Heinz Henning (deceased), Mr. Heinz Jaspers (deceased), Mr. Karl Seitz and Mr. Rolf Schleicher for their many willing suggestions and personal friendships.

Mr. Emil Bürgin, Mr. Arnold Knopp, Mr. Peter Kohns and Mr. Horst Theis for the use of their diaries.

Mr. Thomas L. Jentz for much information and data about the vehicles.

The German Federal Archives in Koblenz and Freiburg/Breisgau.

The Wehrmachtsauskunftsstelle in Berlin.

Mr. Bernd Misteie for technical advice.

Mr. Hartrnut Gerner for his friendly support.

Finally, my family, for their years of help.

The following persons and institutions provided information or pictures:

Walter Alberts (3./schwere Panzerjäger-Abteilung 653)

Kurt Albinus (1./schwere Panzerjäger-Abteilung 653, 2./schwere Panzerjäger-Abteilung 653)

Thomas Anderson

Heinrich Appel (3./Sturmgeschütz-Abteilung 197, 3./schwere Panzerjäger-Abteilung 653)

Bill Auerbach

Frau Baasch

Dr. Herbert Bauermeister (deceased) (Sturmgeschütz-Abteilung 197, schwere Panzerjäger-Abteilung 653, schweres Panzerjäger-Regiment 656)

Isidor Bayerle (Headquarters Company/schwere Panzerjäger-Abteilung 653, 3./schwere Panzerjäger-Abteilung 653)

August Beck (2./Sturmgeschütz-Abteilung 197, 2./schwere Panzerjäger-Abteilung 653, schwere Panzer-Zerstörer-Kompanie 614)

Gerhard Berzel

Ferdinand Biermann (3./Sturmgeschütz-Abteilung 197, 3./schwere Panzerjäger-Abteilung 653)

Josef Bösmüller (Maintenance Company/schwere Panzerjäger-Abteilung 653)

Willi Bohlen (Maintenance Company/schwere Panzerjäger-Abteilung 653)

Heinz Borngässer (2./schwere Panzerjäger-Abteilung 653, Headquarters Company/schwere Panzerjäger-Abteilung 653)

Armin Bortoluzzi

Alfred Bosch (Maintenance Company/schwere Panzerjäger-Abteilung 653)

Georg Bose (Sturmgeschütz-Abteilung 177)

Gerhard Braun (2./Sturmgeschütz-Abteilung 197, 2./schwere Panzerjäger-Abteilung 653, schwere Panzer-Zerstörer-Kompanie 614)

Rudolf Braun (2./schwere Panzerjäger-Abteilung 653)

Anton Brunnthaler (Maintenance Company/schwere Panzerjäger-Abteilung 653)

Bernhard Bredohl (schwere Panzer-Zerstörer-Kompanie 614)

Heinrich Büchele (1./schwere Panzerjäger-Abteilung 653)

Walter Büchner (Headquarters Company/schwere Panzerjäger-Abteilung 653)

Emil Bürgin (1./schwere Panzerjäger-Abteilung 653)

Frau Irmgard Busch (Gerhard Busch: deceased. Headquarters Companies of Sturmgeschütz-Abteilung 197 and schwere Panzerjäger-Abteilung 653 and 1./schwere Panzerjäger-Abteilung 653)

Hermann Cantz (deceased) (1./Sturmgeschütz-Abteilung 197, 1./schwere Panzerjäger-Abteilung 653)

Matthias Carpentier (3./schwere Panzerjäger-Abteilung 653)

Karl Correll (Maintenance Company/schwere Panzerjäger-Abteilung 653)

Hans Creutz (Headquarters Company [Antiaircraft Platoon]/schwere Panzerjäger-Abteilung 653)

Karl-Heinz Oanisch (1./schwere Panzer-Jäger-Abteilung 654)

Johann Oemleitner (Maintenance Company/schwere Panzerjäger-Abteilung 653)

De Meyer, Stefan

Andrew Devey

Herbert von Deyn (1./Sturmgeschütz-Abteilung 197, 1./schwere Panzerjäger-Abteilung 653)

Werner Diehl (Headquarters Company/schwere Panzerjäger-Abteilung 653)

Hans Distler (1./schwere Panzerjäger-Abteilung 653)

Ernst Dörr (Headquarters Company/schwere Panzerjäger-Abteilung 653)

Frau Drews

Wilhelm Duschek (Headquarters Company/schwere Panzerjäger-Abteilung 653)

Heiner F. Duske

Alfred Engelhardt (2./schwere Panzerjäger-Abteilung 653)

Julius Faulhammer (Sturmgeschütz-Abteilung 197 / schwere Panzerjäger-Abteilung 653)

Karl Faust (Headquarters Company/schwere Panzerjäger-Abteilung 653)

Frau Federer

Dieter Fehnle

Hans Fehr (Headquarters Company/schwere Panzerjäger-Abteilung 653)

Karl-Heinz Flick (3./Sturmgeschütz-Abteilung 197, 3./schwere Panzerjäger-Abteilung 653)

Wilhelm Flintrop (1./Sturmgeschütz-Abteilung 197,1./schwere Panzerjäger-Abteilung 653)

Johann Flock (Headquarters Company/schwere Panzerjäger-Abteilung 653, 3./schwere Panzerjäger-Abteilung 653)

Heinrich Frank (deceased) (3./schwere Panzerjäger-Abteilung 653)

Ludwig Gandenberger (Maintenance Company/schwere Panzerjäger-Abteilung 653)

Hans Gardung (2./Sturmgeschütz-Abteilung 197, 2./schwere Panzerjäger-Abteilung 653, schwere Panzer-Zerstörer-Kompanie 614)

Gerhard Garrecht (Headquarters Company [Armored Antiaircraft Platoon]/schwere Panzerjäger-Abteilung 653)

Emil Gaul (3./schwere Panzerjäger-Abteilung 653)

Johann Gebele (Headquarters Company/schwere Panzerjäger-Abteilung 653, 2./schwere Panzerjäger-Abteilung 653)

Max Gierl (Headquarters Company/schwere Panzerjäger-Abteilung 653)

Johann Glanz (deceased) (1./schwere Panzerjäger-Abteilung 653)

Frau Göggere (Kaspar Göggerle [deceased]: 3./schwere Panzerjäger-Abteilung 653)

Josef Göttert (Maintenance Company/schwere Panzerjäger-Abteilung 653)

Horst Golinski (1./Sturmgeschütz-Abteilung 197, 1./schwere Panzerjäger-Abteilung 653)

Karl Gresch (1./schwere Panzerjäger-Abteilung 653)

Bernhard Grethen (Headquarters Company/schwere Panzerjäger-Abteilung 653)

Josef Gruissem (Sturmgeschütz-Abteilung 197, Headquarters Company/schwere Panzerjäger-Abteilung 653 1./schwere Panzerjäger-Abteilung 653)

Nikolaus Haas (1./schwere Panzerjäger-Abteilung 653)

Hans Habeck (2./Sturmgeschütz-Abteilung 197,2./schwere Panzerjäger-Abteilung 653, schwere Panzer-Zerstörer-Kompanie 614)

Frau Haberland

Ernst-August Hagelstein (2/654, Headquarters Company/schwere Panzerjäger-Abteilung 653, 2./schwere Panzerjäger-Abteilung 653)

James Haley

Hans Hanseder (deceased) (Support Company/schwere Panzerjäger-Abteilung 653)

Otto Hecker (deceased) (2./Sturmgeschütz-Abteilung 197, 2./schwere Panzerjäger-Abteilung 653, schwere Panzer-Zerstörer-Kompanie 614)

Albin Heinickel (deceased) (3./Sturmgeschütz-Abteilung 197, 3./schwere Panzerjäger-Abteilung 653)

Heinz Henning (deceased) (1./Sturmgeschütz-Abteilung 197, 1./schwere Panzerjäger-Abteilung 653)

Gustav Hentz (Maintenance Company/schwere Panzerjäger-Abteilung 653)

Alfred Hertel (1./schwere Panzerjäger-Abteilung 653)

Hans Heusel (Maintenance Company/schwere Panzerjäger-Abteilung 653)

Frau Holzapfel

Walter Huleja (2./Sturmgeschütz-Abteilung 197, 2./schwere Panzerjäger-Abteilung 653, schwere Panzer-Zerstörer-Kompanie 614)

Frau Ilse Irmscher

Emil Issler (3./schwere Panzerjäger-Abteilung 653)

Alois Jacob (Maintenance Company/schwere Panzerjäger-Abteilung 653)

Karl Jäger (deceased) (3./schwere Panzerjäger-Abteilung 653)

Gerhard Janoske (3./Sturmgeschütz-Abteilung 197, 3./schwere Panzerjäger-Abteilung 653)

Heinz Jaspers (deceased) (3./Sturmgeschütz-Abteilung 197, 3./schwere Panzerjäger-Abteilung 653)

Markus Jaugitz

Thomas L. Jentz

Frau Jörger (Kriegsverwaltungsrat Erhard Jörger [deceased]: Maintenance Company/schwere Panzerjäger-Abteilung 653)

Prof. Dr. Antonius John

Bruno Kahl (Sturmpanzer-Abteilung 216)

Toni Käfel (2./schwere Panzerjäger-Abteilung 653,schwere Panzer-Zerstörer-Kompanie 614)

Hans Kämmerer (Headquarters Company/schwere Panzerjäger-Abteilung 653)

Edwin Kapitz (Sturmartillerie Association)

Karl Klemme (2./schwere Panzerjäger-Abteilung 653)

Hans Knippenberg (1./schwere Panzerjäger-Abteilung 653)

Hermann Knack (Headquarters Company/schwere Panzerjäger-Abteilung 653, 3./schwere Panzerjäger-Abteilung 653)

Arnold Knopp (Regimental Staff/schweres Panzerjäger-Regiment 656)

Werner Kobrow (2./schwere Panzerjäger-Abteilung 653, schwere Panzer-Zerstörer-Kompanie 614)

Franz Koebergen (Headquarters Company [Antiaircraft Platoon]/schwere Panzerjäger-Abteilung 653)

Johann Köhler (Headquarters Company [Armored Antiaircraft Platoon]/schwere Panzerjäger-Abteilung 653)

Peter Kohns (schwere Panzer-Jäger-Abteilung 654, Headquarters Company/schwere Panzerjäger-Abteilung 653, 2./schwere Panzerjäger-Abteilung 653)

Frau Konnak

Gustav Koss (1./schwere Panzerjäger-Abteilung 653)

Frau Kretschmer

Helmut Kreyenhagen (schwere Panzer-Jäger-Abteilung 654, 3./schwere Panzerjäger-Abteilung 653)

Horst Kürschner (Headquarters Company/schwere Panzerjäger-Abteilung 653, 3./schwere Panzerjäger-Abteilung 653)

Franz Kurrer (schwere Panzer-Jäger-Abteilung 654, 3./schwere Panzerjäger-Abteilung 653)

Frau Leisten

Otto Leister (1./schwere Panzerjäger-Abteilung 653)

Georg Lösch (1./Sturmgeschütz-Abteilung 197, 1./schwere Panzerjäger-Abteilung 653)

Kurt Lohrmann (2./Sturmgeschütz-Abteilung 197, 2./schwere Panzerjäger-Abteilung 653, schwere Panzer-Zerstörer-Kompanie 614)

Hermann Looft (1./schwere Panzerjäger-Abteilung 653)

Walter Lubrich (Maintenance Company/schwere Panzerjäger-Abteilung 653)

Rudolf Ludwig (Headquarters Companies of Sturmgeschütz-Abteilung 197 and schwere Panzerjäger-Abteilung 653)

Fritz Maddaus (deceased) (Sturmgeschütz-Abteilung 197, 1./schwere Panzerjäger-Abteilung 653)

Frau Markmann

Willi Maxheim (3./Sturmgeschütz-Abteilung 197, 3./schwere Panzerjäger-Abteilung 653, 2./schwere Panzerjäger-Abteilung 653)

Kurt Meins (1./schwere Panzerjäger-Abteilung 653)

Josef Möller (1./Sturmgeschütz-Abteilung 197,1./schwere Panzerjäger-Abteilung 653)

Frau Anneliese Moos

Johann Mühlhauser (2./schwere Panzerjäger-Abteilung 653)

Robert Müller (2./schwere Panzerjäger-Abteilung 653)

Karlheinz Münch

Claus Richard Muschick

Frau Mussler (Josef Mussler (deceased): Maintenance Company/schwere Panzerjäger-Abteilung 653)

Frau Muszynski

Gerhard Nahke (3./schwere Panzerjäger-Abteilung 653)

Heinrich Nerger (deceased) (3./Sturmgeschütz-Abteilung 197, 3./schwere Panzerjäger-Abteilung 653)

S. Netrebenko

Karl Neunert (3./Sturmgeschütz-Abteilung 197, 3./schwere Panzerjäger-Abteilung 653)

Johann Nitbauer (Maintenance Company/schwere Panzerjäger-Abteilung 653)

Frau Nitschner

Christian Noethen (3./Sturmgeschütz-Abteilung 197, 3./schwere Panzerjäger-Abteilung 653)

Peter Nonsen (2./schwere Panzerjäger-Abteilung 653, schwere Panzer-Zerstörer-Kompanie 614)

Dr. Günther Northoff (3./schwere Panzerjäger-Abteilung 653)

Wilhelm Opitz (3./Sturmgeschütz-Abteilung 197, 3./schwere Panzerjäger-Abteilung 653)

Kurt Pätzold (Maintenance Company/schwere Panzerjäger-Abteilung 653)

Walter Paulus (deceased) (2./schwere Panzerjäger-Abteilung 653)

Otto Peters (1./Sturmgeschütz-Abteilung 197, 1./schwere Panzerjäger-Abteilung 653)

Willi Petry (3./Sturmgeschütz-Abteilung 197, 3./schwere Panzerjäger-Abteilung 653)

Hans Pfeiffer Headquarters Company/schwere Panzerjäger-Abteilung 653)

Herbert Pietscht (2./Sturmgeschütz-Abteilung 197)

Karl Pitz (Maintenance Company/schwere Panzerjäger-Abteilung 653)

Fritz Poischen (1./schwere Panzerjäger-Abteilung 653)

Dr. Werner Regenberg

Josef Reischer (Headquarters Company [Antiaircraft Platoon]/schwere Panzerjäger-Abteilung 653)

Claus Reißner

Dr. Gerald de la Renotiere (Headquarters Company/Sturmgeschütz-Abteilung 197, 3./Sturmgeschütz-Abteilung 197)

Hubert Retterath (2./schwere Panzerjäger-Abteilung 653)

Albert Riecker (1./Sturmgeschütz-Abteilung 197, 1./schwere Panzerjäger-Abteilung 653)

Willi Ries (3./schwere Panzerjäger-Abteilung 653)

Adam Rihm (2./schwere Panzerjäger-Abteilung 653)

Karl Rist (3./Sturmgeschütz-Abteilung 197, 3./schwere Panzerjäger-Abteilung 653)

Dipl. Ing. Wolfgang Römer (Maintenance Companies of schwere Panzerjäger-Abteilung 653, schwere Panzer-Jäger-Abteilung 654 and schweres Panzerjäger-Regiment 656)

Frau Elfriede Rohne

Ulrich Rohrbach

Walter Roosch (schweres Panzerjäger-Regiment 656)

Friedrich Roth (Maintenance Company/schwere Panzerjäger-Abteilung 653)

Helmut Ruschmeyer (Maintenance Company/schwere Panzerjäger-Abteilung 653)

Rolf Sabrowsky (3./Sturmgeschütz-Abteilung 197, 3./schwere Panzerjäger-Abteilung 653)

Frau Sälzler

Herbert Sauer (2./schwere Panzerjäger-Abteilung 653, schwere Panzer-Zerstörer-Kompanie 614)

Alfred Schab (2./schwere Panzerjäger-Abteilung 653, schwere Panzer-Zerstörer-Kompanie 614)

Frau Anni Schade (Peter Schade (deceased): 3./Sturmgeschütz-Abteilung 197, 3./schwere Panzerjäger-Abteilung 653)

Frau Schäfer

Heinrich Schäfer (deceased) (1./Sturmgeschütz-Abteilung 197, 1./schwere Panzerjäger-Abteilung 653)

Andreas Schauer (1./schwere Panzerjäger-Abteilung 653)

Frau Scheeler

Kurt Scherer (Headquarters Company/schwere Panzerjäger-Abteilung 653)

Alfred Schiestl (deceased) (3./Sturmgeschütz-Abteilung 197, 3./schwere Panzerjäger-Abteilung 653)

Reinhold Schlabs (1./Sturmgeschütz-Abteilung 197, 1./schwere Panzerjäger-Abteilung 653)

Rolf Schleicher (1./Sturmgeschütz-Abteilung 197, 1./schwere Panzerjäger-Abteilung 653, Maintenance Company/schwere Panzerjäger-Abteilung 653)

Johann Schleiß (Headquarters Company/schwere Panzerjäger-Abteilung 653)

Emanuel Schlenska (2./Sturmgeschütz-Abteilung 197, 2./schwere Panzerjäger-Abteilung 653, schwere Panzer-Zerstörer-Kompanie 614)

Erich Schmidhäuser (Sturmgeschütz-Abteilung 197)

Andreas Schmitt (1./Sturmgeschütz-Abteilung 197, 1./schwere Panzerjäger-Abteilung 653)

Wolfgang Schneider

Kurt Schöneckert (Headquarters Company/schwere Panzerjäger-Abteilung 653)

Friedrich Schütz (Headquarters Company/schwere Panzerjäger-Abteilung 653)

Willi Schulmayer (3./Sturmgeschütz-Abteilung 197, 3./schwere Panzerjäger-Abteilung 653)

Frau Schwarz (Fritz Schwarz (deceased): 3./Sturmgeschütz-Abteilung 197, 3./schwere Panzerjäger-Abteilung 653)

Frau Schwarz (Kriegsverwaltungsrat Wilhelm Schwarz (deceased): schwere Panzer-Jäger-Abteilung 654)

Frau Marga Schwarz

Karl Seik (Sturmgeschütz-Abteilung 197, Headquarters Company/schwere Panzerjäger-Abteilung 653, Panzerjäger-Ersatz-Abteilung 17)

Frau Skorpil

Walter Spielberger

Johann Spielmann (1./Sturmgeschütz-Abteilung 197, 1./schwere Panzerjäger-Abteilung 653)

Kolbermoor (city)

Schwetzingen (city archives: Mr. Heuss)

Rainer Statzt (deceased) (schwere Panzer-Jäger-Abteilung 654, 1./schwere Panzerjäger-Abteilung 653)

Andreas Steiger (Headquarters Company/schwere Panzerjäger-Abteilung 653)

Herbert Steinmüller (3./schwere Panzerjäger-Abteilung 653, Headquarters Company/schwere Panzerjäger-Abteilung 653)

Ernst Stenzel (3./Sturmgeschütz-Abteilung 197, 3./schwere Panzerjäger-Abteilung 653)

Georg Sterrenberg (schweres Panzerjäger-Regiment 656)

Herbert Ströll (1./schwere Panzerjäger-Abteilung 653)

Herr Stötter

Hans Tams (Headquarters Companies of Sturmgeschütz-Abteilung 197 and schwere Panzerjäger-Abteilung 653)

Heinrich Teriete (Sturmgeschütz-Abteilung 197, schwere Panzerjäger-Abteilung 653, schwere Panzer-Zerstörer-Kompanie 614)

Horst Theis (Maintenance Company/schwere Panzerjäger-Abteilung 653, 3./schwere Panzerjäger-Abteilung 653)

Heinrich Tillwick (3./Sturmgeschütz-Abteilung 197, 3./schwere Panzerjäger-Abteilung 653)

Kurt Titus (1./Sturmgeschütz-Abteilung 197, 1./schwere Panzerjäger-Abteilung 653)

Frau Else Tumbrink

Helmut Ulbricht (Sturmgeschütz-Abteilung 197, schwere Panzerjäger-Abteilung 653)

Walter Waßmuth (1./schwere Panzerjäger-Abteilung 653)

Fridolin Weber (3./Sturmgeschütz-Abteilung 197, 3./schwere Panzerjäger-Abteilung 653)

Frau Weiß

Ruppert Weiß (3./schwere Panzerjäger-Abteilung 653)

Arthur Weniger (deceased) (3./Sturmgeschütz-Abteilung 197, 3./schwere Panzerjäger-Abteilung 653)

Frau Wilbs

Jürgen Wilhelm

Dr. Maximilian Wirsching (1./schwere Panzerjäger-Abteilung 653)

Max P. Wulff (Headquarters Company/schwere Panzerjäger-Abteilung 653, 3./schwere Panzerjäger-Abteilung 653)

Alois Zeller (Headquarters Company/schwere Panzerjäger-Abteilung 653)

Emanuel Zentgraf (3./schwere Panzerjäger-Abteilung 653)

Willi Zimmermann (Sturmgeschütz-Abteilung 197)

Henning von Zitzewitz (schweres Panzerjäger-Regiment 656)

PUBLISHERS' ACKNOWLEDGEMENTS

We wish to thank all the people who have contributed to the publishing of this book, in particular:

George Bradford: Typesetting
Bo H. Friesen: Translation
Jean Restayn: Color Illustrations and Organizational Diagrams
Hilary Doyle: Plan View Drawings

We also wish to thank you the reader for purchasing this book, and all those of you who have purchased our other books, and have written us with your kind words of praise and encouragement. It gives us impetus to continue to publish translations of the best in-print German-language books on this field of interest and specially commissioned books.

John Fedorowicz,
Michael Olive,
Robert Edwards &
Ian Clunie
JJ Fedorowicz Publishing, Inc.

EDITOR'S NOTE

J. J. Fedorowicz Publishing has a well earned reputation for publishing exceptionally high-quality books on German World War II subjects, and *The Combat History of German Heavy Anti-Tank Unit 653 in World War II* is a prime example. I've been a huge fan of their books for years, and so I jumped at the chance to introduce this book to a whole new audience of readers in an attractive and very affordable edition. Those familiar with the original will note that some changes have been made due to the exigencies of publishing in a new format, but always with a mind to maintaining the same high standards to create a comprehensive photographic survey and detailed historical record of the 653—and its Ferdinands, Elephants, and Jagdtigers—in combat.

Chris Evans
History Editor
Stackpole Books

TRANSLATOR'S NOTE

I took a break from Volume 3 of the "Das Reich" series—published by JJ Fedorowicz Publishing, Inc.—to work on Karlheinz Münch's excellent history of schwere Panzerjäger-Abteilung 653. Having served with heavy tanks for 9 years in the American Army, I was astounded at the similarities in the problems both our formations experienced. The common bane of heavy armored vehicles seems to be mobility. This is not a problem of how fast the vehicle can move, but rather the limitations on where it can move. Like the Elefanten and Jagdtiger, our M1 and M1A1 tanks could find very few bridges that would hold their 65-ton combat weight. This made for many tense moments with our backs to rivers whose bridges could not even support half of our behemoths' weights. Soft ground, snow and even sand presented similar problems. I vividly remember my command tank breaking through the crust of a dry lake bed during the Persian Gulf War and becoming mired in the slime below. It was a completely unexpected event in the middle of the Arabian Desert! The fact that no other tanks or recovery vehicles could get close enough to tow us out compounded the problem. We finally connected several towing cables together and used a series of vehicles to drag the tank free. Another formation actually had to blow up one of its M1A1's when it was unable to recover it from another such lakebed, and this was during an overwhelming victory with complete air superiority!

Maintenance problems are another similarity. Although our M1A1's were not underpowered like the Jagdtiger, the jet turbine engine and transmission were very delicate and finicky devices. Any tank older than two years spent the majority of its time in the motor pool. Repairs and preventive maintenance could not keep up with the rate of mechanical failures. Just like the Jagdtiger and Elefanten of World War II, the American heavy tanks performed magnificently in combat and could take a tremendous amount of punishment. Getting them to the front under their own power was an entirely different matter, however. It is very interesting how history repeats itself, despite great leaps in technology.

This battalion history contains a cornucopia of information in an area where precious little exists. I hope you enjoy reading it as much as I enjoyed translating it.

B. H. Friesen
Major, USAR
Fairview, Texas

1. Batterie

Gruppe Führer

1. Zug

2. Zug

3. Zug

2. Batterie

Gruppe Führer

1. Zug

2. Zug

3. Zug

3. Batterie

Gruppe Führer

1. Zug

2. Zug

Establishment and Operational Deployment of Sturmgeschütz-Abteilung 197

(NOVEMBER 1940 TO JANUARY 1943)

In late November 1940, Sturmgeschütz-Abteilung 192 and Sturmgeschütz-Abteilung 197 were prepared for activation by the VII./Artillerie-Lehr-Regiment (Artillery Instructional Regiment) at Jüterbog, near Berlin. The Army High Command released the officer manning list for Sturmgeschütz-Abteilung 197 on 22 November 1940:

Battalion Commander:	Major Helmut Christ
Adjutant:	Oberleutnant Hanns Liedtke
Battalion Liaison Officer:	Oberleutnant Adrian Gärtner
Battalion Physician:	Assistenzarzt Dr. Herbert Bauermeister
Battalion Paymaster:	Oberzahlmeister Karl Koch
Commander of Headquarters Battery 197:	Oberleutnant Gerald de la Renotiére
	(Leutnant Werner Preusser, Leutnant Karl Seitz)
Commander of the 1./ Sturmgeschütz-Abteilung 197:	Oberleutnant Ulrich Brinke
Commander of the 2./ Sturmgeschütz-Abteilung 197:	Oberleutnant Führ
Commander of the 3./ Sturmgeschütz-Abteilung 197:	Oberleutnant Goebe
Battalion Engineer:	Kriegsverwaltungsrat Rudolf Schaffranek

The date of activation was Monday, 25 November 1940. Home station was the new section of the Jüterbog Training Area.

Sturmgeschütz-Abteilung 197 remained at Jüterbog until early February 1941 and conducted training to prepare it for employment as an assault-gun formation. The more leisurely pace of training during the earlier part of the war allowed for a great deal of ultimate unit cohesion and bonding between and among the battalion personnel.

On 4 February 1941, the assault guns were loaded aboard trains in the Zinna Forest, and the battalion moved to Military District VIII at Brieg (in Silesia, now Poland). Sturmgeschütz-Abteilung 197 was attached to the 262. Infanterie-Division of Generalleutnant Theißen upon its arrival. The 262. Infanterie-

Division was part of the IX. Armee-Korps under General der Infanterie Geyer. The corps headquarters was at Oppeln. The IX. Armee-Korps belonged to the 17. Armee, whose headquarters was in Zakopane. Generalleutnant Theißen visited the battalion on 13 February 1941 and watched the 1./Sturmgeschütz-Abteilung 197 move in close order on the parade field at the Mudra Barracks.

The battalion participated in various training exercises between 17 February 1941 and 25 March 1941 to practice working with infantry units. Various command signal exercises also took place to improve command and control between platoon leaders (sometimes a dismounted noncommissioned officer) and the vehicle commanders. General der Infanterie Geyer reviewed the 3./Sturmgeschütz-Abteilung 197, brought up to full strength with vehicles from the 1./Sturmgeschütz-Abteilung 197, on 26 February 1941. Two other general officers, as well as officers from the IX. Armee-Korps, also attended the review.

Maneuvers also took place with an infantry battalion maneuver also took place, with the 2./Sturmgeschütz-Abteilung 197 (minus its 3rd Platoon) attached.

The battalion received an order by motorcycle messenger on 29 March 1941 to begin preparations for a unit movement. Troop morale soared as everyone anticipated the coming operation.

The Balkan Campaign began on 6 April 1941. The German railways did not provide the necessary personnel and transport cars, so the movement time was continuously moved back. The assault guns and support vehicles finally began loading at the Brieg rail yards on 8 April 1941, and the first transport train began moving at 0358 hours. The route ran from Brieg, through Ostrau (Moravia), then Lundenburg, to Vienna, reaching the city on 9 April 1941. From there, the train passed through Wiener Neustadt, the Semmering Pass (986 meters above sea level) and Graz. The batteries unloaded at various stations (Headquarters Battery/Sturmgeschütz-Abteilung 197 in Wildon, 1./Sturmgeschütz-Abteilung 197 in Kalsdorf, 2./Sturmgeschütz-Abteilung 197 at an unknown location and the 3./Sturmgeschütz-Abteilung 197 in Graz (East). The batteries established billets in the area bounded by Ehrenhausen, Gamlitz and the Yugoslavian border.

Sturmgeschütz-Abteilung 197 was attached to the 132. Infanterie-Division, but it was unable to function as the advance guard for this division because the bridges across the Drau River had been destroyed. The battalion remained idle while waiting for completion of the 16-ton bridge. The battalion finally crossed the river at Pettau on 13 April 1941. From there, it proceeded through Agram towards Karlstadt (Karlovac) without encountering enemy resistance, reaching the city on 16 April 1941. Since Serbia had capitulated in the meantime, the advance, which had reached Banja-Luca with some elements, halted. The battalion remained in Karlstadt. The battalion began its movement back to the Reich on 20 April 1941 in the following order. The march route went through Novaki, Jastrebarsko, Krapinske Toplice and Krapina to Marburg (Maribor). From there, it paralleled the Drau River to Ruden in the Austrian province of Kärnten. The formation reached Villach on 22 April 1941.

The battalion received a 14-day stand-down period to maintain vehicles and the soldiers were billeted in private quarters. During this hiatus, the officers and enlisted personnel made trips into the surrounding areas (Wörther and Mittelstätter Lakes). The batteries conducted maintenance on their vehicles and assault guns.

All vehicles began loading aboard trains at Villach's western rail station during the early morning on 7 May 1941. The train transported the battalion to Glatz in Silesia, arriving there on 9 May. The battalion was billeted in the Moltke Barracks. Between 19 and 28 May 1941, the battalion conducted various terrain exercises at the local training area to improve readiness and incorporate new lessons learned from the last campaign. A large-scale vehicle inspection conducted on 21 May 1941 resulted in the complete satisfaction of the battalion commander.

Starting on 29 May 1941, the battalion prepared to leave Glatz, completing the initiation of the movement on 30 May. The transport trains all steamed towards the East, through Kosel, past Ratibor and Krakow, up to the detraining station at Rzeszow (Reichshof), about 60 kilometers from Przemysl. From there, the battalion conducted a road march north through Sakalow-Jezewe, then through Zawada to Zamosc. The battalion finally reached its march objective in the village of Sahryn. The distance from Rzeszow to Sahryn was 214 kilometers. The battalion, less the 1./Sturmgeschütz-Abteilung 197, later relocated to Turkowice.

The diary of a former member of the 1./Sturmgeschütz-Abteilung 197, Unteroffizier Heinrich Skodell, provides a glimpse into the first, difficult months of combat that the battalion faced in Russia:

MY DIARY—CAMPAIGN AGAINST RUSSIA

Sunday, 22 June 1941. It was 0300 hours. We were 200 meters from the Bug, across from Sokal. The first German gun bellowed at 0315 hours, then hundreds more joined in. Sokal was burning in no time at all and all Hell broke loose there. Combat engineers captured the bridge for us. The assault guns were then called forward.

We crossed the Bug at 0350 hours. We moved through the streets of Sokal, searching for the enemy. A German soldier lay at the first bend, the first casualty. We reached the bunkers 10 minutes later and the fighting began. I was in the command vehicle with my platoon leader, a young lieutenant. We had to make a detour, because we could proceed through the antitank ditches. We were suddenly attacked in a defile by Russians. A short fire fight followed and a brickyard burst into flames. The Russians had run headlong into our guns. We had broken through the bunker line by 0600 hours. I dismounted, got my radio and moved forward. We had to fight our way through the fields. Bullets whistled and shells exploded around us. Some soldiers were hit and medics, covered with blood, ran from one [wounded man] to another.

Fighting took place in the village of Horbkons, but resistance soon broke. The advance continued to Tartakov. We occupied positions there. The city was under heavy artillery fire. We had to move forward twice during the late afternoon, capturing a battery, two tanks and an antitank gun in the process. Gefreiter Smolka, from my platoon, was wounded (shot in the arm). We remained in Tartakov throughout the night.

23 June 1941: Our own artillery fire awakened us and we pursued the Russians. Our [assault] guns conducted a patrol, engaged an enemy battery and drove it to flight. We also destroyed an infantry column. Our platoon leader, Leutnant Ulbricht, was wounded east of Parviatycze. Leutnant Wagner took over the platoon. We were the advance guard that afternoon. Another engagement in the town of Cechov, and we captured two mortars with their prime movers. Gefreiter Eberle was wounded.

24 June 1941: Pursuit and street fighting in Zviniacze, then on to Baremel. Jewish stores gave us their wares without requiring payment. It was very hot.

25 June 1941: Baremel at 0300 hours. We were expecting a large Russian attack. We moved forward, but the Russians had already cleared the area. We had to cross the Styr, but the bridge was destroyed. We moved south through Sipa to cross there, but the bridge was very poor. We had to construct a new one.

26 June 1941: It was 0200 hours in the morning, and the bridge was complete. We moved through Perenyi, Beretecz, across the Styr, Werben and Chryniki. Heavy aircraft attack. Many infantrymen killed. Reached Melnio, our objective for the day. Patrol west of Dubno during the afternoon. Twenty dead Russians, including the first Mongols. Leutnant Wollermann was killed. Leutnant Spielmann wounded.

27 June 1941: We slept well on straw during the night. The weather was very warm. Thorough cleaning. We buried Leutnant Wollermann. Visited the GPU prison in Dubno. A gruesome scene.

28 June 1941: Departed Melnio at 0400 hours. A Russian attack on Sitno at 1800 hours. Attack repulsed. Destroyed 40 armored vehicles and 70 Russian trucks, as well as silenced 2 batteries. Many dead Russians; a horrible scene. Gefreiter Stammen wounded. One assault gun knocked out by a direct hit; had to be sent back for repairs. Knocked out a 52-ton tank.

29 June 1941: Attack at 0900 hours. We preceded the infantry through the remains of the Red Army. Moved cross country. A sudden firefight; three Russians defended desperately in a grain field. One Russian was crushed under the assault gun; the other two were shot. We remained in Kruki for the night.

30 June 1941: Beautiful weather. Enemy fighter made an emergency landing near Kruki. Pilot disappeared. Departed through Poczayov-Nonvy at 1700 hours. Spent the night in Taraz.

1 July 1941: Crossed the Nava. Attacked cross country. Suddenly encountered 3 Russian tanks; we had only one assault gun. Short exchange of fire. One enemy tank destroyed; the fleeing officer was shot. The two other tanks forced to flee. Rested 3 kilometers north of Vieniaviec. Two enemy air attacks inflicted no damage. Received beer: Time for a break!

2 July 1941: It was 0600 hours. The infantry had been fighting since yesterday against desperate Russian attempts to break out at Katrynburg. Our 2nd Platoon supported a battery that had also been fighting there since yesterday. We moved cross country, destroying a tank just before arriving at the town. Then the combat engineers entered the town. The fighting continued for many hours against the superior Russian forces. They attacked over and over again. The fighting was decided by the afternoon. The Reds had taken incredible losses and withdrew. We captured several prisoners. They were Stalin's elite units and fought to the last man. Both of the assault guns of the 2nd Platoon were rendered combat ineffective due to damage and had to be repaired.

3 July 1941: It rained last night. We were in a forest near Horynka, 10 kilometers north of Visniovic. A day of rest. The weather was erratic.

4 July 1941: It rained throughout the night, until 1500 hours this afternoon. We moved all vehicles out of the forest and onto the road before noon. It was a piece of work, because the ground had become soft. Continued forward as the evening commenced. Moved to Vierzoaviec with the combat elements. The field trains had to remain in Visniovic, because the rains had made the roads impassable.

5 July 1941: Rations had to be brought forward by tracked vehicles. Half the vehicles became stuck in the mire. We encountered countless mired vehicles while moving. The weather stabilized; things began to dry. The horse-drawn and dismounted elements had a difficult time moving forward in this thick quagmire. Rations will probably be unavailable for a few days, because our combat elements are moving farther away from the field trains, which cannot follow.

6 July 1941: It was very cool and looked like rain. We struck our tents at 0600 hours and headed to Biatozorka. Rest. We prepared a decent Sunday breakfast for ourselves of fried liver and scrambled eggs. The sun came out. At 1130 hours we crossed the old Russian border in the direction of Kiev. We were the advance guard, together with a heavy machine gun platoon from the infantry. We expected resistance, but the Russians had been routed. We fired a few rounds into a grain field in the direction of fleeing Russians. Riding lessons on Cossack horses. Spent the night in a forest.

7 July 1941: We continued moving east. The Russians could not take the withdrawal. Tired and indifferent, they lagged behind their units and surrendered to their fate. The number of those who surrender increased each day.

8 July 1941: Advance guard again. We caught the Russians along the road to Starokonstantynov. Sizable fireworks; the Russians fled, hardly thinking of resisting. We captured many prisoners and inflicted heavy losses on the Reds. Captured a depot full of ammunition, clothing and provisions. The 2nd Platoon provided security; we heard there were tanks to the right. Tanks appeared suddenly, and we moved forward to fire. Three tanks were destroyed, and the others withdrew quickly. We moved forward cautiously and discovered that they were German tanks. Very unfortunate. We remained in Svinna for the night.

9 July 1941: The weather was very hot. Only moved several kilometers east of Svinna. Heavy thunder and rain during the night.

10 July 1941: The roads were mired. We moved through Starokonstantynov. We hit the Stalin Line southeast of the city; heavy resistance. Unteroffizier Rayd wounded. The enemy fired harassing barrages. A heavy shell landed nearby during the night. I had to find another place to sleep.

11 July 1941: The harassing barrages continued. Our own artillery also fired at this point. As I write these words, I must take cover at any moment because shells land to the left and right continuously. Very uncomfortable . . . the attack on the Stalin Line began during the afternoon at 1530 hours. The Russians put up a desperate defense. When we penetrated, close-quarters fighting ensued in some places, man-to-man. The advance has halted on the right. The attack will probably continue in the morning.

12 July 1941: The right flank withdrew. The Reds fought bitterly. The Russians wanted to abandon their bunkers, but the Commissars chased them back and locked the bunkers from the outside. The Russians have a great fear of their Commissars.

13 July 1941: The fighting continued. The Russians fired upon us with a long-range artillery battery. All efforts by the artillery finding section to locate the enemy battery were unsuccessful. Two Russian air attacks; heavy friendly losses. Leutnant Wagner wounded. We reached Yabloyovka.

14 July 1941: The Russians fired everything they could from their artillery. I carried my radio through the marshland for hours, sometimes sinking up to my torso. It was a good thing that the Russians fired so many duds. It was the first time I almost collapsed. The sun was steaming hot. We reached the town of Skarznitze under those conditions. Air attack. Terrible thunderstorm. The roads are impassable again.

15 July 1941: The Russians appeared to have withdrawn again. Not a single round was fired. The advance continued. The sun was very hot again. We moved through Salinca towards Pagarce. We stayed there; a bridge had to be built. The Russians slowly began destroying everything they left behind.

16 July 1941: We continued east from Pagarce. It was sultry at 1400 hours; a heavy thunderstorm at 1500 hours. We continued as the advance guard. We ran into Russians just outside of the town of Vuyna. Three assault guns, two army antiaircraft guns (20 mm) and two infantry platoons attacked a vastly superior force. After a difficult, three-hour fight, the Russians were forced to flee. The night was crystal clear; we slept in the open.

17 July 1941: We are still in the town of Vunya and await further orders. We slaughtered a pig and roasted it with the most primitive means in the open. The artillery exchanged greetings. We had to take cover now and then, but that did not disturb the roast. Rations and resupply are very poor; we must take care of ourselves. Unfortunately, there was not much available. A Russian captain was taken prisoner. He stated that the Reds intended to attack the village during the night. We made preparations.

18 July 1941: The attack did not take place. We are still waiting in Vunya for fuel, ammunition and rations. The field trains did not arrive because the roads are a mire. We obtained potatoes and turnips and roasted a small pig. You have to know how to take care of yourself. Pouring rain began at 1100 hours. If this continues, we will become stuck here. A sergeant found some flour; we are baking bread. One hour of artillery fire. Shells landed in the immediate vicinity. We were very lucky.

19 July 1941: It rained throughout the night; the roads are impassable. We brought forward fuel, ammunition and rations with halftracks. The infantry pushed the Russians back several kilometers towards evening, so we will have peace in the coming night.

20 July 1941: Today marks the fourth week of fighting the enemy. It is tiring and the poor weather depresses us. Everything is always different from what we anticipated. We moved towards Machnovka during the afternoon. It was supposed to be quiet. Nine Russian fighters shoot at us with machine guns. Perhaps we will advance on Kiev.

21 July 1941: I spent the night in a tent. It looks like rain. Rumors abound, but nobody knows anything specific. It rained again in the evening.

22 July 1941: Weather was not out of the ordinary. Thoroughly cleaned everything again. Ration situation is bad; nothing comes forward.

23 July 1941: Began moving at 0430 hours. Weather very cool until noon. We moved through Berdichev and Zhitomir towards Makaroff. Zhitomir, the first large Russian city with street cars, but no comparison to a German city. The city is destroyed in many places. There is a highway out of Zhitomir towards Kiev.

24 July 1941: Began moving at 1030 hours. War has left its mark along the route. Many dead Russians lay along the road and in the fields, but also many German graves along the way. We halted at the northern outskirts of Andreyevka. The weather was beautiful; the sun very hot. We bivouacked in a cemetery and spent the night there. All the cemeteries are very neglected. Nothing is done with the graves. Forbidden!

25 July 1941: It began raining again during the night. Enemy artillery fire began shortly thereafter, and we had find a more secure place to sleep. The weather was beautiful again during the afternoon. There were many dead Russians nearby and the smell of corpses was very strong, making it necessary for us to bury them today. Our assembly area is preparing for an attack on Kiev. When will the storm break loose?

26 July 1941: The sky was overcast. The sun came out around 1100 hours, and it looked as if it would be a nice day. We spent the time sleeping or frying potatoes. The Russians left us in peace last night. They sent greetings our way before noon, however, and our artillery responded. We endured a terrible artillery fire around 1500 hours. Many dead infantrymen; Kanonier Hütter wounded. Several German bombers arrived at 1700 hours and attacked the Russian positions.

27 July 1941: Our sixth Sunday on Russian soil. It rained until 1230 hours. Little was heard from the Russians, but our artillery spoke out. We are still waiting for the attack. The ring around Kiev probably has not been closed yet. An incredible amount of artillery has moved forward. Will Kiev become a second Warsaw? Enemy artillery fired upon our exact location at 1800 hours. Everyone was surprised that nothing happened. We pulled back several kilometers to thwart any surprises during the night.

28 July 1941: Russian fighters awakened us with low level machine-gun attacks. The noise is greater than the effect. A spy was executed at 1900 hours. It rained again in the evening.

29 July 1941: The weather was beautiful throughout the day. We could hear guns thundering in the distance. We will attack again tomorrow.

30 July 1941: It was 0345 hours, light fog; the weather would be nice. Three different attacks. Moved from Lipovka toward Karolevka to the start point. Fighting in the forest. The Reds suffered heavy losses. Destroyed a cannon at 30 meters, then an entire battery with bravado. Many prisoners. A bullet ricocheted off my helmet. Gefreiter Pohl wounded. Third attack: Combed the woods east of Goleya. The Russians withdrew after heavy artillery fire landed in the woods. Several prisoners. Air attack. Much luck. The bomb landed 20 meters behind us, and two infantrymen were killed. In Karolevka again at 2200 hours. Exhausted; slept on the ground.

31 July 1941: Very hot. Small attack at 1900 hours. We were to capture the town of Maiydonavka. The enemy has fled. We remained in Maiydonavka for the night.

1 August 1941: Our infantry attacked at 0600 hours. They reached their objective with out any problems. We were to probe farther east. Along with a platoon of infantry, we encountered the enemy and opened fire. An assault gun ran over a mine and was immobilized. The crew abandoned the vehicle. The driver, Unteroffizier Kloth, jumped out last and landed directly on a mine. He died immediately. The other assault gun was damaged and had to withdraw. The 25 infantrymen could not hold out because of heavy enemy fire. We all withdrew to the previous attack objective. At 1400 hours, four of us went forward with mine detectors to recover the vehicle and bodies. The Russians had already begun looting the crew's belongings. They began firing wildly when they saw us and we had to withdraw again. We supported an attack at 1700 hours. We advanced despite heavy enemy resistance. The Russians had an incredible amount of artillery that sent "greetings" our way. It was terrible!

Our only remaining armored ammunition carrier ran over a mine. The driver, Kanonier Tschermak, was killed. The assistant driver, Kanonier Cantz, was severely wounded. Russian fighters shot down a German barrage balloon. We moved to Maiydanavka during the night.

2 August 1941: We occupied the northern outskirts of Maiydanavka. Enemy artillery fire became so heavy that we had to withdraw to the southern part of town. The artillery shells started landing closer at 1500 hours, so we withdrew farther - to our field trains in Karolevka.

3 August 1941: We were finally able to pull back to Makaroff to repair our vehicles. I erected my tent right next to a water source. Excellent possibilities for bathing. First delousing.

4 August 1941: The sky was partly cloudy, and the weather was good. We worked on our vehicles. Weapons and personal gear were brought up to par. We will attempt to recover our two dead tonight.

5 August 1941: We only managed to recover one body, Kanonier Tschermak. We had to abandon all other attempts, because the area was under heavy enemy artillery fire. The weather is good.

6 August 1941: The weather was very warm. We washed up and maintained our equipment.

7 August 1941: It has become windy and overcast. "Iron calm!"

8 August 1941: It began raining during the night. We moved to Plissezkoye, south of Kiev, at 0830 hours. We planned to begin fighting immediately, but it turned out otherwise again. We remained in place for the time being. It rained the entire day and was very cool. The weather cleared up around 1500 hours.

9 August 1941: Several thunder showers throughout the day. Otherwise quiet.

10 August 1941: Moved out of Plissezkoye at 0530 hours. We have been transferred to another corps and ended up in Yankovtsche. The situation changed by 1600 hours. We broke camp and moved 25 kilometers south, through Vassilkoff, to Olyschanka. It looks as though we will be assigned to a new division.

11 August 1941: Quiet in Malaya-Olyschanka. Good weather.

12 August 1941: Departed for Peressalenye at 0900 hours. We moved through a drab area. The villages are farther and farther apart.

13 August 1941: The attack at the Dnepr will commence on 15 August. We were to remain here until then, but things always change. The battery suddenly moved out again at 1700 hours. We moved about 50 kilometers southeast to the front line. The infantry was happy to see us. The Russians had counterattacked with tank support the last few days. These attacks left hundreds of dead and wounded Russians on the battlefield. We were to attack that evening, but it was delayed until morning. We spent the night in a town 400 meters from enemy positions. We heard the screams and cries of the Russian wounded very clearly.

14 August 1941: The situation changed again overnight. At 0300 hours, we moved 15 kilometers north to another regiment. The attack will begin tomorrow. It is very hot. Stuka attacks against the bridge.

15 August 1941: Wake up at 0300 hours. Began the attack at 0500 hours in the direction of the Dnepr. The valley containing the city of Kaneff was still shrouded in fog as we opened fire. The commander's vehicle ran over a mine. Nobody injured. We attacked withdrawing Russians and fortified positions. Our infantry moved forward very slowly. We continued that attack during the afternoon. Thunderstorm, completely soaked; the ground was slick. We moved forward without infantry support to a Russian position we had fired upon earlier. Sinister and unseen, rounds hit us at close range. We could not see what was going on, because there were dead and wounded everywhere. We could barely make out those firing upon us. Happy to be out of the area again. Unteroffizier Drohne received shrapnel in his ankle. Both of Leutnant Ulbricht's thighs had been hit, the rounds passing clean through.

16 August 1941: The attack continued. I remained behind today, since most of the 2nd Platoon was out of action. We repaired the platoon leader's vehicle and then moved to Kaneff, where the battery is. Kaneff was captured today. The Russians blew up the railroad bridge across the Dnepr this afternoon. Many prisoners. It was a hot day. Oberkanonier Weller wounded.

17 August 1941: Sunday. We moved about 40 kilometers northwest from Kaneff towards Dratschi. It looks as though we will be in another sector.

18 August 1941: Another hot day. An assault gun returned to us from the maintenance company, but it ran over a mine half way back, wounding Unteroffizier Wirkner. One third of the battery has run over mines. If it continues like this, we can go home soon. Heavy thunderstorm at 2100 hours.

19 August 1941: Nice weather, quiet; waiting for our next operation.

20 August 1941: Day of rest.

21 August 1941: Nice weather. Movement planned for tomorrow.

22 August 1941: Departed at 0400 hours. Moved 40 kilometers north. Remained in Novassilka. Move to the start point at 1800.

23 August 1941: Woke up at 0300 hours. We had to cross high ground under enemy observation, making it necessary to cross while it is dark. Attacked at 0600 hours. Captured the town of Tripoliy without much difficulty. The commander's vehicle ran over amine. The driver, Kanonier Plottnik, is deaf, and Kanonier Schneider received a head injury. A second attack at 1500 hours. We are penetrating enemy bridgeheads. Each time, the Russians had to be pushed across the Dnepr. We remained in Dolena for the night.

24 August 1941: Sunday. Departed at 1300 hours. We moved 25 kilometers to Karlik. The entire battalion assembled here. We will probably move to a new sector.

25 August 1941: It rained sporadically. We prepared for a longer movement. We will join the 17. Armee in the south.

26 August 1941: Departed at 0800, moving through Schependovka, Vincetoska, Bagustaf, Medevia and Lisyanka to Svenigorodka. The weather was nice.

27 August 1941: The march continued at 0600 hours through Vogadschefk, Lodavatka, Schpola, Statopol and Schpalovo to Fedvar. It looks like rain. The movement 300 kilometers south from Kiev is monotonous; always the same picture. Sometimes there are no buildings for 20 kilometers.

28 August 1941: The march continued at 0600 hours. Rain poured down and the roads became a mire. We moved about 90 kilometers southeast and stayed in a small village. We found excellent cooking oil, lard, eggs and flour at a farming collective there.

29 August 1941: The weather was good again. We move 10 kilometers farther to a larger town just before noon to await orders there. We erect our tent in an overgrown garden. I hope things improve soon, because we are all covered with lice.

30 August 1941: Day of rest. Good weather.

31 August 1941: Sunday. Day of rest.

1 September 1941: Very hot. A large attack planned for tomorrow; the advance will resume.

2 September 1941: Departed Mironaka at 0500 hours and moved towards Pavlisch. We waited there to be ferried across the Dnepr. The 2. and 3./Sturmgeschütz-Abteilung 197 crossed over and formed a bridgehead. It is intended for us to create a strong advance guard to push deep into enemy territory. Departed for Plotnikovka at 1700 hours. Spent the night there. Heavy rain at 1800 hours.

3 September 1941: 1100 hours. We crossed the 800-meter-wide Dnepr on ferries. Air attack. We stayed in Solotnischtsche. Slept in a barn. Another air attack at night.

4 September 1941: Awakened at 0400 hours. We were to attack. Canceled again. The bridge across the Dnepr has been completed, incredibly long. The field trains crossed over to our side. Numerous air attacks. It was very cold. The sky was overcast. The Russians repeatedly tried to attack the bridge under the cover of the clouds. Massed fire repulsed them. We moved to Leschtschenki during the afternoon and remained there.

5 September 1941: We moved to the town of Yeristonaka at 1000 hours. We were to attack through the village of Mischtschenki at 1400 hours to the rail line leading east to Krementschug. The Russians were so overcome by the appearance of our assault guns that they simply fled. The Russians suffered very high casualties. Our rounds caused terrible destruction. The regimental commander expressed praise for our assault guns. We remained in the town.

6 September 1941: Departed Lonrikovka at 1600 hours and moved towards Potiki. Tomorrow we will attack across the Psyol. The Russians harassed us with aircraft at every opportunity. There is no indication of German air superiority here. The antiaircraft guns were lucky; a direct hit and a bomber went down in flames. Harassing artillery fire from the Russians all night. The commander reconnoitered the route to the bridge across the Psyol and returned lightly wounded.

7 September 1941: 0600 hours. Our artillery fired a tremendous barrage on the opposite bank of the Psyol. At 0800 hours, we crossed the Psyol on a railroad bridge. Every regiment was screaming for our services. We made the first attack at 1300 hours. We captured more than 100 prisoners and many dead Russians remained behind. The mutilation was horrible. The commander's vehicle was hit by an antitank gun, but everything was alright. The driver, Gefreiter Schlemminger, plus two others, Gefreiter Heynemann and Kanonier Mallowski, were lightly wounded. We destroyed the antitank gun immediately.

8 September 1941: Attack at 0930 hours. We were to cut off Krementschug. The attack proceeded quickly without any appreciable resistance. We destroyed a horse-drawn Russian unit. The Russians fired artillery at us. A direct hit in our battery. Kanonier Lipp dead; Kanonier Titus lightly wounded; Unteroffizier Kläden and Unteroffizier Flintrap severely wounded. We remained in the village for the night. The enemy fired harassing barrages.

9 September 1941: It rained throughout the night. Starting today, I am the gunner for the assault gun. Attack at 1600 hours. It is a strange feeling to acquire a target, finger on the trigger, then simply press with my finger and many people are dead or wounded. Our assault gun experienced engine failure as we reached our objective. We had to go to the maintenance company.

10 September 1941: The weather was overcast and cool. The damage to our assault gun has been repaired. We returned to the battery. No attack today. Eight Russian bombers attacked us at 1700 hours; very uncomfortable, but there were no casualties.

11 September 1941: Awakened at 0400 hours. We were to attack. Then we were to conduct a reconnaissance-in-force, but continuous rain put an end to that idea.

12 September 1941: Attacked the town of Omyelnik at 0830 hours. The Russians had good field positions and were hard to force out. The town was in our hands by noon. Very few prisoners; most of the Russians were dead. Leutnant Preusser, our new platoon leader, was wounded. A round straight through his helmet, but only his scalp was grazed. I observed the incident and took care of the enemy rifleman. We remained in Omyelnik for the night. Light harassing fire from the Russians.

13 September 1941: We depart for the field trains in Romanik at 0800 hours. The 14th Division from Heeresgruppe Kleist has arrived in the sector and will probably take over pursuit of the Russians. We were attached to a new division. Departed at 1300 hours. We crossed the Psyol again. We halted in a grain field outside of Ssilezki and went to sleep for the night in our uniforms. The enemy brought down harassing fire 300 meters from our position.

14 September 1941: Sunday, attacked at 1400 hours. We pushed about 19 kilometers to the northeast. The attack was very successful. Our assault gun destroyed five trucks, one jeep, one prime mover, one heavy gun and one light gun. Also three horse-drawn vehicles. The Russians suffered very heavy losses. The other assault gun in our battery destroyed many enemy batteries. During the night, the enemy fired several shells into the town in which we were sleeping. We noticed that resistance was slowly giving way to flight. The Russian infantry has not been up to par for a long time. They are all older people, some of them have only been soldiers for eight days. The weather was beautiful. Pomp, Piel and Lehmann are missing.

15 September 1941: At 0900 hours, we moved to where we had left off yesterday. We were to attack again. The enemy apparently had enough and bolted. Endless friendly columns moved forward as on the first day of the advance. The weather was very good and morale soared. There was hope once again that the eastern campaign would come to a victorious conclusion this year. The missing soldiers returned at 1300 hours, minus their vehicles. A staff car and motorcycle had fallen into Russian hands. Along with a reconnaissance battalion, we moved out at 1500 hours as the advance guard. Our platoon was at the point. Surprisingly, we pushed 30 kilometers to the east. Captured eight trucks with provisions and destroyed another. Unteroffizier Adam was wounded.

16 September 1941: Continued moving at 0600 hours; five kilometers to the next town. Ambushed a column of 40 trucks. Shot up one staff car and two trucks, which burst into flames. We caught many more trucks throughout the day and another entire column towards the evening. Our achievements for the day: Advanced 30 kilometers; 80 trucks (some captured, some destroyed). Many prisoners. We had enough rations again, since the captured vehicles were crammed full of them. A staff car from our battery went up in flames. An assault gun ran over a mine, but the damage was repaired within two hours. The weather was cool. It rained prior to noon, and the roads are soggy.

17 September 1941: It was very cool. We saw the first enemy tanks this afternoon. A road ran 5 kilometers parallel to us; the Russians were withdrawing along it. A race began. The Russians guarded their withdrawal with tanks. We had an intense firefight with Russian tanks towards the evening. Our assault gun knocked out two tanks. Fired upon an enemy truck column and then had to withdraw because we ran out of ammunition.

18 September 1941: We waited in a stubble field until noon for further orders. We began moving by 1300 hours. We had not traveled far before we had Russian tanks in front of us. The fireworks broke loose. Our assault gun set two of them ablaze. We reached the main road to Poltava. Panic had broken out there among the retreating Russians. Pedestrians, horses, vehicles and tanks swarmed together. We fired into their midst with two assault guns. We dispatched 10 tanks and captured 1,000 prisoners. Towards the evening, we surprised the enemy in his flank and caused unholy confusion. The Russians left an unbelievable amount of materiel and dead men behind. We remained at the Poltava airport for the night. A hit from an antitank gun; Unteroffizier Volger was wounded.

19 September 1941: We returned to the field trains with our assault gun to make some repairs. The weather was cool.

20 September 1941: It was very cool. We no longer sleep in tents; we now stay in the clay huts. The vermin is out in force, very uncomfortable. Our assault gun still is not ready. The other assault guns are engaged in heavy fighting with Russian tanks. One gun has been hit. The entire cupola was torn off and the gunner, Unteroffizier Hacker, was wounded. The rest of the crew's nerves are frazzled. The assault gun was repaired within two days and received a new crew, giving the old one a chance to recover from its shock.

The commander and Obergefreiter König were seriously wounded. The commander will probably lose a leg. The Obergefreiter has shrapnel in his lung. Kanonier Golinski was wounded in the arm. Leutnant Spielmann assumed command of the battery for the time being.

21 September 1941: Our assault gun was ready; we moved to the battery 30 kilometers north of Poltava. We had hardly arrived, when we heard that we would be attached to another division. We returned to Poltava. Just as we found quarters for the night and were happy to be among cultured people again, we were told to get ready to move again. We moved several kilometers out of town, in the direction of Kharkov. We remained there. Traces of fighting could be seen in Poltava.

22 September 1941: We were the advance guard again. After moving several kilometers, we encountered enemy positions. Our assault guns had a devastating effect. The positions were occupied by a battalion of men between 40 and 50 years old, with no communications whatsoever. The commissars were gone. These people were to delay us and they knew absolutely nothing about the situation. The battalion was crushed. Most of them were killed and the rest captured. We continued this afternoon. A sudden attack by four low-flying Russian bombers, but no casualties. We arrived at a wooded area by dusk and slept in the open.

23 September 1941: We had to take our assault gun to Poltava for repairs. It will probably take several days. The battalion commander, Major Christ, was wounded. The new commander arrived today, Hauptmann Freiherr [Baron] von und zu Barisani.

25 September 1941: The weather was nice. Took a stroll through the town, very interesting.

26 September 1941: We waited for the maintenance company. The battery was in Kharkov, fighting against heavy Russian tanks. One of our assault guns went up in flames. The crew barely made it out. That vehicle had already run over mines twice and received a direct hit on 20 September. One of the command vehicles received a direct hit. Leutnant Fellbier, as well as Gefreiter Traub and Gefreiter Schlemminger, were all killed. Kanonier Hütter and Kanonier Jung wounded. Leutnant Spielmann commands the battery. He has been slightly wounded four times, and he is the only remaining one of the six officers who initially deployed with us.

27 September 1941: The advance party from the maintenance company arrived. We moved 2 kilometers to the warehouse that the battery occupies. Air attacks throughout the day.

28 September 1941: Sunday. Work on the assault guns. Air attack.

29 September 1941: It rained the entire day. Not a single Russian aircraft showed itself. The new commander moved the entire battalion to Poltava. The batteries are no longer combat effective. The personnel and materiel losses have been too great. Our battery, 50 men, has suffered 36 wounded and 8 killed to this point.

30 September 1941: Maintenance.

1 October 1941: Maintenance.

2 October 1941: Oberleutnant Liedtke, the battalion adjutant, takes command of our battery. The commander read a message from the Führer to the entire battalion. We have scraped the bottom of the barrel today. We hope to be up to par again in the next few days. Beautiful weather.

3 October 1941: Beautiful weather. Führer's radio message at 1800 hours.

4 October 1941: Promotion party for Wachtmeister Hetzert.

5 October 1941: Mass in the political party building. Pictures of the communist party leaders still adorn the walls.

6 October 1941: It was very cool. The 2. and 3./Sturmgeschütz-Abteilung 197 moved out. Commander of the 3./Sturmgeschütz-Abteilung 197, Oberleutnant Goebe, was killed.

7 October 1941: It is snowing. The Headquarters Battery moved out as well. We must wait several more days. The new assault guns have not arrived yet.

8 October 1941: Delousing today.

9 October 1941: We receive three new assault guns. We will move out on 11 October.

10 October 1941: It rained the entire day. Prepared for movement.

11 October 1941: Frost at night. Moved towards Kharkov at 0600 hours. Terrible weather in the afternoon; snow and rain. The roads were swamped. Spent the night in clay huts.

12 October 1941: Snow and rain the entire day. A small attack during the afternoon. Four buildings occupied by Russians went up in flames.

13 October 1941: Incredible filth outside. We sat in a clay hut and waited. The Russians fired their devilish cannons every now and then.

14 October 1941: Awakened at 0100 hours. We moved forward 10 kilometers to repulse a Russian attack. The attack never occurred. We moved through the dark back to our old quarters. It was terribly cold, almost impossible to remain out in the open. A Rata fighter was hit and disappeared vertically from the sky.

15 October 1941: At 0500 hours, we returned to our old positions and waited. An alert at 1400 hours and we moved to the right flank. Two Russian heavy tanks attacked. A half hour of fireworks and both Russians fled. At our next position, we had to find billets in the dark. Rations only come forward once a day; only cold food.

16 October 1941: The weather has changed again. It did not freeze last night, and a brisk wind was blowing that dried out the roads. At 1300 hours, we relieved the 1st Platoon, which was providing security on the front line. There was nothing going on. We returned to our quarters at dusk.

17 October 1941: We moved out at 0430 hours with bicycle troops and other types of units to form the advance guard. We encountered light resistance just outside a town. We overcame it, capturing 200 prisoners and 3 horse-drawn wagons with food. Leutnant Spielmann was wounded for the fifth time. He has shrapnel in his knee. We reached another town after dark and surprised Russians eating supper in a building. Many new prisoners.

18 September 1941: We continued at 0800 hours. Nothing noteworthy. We occupied billets in a large village. Many deserters.

19 October 1941: Sunday. Finally, a day of rest; only the coffee and cake are missing. A sudden alert at 1530 hours, and we moved several kilometers farther. It rains. We reached our objective after dark. Spent the night in a shack with 20 men, packed like herrings.

20 October 1941: It rained. No wheeled vehicles could move. A cavalry squadron and three assault guns moved towards Kharkov. We reached a solid road and formed the spearhead. Russian trucks and horse-drawn columns were totally bewildered as we suddenly appeared. Several vehicles attempted to flee, but our rounds were faster. The Russians suffered heavy personnel and materiel losses. A town 3 kilometers outside of Kharkov was our objective. We were short on ammunition and fuel. We had to remain awake the entire night, because there were only a few of us. We heard the Russians withdrawing. It was a shame our artillery was not there.

21 October 1941: Reinforcements arrived during the night. The Russians fired into our town.

22 October 1941: The Kharkov suburbs are almost in our hands. Artillery action. Received ammunition today from the 3./Sturmgeschütz-Abteilung 197. We are waiting for fuel and rations.

23 October 1941: The attack on Kharkov was to begin at noon. Fuel was still not here. Attack at 1200 hours; fuel arrived just before that. We attacked 20 minutes after the artillery preparatory fire. We had two assault guns. Destroyed four tanks and many cannon during the street fighting. The houses looked desolate and the bridges were almost all destroyed. We were the first German soldiers in Kharkov. We stayed in some buildings overnight.

24 October 1941: We continued at 0800 hours, fighting block after block. There were barricades and tanks at every corner. Some civilians paid for their curiosity with their lives. There was much destruction today. One cannot describe everything the eyes see on this day. We spent the night in the eastern part of the city. It rained in the evening. Our field trains finally reached a solid road, and we can expect rations soon.

25 October 1941: We moved downtown at 0800 hours. The clearing action continued, but we encountered no resistance. Civilians fired upon soldiers as they searched buildings. They now hang from trees in the middle of the city, even two women. The Reds themselves set the prison on fire so that their disgraceful acts remain obscured.

26 October 1941: Sunday. The weather was beautiful today. We established billets in a large house. Rest. I took a look at the city. There were entire city blocks in need of repair. The backyards were covered with filth. There were, however, wonderful churches built in the oriental style. Unfortunately, they all serve a purpose different than that which had been intended. "Palace of the Proletariat"—a phenomenal structure containing every imaginable luxury. I seriously doubt however, that a worker has ever been permitted to enter this building. It would take too long to describe every impression. At any rate, it is not comparable to a German city.

27 October 1941: Rained the entire day. Rations became even more scarce; apparently, nothing is coming forward. The battery celebrated with Russian wine during the evening.

28 October 1941: It rained continuously. Quiet.

29 October 1941: Slaughtered two cows for the battery as supplementary rations.

30 October 1941: Two civilians were shot because they tried to destroy a bridge.

31 October 1941: Rain, quiet.

1 November 1941: Prepare to move.

2 November 1941: We were to move out today, but fuel still has not arrived. Weather is fair.

3 November 1941: Vehicles bringing fuel forward were towed back by half-tracks, because the roads were impassable.

4 November 1941: Moved out at 0600 hours. We acquired captured fuel today. The improved road ended several kilometers past Kharkov, and the misery began. It was a slow, tiresome advance.

5 November 1941: It was pure torture. The roads were impassable and defy description. We could not even think about eating. Many vehicles have become mired and are considered total losses.

6 November 1941: Movement became even more difficult. The weather became worse. We reached Krasnograd, moving 100 kilometers in three days.

7 November 1941: The battery had to reassemble. We halted for a day. It was raining.

8 November 1941: We continued moving. We were within 40 kilometers of Dnepropetrovsk.

9 November 1941: A stone road. The weather was good. We crossed the Dnepr at Dnepropetrovsk. There were many German soldiers' graves in the city. It was a reasonably good road leading south.

10 November 1941: Crossed the Dnepr on ferries at Dneprostroye. It took half a day. We remained in Saporoshye for the night.

11 November 1941: Destroyed bridges delayed movement considerably. We were within 60 kilometers of Melitopol.

12 November 1941: Reached Melitopol.

13 November 1941: The temperature drops to -10° Celsius [14° Fahrenheit] during the night.

14 November 1941: The cold persisted. Moved out at 1200 hours. Advanced 80 kilometers again.

15 November 1941: Reached Perekop at the long end of the Crimean peninsula. Many soldiers' graves along the way.

16 November 1941: Spent the night in Dzankoye.

17 November 1941: Reached Simferopol, the Crimean capital, by noon.

18 November 1941: Took four trucks to Perekop (306 kilometers). Picked up fuel and oil. It was wet and cold.

19 November 1941: Thoroughly cleaned our clothes. The lice tortured us more and more.

20 November 1941: It was snowing and bitterly cold. The assault on the Sevastopol fortress is to start on 26 November.

Unteroffizier Skodell's diary ends here.

On 1 November 1941, Hauptmann Steinwachs assumed acting command of the battalion in Kharkov. The Army High Command ordered the battalion transferred from the 6. Armee to the 11. Armee-Korps (Crimea) on 3 November 1941. The field-army group made the route of march optional, so the headquarters staff reconnoitered and established a route every day. It continued through Krasnograd, Dnepropetrovsk, Saporoshye, Melitopol and Nikolayev up to the Strait of Perekop. This 900-kilometer march along the worst roads and in the worst weather, after four months of combat without any sort of reconstitution, inflicted considerable losses upon the battalion. The movement had to take place as quickly as possible, so the battalion's batteries moved as separate march units.

The assault guns survived this forced march the best. Seventy percent of the wheeled vehicles broke down. The maintenance section repaired broken-down vehicles and then took charge of moving them further. The maintenance section did not reach the Crimea until January 1942, but it succeeded in repairing all vehicles that broke down along the route.

Hauptmann Steinwachs reported to the Commander-in-Chief of the 11. Armee, Generaloberst von Manstein, on 13 November 1941. The battalion reached the Ukrainka area, north of Simferopol, where it was staged. Once it was there, the maintenance section of Sturmgeschütz-Abteilung 190 provided invaluable assistance.

After several briefings and some reconnoitering, the battalion was allocated to the LIV. Armee-Korps. Hauptmann Steinwachs' recommendation to employ the entire battalion within the sector of the 22. Infanterie-Division, because of the favorable terrain there, was turned down. The batteries were divided among three divisions.

The first major German attack on the Sevastopol fortress began on 17 December 1941. The 1./Sturmgeschütz-Abteilung 197, advancing on the right wing of the attack, crossed completely open terrain and was quickly shot up by the heavy Russian artillery. The advance continued in stages—under unspeakable terrain and weather conditions, through minefields, against fortified artillery and retractable armored turrets—making unbelievable demands upon the infantry and engineers. The 2. and 3./Sturmgeschütz-Abteilung 197, attached to Sturmgeschütz-Abteilung 190, exhausted themselves carrying the attack forward and gaining ground. When Russian forces landed at Kerch and Eupatoria at the end of December, the German attack had to be called off (31 December 1941). The forward German lines were pulled back considerably. Generalleutnant Wolf, the commander of the 22. Infanterie-Division, thanked Hauptmann Steinwachs for the support of his assault guns.

Major Helmut Christ then arrived back at the battalion and assumed command of the formation again. He relinquished command again shortly thereafter, however, due to illness. After a short leave, Hauptmann Steinwachs was designated as the commander of the battalion.

The severely depleted battalion received a battlefield reconstitution in January and February 1942. The maintenance section, under the leadership of Kriegsverwaltungsrat Schaffranek, worked tirelessly and successfully to restore the battalion's total combat power. The 1./Sturmgeschütz-Abteilung 197 received six new assault guns. In January 1942, the 3./Sturmgeschütz-Abteilung 197 was detached from the battalion for a short time to take part in the successful counterattack that recaptured Fedosia from the Russians.

On the morning of 27 February 1942, the tremendously superior Russian forces along the Parpatsch front and Kerch Peninsula began the awaited offensive ("Stalin Offensive") to recapture the Crimea. Sturmgeschütz-Abteilung 197 had only its first two batteries—a total of eleven assault guns—available for combat. Both batteries took part in the defensive effort under a variety of formations, including the 10. Infanterie-Division and the 170. Infanterie-Division. The massed Russian armor and infantry attacks continued until 25 March 1942.

The battalion made an outstanding contribution to the defense against this Russian attack, destroying some 80 enemy tanks in the process. The battalion was recognized in the Wehrmacht Daily Report for 15 March 1942: "During fighting on the Kerch Peninsula, a platoon from an assault gun battalion, under the command of Leutnant Spielmann, destroyed 14 enemy tanks on 13 and 14 March."

The battalion was favorably mentioned again in the report dated the next day: "During the fighting on 13 March 1942, Oberwachtmeister Schrödel, commander of a assault gun in an assault-gun battalion, destroyed eight enemy tanks, including three heavy tanks."

The battalion was mentioned once again in the report dated 4 April 1944: "Sturmgeschütz-Abteilung 197 has destroyed 200 enemy tanks since the beginning of the Eastern Campaign."

(Oberwachtmeister Schrödel was awarded the German Cross in Gold on 11 April 1942. On 11 April 1942, Oberleutnant Johann Spielmann (promoted effective 1 July 1941) received the Knight's Cross to the Iron Cross.)

The battalion was brought up to full combat strength again after its return to the Ukrainka staging area. Simultaneous preparations begin for Operation "Bussard Hunt," recapturing the Crimea. Sturmgeschütz-Abteilung 197 (minus its 3./Sturmgeschütz-Abteilung 197) moved out with the 50. Infanterie-Division on 8 May 1942 for the breakthrough attack. The 3./Sturmgeschütz-Abteilung 197 was attached to the 170. Infanterie-Division.

The commander of the 1./Sturmgeschütz-Abteilung 197, Oberleutnant Liedtke, was seriously wounded shortly after the start of the attack, and Oberleutnant Spielmann assumed acting command of the battery. Rain and mud initially prevented a rapid advance. All the assault guns of the 3./Sturmgeschütz-Abteilung 197 became completely stuck in the mud on the second day and had be towed out with prime movers. The weather improved and the 22. Panzer-Division advanced. The battalion also supported the advance of the 28. leichte Division at various times with great success. The last Russian resistance in Eastern Kerch was broken on 20 May 1942.

Soldiers of Sturmgeschütz-Abteilung 197 received a large number of awards and commendations for these operations. Unfortunately, they also suffered considerable personnel losses, among them the death of the commander of the 2./Sturmgeschütz-Abteilung 197, Oberleutnant Haager. Oberleutnant Eberhard Kuntze assumed command of the battery. The most difficult task still lay before the 11. Armee, however: Capturing the Fortress of Sevastopol.

Sturmgeschütz-Abteilung 197 was reconstituted and became ready for full operational deployment. Along with other equipment, the battalion received six new long-barreled assault guns (Sturmgeschütz III L/48 75 mm). The attack upon the city and fortress of Sevastopol began on 7 June 1942. The battalion, minus the 3./Sturmgeschütz-Abteilung 197, supported the attack of the 50. Infanterie-Division, while the 3./Sturmgeschütz-Abteilung 197 deployed in the northeast sector with the 24. Infanterie-Division. The Russian defenders had reinforced the positions and forts considerably. The difficult terrain and enormous heat also made things tough for the assault artillerymen. The assault guns supported the infantry and engineers in bitter close combat. On 13 June 1942, the Wehrmacht Daily Report announced:

During the fighting outside of Sevastopol, Knight's Cross recipient Oberleutnant Spielmann, battery commander in an assault-gun battalion, and Oberleutnant Frank, company commander in an infantry regiment, distinguished themselves with exceptional bravery.

On 17 June 1942 the 24. Infanterie-Division, supported by Sturmgeschütz-Abteilung 197, captured the forts "Molotov," "GPU" and "Dnepr." Together with the 50 Infanterie-Division, the Gaytani Heights and a bridgehead across the Tschornaya were captured. It was a horrible experience for the members of the battalion as the Russians blew up the granite fortification "Inkermann" with its entire garrison and a field hospital still inside.

The battalion's last remaining operational assault gun carried the attack of the 50. Infanterie-Division across the antitank ditches and into Sevastopol. This extremely difficult and very costly victory was completed on 1 July 1942. The battle for Sevastopol was over. Sturmgeschütz-Abteilung 197 fought in this sector in a series of extraordinary operations. Every soldier, from driver to mechanic, applied himself at every moment. This was universally recognized at all levels of the chain of command.

After a well-deserved, but short, period of rest, the battalion was transferred to the Voronesh area and allocated to the VII. Armee-Korps. In this sector, the battalion supported various divisions—340. Infanterie-Division, 377. Infanterie-Division and the 387. Infanterie-Division—defending against many intense Russian attacks. In doing so, it destroyed a large number of enemy tanks. Unfortunately, the commander of the 3./Sturmgeschütz-Abteilung 197, Oberleutnant Gerald de la Renotière (German Cross in Gold, 28 July 1942) was severely wounded on 14 August 1942.

The Russians forces halted their costly attacks in this sector of the front on 17 August 1942. The battalion received movement orders on 23 August 1942, apparently a transfer to the 2. Panzer-Armee in Orel. Once there, the battalion was assigned to the LIII. Armee-Korps (General Clößner) and received the following mission: "Relieve the infantry from the continuous, vicious enemy armored thrusts—free rein."

After immediate terrain reconnaissance and preparations, the battalion conducted a surprise attack that destroyed seven KV I tanks within several days. This fulfilled the battalion's mission.

In October 1942, the battalion was transferred to the 4. Armee at Spass-Demensk as the field-army reserve for the sector of the LVI. Armee-Korps. Apart from occasional alerts, the time was spent training, conducting reconnaissance, preparing for combat, wargaming and attending briefings. On 23 December 1942, the Commander of the 4. Armee, General Röttiger, presented the battalion commander with the following order: "The personnel of the [battalion] will soon move to Jüterbog to be outfitted with heavy assault guns."

The battalion was relieved in early January 1943 by personnel of Sturmgeschütz-Abteilung 270 arriving from France. It took over the weapons and equipment. The entire battalion assembled before the commander, Major Steinwachs, at 1400 hours on 20 January 1943 to receive a briefing on the upcoming reorganization and redesignation. Then the personnel climbed aboard waiting trucks for the move to Spass-Demensk, where trains arrived to take them back to Germany.

The return trip began on 21 January 1943. The trains rolled through Smolensk, Minsk and Warsaw, finally reaching Berlin on 29 January 1943. The batteries occupied quarters in the new camp at Jüterbog on the same evening. There the soldiers received the joyous news that almost all of them were allowed to depart for a three-week leave.

The following list of engagements was appended to the Wehrpaß (military identification booklet that contained a wealth of information about an individual soldier) of the assault gunners of the 1./Sturmgeschütz-Abteilung 197 for the period running from 9 April 1941 to 12 June 1943:

Balkans

9 April 1941: Breakthrough at the Yugoslavian border fortifications.

10 April–12 April 1941: Fighting to capture Agram and Belgrade.

13 April–18 April 1941: Capture of Belgrade; pursuit to Sarajevo.

18 April–22 April 1941: Securing the former Yugoslavian area.

Russian Campaign

22 June–12 July 1941: Frontier fighting in Bessarabia, Galicia and Volhinia

22 June–28 June 1941: Frontier fighting between the Bug and Styr

23 June–12 July 1941: Fighting between the Styr and Stalin Line

25 June–4 July 1941: Advance across the Horyn to the Stalin Line

2 July–25 July 1941: Penetration to Kiev and advance to the Dnepr

2 July–25 July 1941: Penetrating the Stalin Line

8 July–16 July 1941: The Battle of Cudno-Berdichev

11 July–24 July 1941: Fighting outside of Kiev

14 July–24 July 1941: Fighting in the area north of Zhitomir

Battles of Pursuit Toward the Dnepr and Attacks Across the Dnepr

26 July–29 August 1941: Battles of pursuit to the Dnepr

31 August–12 September 1941: Attack across the Dnepr

13 September–5 October 1941: Battles of pursuit across Poltava

21 August–27 September 1941: Battle for Kiev

1 October–10 October 1941: Pursuit up to the Donetz

1 October–10 October 1941: Battles of pursuit at Psiol and along the Vorskla

17 October–25 October 1941: Fighting at Kharkov and Belgorod

26 October–16 November 1941: Employment in the operational area

Battle for Crimea

17 November–16 December 1941: Securing the Crimea

17 December–31 December 1941: Attack on Sevastopol

1 January–18 January 1941: Fighting at and northwest of Fedosia

19 January–7 May 1942: Defensive fighting at the Parpatsch Position

8 May–21 May 1941: Fighting on the Kerch Peninsula and capture of Kerch

22 May–1 June 1942: Securing the Crimea

2 June–4 July 1942: Attack and Capture of the Sevastopol Fortress

5 July–31 July 1942: Securing the Crimea

1942 Eastern Offensive

1 August–25 August 1942: Defensive fighting at Voronesh

Positional Fighting in the Area of Operations of Heeresgruppe Mitte

26 August 1942–20 January 1943

26 August–12 September 1942: Offensive and defensive operations in the area south of Belev-Koselsk-Szuchinitschi

13 September–20 January 1943: Employment in the operational area

21 January–12 June 1943: Employment in the operational area

COMMANDERS OF STURMGESCHÜTZ-ABTEILUNG 197

25 November 1940 to 9 September 1941: Major Helmut Christ

9 September 1941 to ? October 1941: Hauptmann Kurt von Barisani

1 November 1941 to ? December 1941: Hauptmann Heinz Steinwachs

December 1941: Major Helmut Christ

January 1942 to 1 April 1943: Major Heinz Steinwachs

The "C" version of the Sturmgeschütz III from the Artillerie-Lehr-Regiment in at Berlin in November 1940. Chassis number 90 111. The vehicle is Gun A of a training battery. The training regiment unit insignia is visible on the right fender and to the left of the driver's vision port.

Winter training and first gunnery exercise for the 1./Sturmgeschütz-Abteilung 197 at the Jüterbog Training Area on 2 January 1941. TAMS

Forming up to move out in the new assault guns. The crews wear the short-lived crash helmet/beret combination, which proved both unwieldy and unpopular. It was soon discarded in favor of soft caps. RIECKER

Officers of Sturmgeschütz-Abteilung 197 at Jüterbog in January 1941. From left to right: Leutnant Ulbricht, Oberleutnant Brinker (Commander of the 1./Sturmgeschütz-Abteilung 197), Leutnant Spielmann and Leutnant Wollermann (KIA). PETERS

The "Cannon Eagle" crest of
Sturmgeschütz-Abteilung 197.
Individual batteries had different colors.
Green: Headquarters Battery;
white: 1./Sturmgeschütz-Abteilung 197;
red: 2./Sturmgeschütz-Abteilung 197;
yellow: 3./Sturmgeschütz-Abteilung 197;
and blue: Maintenance Battery.

The entire battalion rail loading at Jüterbog (Forst Zinna) on 4 February 1941 for transport to Brieg in Silesia (Military District VIII). RIECKER

The entire 1./Sturmgeschütz-Abteilung 197 assembles at the Mudra Barracks in Brieg (Silesia) on 13 February 1941 for an inspection by General Theißen, the commander of the 262. Infanterie-Division. PETERS

This picture of Gun A of the 3./Sturmgeschütz-Abteilung 197 was taken at the Oppeln Training Area. All assault guns display the battalion crest at this point. DR. RENOTIÉRE

The guns on display for Armed Forces Day on 23 March 1941.

The battalion received orders for employment in the Balkans Campaign by the end of March 1941, but the assault guns were unable to entrain at the Brieg freight yards until 7 April due to a shortage of rail cars. LOHRMANN

Assault guns of the 2./Sturmgeschütz-Abteilung 197. BECK

The battery command vehicle of the 1./Sturmgeschütz-Abteilung 197 was equipped with an MG 08/15 and retained this antiquated weapon until the end of April 1941. PETERS

Gun A of the 1./Sturmgeschütz-Abteilung 197 during a road march in Yugoslavia. PETERS

Although the battalion was not involved in combat, the maintenance sections and company kept busy, since the poor and mountainous march routes placed heavy demands on the wheeled and tracked vehicles. PETERS

In preparation for the attack on the Soviet Union, the battalion was moved from Glatz (Silesia) to eastern Poland on 30 May 1941. The batteries occupied wooded areas near the towns of Sahryn and Turkovice.

Three guns from the 3./Sturmgeschütz-Abteilung 197 (C, D and E) occupy the new assembly area along the Bug. Tarpaulins cover the assault guns to protect them from the dust and rain. Notice the letters painted on the tarpaulins. This photograph was taken on 20 June 1941. DR. RENOTIÉRE

Crew of the air-defense vehicle (Kfz. 4) of the 3./Sturmgeschütz-Abteilung 197 during final preparations. Maintenance and weapons cleaning. DR. RENOTIÉRE

Ammunition loading begins. DR. RENOTIÉRE

A quick letter to the family. DR. RENOTIÉRE

The batteries of the battalion crossed the Bug at Sokal at 0530 hours on 22 June 1941. The 1./Sturmgeschütz-Abteilung 197 was detached from the battalion immediately thereafter and attached to the 75. Infanterie-Division for a few days.

A gun commander intently scans the terrain. This was very often a dangerous task, since Russian snipers made special efforts to eliminate the commanders. NERGER

Examining a captured Russian T 26 tank. TAMS

A view of the loader, who also served as the vehicle's radio operator. The soldier plays a harmonica. The on-board submachine gun hangs ready on the rear bulkhead. TERIETE

The assault gun quickly proved itself as a fearsome weapon, not only in the infantry-support role, but also against tanks. This gun from the battalion displays 14 "kills" on the cannon's armor glacis. PETERS

Devastating hit on a gun from the 2./Sturmgeschütz-Abteilung 197. NERGER

Examining a captured Russian T 35. The combat value of this enormous Russian tank was questionable. It often fell prey to its own lack of maneuverability. TERIETE

A mired Russian KV 2 (152 mm cannon). DR. RENOTIÉRE

The 3./Sturmgeschütz-Abteilung 197 captured two T 34's at Poltava in October 1941. Both tanks were repaired by the maintenance company, adorned with white German crosses and sent into combat under new ownership. DR. RENOTIÉRE

In early November 1941, the battalion moved from Kharkov to Crimea. This road march of over 900 kilometers involved considerable breakdowns. The vehicles struggled along the mired paths and roads. The Sturmgeschütz had to pull the wheeled vehicles on some occasions.

One of the last "B" versions of the Sturmgeschütz III used by the battalion in the Crimea. After the unsuccessful attack against Sevastopol on 17 February 1942, almost all guns of this version were no longer serviceable. TAMS

This picture was taken in Ukrainka (Crimea), north of Simferopol, in March 1942. This "E" version Sturmgeschütz III offers an excellent example of a wavy camouflage pattern. TAMS

RIECKER

RIECKER

In the early spring of 1942, the vehicles and assault guns of the battalion were given a camouflage finish over their basic gray color. This observer's vehicle (SdKfz. 253) from the 1./Sturmgeschütz-Abteilung 197 was christened "Little Claire".

This observer's vehicle (SdKfz. 253) from the 1./Sturmgeschütz-Abteilung 197 received a pointblank hit from an anti-tank rifle during an attack on the Pabalsch Position on 8 May 1942. Wachtmeister Raydt was killed. RIECKER

Assault Gun "Z2" of the 1./Sturmgeschütz-Abteilung 197. To the left is Knight's Cross recipient, Leutnant Spielmann, who is conducting terrain reconnaissance shortly before the large-scale German attack on the Sevastopol fortress.

Assault Gun "D" of the 1./Sturmgeschütz-Abteilung 197. The center return roller was shot off during the attack on Fort "GPU" on 17 June 1942. BUSCH

The fighting for the Fortress of Sevastopol ended in a victory for the Germans on 3 July 1942. Officers and men of the battalion take in the destroyed fortifications of Fort "Maxim Gorki". BUSCH

An assault gun from the 3./Sturmgeschütz-Abteilung 197 after the end of the fighting for Crimea. Standing in front of it are its driver, Obergefreiter Heinrich Appel (left), and Gefreiter Paul Rost. APPEL

DR. RENOTIÈRE

DR. RENOTIÈRE

Assault Gun "A" of the 1./Sturmgeschütz-Abteilung 197 received a direct hit in the engine compartment on 14 August 1942 and caught fire. It exploded 15 minutes later.

The first long-barreled assault guns for the battalion arrived at the combat trains in Semlyansk on 17 August 1942. They were sprayed with sand-colored primer at the factory. DR. RENOTIÉRE

Guns from the 3./Sturm-geschütz-Abteilung 197 stand by for rail loading at the Orel train station on 2 October 1942 for the trip to Smolensk. All three batteries had a mixture of older and newer versions of the assault gun. APPEL

Oberleutnant Johann Spielmann, Battery Commander of the 1./Sturmgeschütz-Abteilung 197, together with the Battalion Commander, Hauptmann Steinwachs. This picture was taken shortly before the battalion's return to German territory. BUSCH

These two pictures of a Sturmgeschütz III (Chassis No. 91 284) from the 1./Sturmgeschütz-Abteilung 197 were taken during training near Spass-Demensk in January 1943. Gun Commander: Unteroffizier Heinz Henning.

Schweres Panzerjäger-Regiment 656 – July 1943

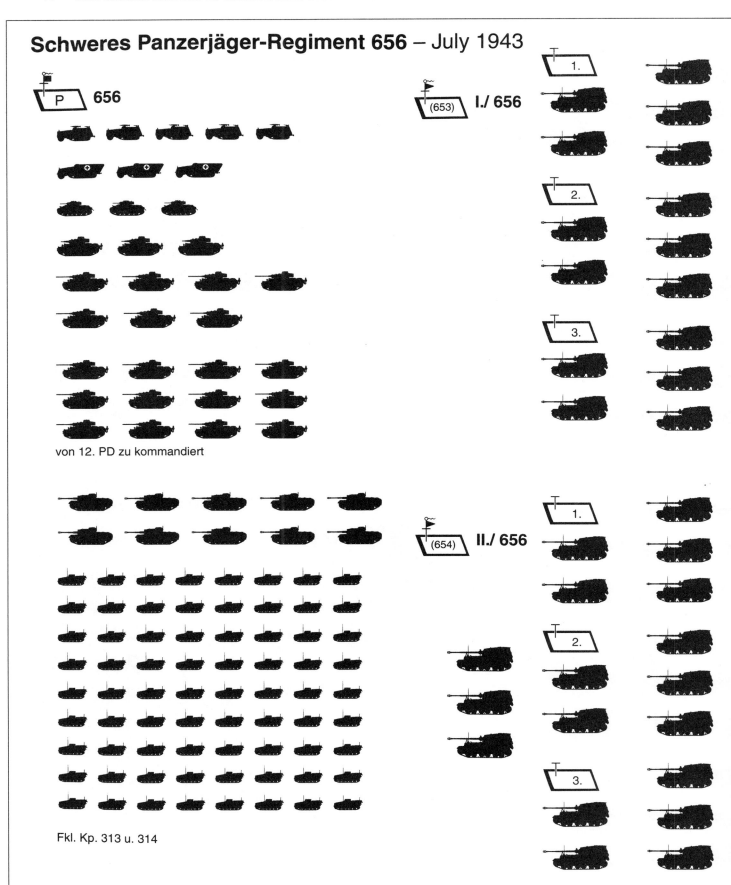

P 656

von 12. PD zu kommandiert

Fkl. Kp. 313 u. 314

(653) I./ 656

1.

2.

3.

(654) II./ 656

1.

2.

3.

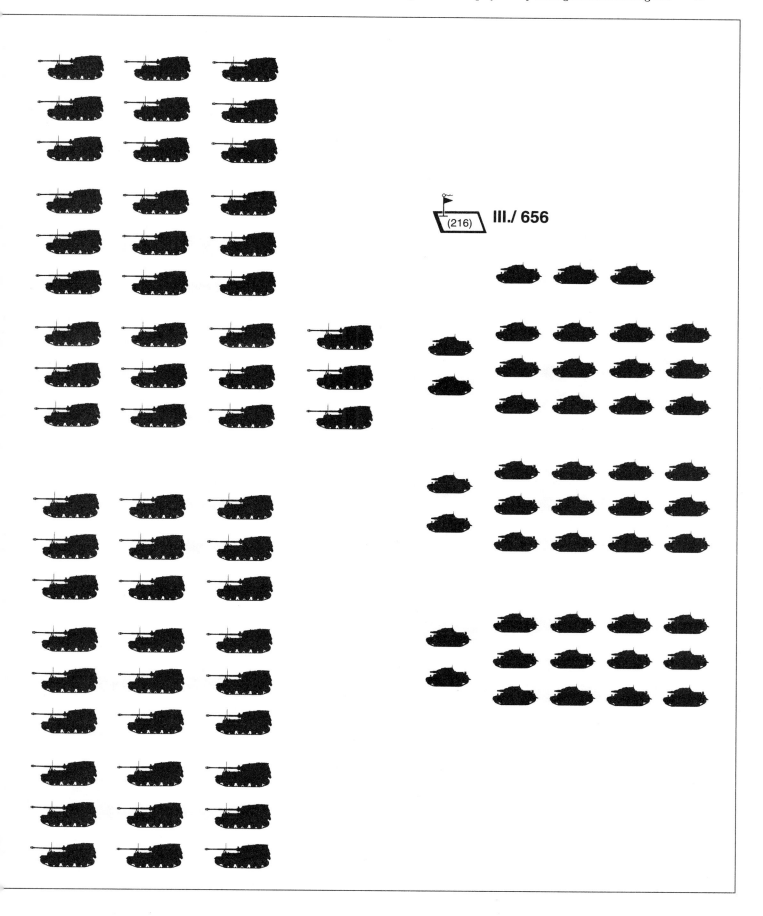

III./ 656

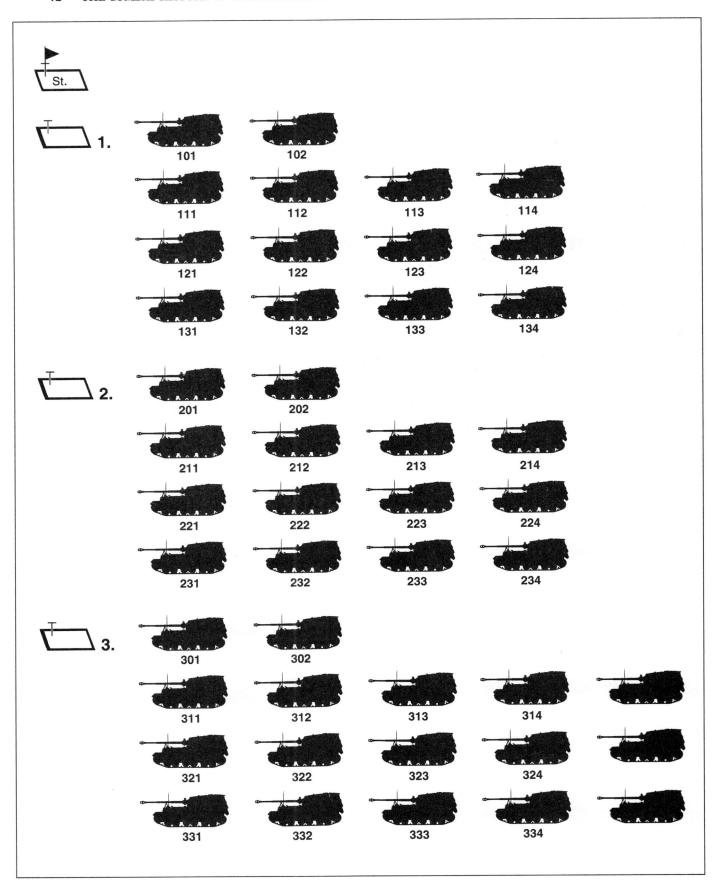

Formation and Employment of schwere Panzerjäger-Abteilung 653

(APRIL 1943 TO DECEMBER 1943)

On 1 April 1943, Sturmgeschütz-Abteilung 197 was redesignated as schwere Panzerjäger-Abteilung 653 at Bruck an der Leitha in Austria. It is also transferred from the assault artillery branch to armor. The officers, noncommissioned officers and soldiers of the former Sturmgeschütz-Abteilung 197 formed the cadre for the redesignated battalion. The commander was Major Heinrich Steinwachs. Oberst Hoffmann-Schoenborn, the senior officer of the assault artillery branch, bid farewell to the assault artillerymen on 14 April 1943 in a solemn ceremony.

The arrival of new personnel brought the battalion up to a strength of almost 1,000 men. In May 1943, it received the Ferdinand tank destroyer (Sd.Kfz. 184) as its combat vehicle. The tank destroyer, named after its designer, Professor Ferdinand Porsche, was the heaviest tank destroyer in the German armed forces at the time. A total of 90 Ferdinande were produced in this series.

TECHNICAL DATA FOR THE "FERDINAND" (SD.KFZ. 184)

Empty Weight:	65 tons
Combat Weight:	70 tons
Engines:	2 Maybach HL 120 TRM engines
Transmission:	Gasoline-Electric Porsche/Siemens
Maximum Speed:	35 kilometers per hour
Range (road/cross country):	150/90 kilometers
Fuel Consumption:	12 liters per kilometer
Crew:	6
Main gun:	one 88 mm Pak 43/1 L/71 (55 rounds in the basic load)
Auxiliary armament:	one MG 34 (600 rounds)

The Ferdinande were assembled at the Nibelungen Works in St. Valentin (Austria). The officers, vehicle commanders and drivers received several weeks of orientation there. The crews helped with portions of the final vehicle assembly. During this period, the soldiers lived in the Ennsdorf camp at Enns an der Donau or in Haag. The Nibelungen Works delivered the final Ferdinand (chassis number 150100) on 8 May 1943. After leaving the assault artillery branch, schwere Panzerjäger-Abteilung 653 relocated to Neusiedel am See. The battalion was billeted in the old Hungarian Hussar barracks.

The Army High Command ordered the first production batch of 45 Ferdinande delivered to Rouen (France). The battalion provided the transport personnel. The battalion's sister formation, schwere Panzerjäger-Abteilung 654, had been at Rouen since mid-April 1943. This battalion received its complement of vehicles first. After delivering the Ferdinande, the transport personnel from schwere Panzerjäger-Abteilung 653 returned to Neusiedel.

VEHICLE COMPLEMENT OF SCHWERE PANZERJÄGER-ABTEILUNG 653

(Source Federal Archives/Freiburg Military Archives)

As of 7 May 1943

	Required	Actual
Kr.Pz.Wg. 251/8	1	0
Stl.Sd.Kfz. 7/1	6	0
s.Zgkw. 18t Sd.Kfz. 9	15	15
Zgkw. 35t Sd.Kfz. 20	2	0
"Tiger (P)" Sd.Kfz. 184	45	8

As of ?

	Required	Actual
Kr.Pz.Wg.251/8	1	0
Stl.Sd.Kfz.7/1	6	2*
s.zgkw. 18t Sd.Kfz.9	15	15
Zgkw. 35t Sd.Kfz.20	2	0
"Tiger (P)" Sd.Kfz.184	45	40

* one en route

The battalion started combat training at the Bruck Training Area. The maintenance company and forward maintenance section attempted to work out all the "growing pains" affecting the Ferdinand tank destroyer.

Generaloberst Heinz Guderian, the Inspector General of the Armored Forces at the time, visited the battalion on 24 and 25 May 1943. He singled out the 1./schwere Panzerjäger-Abteilung 653, under the command of Knight's Cross holder Hauptmann Johann Spielmann, for special recognition. The 3./schwere Panzerjäger-Abteilung 653 conducted a minefield-crossing demonstration for the general, using radio controlled explosive charge carriers (Borgward IV's) and engineers. After the demonstrations, all of the drivers successfully bring their Ferdinande back the 42 kilometers from the training area to Neusiedel without a single breakdown. (Guderian's aide de camp verified this improbable fact for the incredulous general.) After a briefing about the impending offensive in the Kursk salient, Generaloberst Guderian bid farewell to the battalion' s soldiers.

Effective 8 June 1943, schweres Panzerjäger-Regiment 656 was established in St. Pölten (Austria). The commander was Oberstleutnant Baron Ernst von Jungenfeld. The cadre for the staff came from Panzer-Regiment 35 (home station: Bamberg)

Schweres Panzerjäger-Regiment 656 was assigned three battalions:

- I./schweres Panzerjäger-Regiment 656 (schwere Panzerjäger-Abteilung 653). Commander: Major Heinrich Steinwachs
- II./schweres Panzerjäger-Regiment 656 (schwere Panzer-Jäger-Abteilung 654). Commander: Hauptmann Karl-Heinz Noak
- III./schweres Panzerjäger-Regiment 656 (Sturmpanzer-Abteilung 216). Commander: Major Bruno Kahl

(To avoid confusion, all of the above named battalions will be referred to by their original designations in the text, unless specifically noted otherwise.)

The regiment also received two radio-controlled armor companies, Panzer-Kompanie 313 (Fkl), under Oberleutnant Fritschken, and Panzer-Kompanie 314 (Fkl), under Hauptmann Braam. These two companies had a total of 72 B IV's as part of their inventory.

Schwere Panzerjäger-Abteilung 653 moved to Russia aboard 11 transport trains (transport numbers 326281-326291) from 9-12 June 1943. The loading site was Parndorf (Austria). The battalion moved through Brünn, Modlin, Brest-Litovsk, Minsk, Briansk, Karatchev and Orel to its staging area. The detraining site was the Smiyevka train station, 35 kilometers south of Orel. From there, the individually arriving companies moved to their assembly areas (Davidovo for the 3./schwere Panzerjäger-Abteilung 653; Gostinovo for the 2./schwere Panzerjäger-Abteilung 653; and Kuliki for the 1./schwere Panzerjäger-Abteilung 653). The companies occupied those areas until 30 June 1943. Additional technical training was conducted there, and the vehicle commanders received terrain orientations.

Starting on 1 July 1943, the attack forces of the 9. Armee began moving in small groups to their forward assembly areas behind the front (Ssorotschi Kusty). All vehicles refueled and rearmed there. On 2 July 1943, the vehicles moved forward another 15 kilometers and occupied positions in the town of Novopolevo. During the evening twilight of 3 July 1943, the Ferdinande of schwere Panzerjäger-Abteilung 653 moved to their start point in Glasunovka, directly on the Orel-Kursk rail line. Schweres Panzerjäger-Regiment 656 assembled there as part of the XXXXI. Panzer-Korps (General der Panzertruppen Harpe). The Regimental Commander, Oberstleutnant Ernst von Jungenfeld, spoke to the assembled soldiers on the evening of 4 July 1943.

VEHICLE COMPLEMENT OF SCHWERE PANZERJÄGER-REGIMENT 656 (4 JULY 1943)

	Assigned	Available	Repairs
Sd.Kfz. 250/5	5	5	.
Sd.Kfz. 251/8	3	3	
Sd.Kfz. 30 I	72	72	
Stug. III	10	10	
Bef.Pz. III L/42	5	5	
Bef.Stu.Pz. (15 cm)	3	3	
Stu.Pz. IV	42	39	3

continued

VEHICLE COMPLEMENT OF SCHWERE PANZERJÄGER-REGIMENT 656 (4 JULY 1943)

	Assigned	Available	Repairs
Ferdinande	89	83	6
Pz. III L/42	12	10	2
Pz. III L/60	7	7	
Pz. III 7.5 cm	3	3	
Pz. II	3	3	

(12 Panzer III's transferred to the 12. Panzer-Division)
(Source: Federal Archives / Freiburg Military Archives)

On 5 July 1943 at 0330 hours, the entire 9. Armee launched its portion of the attack for Operation "Citadel".

OFFICER DUTY POSITIONS WITHIN SCHWERE PANZERJÄGER-ABTEILUNG 653 (AS OF: 5 JULY 1943)

Commander:	Major Heinrich Steinwachs
Adjutant:	Leutnant Bernhard Konnak
Liaison Officer:	Leutnant Werner Haberland
Battalion Surgeon:	Dr. Herbert Bauermeister (transferred to the staff of schweres Panzerjäger-Regiment 656)
Battalion Surgeon:	Dr. Wolfgang Prellwitz
Paymaster:	Oberzahlmeister Karl Koch
Battalion Engineer:	Kriegsverwaltungsrat Schaffranek
Headquarters Company:	Oberleutnant Karl Seitz
1./schwere Panzerjäger-Abteilung 653:	Hauptmann Johann Spielmann
2./schwere Panzerjäger-Abteilung 653:	Hauptmann Eberhard Kuntze
3./schwere Panzerjäger-Abteilung 653:	Oberleutnant Hanns Wegelin
Maintenance Company:	Oberleutnant Lange

FERDINAND VEHICLE COMMANDERS (OREL, 5 JULY 1943)

1./schwere Panzerjäger-Abteilung 653

Ferdinand 101	Hauptmann Johann Spielmann
Ferdinand 102	Hauptfeldwebel Fritz Madaus
Ferdinand 111	Oberleutnant Helmut Ulbricht
Ferdinand 112	Stabsfeldwebel Willi Slanarz
Ferdinand 113	Feldwebel Karl Wedler (?)
Ferdinand 114	Unteroffizier Erich Prezler (?)
Ferdinand 121	Leutnant Herrmann Löck
Ferdinand 122	Feldwebel Wilhelm Flintrop (?)

Ferdinand 123	Unteroffizier Werner Kühl (?)
Ferdinand 124	Feldwebel Rolf Schleicher / Feldwebel Hans Huber
Ferdinand 131	Feldwebel Gustav Koss (?)
Ferdinand 132	Unteroffizier Horst Golinski (?)
Ferdinand 133	Feldwebel Heinz Rempel (?)
Ferdinand 134	Unteroffizier Reinhold Schlabs

2./schwere Panzerjäger-Abteilung 653

Ferdinand 201	Hauptmann Eberhard Kuntze
Ferdinand 202	Hauptfeldwebel Willi Schmidt (?)
Ferdinand 211	Leutnant Karl Schrader (killed 15 July 1943)
Ferdinand 212	Stabsfeldwebel Ebel (?)
Ferdinand 213	Feldwebel Franz Blaschke (?)
Ferdinand 214	Unteroffizier Erhard Rau (?)
Ferdinand 221	Leutnant Göttelmann KIA)
Ferdinand 222	Feldwebel Kurt Albinus (?)
Ferdinand 223	Feldwebel Emanuel Schlenska (?)
Ferdinand 224	? Albin Weiskopf (?)
Ferdinand 231	Oberfeldwebel Friedrich W. Meigen (?)
Ferdinand 232	Feldwebel Otto Hecker (?)
Ferdinand 233	Feldwebel Heinz Borngässer (?)
Ferdinand 234	Unteroffizier Fritz Walkenhorst (?)

3./schwere Panzerjäger-Abteilung 653

Ferdinand 301	Oberleutnant Werner Salarnon
Ferdinand 302	Wachtmeister Franz Czichochewski
Ferdinand 311	Oberleutnant Lange
Ferdinand 312	Oberfeldwebel Emil Issler (?)
Ferdinand 313	Feldwebel Fritz Schwarz (?)
Ferdinand 314	Wachtmeister Ferdinand Biermann (?)
Ferdinand 321	Oberwachtmeister Speidel (?) (KIA)
Ferdinand 322	Wachtmeister Heinrich Teriete (?)
Ferdinand 323	Unteroffizier Christian Noethen (?)
Ferdinand 324	Unteroffizier Willi Petry (?)
Ferdinand 331	Leutnant Franz Kretschmer
Ferdinand 332	Feldwebel Albin Heinickel
Ferdinand 333	Wachtmeister Benno Schardin
Ferdinand 334	Fahnenjunker (Officer Candidate) Wilhelm Opitz
Ferdinand	?*
Ferdinand	?
Ferdinand	?

* The three Ferdinande issued for the Headquarters Company were attached to the 3./schwere Panzerjäger-Abteilung 653. These vehicles were received without tactical markings. Vehicle commanders designated with a (?) have not been associated with a specific vehicle number until now.

After a mighty artillery barrage and heavy bomber attacks by the Luftwaffe, the Ferdinande of the battalion, along with the infantry of the 292. Infanterie-Division and the 86. Infanterie-Division, moved forward along a broad front. Behind them, in the second wave, were the Sturmpanzer (assault tanks) of Sturmpanzer-Abteilung 216—150 mm assault howitzers on a Panzer IV chassis and referred to after the war as the Brummbär ("Grizzly Bear")—and the assault guns of Sturmgeschütz-Abteilung 177 and Sturmgeschütz-Abteilung 244.

The objective was the first network of Russian positions on Hill 257.7, named "Tank Hill", which was the cornerstone of the Russian defensive networks at Malo-Archangelsk and Olchovatka. The barren terrain was very heavily mined and the radio-controlled explosive-charge carriers employed there were unable to accomplish the task. The Ferdinande of schwere Panzerjäger-Abteilung 653 made very slow progress through the minefield. Many vehicles were immobilized with broken tracks and damaged idler arms. The commander of the 1./schwere Panzerjäger-Abteilung 653, Hauptmann Spielmann, was severely wounded by a Russian antipersonnel mine while dismounted and guiding his driver, Unteroffizier Karl Gresch. Oberleutnant Helmut Ulbricht took assumed acting command of the company.

In a memorandum about the employment of radio-controlled weapons during the period from 5–8 July 1943, the Commander of Panzer-Abteilung 301 (Fkl), Major Reinel, described the actions of the radio-controlled companies during Operation "Citadel" (Source: Federal Archives / Freiburg Military Archives):

SECRET

Reinel
Major
Commander
Panzer-Abteilung (Fkl) 301

23 July 1943

Three separate radio-controlled tank companies were employed in the area of operations of the 9. Armee during the attacks south of Orel on 5 July. Two companies were attached to schweres Panzerjäger-Regiment 656 and one to schwere Panzer-Abteilung 505. The companies were employed as organic wholes and led by their company commanders, who directed their platoons to work closely with the forward-employed companies of the larger formations.

The combat mission was the same for all the companies, specifically: Aggressive combat reconnaissance; detection of minefields and clearing lanes through them; destruction of hard to overcome positions, such as fortified antitank weapons; as well as super-heavy enemy tanks. Inquiries among the units about the combat operations presented the following picture:

1) Employment of Panzer-Kompanie 314 (Fkl) with the 1./schweres Panzerjäger-Regiment 656 [schwere Panzerjäger-Abteilung 653].

A very dense, echeloned minefield blocked approaches to the Russian main line of resistance, which was simultaneously blocked by heavy artillery barrages. In accordance with its attack orders, the company began clearing three lanes through the minefield. Due to the great depth of the minefield, a total of 12 B IV's were expended in the process. The control tanks traversed these lanes without suffering any damage from mines. The breaching of these lanes by combat engineers, as outlined in the order, was unsuccessful, however, because they could not move forward through the overwhelming artillery fire. This caused a halt in the attack. The numerous artillery explosions on the battlefield made it impossible for the heavy tank destroyers (Ferdinande) to recognize the lanes cleared through the minefields by the B IV's. Even the B IV tracks were not visible in the thick sod. This caused losses among the Ferdinande, despite the lanes cleared through the minefields. During the rest of the attack, a total of seven B IV's were employed. Of these, one landed in a trench occupied by infantry, whom it destroyed as they attempted to attack it with hand grenades and close-combat weapons. Two B IV's were steered towards a heavily occupied wooded area against which our infantry could not advance and then detonated within it. There was no further resistance there after that. Four B IV's were destroyed by artillery shells during the course of the offensive operations. One already had its fuse armed, and it detonated; the other three caught fire.

2) Employment of Panzer-Kompanie 313 (Fkl) with the II./schweres Panzerjäger-Regiment 656 [schwere Panzer-Jäger-Abteilung 654] took place under the same conditions. Four B IV's were destroyed when one of the company's platoons crossed an unknown friendly minefield on approach to the front line. As a result, the other platoon was only able to clear one lane through the Russian minefield, expending 4 B IV's in the process. Artillery fire struck and detonated one B IV in the assembly area and set two more ablaze. The undersigned could not clearly determine the cause of this incident, because the B IV driver and [nearby] combat engineers were all killed. It is suspected that the fuses were already in place and the heat of the burning charge detonated them. Another B IV was hit by artillery during its radio-controlled approach and also exploded. Later in the attack, three B IV's destroyed antitank nests and a bunker, achieving both a tactical success and rise in morale.

3) Employment of the Panzer-Kompanie 312 (Fkl) with schwere Panzer-Abteilung 505.

The company deployed forward of the Tiger tanks as a combat reconnaissance force in accordance with tactical requirements and had the following successes: One B IV was detonated at a distance of 800 meters in an antitank nest of 2 or 3 guns, destroying all the infantry clustered around it. Another B IV was deployed against a T 34 at a distance of 400 meters. The T 34 tried to ram the B IV and was destroyed as it detonated. Three B IV's were steered towards three heavy bunkers at distances of 400 to 600 meters, destroying all three bunkers when detonated. One B IV moved towards an antitank bunker and destroyed it, even though the vehicle was set ablaze 10 meters short of the bunker before exploding. Two B IV's were committed at a distance of 800 meters against an antitank crew and infantry gun, destroying both. One B IV reached a Russian position and was attacked with Molotov cocktails, detonating it. The explosion had a terrible effect upon the enemy position. Four B IV's were destroyed by enemy defensive fire during their approaches. On two occasions, we successfully recovered the radio control devices, but the other two burned. A total of 20 B IV's were deployed during four days of fighting.

Tactical Evaluation of the Operation [Excerpts]

1) Employment of the radio-controlled companies, which are a potent offensive weapon, succeeded in two cases in conjunction with the heavy tank destroyers and in only one case together with a proven offensive weapon, a Tiger battalion. With regard to the heavy tank destroyers, the heavy weight of the Ferdinande restricted the offensive momentum of the radio-controlled units. The latter quickly won ground, but the sluggishness of the Ferdinande during the attack resulted in offensive successes not being exploited quickly enough. The advancing control tanks had to wait too long for the Ferdinande to arrive and suffered heavy losses from enemy weapons. On the other hand, the coordination with a pure tank unit, the Tiger battalion, worked much better. Especially qualified and trained as offensive weapons, both technically and tactically, they won ground during the attack and held together well. The operation proved that radio-controlled weapons can only achieve total success when working in conjunction with pure tank formations.

2) Employment of Panzer-Kompanie 313 (Fkl) and Panzer-Kompanie 314 (Fkl) (within schweres Panzerjäger-Regiment 656), along both sides of the Orel-Kursk rail line, was con-

ducted against a deeply echeloned position with heavy minefields in its forward areas. The extremely powerful effect of the enemy artillery made the attacker's mission considerably more difficult . . . Both companies were spread along a wide regimental sector and each attached to a Ferdinand battalion. They used up their combat power very quickly. Due to shortages of reserves, they could not cover their losses in the forward-deployed platoons, much less sustain the thrust deep into the enemy main battle area. There was no mobile reserve available, which a higher-level radio-controlled unit commander could have deployed at a weak area to turn a penetration into a breakthrough. The close coordination with the Ferdinande, which was necessary for complete success, was well achieved through planning and tactical exercises. In combat, however, this coordination soon collapsed in the face of heavy enemy weapons and could not be re-established despite energetic efforts by the radio-controlled unit commanders, because they could not overrule the orders of the battalion commanders. A higher-level radio-controlled leadership could have contributed to success here as well. Eight of the twelve available control tanks had to be deployed on the front line. The remaining four had to move forward a short time later to cover the resulting losses. Due to the lack of reserves, the attack soon lost momentum and became stuck in enemy positions.

With only 12 operational Ferdinande remaining, schwere Panzerjäger-Abteilung 653 reached its objective for the day at 1700 hours on 5 July 1943. During the next two day, the Ferdinande took part in extremely difficult operations around the town of Ponyri. Major Steinwachs then had to order a recovery day for the battalion, because all the vehicles were effectively out of action and in dire need of repairs.

Former Gun Commander, Unteroffizier Reinhold Schlabs, described the loss of Ferdinand 134 in a letter to the author on 22 January 1991:

It must have been the last day of the attack when I arrived back at my company with vehicle number 134. It had been undergoing repairs at the maintenance section at the rail embankment. After his gun was damaged, Oberleutnant Ulbricht climbed aboard my vehicle. We moved forward—I remember it to this day—we were the only operational vehicle, and we found safety in the concealment of a sandy depression. After a short time, we came under fire from our own artillery and received a direct hit in the rear track. We were no longer able to move. We halted the artillery barrage by firing a flare. Oberleutnant Ulbricht immediately concerned himself with the recovery of his vehicle, while my crew and I held out in our vehicle until dark. The Russians attacked during the night, but made a wide detour to the left and right around the depression. Since there was no possibility of recovering the vehicle in this situation, we evacuated the vehicle and destroyed it, making our way back to the rail embankment on foot. It seemed like a miracle when a Panzer IV overtook us on the way back and took us aboard. We reached the battalion command post around 0300 hours and I reported, to the great surprise of our commander, Major Steinwachs, that my crew (although without a vehicle) had returned safely.

The Russian 3rd Tank Army—four corps with 1,460 tanks and 21 divisions; a total strength of 230,000 men—received orders on 11 July 1943 to conduct the offensive at Orel. The prelude concentrated on the XXXV. Armee-Korps under General der Infanterie Rendulic. Schwere Panzerjäger-Abteilung 653 moved to Rendulic's sector during the night of 13/14 July 1943 and occupied defensive positions. On 14 July 1943, the 36. Panzergrenadier-Division was the target of a frontal attack by almost 400 Russian tanks. The Ferdinande of schwere Panzerjäger-Abteilung 653, together with the antitank elements of the mechanized infantry division, became rescuers of the highest degree. Despite a lack of both time and familiarity with the terrain, a consolidated battle group of all three tank-destroyer companies, under the command of Leutnant Heinrich Teriete, succeeded in repulsing the attack. Leutnant Teriete received the Knight's Cross to the Iron Cross on 22 July 1943 for the destruction of 22 Russian tanks during this engagement. (Teriete's driver was Alois Schäfer and his gunner was Kurt Titus.)

Notes from a source within the 36. Panzergrenadier-Division illuminate operations of schwere Panzerjäger-Abteilung 653 and schwere Panzerjäger-Abteilung 654 during this second phase of Operation "Citadel" (after 12 July 1943):

13 July 1943: Voroschilovo Train Station. Three Ferdinande of schwere Panzerjäger-Abteilung 653 together with seven Hornissen ["Hornets": a lightly armored tank destroyer based on a Panzer III/Panzer IV chassis and armed with the formidable 8.8 centimeter Pak 43/1 L71] unload at Voroschilovo (West) during the night.

14 July 1943: 24 Ferdinande from schwere Panzerjäger-Abteilung 653 and 30 assault guns from Sturmgeschütz-Abteilung 185 moved to the Beresovez-Ponikovez area: 53. Infanterie-Division and 36. Panzergrenadier-Division. During the early morning hours, 34 Ferdinande from schwere Panzerjäger-Abteilung 653 were in position on the left flank of Kampfgruppe Gollnick. 26 Ferdinande from schwere Panzer-Jäger-Abteilung 654 have been in this sector since 12 July. At 0500 hours, Pionier-Bataillon 36 [36. Panzergrenadier-Division], with attached assault guns from Sturmgeschütz-Abteilung 185 and 4 Ferdinande from schwere Panzerjäger-Abteilung 653, attacked dug-in enemy tanks in Shelyabug (South) (southeastern portion). The combat-engineer battalion was minus its 3rd Company. This company, along with 4 Ferdinande from schwere Panzerjäger-Abteilung 653, under the command of Leutnant Kretschmer, was sent to the location of the 12./Grenadier-Regiment 87 in Shelabugskiye-Wiss. Additionally, 20 assault guns and 4 Ferdinande from schwere Panzer-Jäger-Abteilung 654 were in firing positions in Podmasslovo (Southeast), oriented towards Hill 267.3. Around 0800 hours, 6 Ferdinande from schwere Panzerjäger-Abteilung 653 and 6 self-propelled guns from Panzerjäger-Abteilung 36, occupied positions in Kotschety (northern edge) under the command of Leutnant Kothe. At 1630 hours, the 4 Ferdinande from schwere Panzerjäger-Abteilung 653 held in reserve and the 3./Sturmgeschütz-Abteilung 185 were attacked by enemy tanks that had broken through. At 1700 hours, enemy tanks broke out of Krassn. Niva and overran the 10./Grenadier-Regiment 118 of Hauptmann Nicklas. Twenty-two tanks in the first wave were destroyed by Leutnant Teriete's Ferdinand firing from the right flank near the command post of Grenadier-Regiment 118.

15 July 1943: During regrouping, 9 Ferdinande from schwere Panzerjäger-Abteilung 653 were sent to occupy positions on a hill one kilometer southeast of Zarevka.

16 July 1943: Schwere Panzer-Jäger-Abteilung 654 occupied defensive positions in the sectors of the 292. Infanterie-Division and the 36. Panzergrenadier-Division (minus Grenadier-Regiment 118) up to and including Zarevka. The Ferdinande of schwere Panzerjäger-Abteilung 653 were with Infanterie-Regiment 36 (mot.) of the 36. Panzergrenadier-Division and the 8. Panzer-Division.

The high rate of maintenance problems with the Ferdinande caused Major Steinwachs to form small Kampfgruppen that supported various division (among them: the 78. Sturm-Division, the 262. Infanterie-Division and the 299. Infanterie-Division).

The following lists of engagements for the battalion are taken from the Wehrpaß of Gefreiter Johann Schleiß, a medic from the Headquarters Company of schwere Panzerjäger-Abteilung 653:

Day	Date	Area
1	5 July 1943	Orel-Kursk
2	6 July 1943	Prilepy
3	7 July 1943	Ponyri
4	8 July 1943	Ponyri
5	9 July 1943	Polevaya-Stream
6	13 July 1943	Setucha
7	14 July 1943	Shelyabug-South
8	15 July 1943	Podmasslovo
9	17 July 1943	Prilepy
10	18 July 1943	Vinniza
11	19 July 1943	Kasinka
12	20 July 1943	Maiski-Kasinka
13	21 July 1943	Telegino
14	22 July 1941	Mochovskiy
15	23 July 1943	Krassny-Svesda
16	25 July 1943	Krynkovka

Suffering 24 killed and missing, 126 wounded and 13 totally destroyed guns, the battalion destroyed 320 Russian tanks and a large number of guns, antitank guns and trucks during the period from 5 to 27 July 1943.

Totally Destroyed "Ferdinande," schwere Panzerjäger-Abteilung 653

- 1./schwere Panzerjäger-Abteilung 653: 6 Ferdinande (Guns 111, 112, 113, 122, 132, 134)
- 2./schwere Panzerjäger-Abteilung 653: 1 Ferdinand (Gun 232)
- 3./schwere Panzerjäger-Abteilung 653: 4 Ferdinande (Guns 311, 323, 331, 333)
- two Ferdinande from the vehicle reserve

Unteroffizier Böhm wrote about the first combat operations of the Ferdinande in a report dated 19 July 1943 to Generalmajor Hartmann in the Speer Ministry. (Source: Federal Archives / Freiburg Military Archives)

Honorable General Hartmann!

Please permit me to report to you about the combat operations of our Ferdinande. On the first day of combat, we successfully defeated bunkers, infantry, artillery and antitank positions. Our guns were under artillery barrages for three hours and still maintained their ability to fire! Several tanks were destroyed during the first night, and the others fled. Artillery and antitank crews fled before our guns after we fired upon them repeatedly.

In addition to many batteries, antitank guns and bunkers, our battalion destroyed 120 tanks during the first round of fighting. We suffered 60 casualties during the first few days, mostly from mines. Everything far and wide was mined and the "mine dogs" [Author's note: B IV explosive-charge carriers] were insufficient. Unfortunately, we even crossed one of our own minefields!

We had much to do, but got everything accomplished! Inspector General Guderian was also with us. The Russians have increased their number of weapons greatly! They had artillery here in amounts we had never seen before and fired at individual soldiers with it! They have numerous antitank guns and their handheld antitank weapons are very good (I measured a penetration 55 millimeters into a Ferdinand). We had 6 total losses during the first operation, one of which received a direct hit in the open driver's hatch while halted and caught fire— one killed, three wounded. One caught fire due to unknown reasons (presumably an exhaust leak) and another was burnt out when its generator caught fire from overuse attempting to extract itself from a swamp. Three others were immobilized by mines and had to be destroyed by the crews during an enemy counterattack.

We also had some bad luck. It was at the rail embankment when a Panzer III on the other side received a direct hit and flew through the air, landing on the front part of the Ferdinand, breaking the gun tube, aiming device and engine grating. The other battalion had a heavy shell penetrate the roof of a vehicle.

We were more successful during the second operation, defending east of Orel. Only two total losses (one destroyed by crew). One gun under Leutnant [Teriete] destroyed 22 tanks in one engagement. The total number of tanks destroyed is high and the Ferdinande contributed substantially to the defense, just as with the penetration. One gun commander destroyed seven of the nine American-built tanks that approached him.

The main gun is very good. It destroys every tank with one or two rounds, even the KV II and the sloped American ones. The high-explosive rounds, however, cause many stoppages when the cartridges become jammed—sometimes very distressing. One gun tube was hit, another burst and a third exploded from too much pressure. These were replaced with tubes from destroyed vehicles, and parts were cannibalized, since we had managed to recover all of our broken vehicles. W are also placing protective covers over the gratings now, which was my suggestion, because the Russians fire at us with phosphorus shells and the aircraft drop the same.

The Ferdinand has proved itself. They were decisive here, and we cannot go against the mass of enemy tanks today without a weapon of its type. Assault guns are not enough. The electric transmission has proved itself completely, pleasantly surprising both drivers and crews. There were very few engine and electrical malfunctions. The engine is recognized as weak for the tonnage and the track is a bit narrow. If the vehicle is modified according to combat experiences, it will be fantastic!

One Ferdinand was mistakenly hit in the superstructure by a Panzer IV. The gun commander was cut in two. An antitank gun hit another in the sprocket. Yet another was hit in the hull by a T 34 at a range of 400 meters (seven T 34's surrounded it). The entire round penetrated without causing any damage. One Ferdinand occupying a forward position at night was damaged and blinded by infantry in close combat and landed in a ditch. A machine gun at the front is needed for such occasions. The side hatches are too small and one cannot aim through them.

A large error on our part is letting enemy guns and tanks remain on the battlefield instead of employing special units to either recover or destroy them. If, for example, 45 enemy tanks remain in no-man's-land overnight, then 20 of them are missing the next morning. The Russians will have recovered them with half-tracks during the night. The tanks we destroyed last summer and left on the battlefield fell into Russian hands again this winter. In several weeks, perhaps 50 of them will be operational again, and we wonder where all those Russian tanks come from. This costs us work and blood. During our first operation, for example, all knocked out Russian tanks remained in place, as did the cannon and antitank guns, some of them intact and with ammunition. The dug-up mines remained out in the open. When the front had to be withdrawn, everything fell back into Russian hands.

It was the same here. The American tanks remained in place. We should consider recovering these items as raw materials to create new weapons. This would give us the means to acquire good raw materials (which are often hard for us to obtain) for production of new heavy weapons. Thousand of tons could be brought in this way while depriving the enemy of recovering their losses in a short time through repairs or cannibalization. There are already scrap-metal collection points, but this could be pursued more intensively. Empty rail cars sometimes sit at stations for long periods, when they could be filled in the interim.

I have heard that all broken down Ferdinande from our battalion were recovered. They arrived too late and there were too few. We need 10 times as many, then we would make progress. I hope the new type is almost ready for production. Other than that, I am well and hope that the General is also in the best of health again.

Heil Hitler!

/signed/ Unteroffizier Böhm

The poor mechanical condition of the vehicles of schweres Panzerjäger-Regiment 656 forced the Regimental Commander, Oberstleutnant von Jungenfeld, to send the following report to the 2. Panzer-Armee:

SECRET

schweres Panzerjäger-Regiment 656   Regiment Command Post
24 July 1943

Commander
No. 250/43 SECRET

To
Headquarters, 2. Panzer-Armee
SUBJECT: Status report of schweres Panzerjäger-Regiment 656

As dictated by the tactical situation, the regiment has been in combat without interruption since 5 July. Only the [I./schweres Panzerjäger-Regiment 656] had a 24-hour period to conduct maintenance. Since the Ferdinand tank destroyers, like the Sturmpanzer, had an extraordinary number of mechanical problems, it was planned to withdraw them for 2–3 days following a 3–5 day operation—and for longer periods after longer operations—to effect repairs. The maintenance units have worked day and night to repair damaged vehicles, so that sufficient vehicles are available to face the enemy.

Due to the excessive demands placed upon all vehicles by the tactical situation, they all need an immediate 14–20 day overhaul. Their mechanical condition is such that there are more cases every day of newly repaired vehicles breaking down on the way from the maintenance sections to their formations with new or different problems. Planning for operations with a certain number of vehicles, as well as forecasting the number of combat-ready vehicles, has become impossible. We can only count on the vehicles that have survived the trip between the maintenance unit and the front to oppose the enemy.

Consequently, I must report to the 2. Panzer-Armee that my regiment will no longer be combat ready due to mechanical reasons in a very short time, if it is not possible to give all vehicles at least one week for thorough maintenance.

The regiment still has available:

54 Ferdinande

41 Sturmpanzer

Of which, the following are operational:

25 Ferdinande (4 only conditionally operational)

18 Sturmpanzer

Even these operational vehicles" are on their last legs.

I therefore urge you to withdraw the Ferdinande from the front line, dissolve the various groups and leave only 3 groups 5-8 kilometers behind the front as a mobile reserve. All other Ferdinande will go to the maintenance units. Overhauled Ferdinande will then relieve those at the front.

Recommendations:

Kampfgruppe I:

Location: Near Krutaya Gora. Operations in the Schumalovo-Domnino-Mal Dyabzevo sector.

Kampfgruppe II:

Location: Stanovoi-Kolodes. Operations in the sector from the field-army boundary to Schumalovo.

Regimental command post in the immediate vicinity of the Headquarters of the 2. Panzer-Armee. Telephone communications through the Headquarters of the 2. Panzer-Armee (Codeword: Schankwirth). Radio contact with both Kampfgruppen every half hour from 0400 to 2400 hours. Transport orders for all non-operational vehicles are being disseminated and will be carried out on 27 July 1943.

The regiment also reports that employment of vehicles in Kampfgruppe Kahl along the Orel-Mzensk road is only possible up to Orel, because of the presently mired roads.

/signed/

von Jungenfeld

The first combat lessons for the Ferdinand, from the mechanical viewpoint, were written by Heinz Gröschl, attached to schwere Panzerjäger-Abteilung 653 from the Porsche Company as an advisor, in a report to the Porsche Company dated 26 July 1943 Source: Federal Archives / Freiburg Military Archives):

Our vehicles have been in combat for three weeks and, along with the previous kilometers, have covered an average total of 500 kilometers each. I have accumulated enough information to present you with a picture of the positive and negative qualities of our vehicles. I concur with the majority of the gentlemen in the battalion that the weapon has been successful, and it is a universal regret that there are so few of them available. With an average of 15 enemy tanks destroyed per vehicle, we can certainly speak of success. I must stress above all things that this figure could have been considerably higher. Unfortunately, the majority of the vehicles are always undergoing repairs. This condition becomes worse with every passing day, because the already insufficient supply of repair parts has been exhausted with the increasing wear on all parts. There has been practically no re-supply of repair parts to speak of. There are 17 vehicles missing from the original total of 44. Seven of these have been transferred to other battalions on orders from the regiment. The other 10 were total losses. I will now report on the most serious damage and problems.

Tracks and Suspension (Idler Arm Assemblies)

Despite expectations, there was no damage due to overloading. The soft ground played an important role. The wear-out of rubber pads (especially on the two rear idler arms) and rubber rings (usually the 5th roadwheel under the exhaust) was very great. Slot and key nuts did not become loose, although most of the vehicles still have the old tin washers. A mass replacement of curled roadwheel rings is necessary. Torsion bars have not broken since Neusiedl. Joint supports hold up with no problems. Enemy actions have rendered approximately 20 idler arm assemblies (idler arms with spring housings) and a larger number of idler arms inoperable. Damaged idler arms, cracked spring housings, every slot and key nut ripped out and frequently deformed idler arms were the most common types of damage, mostly caused by mines. The fifth roadwheel will not hold grease because of the high temperature in that area. Support trunnion breakage on the forward idler arm assemblies was probably caused by mines as well. Unfortunately, replacement parts were and still are not available in sufficient quantities. Parts from destroyed vehicles were used whenever possible.

Forward Drive

Except for one incident in Neusiedl—undoubtedly brought up by Herr Zadnik—there have been no problems. You are certainly aware of worn-down sprocket bolts by now.

Steering Assembly and Brake

Herr Zadnik is aware of several cases of brake damage in Neusiedl. No problems since then. Two vehicles that remained in combat for a day or two after being damaged each had a brake drum shot through. Naturally, the inner parts were completely destroyed.

Track

Has become one of the most difficult problems recently. One third to one half of the track pins on most vehicles have broken once or twice. Repair parts are completely non-existent. Mines and main-gun fire have made a large number of joints completely unserviceable.

Hull

Has proved itself almost impervious to rounds. Except for one penetrating hit to the side near the rear ventilation motor housing (76 mm) and besides many scars, everything has remained intact. It should be mentioned that even the single penetrating round did not have any ill effects. Practical experience has shown however, that the engine gratings are a weak area. Along with Molotov cocktails, a direct hit from artillery or a [bomb] on or near the gratings can set the vehicle ablaze. Shrapnel penetrates the fuel tank or damages other important parts, such as water lines. The temperature in the engine compartment was so high that the fuel actually began to boil within its containers in isolated instances. Attaching winches, equipment and cables to the outside of the vehicle was wrong. It should have been predicted that these items would be destroyed in a short amount of time.

Superstructure

Penetrated in the side on two occasions. A tight seal between the superstructure and the engine gratings on the hull is either insufficient or missing entirely. Very small, but not harmless, pieces of shrapnel enter through the gun tube shield. This caused wounds among the crew. The temperature in the crew compartment is still too high. Ammunition for the flare pistols ignited on several occasions. According to the vehicle commanders and gunners, the preheated rounds caused [them] to shoot over their mark.

Spark Ignition Engine

There have been many engine failures lately. The following problems are prevalent: Bent or torn valves (as a result of shattered piston heads), bent or broken piston rods and cracked cylinder heads. Cracked cylinder heads and leaking cylinders are probably caused by overheating. Experience dictates that a loss of more than 10 liters of water is not sustainable. The gaskets on the exhaust header usually fail after a short time. This presents a constant fire hazard. Installing new gaskets, which are known to be unreliable, is an exceptionally difficult and time consuming task. Right now it is impossible to exchange defective engines because there are no replacements.

Cooling System

Leaking radiators and failed ventilators have often caused us much work. The radiators usually leak at the welds to the lower supports. I suspect that the short, inflexible pipe connection between the lower support of two radiators is the cause. In the ventilators, the power flanges become welded to the ventilator housing. Repair parts are not available.

Generators and Electrical Motors

We had the last generator problem in Neusiedl. It was the well-known short circuit with the lower facing prong contact. Since then, all devices have run without problems. I must stress, however, that we have had predominantly dry weather until now and that the vehicles are seldom cold. The collection of dust in the generators is very noticeable, but it does not seem to affect their performance.

Gearshift

Has not experienced any noteworthy problems. Three vehicles have each had a reverse rheostat replaced. The collection of dust here also leaves much to be desired.

Alternator, Battery

The reverse rotation alternator has led to the greatest complications. It has directly contributed to the total loss of a vehicle. Every day there were more vehicles with burned-out fuses and, therefore, dead batteries. Herr Zadnik will have briefed you about this already. We have returned to installing the alternators with their original rotation and have already completed this work on nine vehicles. This has stopped the problems. Herr Scharpf, from the Bosch Company, assisted us with these modifications and, unfortunately, died in the process. The battery is poorly secured. The first day of the attack alone cost us more than 30 batteries. Every mine that was hit resulted in damage to at least one and, in many cases, both batteries. In all instances, the housing had either burst or was completely destroyed. A hit by a round often had the same effect. Both radio batteries have heavy demands placed upon them and must often be recharged outside the vehicle.

Bowden Wire Devices, Tachometers

There are also problems with Bowden wire devices, which can only be overcome with the greatest difficulties, since it is not exactly the smallest repair part we have. Tachometers have failed on many vehicles. The vehicles drive without a "tach". Such difficult-to-obtain items should function with greater reliability, because there is no time to repair them during combat.

Weapons

The main gun works extremely well, but is almost constantly in need of repair. Panels break off the tube for inexplicable reasons and the casing ejector does not function. The casings are often extracted with a hammer and chisel. Moving into combat with an unsupported gun tube knocks lateral and vertical traverse devices out of alignment to such an extent that up to 20 centimeter deviations exist at the muzzle of the gun tube. The lateral traverse devices often jam when the vehicle becomes hot. The alignment must be reset after a short time in combat. The forward gun tube support is sometimes shot away during combat. Stabsfeldwebel Brunnthalter has given the commander of schwere Panzerjäger-Abteilung 653 a more detailed report for him to forward.

Major Steinwachs, who commanded the battalion throughout the fighting at Orel, was ordered to attend a regimental command course in Berlin in mid-July 1943. He remained with his battalion, however. In this he was protected by General Rendulic, and he commanded it until the conclusion of these difficult days of fighting. In mid-August 1943 he relinquished command of the battalion to his successor, Hauptmann Georg Baumunk.

The Wehrmacht Daily Repot of 6 August 1943 announced:

During the defensive fighting at Orel, during the period of 5–27 July 1943, schweres Panzerjäger-Regiment 656 knocked out 502 Soviet tanks and destroyed more than 200 antitank guns and 100 field pieces.

The withdrawal of schweres Panzerjäger-Regiment 656 was very problematic due to the vehicles' maintenance problems and heavy weight of the Ferdinande. A precise reconnaissance of the march route was necessary, and the guns had to be transported on special rail cars. Two documents from the Federal Archives / Freiburg Military Archives provide information about these difficulties:

SECRET COMMAND MATTER
schweres Panzerjäger-Regiment 656
Regiment Command Post, 1 August 1943
Regimental Operations No. 49/43 (SECRET COMMAND MATTER)
SUBJECT: March from Karatchev to East Briansk
TO: Headquarters, 2. Panzer-Armee
THROUGH: XXIII. Armee-Korps

The regiment conducted a reconnaissance of possible march routes for Ferdinande from Karatchev to the west today. The results are as follows:

1) The first bridge west of Karatchev is about 50 meters long and has a capacity of 60 tons. Crossing there with the Ferdinand is possible only in an emergency. Another important point must be mentioned here. A bridge of this length makes it difficult to make steering movements with the tank. The greatest danger with such steering movements is that the 70-ton weight of the Ferdinand would destroy the bridge, rendering it unusable for other vehicles. A detour bridge beside the above-mentioned bridge collapsed today when a Panther crossed it.

2) The next available bridge has a length of 25 meters and is in the process of being reinforced to a 60-ton capacity. The same dangers are present with this bridge as in 1) above.

3) Five other small bridges have lengths of 4-10 meters and capacities of 24 tons. They can be crossed only in extreme emergencies and without concern for their future usability.

4) The road itself is easily negotiable up to the corduroy lanes. There are no detours around the corduroy lanes, but a single lane is not wide enough for the tank's width, making it necessary for them to travel along both lanes. This would make it necessary to completely block all traffic along that road and probably make the road impassable to other vehicles afterwards.

5) The regiment has therefore come to the conclusion that the Ferdinande presently in Karatchev must be loaded aboard rail transport for their movement west. If not, then the road and bridges traversed will probably be destroyed or at least made less trafficable.

The poor mechanical condition of the tank destroyers makes it very likely that most of them will break down along the route from Karatchev to Briansk (about 40 kilometers). The 4 or 5 available prime movers would than have to tow these vehicles, causing still more traffic problems along all routes.

The regiment therefore considers it absolutely necessary to recommend that the Ferdinande be loaded aboard rail transport. Eight Ssym rail cars are required, and must be positioned in Karatchev. A maximum of two hours will be required for loading operations.

/signed/

von Jungenfeld

schweres Panzerjäger-Regiment 656
Regimental Command Post, 5 August 1943
Regiment Operations No. 294/43 SECRET
SUBJECT: Route Reconnaissance
TO: Headquarters, 2. Panzer-Armee
    XXIII. Armee-Korps

The regiment has conducted reconnaissance of various routes to deploy the Ferdinande as ordered and report the following:

I) Karatchev Area:
    a) North: 4 Ferdinande are in positions approximately 2,800 meters north of the
       Karatchev train station along the Pessotschnya.
    Control over:
The large bridge south of the above-named town, the town itself, all terrain to the west and east and Krassny Pachar. Distances are recorded range diagrams. Crossing the bridge itself is possible, but the approaches to it are very marshy. Even staff cars get stuck there. Mov-

ing these guns directly east to Kasnika is impossible, because the entire terrain consists of marsh and swamp, impassable to even the lightest vehicles.

   b) 4 Ferdinande, 2 Sturmpanzer are in positions 800 meters south of the Karatchev train station.

Operational Options:

   1) Reinforce the 4 Ferdinande at the Pessotshnya bridge.
   2) Occupy reconnoitered positions south of Odrino.
   3) Route of March:

Karatchev—unimproved road through Hill 209.4 to Odrino Positions are about 500–800 meters south of the town of Koroteyevka.

We control the river crossings and the large bridge itself, as well as Odrino to the center of town. The northern part of town slopes down to the north and is not visible.

The bridge at Odrino will support 60 tons. The Ferdinande could only occupy positions 800–1,000 meters north of the town and have only a limited field of fire there (less than 1,000 meters). The position south of Koroteyevka is therefore more advantageous to block the river crossing.

   c) Blocking the Orel-Karatchev Road

A bridge with 24 ton capacity and poor detours; use only in emergencies. Assembly area behind Hill 246.1. From here, you can control this road and the road from Chotynez.

   d) To the South

The road is trafficable in a southern direction only as far as Nov Isvet. A crossing cannot be blocked here because it lies between Nov Isvet and Gora Kryas. We cannot use the southern route to Inrassovo because the bridge leading out of Nov Isloboda will not support a Ferdinand.

   e) To the Southwest

The only route under consideration is from the southwestern outskirts of Karatchev to the village of Baschkatost, then directly south to the village of Belyayev-Dvory, the field road southeast. All the bridges are very weak. Detours are too narrow, too steep and sometimes too wet for the Ferdinande.

Most of the vehicles would not complete the almost 35 kilometer march in their present poor mechanical condition. They would not be able to withdraw to the Hagen Line under any circumstances. Recovery operations in this terrain would also be virtually impossible. The route seems passable for assault guns and Panzer IV vehicles.

II) Area Behind the Hagen Line

   a) Main road:

Trafficable from Briansk to our positions, however we would cause considerable damage to the road (destroying it for other vehicles). The last part of the route, just before the positions, consists of very narrow corduroy road, to the right and left of the swamp. Very limited fields of fire. 4 properly emplaced 75 mm antitank guns can block the entire highway.

   b) To the South:

Route through the forest virtually impassable, much preparation necessary. Swamps and marshes at the edges of the forest, only marginally passable after long dry spells. Distance from Briansk to the engagement area is approximately 30 kilometers. The Ferdinande would have a difficult time on this route as well, given the present condition of their tracks and automotive components.

   c) To the North has not been reconnoitered yet:

The terrain and distances, according to the 4. Panzer-Division, which is in this sector, are not conducive to operations by Ferdinande.

In conclusion, the regiment reports again that the Karatchev - Briansk route does not seem passable for Ferdinande. Such a movement could destroy or endanger the bridges themselves, halting all traffic along the road. Additionally, the condition of the tank destroyers and assault tanks in Karatchev is such that they would not be able to complete such a march, and the recovery operations would cause great congestion along the march route.

We therefore request rail loading these vehicles for movement.

/signed/

von Jungenfeld

Schwere Panzerjäger-Abteilung 653 was finally able to recover in Briansk beginning in August 1943. What was left of schwere Panzer-Jäger-Abteilung 654 also arrived there, having suffered heavy losses in vehicles during the fighting at Orel. The Führer Headquarters ordered schwere Panzer-Jäger-Abteilung 654 to turn its 19 remaining Ferdinande over to its sister battalion and was sent back to France with only its cadre. On personal orders from Adolf Hitler, the remaining two battalions of schweres Panzerjäger-Regiment 656—schwere Panzerjäger-Abteilung 653 and Sturmpanzer-Abteilung 216—was sent to Dnepropetrovsk for maintenance on 25 August 1943. The tracked vehicles proceeded by rail, while some of the wheeled vehicles conducted a road march.

ORDER

26 August 1943 schweres Panzerjäger-Regiment 656

The regiment, composed of schwere Panzerjäger-Abteilung 653 and Sturmpanzer-Abteilung 216, is currently moving to Dnepropetrovsk for maintenance. The Porsche, Alkett and Siemens Companies have sent many inspectors to assist with the maintenance and refitting of these vehicles. They will install the newest improvements.

The second Ferdinand battalion—654—has been transferred to the Orleans areas as a cadre unit for retraining with Jagdpanther [tank destroyers].

It is recommended that schweres Panzerjäger-Regiment 656, with [schwere Panzerjäger-Abteilung 653] and Sturmpanzer-Abteilung 216, also be transferred to the Western Theater, because these formations can only conduct limited operations in the east during the next few months due to mud and winter mobility limitations. (Federal Archives / Freiburg Military Archives)

The battalion's transport and march from Briansk caused great difficulties, however. Finding an appropriate repair installation in Dnepropetrovsk was also difficult, so various delays always occurred. These difficulties caused the Army High Command to conduct an inspection of the movement and transfer by an armor officer from the general staff:

SECRET

Armor Officer of the Chief of Army General Staff
Headquarters, Army High Command, 1 September 1943
Report No. 1309/43 SECRET

Report on the Visit to the Ferdinand and Sturmpanzer Battalions

A) Ferdinand Battalion

The following observations were made during the investigation:

I. Why was maintenance not scheduled to begin until 1 September ?

1. First elements (parts of the maintenance company and four Ferdinande) arrived on 26 August
2. Difficulties finding a repair facility
   a) Assignment difficulties because all facilities had been assigned according to the "Ivan Program"; lengthy meetings before arriving at a decision.
   b) Clearing out the facility concluded on 29 August.
   c) Preparing the facility properly (laying down steel plates, filling underground canals with debris to support the weight of the Ferdinande).
   d) Securing a water supply.
   e) Securing electricity.
3. The heavy weights involved, including repair parts (example: side panels weigh 1,200 kilograms), made the use of cranes necessary during loading and unloading, consuming much time.
4. The battalion has arranged for a long-term, thorough overhaul in every way and made the corresponding preparations.

II. Why was the maintenance supposed to take 4–6 weeks?

1. The majority of the vehicles needed a complete overhaul, since the battalion was in combat for three continuous weeks and had no opportunity to conduct maintenance and repairs. (The proper procedure would have been to conduct a halt for maintenance every 5–6 days.)
2. All vehicles needed additional modifications. See Attachment 1 for specific information. The critical modifications were:
   a) Improving the engine grating covers.
   b) Shielding the fuel line.
   c) Flexible attachment for the water pipe.
   d) Modifying the alternator.

III. How many vehicles can be expediently repaired without a complete overhaul?

1) Ten Ferdinande were conditionally combat effective one week after their arrival in Dnepropetrovsk.
2) Expedient repairs of remaining Ferdinande were not possible, because all repairs requiring removal of the superstructure will take longer.
3) Battalion Commander recommended against these quick repairs or [stated that] he could be responsible for the reliability of the vehicles in combat.
4) An immediate decision, either complete overhaul of all Ferdinande or expedient repairs for these 10 Ferdinande, is necessary due to the difference in actions that must be taken.

IV. Technical details about damage to Ferdinande.
See Attachment 2.

V. What can the Army General Staff do to speed up the repairs?
1. Speed up transports.
2. Fastest possible delivery of:
   a)   60 engines (Otto HL 120 TRM).
   b)   100 square meters of armor plating (10 mm).
   c)   50 square meters of armor plating (30 mm).

B) Sturmpanzer Battalion
The following observations were made during the investigation:

I. Why was maintenance not scheduled to begin until 1 September ?
1. The first Sturmpanzer did not arrive in Dnepropetrovsk until 30 August
2. Ten Sturmpanzer were repaired before rail loading in Briansk.

II. Why should the maintenance take 4–6 weeks?
A complete overhaul for the Sturmpanzer Battalion will only take 14 days to 3 weeks.

III. How many vehicles can be expediently repaired without a complete overhaul?
All 38 Sturmpanzer can be expediently repaired within 10 days of their arrival at Dnepropetrovsk without a complete overhaul.

IV. Technical details about damages to the Sturmpanzer.
1. Main damage to 75% of the vehicles: The main gun has drooped, must be raised.
2. Mechanical repairs.
3. Final drives.
4. Side panels.
Spare parts for these repairs are available.

V. What can the Army General Staff do to speed up the repairs?
Speed up transports.

C) Additional observations for both battalions

I. Maintenance will be conducted:
1. At the Ferdinand Battalion:
   a)   Maintenance Company of schwere Panzerjäger-Abteilung 653.
   b)   Maintenance Company of schwere Panzerjäger-Abteilung 654.
2. At the Sturmpanzer Battalion:
   a)   Most of the vehicles at the attached 545th and 552nd Maintenance Companies.
   b)   Some vehicles within the organic maintenance platoon.

II. Transport Situation
1. Two transports have been leaving Briansk daily since 21 August.
2. Arrived in Dnepropetrovsk since 30 August: 6 transports (including 14 Ferdinande and no assault tanks)

3. One transport arrived in Dnepropetrovsk on 31 August; one transport arrived in Dnepropetrovsk on 1 September

4. Last transport departed Briansk: On 31 August, including the elements in combat until 29 August.

5. Difficulties with transport:
   a) Trains must halt up to 20 hours during the movement.
   b) Many vehicles overheating.
   c) Rails breaking during the loading of Ferdinande aboard rail cars (75-ton combat weight).
   d) Lost to bandits: 2 Maultier utility vehicles.

2 ATTACHMENTS
Attachment 1 to Report No. 1309/43 SECRET
Armor Officer of the Chief of Army General Staff

Critical Modifications to the Ferdinand

The following modifications are considered necessary to improve the combat power and reliability of the Ferdinand tank destroyer.

A. Fire Suppression.
   1. Modify the gratings for better protection against shrapnel.
   2. Shield the fuel line from the exhaust.
   3. Modify connections to the exhaust collection pipe.
   4. Oil leakage shield on the ventilator housing.
   5. Prevention of leaves etc. accumulating on the exhaust pipes.
   6. Improve access to the engine compartment from the crew compartment.
   7. Installation of a fire extinguishing system comprised of two carbon dioxide extinguishers with a capacity of 5 liters each.

B. Improvement Against Mine Damage.
   1. Flexible attachment of the battery.
   2. Remove tie down legs from generator housing.
   3. Improve alternator attachment.

C. Overcoming the Source of Failures of the Low-Voltage Electrical System.
   1. Installation of alternators with new anchors prepared by the Bosch company.
   2. Supplying the generators with 12 volts (instead of 24) to improve communication conditions.
   3. Reducing communication disruption by the superstructure and hull.
   4. Protecting the ampere meter from damage.

D. Drive System.
   1. Making the floating clutch rigid.
   2. Installing larger gears in the drive.
   3. Delivery of new tracks.
   4. Replacing rubber pads on the tracks.

E. High-Voltage Electrical System
1. Adjusting K 58.8 resistance (protection against surges).
2. Replacing high ohm resistance with fixed ground.
3. Complete cleaning of all electrical equipment and switches.
4. Removing generator casing underneath the air-flow shield.

F. Superstructure.
1. Installing rain gutters on the forward side.
2. Sealing the driver and radio operator hatches on the front deck.
3. Sealing the seam between the hull and superstructure.
4. Covering the gratings with mesh.
5. Increasing tension on the springs of the driver and loader hatches.
6. Welding feelers onto the hull forward of the superstructure.
7. Attaching spare track blocks, tools and equipment boxes to the rear of the superstructure.
8. Installing rain and glare shields above the vision blocks.
9. Installing air flow shield under the rear protective deck.
10. Improving welds on the engine compartment access plate.

G. Other Modifications.
1. Changing shape and angle of the gun shield.
2. Shrapnel protection behind the ball shield.
3. Stiffening or strengthening the superstructure deck plating. (Recommendation: Weld shut loader's hatch, only if number 4 below is carried out).
4. Emergency exit through maintenance hatch in the rear of the superstructure.
5. Cupola with vision blocks for commanders.
6. Recommendation for a machine gun that can be inserted into the gun tube.
7. Service forward gun area from driver's compartment.
8. Vision block for radio operator.
9. Machine telegraph between the commander and driver.
10. Better rubber seals for vision blocks.
11. Improving cooling system and air ventilation.
12. Improving fastening of water-filling points; attach caps to points with a chain.
13. Improve fastening of rear protective hood.
14. Modify nuts on track connecting rods (tighten with a hexagonal key).
15. Modify exhaust port (strong track deflector necessary).

The tasks outlined above can be completed within six weeks of the arrival of all necessary modification parts and materials, given favorable work conditions and with the combined efforts of all available maintenance services.

Attachment 2 to Report No. 1309/43 SECRET
Armor Officer of the Chief of Army General Staff

[next page]

STATUS OF THE REQUIRED MAINTENANCE PERFORMED ON FERDINANDE OF SCHWERE PANZERJÄGER-ABTEILUNG 653

Running number	a) Unit Number b) Chassis number	Damage sustained	Maintenance days
1	a) 101 b) 150014	Replace both gasoline engines. Replace oscillating mount for both sets of engines. Complete overhaul of entire cooling system. Install new slot keys and drive flanges for ventilators, also on the floor ventilators. Replace high voltage lines; replace rubber washers on all roadwheels. Replace alternators and reinforce alternator mounts. Short-term tasks: Replace tracks, exchange mudguards, repair lighting system, conduct welding operations on the superstructure, remount belt rollers.	14
2	a) 102 b) 150024	Rebuild all springs (rubber padding) to specifications. Replace rubber washers on all roadwheels. Overhaul drive and steering sprockets. Inspect entire cooling system in conjunction with radiator maintenance and cleaning. Install new ventilator rods. Exchange alternator and reinforce mounts. Rework lateral gun traversing mechanism. Short-term tasks: Replace tracks, repair track guards, insulate alternator regulator.	9
3	a) 114 b) 150083	Inspect Maybach engines. Overhaul cooling and ventilation systems. Remount belt adjustments. Replace ignition cables. Adjust ignition. Construct and weld engine compartment access plate hinges. Overhaul drive and steering sprockets. Short-term tasks: Replace tracks, replace rubber washers on 4 roadwheels.	8
4	a) 121 b) 150080	Exchange a gasoline Engine. Replace floating clutch. Remount radiator (under pressure). Replace slot keys and drive flanges on ventilators. Install radio anti-interference devices. Rework the gun elevation and traversing mechanism. Short-term tasks: Welding on superstructure.	10
5	a) 123 b) 150093	Exchange right gasoline engine. Overhaul cooling system. Repair ventilator drive. Weld hinges onto engine access plate. Replace Bowden wire system. Short-term tasks: Replace support rod mounting plate on rear idler arms. Adjust and weld track covers.	9
6	a) 124 b) 150012	Exchange gasoline engines. Repair and clean entire cooling system. Replace slot keys and drive flanges on ventilators. Short-term tasks: Insulate alternator regulator, replace tachometer, weld gun-tube supports, replace tracks.	12
7	a) 131 b) 150077	Exchange gasoline engines. Complete overhaul of entire cooling system. Replace ventilator system. Reinstall belt adjustments and widen the span. Install new alternator and regulator. Block clutch with blocking plates. Install ground for electrical system. Short-term tasks: Replace rubber washers on 4 roadwheels. Repair towing connections. Realign grating plates.	14

STATUS OF THE REQUIRED MAINTENANCE PERFORMED ON FERDINANDE
OF SCHWERE PANZERJÄGER-ABTEILUNG 653

Running number	a) Unit Number b) Chassis number	Damage sustained	Maintenance days
8	a) 133 b) 150019	Rewire high-voltage cables. Repair electrical steering system. Repair battle damage in hull by welding. Replace idler arms. Short-term tasks: Fabricate and weld lifting hooks to superstructure.	7
9	a) 201 b) 150020	Exchange gasoline engines. Repair cooling system. Repair ventilator drive. Connect ground to electrical system. Realign and fasten grating plates.	7
10	a) 202 b) 150017	Exchange gasoline engines. Refurbish radiator. Remount radiator. Install new alternator and generator. Realign and fasten grating plates. Adjust and re-fasten gun span. Short-term tasks: Replace tracks. Adjust and weld track covers. Repair lateral gun traversal device.	11
11	a) 211 b) 150028	Replace oscillating metal mounts on both sets of generators. Install new Bowden wire device. Remount tension rollers for belt adjustments. Weld hinges on engine access plate. Rebuild supplementary springs. Short-term tasks: Replace tracks.	7
12	a) 212 b) 150067	Repair crew compartment floor. Fabricate and attach air filter mount.	4
13	a) 213 b) 150074	Exchange gasoline engines. Overhaul and clean cooling system. Replace rubber washers on roadwheels for rear idler arms. Replace Bowden wire device. Overhaul steering sprockets. Rewire high-voltage system. Repair lateral gun traversing device.	12
14	a) 214 b) 150081	Exchange right gasoline engine. Repair engine access plate. Re-fasten forward slope supplemental armor. Fabricate and install new access plate for optical sight. Short-term tasks: Replace tracks. Repair support strut mounting plate on rear idler arm.	10
15	a) 221 b) 150086	Overhaul suspension. Short-term tasks: Install new alternator. Replace temperature sensor for electrical motor. Exchange track blocks.	7
16	a) 222 b) 150087	Overhaul steering sprockets. Adjust and repair tracks. Replace tension roller mounts for belt adjustments. Short-term tasks: Replace tracks. Adjust track covers.	5
17	a) 223 b) 150089	Replace gasoline engines. Repair electric steering. Short-term tasks: Replace tracks. Exchange roadwheels. Weld track cover.	9
18	a) 224 b) 150092	Correct oil loss in right gasoline engine. Repair electric steering. Install new alternator. Insulate regulator. Overhaul suspension. Short-term tasks: Replace tracks. Repair track cover.	5

STATUS OF THE REQUIRED MAINTENANCE PERFORMED ON FERDINANDE
OF SCHWERE PANZERJÄGER-ABTEILUNG 653

Running number	a) Unit Number b) Chassis number	Damage sustained	Maintenance days
19	a) 231 b) 150094	Exchange right gasoline engine. Repair penetration of left side armor. Overhaul electric steering. Replace bolts on supplemental armor. Replace rubber washers on all roadwheels. Short-term tasks: Replace tracks. Fabricate and Weld on new turret hooks.	10
20	a) 233 b) 150097	Complete overhaul of entire cooling system. Repair superstructure hatches (damaged by projectiles). Fabricate and weld on new protective shield for crew compartment ventilator. Overhaul support wheels. Repair mechanical steering. Short-term tasks: Replace tracks and rubber washers on roadwheels.	7
21	a) 234 b) 150100	Repair, adjust and attach new grating plates. Reattach bottom plates on the hull. Overhaul steering sprockets. Replace rubber washers on all roadwheels. Clear faults from radio system. Short-term tasks: Replace tracks. Fabricate and install equipment boxes.	12
22	a) 301 b) 150079	Exchange right gasoline engine. Repair cooling system. Install new slot keys and drive flanges in ventilator drive. Install new alternator and regulator. Clear faults from radio system. Repair ejection device on elevation traversing mechanism. Short-term tasks: Welding on superstructure.	10
23	a) 302 b) 150098	Overhaul cooling system. Repair, adjust and install new grating plates. Replace Bowden wire device. Overhaul steering sprockets. Repair work on mechanical steering. Short-term tasks: Replace tracks. Replace rubber washers on roadwheels	7
24	a) 312 b) 150082	Complete suspension overhaul. Correct oil loss in left engine. Repair and adjust mechanical steering. Install new alternator and regulator. Short-term tasks: Repair track covers. Repair armatures.	8
25	a) 313 b) 150015	Repair electric steering. Replace tracks. Replace roadwheels. Weld track covers.	4
26	a) 314 b) 150021	Replace tracks. Repair track covers. Replace armatures.	3
27	a) 321 b) 150075	Exchange right gasoline engine. Repair ground in electrical system. Repair electric steering. Replace rubber washers on all support rollers.	5
28	a) 322 b) 150013	Overhaul steering sprockets. Replace Bowden wire device. Replace belt adjustment mounts. Repair and clean cooling system. Replace alternator. Short-term tasks: Replace tracks. Repair track covers. Repair armatures.	7

STATUS OF THE REQUIRED MAINTENANCE PERFORMED ON FERDINANDE
OF SCHWERE PANZERJÄGER-ABTEILUNG 653

Running number	a) Unit Number b) Chassis number	Damage sustained	Maintenance days
29	a) 324 b) 150073	Exchange right gasoline engine. Overhaul steering sprocket. Replace idler arms. Repair Bowden wire device. Short-term tasks: Repair and weld track covers.	7
30	a) 332 b) 150095	Repair electric steering. Replace bolts on forward supplemental armor. Short-term tasks: Replace tracks.	4
31	a) 334 b) 150018	Overhaul and clean cooling system. Repair Bowden wire device. Replace electric starter.	6
32	a) 511 b) 150040	Exchange gasoline engines. Overhaul entire cooling system. Complete suspension overhaul. Remount alternator. Rewire high-voltage electrical system. Replace tracks. Attach track covers. Repairs to superstructure.	16
33	a) 512 b) 150033	Overhaul suspension. Replace ventilator drive. Replace tracks.	7
34	a) 513 b) 150036	Exchange one gasoline engine. Repair and clean cooling system. Replace one idler arm. Replace rubber washers on roadwheels. Install rubber pads on springs. Replace tracks.	7
35	a) 521 b) 150064	Exchange gasoline engines. Complete suspension overhaul. Clean and overhaul cooling system. Replace ventilator drive. Repair floor ventilator. Repair track covers. Repair superstructure damage. Re-fasten grating plates.	12
36	a) 532 b) 150046	Complete suspension overhaul. Replace ventilator drive. Repair mounts for one alternator. Replace floor ventilator drive. Repair track covers. Repair superstructure damage. Re-fasten grating plates.	6
37	a) 533 b) 150044	Complete overhaul of entire cooling system. Repair alternator mounts. Repairs to superstructure.	7
38	a) 534 b) 150030	Clean and repair cooling system. Overhaul ventilator drive. Remount tension rollers. Overhaul steering sprockets. Repair floor ventilator. Replace tracks.	7
39	a) 611 b) 150062	Replace exhaust seal. Replace left ventilator drive. Repair right steering sprocket. Complete suspension overhaul. Repair main-gun traversing system.	5
40	a) 612 b) 150022	Replace Bowden wire device. Overhaul cooling system. Repair suspension. Replace ventilator drive.	6
41	a) 613 b) 150050	Exchange gasoline engines. Overhaul suspension. Replace ventilator drive. Repair alternator drive.	12
42	a) 621 b) 150068	Overhaul suspension. Repair cooling system. Replace floor ventilators.	7
43	a) 622 b) 150076	Repair cooling system. Replace ventilator drive. Re-mount belt adjustments. Replace exhaust seal.	4

STATUS OF THE REQUIRED MAINTENANCE PERFORMED ON FERDINANDE
OF SCHWERE PANZERJÄGER-ABTEILUNG 653

Running number	a) Unit Number b) Chassis number	Damage sustained	Maintenance days
44	a) 631 b) 150069	Exchange gasoline engines. Repair cooling system. Replace ventilator drive. Re-mount alternator.	13
45	a) 632 b) 150060	Repair engine and cooling systems. Overhaul suspension.	4
46	a) 633 b) 150071	Exchange gasoline engines. Replace idler arms Overhaul and clean cooling system. Repair floor ventilators. Re-fasten alternator.	9
47	a) 702 b) 150057	Overhaul suspension. Replace tracks.	3
48	a) 714 b) 150034	Repair track tension device. Replace rubber washers on roadwheels. Replace rubber pads. Install new floor ventilators. Repair Bowden wire device.	8
49	a) 722 b) 150047	Exchange gasoline engines. Repair cooling system. Replace ventilator drive. Replace rubber washers on roadwheels. Replace tracks.	7
50	a) 721 b) 150055	Replace seal on right gasoline engine. Replace one electrical starter. Repair track covers. Re-fasten grating plates.	6

A total of 50 Ferdinande survived the Battle of Orel and the withdrawal that followed. The maintenance companies of the two Ferdinand battalions were combined into a single unit. Oberleutnant Wolfgang Römer of schwere Panzer-Jäger-Abteilung 654 and Kriegsverwaltungsrat Rudolf Schaffranek shared the responsibility for maintenance.

Shortly after the arrival of the first rail transports in Dnepropetrovsk, schweres Panzerjäger-Regiment 656 received an order to form a mixed Kampfgruppe consisting of Ferdinande and Sturmpanzer. Using all available resources, a "quick repair" produced 15 operational Ferdinande and 25 operational Sturmpanzer in 7 days. Everybody in the maintenance units gave one hundred percent to this task, improvising to outfit the vehicles with tracks and, sometimes, new engines. The mixed unit (12 Ferdinande and 13 Sturmpanzer), under the command of Hauptmann Baumunk, loaded aboard rail transports in Dnepropetrovsk on the morning of 11 September 1943. The objectives were Ssinelnikovo and Pavlograd, in the direction of the Soviet penetration into the northern sector of Heeresgruppe Süd. The Kampfgruppe had orders to hold open the Ssinelnikovo-Pavlograd rail line and the Pavlograd-Dimitriyevka road. There was very little enemy contact during this operation, with one armored car destroyed and five 76.2 mm antitank guns captured. For this meager result, the deployed vehicles fell victim to the strain of prolonged movement and had be recovered laboriously.

The withdrawal of the entire German Central Front in mid-September 1943 interrupted the large-scale maintenance efforts on the Ferdinande and Sturmpanzer in Dnepropetrovsk. The entire maintenance battalion, other repair services and field trains relocated to Nikopol, in order to continue the urgent repairs there. On 19 September 1943, schweres Panzerjäger-Regiment 656 received orders from the Army High Command to deploy all available forces to the Saporoshye Bridgehead. This bridgehead, on the eastern side of the Dnepr, was to be held at all costs. It protected the largest dam in Europe—760 meters long—whose turbine power plants provided the entire western Ukrainian industrial area with electricity.

The bridgehead was in the sector of the XXXX. Panzer-Korps (Generalleutnant Henrici). It consisted of six divisions and schweres Panzerjäger-Regiment 656 as a mobile reserve. Two Kampfgruppen were formed, each under one of the battalion commanders. Gruppe Nord (Group North), under Major Georg Baumunk (schwere Panzerjäger-Abteilung 653), and Gruppe Süd (Group South), under Major Bruno Kahl (Sturmpanzer-Abteilung 216). The latter battle group was also commanded on occasion by both Hauptmann Horstmann and Hauptmann Klett, both from Kahl's battalion.

The regiment's vehicle situation was catastrophic. Almost 40 Ferdinande and two thirds of the Sturmpanzer were still undergoing major repairs in Nikopol. Even so, the deployed vehicles always provided relief at various fronts along the bridgehead with their enormous firepower. The sparring for the town of Novo-Alexandrovka, in the southern sector, was particularly hard. The Ferdinande and Sturmpanzer turned back a Russian armor attack there on 10 October 1943. The regiment reported 48 destroyed Russian tanks. The Ferdinande were pulled out of the bridgehead during the early morning hours of 13 October 1943. The gigantic vehicles rolled slowly across the dam to the western bank of the Dnepr. The dam was then destroyed on 15 October 1943. The Saporoshye Bridgehead was evacuated at the same time.

OPERATIONS OF SCHWERES PANZERJÄGER-REGIMENT 656
IN THE SAPOROSHYE BRIDGEHEAD

Date	Situation
1 October 1943	Operations with Gruppe Henrici as schwere Panzerjäger-Gruppe Ferdinand (Heavy Antitank Group "Ferdinand")
2 October 1943	3 Ferdinande each with the 333. Infanterie-Division and the 123. Infanterie-Division.
5 October 1943	Operations in the Vassilyevski area.
7 October 1943	Operations with the 16. Panzergrenadier-Division (complement of 20 armored vehicles)
9 October 1943	6 Ferdinande defended against enemy penetration at Saporoshez-Krugilik. 19 armored vehicles.
10 October 1943	9 Ferdinande in operations at Krinitschny. One group of Ferdinande with the 125. Infanterie-Division.
11 October 1943	14 tanks operational; 4 undergoing short-term repairs; 30 undergoing long-term repairs.
15 October 1943	Schwere Panzer-Abteilung 506 attached. Formed a combat group in the north at Maryevka and in the south at Shirokoye with the 16. Panzergrenadier-Division.
16 October 1943	Complement: 15 operational vehicles; 5 undergoing short-term repairs; 28 undergoing long-term repairs.

Source: Federal Archives / Freiburg Military Archives.

Transfers created many changes in the leadership positions of schwere Panzerjäger-Abteilung 653:

Commander:	Major Georg Baumunk
Adjutant:	Oberleutnant Becker
Headquarters Company:	Oberleutnant Karl Seitz
1./schwere Panzerjäger-Abteilung 653:	Oberleutnant Helmut Ulbricht
2./schwere Panzerjäger-Abteilung 653:	Oberleutnant Werner Salamon
3./schwere Panzerjäger-Abteilung 653:	Oberleutnant Lange
Maintenance Company:	Oberleutnant Hanns Wegelin

The commander of the 3./schwere Panzerjäger-Abteilung 653, Oberleutnant Lange, was seriously wounded by bomb shrapnel on 23 October 1943 and succumbed to his wounds. Oberleutnant Bernhard Konnak assumed command of the company.

A very disruptive period began for schweres Panzerjäger-Regiment 656. It was divided among three army corps. Fourteen vehicles went to the LVII. Armee-Korps near Krivoy-Rog, of which 6 Ferdinande were attached to the 11. Panzer-Division in a blocking position to prevent the fall of this important, ancient city. Four guns went to the XXX. Armee-Korps and three guns to the XVII. Armee-Korps. The Ferdinande and Sturmpanzer of the regiment were in continuous combat and often formed the last defense for the hard-pressed German front.

The following operational dates and locations for the period 20 September 1943 to 6 November 1943 are contained in the Wehrpaß of the medic, Gefreiter Johann Schleiß (Headquarters Company of schwere Panzerjäger-Abteilung 653):

Running Count	Date	Location
1	20 September 1943	Nikolayevka
2	26 September 1943	Grigoryevskiy
3	30 September 1943	Novo-Alexandrovka
4	1 October 1943	Vassilyevskiy
5	2 October 1943	Vassilyevskiy
6	3 October 1943	Vassilyevskiy
7	9 October 1943	Vischnevy
8	10 October 1943	Schvetschenko
9	11 October 1943	Ivanovskiy
10	12 October 1943	Hynzernovskiy
11	28 October 1943	Radyanka
12	31 October 1943	Dolgaya
13	4 November 1943	Petropol
14	5 November 1943	Herrmannsdorf
15	6 November 1943	Volniy

The total amount of enemy equipment destroyed by all of schweres Panzerjäger-Regiment 656 from 5 July 1943 to 5 November 1943 consisted of:

582 tanks

344 antitank guns

133 cannon

103 antitank rifles

3 aircraft

3 armored cars and

3 assault guns

Beginning on 10 November 1943, the regimental staff location was the former German expatriate village of Blumenfeld, near Petropol. From there, the operational combat vehicles moved to the Nikopol bridgehead on 13 November 1943, which was required be held throughout the winter of 1943/44.

The first defensive fighting at the bridgehead began on 20 November 1943. The villages of Maryevka (20 November 1943) and Katerinovka (23 November 1943) were particularly critical areas in the German defensive line. The Ferdinande had tremendous success during the engagement at Koschasovka/Miropol from 26–27 November 1943. They destroyed 54 Russian tanks: 21 by Leutnant Franz Kretschmer and his crew (Gunner: Unteroffizier Alois Moosdiele; Driver: Unteroffizier Heinrich Appel; Radioman: Obergefreiter Peter Schade; 1st Loader: Kanonier Otto Isen; 2nd Loader: Kanonier Paul Schmidt). Leutnant Franz Kretschmer was awarded the Knight's Cross to the Iron Cross on 17 December 1943.

Schweres Panzerjäger-Regiment 656 received special recognition Wehrmacht Daily Report dated the 28 November 1943:

From the Führer Headquarters, 26 November 1943

Dnepr Bridgehead

The Armed Forces High Command reports: Soviet attacks at the Nikopol Bridgehead and in the Great Dnepr Bend were generally repulsed in bitter fighting lasting into the night. There is still intense fighting at a penetration point southwest of Krementschug. The enemy lost 112 tanks yesterday. Schweres Panzerjäger-Regiment 656, under Oberstleutnant von Jungenfeld, destroyed 54 tanks. Leutnant Kretschmer particularly distinguished himself during the fighting, destroying 21 enemy tanks with his tank destroyer.

Schweres Panzerjäger-Regiment 656 destroyed 654 tanks and 610 guns during the previous four months.

Vehicle Status in schweres Panzerjäger-Regiment 656 (29 November 1943)

I./schweres Panzerjäger-Regiment 656 (schwere Panzerjäger-Abteilung 653)

Ferdinande: 4 operational; 8 in short-term repair; 30 in long-term repair; 4 total losses

3./schweres Panzerjäger-Regiment 656 (Sturmpanzer-Abteilung 216)

Sturmpanzer IV: 2 operational; 43 in long-term repair

This vehicle situation, along with the distinctly poor performance of the Ferdinande and Sturm-panzer during the winter, brought the senior army leadership to the conclusion that the entire regiment had to be withdrawn. It was to be sent to St. Pölten and St. Valentin in Austria for depot-level mainte-nance. Schweres Panzerjäger-Regiment 656 received the following order on 10 December 1943:

> Schweres Panzerjäger-Regiment 656 is transferred from the sector of Heeresgruppe Süd [Krivoy-Rog / Nikopol area] and moves with schwere Panzerjäger-Abteilung 653 and Sturm-panzer-Abteilung 216 to be reconstituted at St. Pölten.

The second large Russian offensive against the Nikopol Bridgehead took place in the middle of the regiment's rail movement. A Kampfgruppe of operational Ferdinande and Sturmpanzer, under the com-mand of Leutnant Kretschmer, was ordered back into the bridgehead to support the endangered infantry divisions east of the Dnepr. The Southern River Engineer Command provided a 1,000-ton ferry for this mis-sion. The soldiers participating in this operation were personally decorated by Generalfeldmarschall Schörner. The withdrawal of the Kampfgruppe to the western side of the Dnepr began on 25 December 1943 with engineer ferries. An immediate advance by Russian forces against the German elements loading the Ferdinande aboard ferries made it necessary for a section under the command of Feldwebel Alfred Schiestl (Gun 334) to clear up the situation.

The entire regiment moved back to German territory in 21 transport trains during the period from 16 December 1943 to 10 January 1944. The desperately needed depot-level maintenance of the Ferdi-nande and Sturmpanzer began towards the end of December in the Nibelungen Works in St. Valentin and the Vienna Army Arsenal.

FERDINAND STATUS FOR SCHWERE PANZERJÄGER-ABTEILUNG 653 AND SCHWERE PANZER-JÄGER-ABTEILUNG 654 (30 JUNE 1943 TO 30 NOVEMBER 1943)

SCHWERE PANZERJÄGER-ABTEILUNG 653

Date	Assigned	Operational	In Maintenance	Loss
30 June 1943	44	41	3	—
5–14 July 1943				schweres Panzerjäger-Regiment 656 lost a total of 19 Ferdinande
29 July 1943	31	10	21	13
31 July 1943	31	13	18	—
1 August 1943	—	27	38	—
20 August 1943	50	12	38	—
1 September 1943	50	10	40	—
30 September 1943	49	20	29	—
31 October 1943	48	10	38	—
1 November 1943	48	9	39*	—
30 November 1943	42	7	35	—
20 November 1943**				

* plus three recovery versions of the Ferdinand
** Ferdinand status of schweres Panzerjäger-Regiment 656: 4 operational; 8 in short-term repair; 30 in long-term repair; and 4 total losses

SCHWERE PANZER-JÄGER-ABTEILUNG 654

Date	Assigned	Operational	In Maintenance	Loss
30 June 1943	44	43	3	—
5–14 July 1943*				
29 July 1943	19	13	6	—
31 July 1943	19	13	6	—

* See above concerning the total losses of the regiment
(Source: Federal Archives / Freiburg Military Archives)

EXCERPTS FROM LETTERS AND DIARIES FROM PERSONNEL OF SCHWERE PANZERJÄGER-ABTEILUNG 653 AND SCHWERES PANZERJÄGER-REGIMENT 656 DURING THE PERIOD FROM 1943 TO 1944

In a letter dated 2 October 1992, former Unteroffizier Karl Neunert (3./schwere Panzerjäger-Abteilung 653) wrote the following to the author:

Reminiscences
Beginning of the Offensive at Orel: 5 July 1943

Moving to the assembly area during the night brought an unexpected spectacle with it. The throbbing of our engines prompted the Russians to employ the spotlights from all their anti-aircraft batteries. They were expecting a bombing attack.

We initially had to overcome heavily mined areas and positions (trenches) during our attack. Small, armored tracked vehicles were committed, carrying explosive charges. They would detonate themselves, blowing up mines in a large radius around them. Strong defense from the Russian trenches. Russian fighters and bombers (even American Boston Bombers) were deployed. The Ferdinand (Gun 331), in which I was the gunner, ran over many mines (5?) on the first day, without suffering significant damage. The infantry deserve special recognition. They fought magnificently under the protection of the Ferdinande.

The offensive stalled after a few days. An infantry captain asked us and the crew of another Ferdinand not to withdraw during the night...He wanted us to stay in a large, flat area (near the town of Alexandrovka) with his infantrymen, or they would not be able to hold this area. We stayed. In the gray of dawn, we saw Russian infantry on the other Ferdinand (Gun 333. Commander: Wachtmeister Benno Schardin; Gunner: Unteroffizier Karl Leukel) about 200 meters away. The vehicle's hatches were open! Our infantry had withdrawn during the night without informing us. We withdrew, driving in reverse, but had to cross a ditch after several hundred meters. The tank sank in at the deepest point, right up to the hull. Russian infantry passed us on the high ground at a distance on the left and right, without shooting at us. We tried every trick, throwing blankets and coats, whatever we had, under the tracks. Everything slid through. I prepared the gun for demolition and we ran for our lives. The tube did not explode, however. I still do not know to this day why it did not. We were lucky and reached our company. Hauptmann Wegelin, who first inquired about the condition of the soldiers and then about the vehicle, apparently tried to have Stuka dive bombers destroy both Ferdinande. Results: Unknown.

Saporoshye, 2 October 1943

Operations in the bridgehead. During the morning hours of 2 October, our gun received a direct hit while advancing. The protective shield over the gun mantle was hit. Many small and tiny pieces of shrapnel entered the fighting compartment through the 1 centimeter wide opening (slit) in the gun mantle. Each one of the 4 crewmembers in the fighting compartment was wounded, but the driver brought the vehicle back safely. As the gunner, I had my hand on the lateral traversing device and received a wound to the main artery in my inner, left arm, in addition to negligible injuries to my right leg. Despite their own wounds, my comrades immediately and skillfully took care of my injury. After being looked at by our medical Feldwebel, Leitner, I was moved to the main aid station (undergoing an operation), then 2–3 days in the field hospital in Saporoshye and then home. This ended my time with schwere Panzerjäger-Abteilung 653.

Unteroffizier Horst Theis describes his combat experiences with schwere Panzerjäger-Abteilung 653 in this first-hand account:

On 20 January 1943, Sturmgeschütz-Abteilung 197 was loaded aboard rail cars in Spass-Demensk and transported to Jüterbog, where it arrived on 30 January 1943. A three-week leave period followed and then orders to proceed to the Nibelungen Works at St. Valentin in lower Austria as an armored vehicle radio operator. The radiomen were trained there as replacement drivers for our newest weapon, the Ferdinand. The gun had a 6-man crew and was equipped with an 88 mm super-long main gun and one machine gun in the fighting compartment.

I was designated as the radio operator in the vehicle of the headquarters company commander. The company commander was Oberleutnant Seitz. The battalion received its own maintenance company and left the assault artillery branch of the artillery on 1 April 1943. From that point forward, it was designated as schwere Panzerjäger-Abteilung 653. In mid-April, the battalion moved to Neusiedel on Lake Neusiedl, near the Bruck an der Leitha Training Area in Austria. At the end of May 1943, the battalion moved by expedited rail movement (4 days) to the area south of Orel.

The headquarters company's tank-destroyer platoon, with the exception of me, was transferred to the line companies, because the staff did not have any combat vehicles. Oberleutnant Seitz dismissed my complaints. Since I stubbornly requested a transfer every week, however, he finally let me go as an officer candidate. First, I was a radio operator in a command tank (Panzer III) and then assigned as the radio operator in the vehicle of Oberleutnant Lange (commander of the maintenance company) at the beginning of the offensive on 5 July 1943, working directly behind the front line. After unloading from the trains in Smiyevka and occupying assembly areas near Gagarinka, we initially advanced towards Belgorod. Besides us, schweres Panzerjäger-Regiment 656 consisted of schwere Panzer-Jäger-Abteilung 654, whose vehicles we later received, Sturmpanzer-Abteilung 216 and a signal battalion.

The Luftwaffe provided effective support during the first few days. By 19 July 1943, however, the objective of the offensive—collapsing the large salient in the front between Orel and Kursk—had failed, despite 20-hour attacks during the long summer days. The withdrawal began: From Yamskoy, through Stovo-Kolodes and Mal-Gat, to Orel. By 30 July 1943 we had moved through Karatchev and were in Briansk. We had hardly been able to sleep during the short nights of the last few weeks. We were unable to even think about changing positions until after dark. Fuel (pumped by hand out of barrels, 600 to 700 liters per vehicle), ammunition and rations were usually brought forward during the night. Twilight began already at 0400 hours.

On 1 August 1943 I contracted jaundice as a result of exhaustion and was taken to the dispensary. Our medical Oberfeldwebel, Schürwanz, would only feed me "tea and biscuits" however, so I made myself scarce and paid dearly for doing so.

My wish was finally fulfilled on 16 August 1943, and I became the radio operator for the commander's gun (tactical number 621) under Feldwebel Müller. On 18 August 1943, Hauptmann Baumunk took over command of the battalion from the future Oberst Steinwachs. The battalion loaded aboard trains for Dnepropetrovsk on 22 August 1943. We took along a sack of fresh potatoes to ensure our subsistence. In Dnepropetrovsk, we occupied private quarters in the suburbs. They were much cleaner than those we had in the central sector. After the maintenance company overhauled the vehicles, we loaded aboard trains again on 11 September 1943, along with elements of the 3./schwere Panzerjäger-Abteilung 653, and moved through Ssinelnikovo to Pavlograd. From there, we pushed forward, together with the first new Panthers, to 50 kilometers east of Pavlograd. The Russians retreated so fast that we only managed to snag a few armored cars.

This eight-day excursion took us to an area where there was more sustenance. We captured a lot of materiel in Petrograd while clearing a supply depot, because the paymaster became totally confused when several T 34's appeared outside the city. After a short rest, we loaded aboard trains again in Dnepropetrovsk on 23 September 1943, managing to outfit ourselves well in the process of evacuating a Luftwaffe clothing depot. This time we proceed to Dnyeprostoy and then across the Dnepr dam to Saporoshye. Difficult fighting in the bridgehead followed and we participated in it, initially with the 1./schwere Panzerjäger-Abteilung 653 and then with the 3./schwere Panzerjäger-Abteilung 653. Our gun knocked out its first enemy tanks on 1 October 1943, with more combat operations following on 3, 4, 9 and 10 October 1943.

On the morning of 13 October 1943 . . . we withdrew across the dam. We occupied security positions along the Dnepr about 10 kilometers north of the city, together with Unteroffizier Schiestl's vehicle and a Sturmpanzer. Since "Ivan" succeeded in forcing a bridgehead at Dnepropetrovsk, we were thrown into the gap along the road between Saporoshye and Dnepropetrovsk. We were in combat on 24, 25 and 26 October 1943, during which we destroyed one of the new Russian SU 152 assault guns equipped with a 152 mm main gun. Oberleutnant Lange was killed the night before his leave was to begin.

Our vehicle suffered considerably heavy damage during the last few operations, so we had to go to the maintenance company in Nikopol on 31 October 1943. Since repairs were to take 2 to 3 weeks, the crew moved to the location of the Headquarters Company in Katharinental for that period. We spent three quiet weeks there. Our sled was ready on 20 November 1943, and an engineer ferry brought it across to the bridgehead at Nikopol. We were attached, as we had been since Saporoshye, to the 3./schwere Panzerjäger-Abteilung 653, while the 2./schwere Panzerjäger-Abteilung 653 conducted the well-known counterattack at Krivoy-Rog. A great achievement by our battalion followed on 24 November 1943, when only 3 Ferdinande repulsed a Russian armor attack of about 70 T 34's. We destroyed 47 enemy tanks without suffering any casualties. Leutnant Kretschmer was able to claim the lion's share of the kills for himself and received the Knight's Cross.

The three weeks that followed brought continuous combat for our remaining three guns and a few Sturmpanzer. This was under extremely bad conditions, such as rain, mud, snow and ice. Our beards grew longer and longer. We had to use a blow torch inside the crew compartment to carefully thaw the ice our breath created in the extremely low temperatures. We received a visit here by future Generalfeldmarschall and recipient of the Diamonds to the Knight's Cross, Schörner, who was still a General der Gebirgstruppen at the time. He impressed us all considerably when, during a speech, he was the only one who remained standing during an artillery attack. We all sought cover in the snow. While most of the regiment had already departed home for depot-level maintenance, I was wounded during an offensive operation on 14 December 1943. I passed through the main aid station in Kamenka and then traveled by hospital train from Nikopol, reaching Cholm, near Lublin, the afternoon of Christmas Eve. After the difficult days in the cold and filth, the hospital train, with its covered, two-tier beds, seemed like a small wonder to me. A sentimental Christmas celebration followed, as we were all thankful to be away from the front and in the peaceful field hospital.

The radio operator of a Panzer III converted to be an armored ammunition carrier, Franz Kurer (both schwere Panzerjäger-Abteilung 653 and 654), presented the author with the following chronology of operations during his time with schwere Panzerjäger-Abteilung 653 on 28 June 1992:

3 April 1943	I was assigned to the convalescent company of Panzerjäger-Ersatz- und Ausbildungs-Abteilung 7 (7th Tank Destroyer Training and Replacement Battalion) Replacement Battalion in Munich and on 9 April 1943 to the march element [scheduled to move to the field]. I received training as a radio operator there.
19 June 1943	Transfer to schwere Panzer-Jäger-Abteilung 654.
22 June 1943	Departed Munich (total of 6 men) for Rouen in northern France.
1 July 1943	Departed for Orel, with 20 men, 3 ammunition carriers, one car full of lumber and 2 passenger cars. We were always attached to freight trains.
11 July 1943	Arrival in Smiyevka near Orel; unloaded there. Departed with ammunition carriers to Glasunovka to the battalion command post. Continuous operations along the Orel-Kursk rail line.
31 July 1943	Loaded aboard trains in Orel for Briansk.
10 August 1943	Transferred, with carriers, to schwere Panzerjäger-Abteilung 653.
25 August 1943	Loaded aboard trains in Briansk, through Krementschug to Dnepropetrovsk.
1 September 1943	Arrival and unloading of rail cars.
11 September 1943	Dnepropetrovsk. Boarded trains to Pavlograd. Operations in Pavlograd at the bridge with 3–4 guns.
15 September 1943	Loaded aboard trains again at Pavlograd.
16 September 1943	Reached Sinelnikovo and unloaded.
19 September 1943	Engineer elements destroyed rail facilities and larger buildings in Sinelnikovo, most of the city is in flames.
21 September 1943	Boarded trains in an open field in Itlarinovo; combat engineers have built a loading ramp for this purpose.
25 September 1943	Unloaded in Dnepropetrovsk, then across the dam to Saporoshye.
29 September 1943	From this day forward, daily operations along the rail line, in the fruit orchards and at the airfield.
2 October 1943	Driver Heinz Wagner wounded; replaced by Heinrich Bach.
10 October 1943	Heavy artillery fire and air attacks for 3 hours.
12 October 1943	Departed for Tschapayevka, across the dam.
15 October 1943	Destroyed the dam and moved to Nikoleifeld.
5 November 1943	Attacked Hermannsdorf-Volny. A recovery vehicle exploded while towing a tank destroyer. The driver was seriously burned.
6 November 1943	Driver Hermann Bach wounded, replaced by Heinrich Adolf.
11 November 1943	Loaded aboard trains at Petropol.
13 November 1943	Unloaded in Nikopol and moved to Kamenka by ferry.
16–19 November 1943	Remained in Snamenka.
21 November 1943	Reached Dneprovka.
24 November 1943	Stachonov (chicken farm).
26–27 November 1943	Large Russian attack. Leutnant Kretschmer destroyed 21 tanks and received the Knight's Cross. Difficult days for the ammunition drivers.
5 December 1943	Carrier broke down from engine damage, towed to Dneprovka.

6 December 1943	Received the Iron Cross, 2nd Class for operations in Nikopol.
22 December 1943	Loaded aboard trains in Nikopol.
23 December 1943	Departed for Vienna, St. Valentin and St. Pölten.
2 January 1944	Arrived in Vienna.
3 January 1944	Unloaded at the Vienna Arsenal.
10 January 1944	Turned over carriers at the Vienna Arsenal.
11 January 1944	Arrived at St. Pölten.
14 January 1944	Joined the guard force at the Nibelungen Works. Remained in Sternberg until 1 February 1944.

Notes taken by Radioman Arnold Knopp (Panzer-Regiment 35), a former member of the staff of schweres Panzerjäger-Regiment 656, provide a glimpse into the period from 21 June 1943 to 2 January 1944.

June 1943

21   We arrived at our objective in Gagarinka (Orel sector) and reported to the command staff. Assigned to the work force. Very hot. First bombing attack by Russian aircraft at 2130 hours (1 wounded).

22   Nothing special. Very hot.

23   As on the 22nd, very dusty on the roads.

24   Still hot. Laid heavy field cable. Became mired in the marshland in a [Sd.Kfz. 250]. Recovery with a tracked vehicle.

25   Assigned as a radio operator in a halftrack. Prepared the vehicle.

26   The heat subsided. Vehicle maintenance.

27   Rainy weather. No duty.

28   Three hour road-march exercise in the morning. Moved 26 kilometers cross-country with the halftrack in the afternoon. Heavy dust on the vehicle. Guard duty at night.

29   Radio equipment maintenance during the afternoon. Weather was nice again. Very windy.

30   No change in the weather. Radio equipment maintenance. A Fieseler Storch aircraft landed on a meadow nearby at 0900 hours. It took off again around 1100 hours. Lively air activity by German fighters during the afternoon.

July 1943

1   No change in the weather. Lively air activity. Prepared vehicle for movement. Departed at 2100 hours for the first assembly area. Enemy aircraft at night.

2   We were in a sandy depression. No possibility of working during the day! Departed at 2200 hours for the second assembly area. Muddy roads, poor progress.

3   Arrival in Glasunovka at 0200 hours, 5 kilometers from the front. Lively air activity. Artillery shells landed in the vicinity. Our artillery responded from nearby.

4   No change in the weather. Slept in a ditch under the halftrack. German air activity and artillery fire from both sides. Otherwise quiet. The Führer order was read aloud.

5   Guard duty from 1200 to 0200 hours. Heavy enemy artillery fire at 0100 hours. Many squadrons of German aircraft attacked the enemy positions during the early morning. The attack began at 0400 hours. Heavy enemy artillery fire on our departure point. We were under artillery fire for about one hour. Enemy withdrew 8 kilometers. Heavy aerial combat, many aircraft shot down. Artillery fire stopped. Enemy air attacks during the night.

6   Heavy artillery fire on both sides. The formations continued to advance. Eight enemy aircraft shot down within 4 hours in our sector. German air superiority.

7   Heavy artillery fire on both sides, numerous aerial engagements. A German aircraft made an emergency landing. We moved to the most-forward positions. Artillery shells struck all around us. The enemy withdrew farther. Enemy aircraft dropped a few bombs during the night.

8   Artillery fire on both sides. Enemy attack reinforced by tanks. Many enemy tanks knocked out. Heavy German air activity. Moved forward again, occupied a bunker. More enemy aircraft shot down.

9   Heavy artillery fire. We moved into open terrain. Enemy artillery struck near us. Command vehicle ran over a mine on the front line and was out of action. Crew was fighting enemy infantry. We moved forward to help. I remained behind in an infantry trench. The Leutnant and driver moved forward to the enemy. The Leutnant was seriously wounded. The driver, also seriously wounded, brought the vehicle back to the German lines. The vehicle had been hit numerous times by enemy antitank rifles. A sergeant brought the vehicle farther to the rear.

10   Moved to a rest position for three days. There was still heavy artillery fire, many aerial engagements.

11   Occupied rest positions. Many enemy aircraft shot down. The Luftwaffe attacked the enemy with powerful formations at 1800 hours. We could observe the attack very well. Count at least 100 Stukas, one Ju 88 squadron and one He 111 squadron. Thick clouds of smoke over the enemy positions. The attack lasted about 1.5 hours. Heavy artillery fire throughout the day.

12   Still occupied rest positions. Artillery fire subsided, little air activity. No change in the weather.

13   As yesterday.

14   Moved to a new rest position in a small patch of woods 2 kilometers away. Built an expedient bunker there.

15   Heavy rain in the morning. Our vehicle was repaired. Moved forward again to the battalion command post at 1500 hours. Heavy artillery fire throughout the day. The Russians attacked our front with armor and artillery support during the morning. They were repulsed. Heavy air activity.

16   Our infantry changed positions. We moved back 2 kilometers to a destroyed village. We were relieved at 0900 hours. Back to the rest position. Prepared for the withdrawal at 1100 hours The Russians attacked friendly positions with about 100 fighter and bomber aircraft. Numerous bombs landed about 50 meters next to our rest position in the woods. One tank destroyer was put out of action. After the bombing raid, we withdrew 5 kilometers farther to a new rest position. Another heavy air attack by the Russians at 1500 hours. The same at 1800 hours. Artillery fire.

17   Awakened up at 0600 hours. Heavy air attack at 1100 hours, again at 1500 hours and 1800 hours, just like the previous day. Friendly antiaircraft guns shot down several aircraft. A German barrage balloon tore loose and was shot down by our friendly antiaircraft guns. Artillery fire throughout the day.

18   Moved forward again during the morning to relieve the front. Comrade Schäfer wounded by a shell fragment. Heavy artillery fire on both sides. Built an expedient bunker as a precautionary measure.

19   The Russians attacked on the right flank. They were repulsed. Very heavy artillery fire on both sides. We withdrew around 2300 hours. Enemy aircraft dropped a few high-explosive bombs.

20   Awakened at 0600 hours. Waited for the order to deploy. Departed at 1400 hours for the Glasunovka train station. Departed there around 2000 hours. Track broken along the way (artillery fire); returned again. Continued along another track. Air activity during the night.

21   Arrive in Orel at 0300 hours. Unloaded from the train and continued cross country. Very hot. Bathed in a pond.

22   Continuous operations by Luftwaffe elements throughout the day. Weather the same as yesterday.

23   Awakened at 0500 hours. Departed at 0600 hours, across the Obtucha, to the most forward positions. No artillery fire. Luftwaffe heavily engaged. Withdraw 10 kilometers behind the front (rest position) at 1600 hours.

24   Very hot for a while, heavy rainfall. Radio watch in the tank. German aircraft attack.

25   Awakened at 0600 hours, then cleaned weapons. Weapons inspection at 1000 hours. Radio watch starting at 1100 hours. Heavy thunderstorm. It rained the entire night No air activity. Otherwise very quiet.

26   Severe thunderstorm. Russian aircraft arrived; 3 were shot down. Powerful German bomber and Stuka elements continuously attacked the enemy positions. We moved forward to the 1st Battalion [schwere Panzerjäger-Abteilung 653] during the afternoon, our armored car will provide radio traffic support.

27   Russian artillery fired into the village where we occupied rest positions. Radio watch during the day. Heavy rainfall. The command post withdrew farther to the rear during the night. We moved back to Luyanova along the Rybnitza. Roads were completely mired.

28   Much work due to vehicle cleaning. Artillery strikes in front of the village. Heavy artillery action along the front.

29   Scattered rain showers. Artillery shells landed before noon again. Russian aircraft, as always, in the evening.

30   The same as yesterday.

31   0700 hours: We returned to the regimental staff in Orel. The road was almost impassable. The mud on the roads is about 1/2 meter deep. Arrived in Orel at 1000 hours. We met our comrades and moved with them to Karatschev, 75 kilometers west of Orel. Vehicle after vehicle on the road, endless columns. Made poor progress. Arrived in Karatschev at 1500 hours. We remained there initially. Organized our vehicle. Heavy air activity.

August 1943

1   We washed all our dirty uniforms. Nice weather. It was Sunday. We fried potatoes and cooked applesauce on our homemade oven. The Luftwaffe continuously attacked the enemy positions with Stukas and bombers. We observed an aerial engagement during the evening. Mail finally arrived today, and I received one package; wrote letters.

2   Aerial engagements over Karatschev at 0400 this morning. Lively air activity by the Luftwaffe throughout the day. Very nice weather.

3   The same as yesterday. Guard during the evening. Enemy aircraft at night.

4   Guard during the day.

5   The same as yesterday. Lively air activity.

6   0200 hours: We withdrew to Briansk. Enemy aircraft attack the Karatschev airport. Arrived in Briansk at 1700 hours. Occupied quarters on a lake. Change quarters on the same day to a town near Briansk. Enemy aircraft were coming. The town is called Grylovka.

7   Cleaned the vehicle for inspection. Very hot.

8   The same as yesterday.

9   Vehicle inspection at noon. Cleaned weapons. Still hot.

10   The same as yesterday. Weapons inspection from 1700–1800 hours.

11   Awakened at 0500 hours. Strenuous exercise from 0600–0700 hours. Cleaned our clothing for a uniform inspection. Dressed in black [Panzer uniform] for the morning. Orders for the afternoon: Move to halftrack number RN 6. Prepared to move due to attachment to the 3rd Battalion [Sturmpanzer-Abteilung 216]. Remained on alert.

12   Awakened at 0600 hours. Assembled at 0700 hours. The departure was delayed. Reported to the commander at 1400 hours: "Promotion to Gefreiter effective 1 August 1943.

13   Commander flew to Berlin. Ready to move at 1500 hours. Loaded aboard trains at 1800 hours. Moved to Roslavl during the night. Back to Briansk again.

14   We were at the Briansk train station. Departed for Brasovo at 1400 hours. Partisan alert. Arrived in Brasovo at 2100 hours. We spent the night on straw next to a building near the train station.

15   Departed for the front at 0700 hours. Occupied quarters near a lake (30 kilometers from the front). We were approximately 100 kilometers southeast of Briansk. Lunar eclipse.

16   Rained during the night. Prepared for the eventual return trip, but did not depart yet.

17   Assembled at 0600 hours. Briefing for the march. Lively air activity.

18   Still in the same village. Rained from time to time.

19   Prepared everything for combat. Nice weather. Very cold at night. Vehicles moved to the front. We followed one hour later. Dusty roads. Occupied a wooded hollow. Very pretty countryside. In the vicinity of an estate. The front was 7 kilometers away. Heavy artillery occupied positions not far away.

20   Had guard duty. Heavy rain. Otherwise nothing special. Had been away from the regimental staff for one week. Received sundry packet.

21   The weather remained the same. Still occupied the hollow. Reasonably quiet during the day. Could hear artillery firing and shells exploding.

22   Very nice weather. Commander was with us. German bombers attacked the Russians towards evening. Heavy antiaircraft fire from the Russians.

23   Nice weather during the day. Lively enemy air activity during the night.

24   Nice weather continued. Still occupied the defile.

25   Ordered to move at 1400 hours. Prepared everything. We departed with the vehicles at 1700 hours. March distance was about 30 kilometers. Moved through partisan territory during the night. Weapons at the ready. No significant incidents. Air activity. We halted at 2300 hours and spent the night in a forest.

26   Awakened at 0400 hours. Received rations. Departed at 0500 hours. Move about 5 kilometers and then halted in a tiny forest. Expansive and open hilly terrain was in front of us. It was still 15 kilometers to the front. Powerful enemy air elements flew overhead in waves during the day, dropping bombs and strafing. Artillery shells struck. At 0900 hours, our vehicle was ordered forward with the battalion's armored vehicles. We came under heavy enemy artillery fire (infantry mortars and "Stalin Organ" rocket launchers) about 5 kilometers from the front. We took cover in a gully. Then we moved across the high ground and into a burning town just short of the front line. Continuous artillery fire. Heavy enemy air attack during the afternoon. We moved up to the front line at 1700 hours as a replacement for the lieutenant's vehicle, which was put out of action. A middle-wave radio operator from the battalion took over my position in the vehicle. I returned with the damaged Sturmpanzer.

27 I moved forward again with an amphibious staff car to orient a platoon sergeant. Met my comrades. Moved back again. Order: "Get ready to move!" We were to board a train again. Our halftrack was still at the front with the Ferdinande, so I took another halftrack in the direction of the train station. We remained in a forest outside the town of Navlya until we begin loading.

28 Nice weather. Waited in the forest for the return of the other halftrack, which was still at the front. It arrives around 1700 hours. Cleaned the vehicle. Thunderstorm.

29 It was Sunday. Rain showers throughout the day. Prepared for rail loading tomorrow morning.

30 Foggy and rainy weather. Awakened at 0400 hours. Departed for the Navlya train station at 0500 hours. Then we loaded aboard the trains. We remained at the train station until noon. Departed at 1300 hours for Briansk. Our locomotive detached 9 kilometers outside of Briansk. Remained on a siding until 0900 hours the next morning. Very cold at night.

31 Departed at 1000 hours, moving south of Briansk, towards Gomel. The locomotive detached at Unetscha. The train remains there until the next day.

September 1943

1 Stationary at the Unetscha train station. Departed at 1500 hours. Halted again 70 kilometers outside of Gomel. The locomotive remained with the train. Demolitions blocked the tracks.

2 Train departed around 0900 hours. The cause of the delay was a train that had been blown up by partisans and blocked the way. The train's engineer and fireman were both dead. The wreckage was still smoldering. Our transport passed Gomel moving south. A two-hour delay 10 kilometers south of Gomel to change locomotives. Continued to Chernikov. Remained there until the next day.

3 Remained in the Chernikov train station. Cloudy weather.

4 Overcast and rainy weather. Rail line blocked by demolitions. Finally departed at 1600 hours; partisan alert. Installed machine gun. The train moved very carefully.

5 Moved the entire night. Sergeant remained behind in Grabneka. The transport left without him. Very nice weather. Transport continued east, towards Poltava. Branched off south during the morning. Crossed the large Dnepr bridge at Krementschug towards evening. Very cool during the night.

6 Arrived a Dnepropetrovsk at 0500 hours. Unloaded between 0700 and 0800 hours. Moved through the city back to the regimental staff. Very nice weather. Occupied positions on the bank of the Dnepr. Nice view.

7 Awakened at 0430 hours. Exercised from 0600–0700 hours. Perform radio maintenance.

8 Awakened at 0530 hours. Calisthenics. Russian bombers attack during the morning. Guard and officers' social during the evening.

9 Awakened at 0600 hours. Italy has capitulated. Went to the movie theater during the evening.

10 Ready to move with RN 5. Going into combat again. Everything ready at 1700 hours. Received soap. Company social at 1900 hours. Nice program: Luftwaffe band, magicians, accordion player. Commander was present. Good supper. Heavy antiaircraft fire around 2200 hours. Ivan was attacking. We did not let it bother us. Conversation and good spirits. Went to bed at 0130 hours.

11 Awakened at 0230 hours. Got everything ready to move. Waited until 0700 hours. Hazy weather. Departed for the front at 0700 hours, moving east across the large Dnepr

bridge. Moved about 80 kilometers to Pavlograd. Individual enemy tanks had pushed through to the main road. The city was burning, presumably destroyed by withdrawing German forces. The supply depot was blown up. It was not far to the front line. Rainy weather. Radio traffic until 2400 hours. Radio receiver was defective.

12   Radio contact reestablished at 0420 hours; a new receiver. There was almost nobody besides us remaining in the city. The buildings were empty. There was an intact piano in one building and another in the park next to us. The other halftrack from our unit did not return until night.

13   We occupied an assembly area about 6 kilometers east of Pavlograd. Successful attack at 0800 hours; no resistance. Advanced 20 kilometers without seeing any enemy. Many trucks still burning along the highway. We halted in Dmitriyevka and remained there until the following day.

14   Rations were distributed. Russian fighters circled overhead. A group of Stukas returned from operations All regimental staff vehicles, except ours, returned to Pavlograd. We maintained the radio link between the battalion and regiment. Radio watch every two hours throughout the night.

15   Departed for Vassilkovka at 0600 hours. A four-hour delay at the entrance to the town. During this time, a motorized division rolled by on its way to the front. All heavy and very heavy weapons. At 1100 hours we also continued towards the front. First enemy contact around 1300 hours in Grigoryevka. An enormous orchard between Vassilkovka and Grigoryevka. Harvested a large number of apples. Artillery fire and explosions in Grigor. All types of tanks attacked. Russian aircraft arrived. We halted at a farm.

16   Returned to Vassilkovka at 0700 hours. Our halftrack collides with a staff car along the way. Front wheels were badly bent. We could continue, but only slowly. The battalion commander had ordered us back to the regiment, about 45 kilometers away. We could only move slowly. We saw a large railroad bridge blown up in Vassilkovka. We reached the regiment in Ssinelnikovo at 1600 hours. Received rations. It rained sporadically throughout the day.

17   Awakened at 0700 hours. Picked up potatoes with a truck. Made slow progress because the roads were mired. Returned around 1300 hours. Loaded tank tracks. The regimental staff moved to Dnepropetrovsk. We remained in Ssinelnikovo and maintained radio contact with the regiment.

18   Awakened at 0800 hours. Radio maintenance thereafter. There were rumors that we would move to Saporshye. Demolitions were heard in the city, and the buildings burned late into the night. Russian aircraft were above the city during the day. It looked as though the city would be abandoned.

19   Awakened at 0700 hours. Prepared to move. A cloud of black smoke hung over Ssinelnikovo. Buildings were ablaze everywhere. At 1000 hours, we moved about 25 kilometers to the west, to Illarionovo (15 kilometers outside of Dnepropetrovsk). Russian combat aircraft attacked the main road. Quadruple Flak provided security. It was Sunday. We were in a reasonably clean house, occupied by a woman with many children.

20   Very nice weather. Russian aircraft continuously attacked the town throughout the day. German planes joined in. One German fighter was shot down, the pilot escaped using his parachute. Large columns of vehicles moved past us to the Dnepr. We moved to the train station in the evening. Ssinelnikovo had meanwhile become the front line. Villages and cites were burning far along the entire horizon.

21   We loaded aboard a train early at 0300 hours. We departed at 0500 hours in the direction of Dnepropetrovsk. We halted at a train station along the Dnepr. The beautiful city

of Dnepropetrovsk was on the other side of the river. Russian combat aircraft attacked us twice during the morning. Our air defense was heavy. A 20 mm quad Flak shot down an aircraft. No more attacks after that.

22   We continued moving at 9500 hours. Long delay at the bridge over the Dnepr. Upon moving again, we passed our former quarters. The train halted in Apostolovo until the next morning.

23   Departed Apostolovo at 0900 hours. Only 130 kilometers to Saporoshye. After 80 kilometers, our train had to halt and move to a siding. The main track was blocked. Continued moving at 2000 hours.

24   Arrive in Saporoshye at 0500 hours. Unloaded. Waited along the road for orders to move to our new area. Moved with [Sturmpanzer-Abteilung 216] to Neuendorf [a former German settlement], about 25 kilometers northwest of Saporoshye. Our regimental staff occupied a school in Saporoshye. Our halftrack was ordered there. We left the battalion and crossed two Dnepr bridges. We saw the largest dam in Europe. Antiaircraft guns encircled the city. We arrived at the regimental staff at 1500 hours. Finally a decent bed again. Air activity during the night.

25   Cleaned the vehicle. Noncommissioned officers' social. Guard. Russians dropped bombs.

26   No duty on Sunday. Nice weather. Trip to the island of Cortizze with friends. Grapes were nice and ripe.

27   Radio maintenance. Straightened out our vehicle.

28   The same as yesterday. Nice weather.

29   Awakened at 0515 hours. Departed for combat at 0600 hours with our halftrack. The Russians had forced a wedge into our positions. Stukas attacked. Heavy artillery barrage. A shell landed 2 meters from us. Changed positions. Constantly moving because the enemy always zeroed in on us. Heavy bombing attack by Russian aircraft at 1630 hours. Moved around disoriented for 3 hours in the evening. Returned to Saporoshye around 2100 hours.

30   Radio maintenance. Clean vehicle. A bath in the city during the afternoon. Nice weather.

October 1943

1   Awakened at 0530 hours. Heavy Russian artillery (152 mm) fired into the city. Shells landed in our vicinity. The Russians attempted to penetrate but were repulsed. Established radio contact in the halftrack beginning at noon.

2   Nice weather. Radio contact with the front. Four enemy tanks destroyed. We heard heavy artillery fire. The Russians attacked repeatedly but were repulsed every time. Saporoshye was mentioned for the first time in the Wehrmacht Daily Report.

3   Nice weather. Radio duty.

4   All civilians had to leave the city by today and move to rear areas. Radio duty.

5   Nice weather. Radio watch. Evacuation of the civilians continued. Enemy aircraft flew over the city without dropping any bombs. The front had shifted farther east, and the enemy has been pushed back a bit.

6   The weather is still nice. Radio watch. Increased level of alert. Buildings were blown up and large fires burned in the city.

7   Nice weather. Continuous explosions in the city throughout the day. We were on alert.

8   Awakened at 0430 hours. Radio watch. Weather has not changed; still nice.

9   Awakened at 0500 hours. Radio duty at 0600 hours. The Russians attacked from two sides. Heavy artillery fire. Shells landed in our vicinity. Cloudy weather, light rain, dry again towards evening. Discovered that the Kuban Bridgehead had been abandoned.

10   Heavy barrage in front of the city commencing at 0400 hours. The Russians attacked with reinforced elements. Air attacks. Radio traffic. The weather was very windy. The Russians were repulsed.

11   Fairly cold. Stormy weather. Radio watch. The Russians attacked continuously. Stuka elements engaged. In the evening, we received the order: "Prepare to move!" We started packing.

12   Do not get to bed until 0230 hours. Two halftracks and one armored vehicle remained in Saporoshye as a radio station. The other vehicles crossed the Dnepr and moved to positions in the rear. Russian aircraft attacked. Artillery fired into the city. Radio watch. Prepared the halftrack for the move. Cool and stormy weather.

13   Both sides continually fired artillery into the city. Buildings burned. Our quarters trembled from the explosions. There was a full moon. The city was brightly lit. The crashing of bombs was mixed in with all of this. We departed Saporoshye in our halftrack at 0430 hours. The route took us across the dam to Cortiza, about 15 kilometers west of Saporoshye. We remained there. German and Russian aircraft conducted attacks throughout the day. Stormy, cold weather.

14   Windy and cool. Radio watch. Artillery fire on both sides. The dam was blown up towards evening.

15   The weather was the same as yesterday. Radio watch. It began raining in the afternoon. Another demolition charge blew up the remainder of the dam. We were in Cortiza.

16   Departed at 0700 hours for the regimental headquarters in Vladimirsky, about 35 kilometers west of Cortiza. Quarters were widely dispersed. We occupy quarters with the 4-man radio crew, about one kilometer away.

17   Sunday; it rained throughout the day. Duty at the radio station. Meals were brought forward to us.

18   No duty. Overcast weather. Ten men departed on leave.

19   Radio duty. No change in the weather.

20   No duty. Russian combat aircraft attack, two were shot down. Four more were shot down during the day.

21   No change in the weather. Radio duty. Plagued by mosquitoes. Air activity decreased. The Russians have allegedly broken through at Krementschug.

22   Very nice weather. Radio duty. Russian defense troops occupying the room next to ours departed for Krivoi-Rog to fight partisans. Prepare halftrack RN 5 for detachment to the 1st Battalion [schwere Panzerjäger-Abteilung 653] during the afternoon. Departed for Neuendorf, west of Saporoshye, at 1500 hours. Arrived at 1700 hours. Remained there until the next morning. Comrades Schmidt and Lietz transferred to RN 5 and remained with the 1st Battalion.

23   Departed for Vladimirsky at 0700 hours. Packed our gear at 2200 hours and transferred to halftrack RN 6. Bombs landed near the radio station during the night.

24   Awakened at 0300 hours. Everything had be prepared to move by 0400 hours. Very cold. Moved with the combat staff to Neuendorf and farther down the highway towards Dnepropetrovsk. Russian artillery fired upon the highway. The march continued west of the highway, until approximately 20 kilometers outside of Dnepropetrovsk. Hot and dusty during the day. Our halftrack has a 3-man crew and we occupied quarters in a village.

25   Awakened at 0530 hours. Initially foggy, then more cheerful weather. Radio duty. Departed at 1000 hours and moved about 40 kilometers southwest to the town of Garkuschino. Russian aircraft attacked during the march. Occupied quarters in a school. Radio duty. The front was moving closer and closer. The Russians were pushing us firmly.

26   Cool in the morning, nice weather later. Combat engineers have also occupied quarters in the village. Half of the regimental staff moved to Vladimirsky again. We remained here with the Leutnant and 10 soldiers. The Russians assembled their strongest forces for an attack. We evacuated Dnepropetrovsk. The Russians pushed across the Dnepr. Krivoi-Rog was already a battlefield. We were in the pocket.

27   Rainy. Heavy Russian attack. Continuous artillery fire at the front, which has moved far to the west already. The Russians captured a portion of the main road. The Russians exerted heavy pressure against the German positions at Krivoi-Rog, Krementschug and Dnepropetrovsk. We were now about 100 kilometers northwest of Saporoshye and about 40 kilometers southwest of Dnepropetrovsk.

28   Got everything ready. Departed at 1000 hours for Novaya Nikolayevka, about 40 kilometers north of Nikopol. Our vehicle's axle broke along the way and we had to halt. Constructed an expedient axle and another wheel. Attempted to continue, moving slowly. Reached Tchumaki towards evening and spent the night at the outskirts of the town.

29   A recovery vehicle was supposed to be en route, but it never arrived. We attempted to continue moving slowly at 1300 hours, using the main road towards Nikopol. We encountered the recovery crew along the way. Two of us climb aboard the Volkswagen staff car that accompanies them, taking all our belongings with us. Moved to the staff location at Novaya Nikolayevka. Arrived towards evening. Transferred to halftrack RN 8.

30   Departed at 0400 hours for Novo Ukrainka, about 10 kilometers northeast of Krivoi-Rog. A distance of 90–100 kilometers to the west. We arrived at 1100 hours. First frost. Radio contact. All leaves canceled in the southern sector.

31   Cloudy, not as cold as yesterday. Radio traffic. The field trains were withdrawing 130 kilometers to the west. We were not moving yet.

November 1943

1   Awakened at 0600 hours. Overcast weather. It was All Saints Day. We also withdrew today. Departed at 0930 hours; moved 104 kilometers to Tomakovski. The Germans have pushed back the Russians at Krivoi-Rog. The Russians lost many tanks.

2   Erected a secure radio station. Windy, cold weather. Police evacuated the village. The front was farther away. We have moved about 450 kilometers in the last few days.

3   Cold, overcast weather. Radio watch. Cleaned weapons, straightened out equipment.

4   Prepared halftrack RN 8. Departed for Tomakovka at 1100 hours. A 70-kilometer move. Radio station at corps. Nice quarters. We were detached as a signal unit at the corps headquarters.

5   Departed for the front at 1100 hours. Moved 60 kilometers to the location of the 304. Infanterie-Division at Petropol. The main road was under heavy artillery fire. As a result, we had to take another route to our objective. Arrived at 1430 hours. At 1500 hours we accompanied the other halftracks on an attack. The commander of the 1st Battalion [schwere Panzerjäger-Abteilung 653] was with us. Heavy antitank and artillery fire. Russian combat aircraft joined in. Very cold. Slept in the vehicle during the night. Enemy air activity during the night.

6   Return to the staff at 0500 hours; 65 kilometers. We were in Tomakovski again around 0800 hours. Very cold. Received 10 kilograms of flour and 1 kilogram of sugar. Sent the groceries home.

7   It was Sunday. Cold, windy and rainy. Received much mail.

8   Stormy weather. Radio duty. The Führer gave a speech over the radio.

9   Foggy, rainy weather. Went to the support point with a truck. Roads were muddy.

10   Hazy weather with light rain. Radio duty.

11   Comrade Sterrenberg went to the field hospital. I was detached to the combat staff. Moved to Nikopol at 1000 hours. Misty weather; muddy roads. We reported to the regimental maintenance company and remained there overnight. Slept in a bunker. Waited for recall.

12   Awakened at 0430 hours. We received word at 0600 hours: Continue to Prokoskoye along the Dnepr, about 20 kilometers west of Nikopol. The first snowfall, but none remained on the ground. Radio duty in the halftrack. It was freezing cold.

13   Radio duty. A part of our staff also arrived here to join the combat staff. The weather was misty. Heavy rainfall in the evening, everything was a mire. The village of Prokoskoye is on the northern arm of the Dnepr, flowing west here. The terrain is marshy and covered with thick forests. Forests appear very seldom in the Ukraine. Instead of fueling the ovens with the usual straw, we used wood here. There was a partisan alert.

14   The rain has stopped. Radio duty in the halftrack.

15   Overcast, but dry, weather. Combat aircraft attacked in the entire area throughout the day. Radio duty.

16   The weather was the same as yesterday. Radio duty in the halftrack. An attack by von Horstmann today [Commander of Sturmpanzer-Abteilung 216].

17   Overcast, foggy weather. Radio duty in the halftrack. Cleaned weapons.

18   The weather was the same as yesterday, but colder. Radio duty in the halftrack. Watched a movie in the evening. The film was entitled "A Summer Companion".

19   Very cold, cloudy. Heavy radio traffic.

20   The same weather as yesterday. Greater than usual radio traffic throughout the day until 2300 hours. Our forces attacked the enemy. The Russians attempted to break through with strong armored forces. More than 200 tanks were destroyed along the front in front of us, 150 of them in a corps sector containing one of our battalions. Heavy Russian barrages and repeated air attacks on Nikopol and the main roads. Heavy enemy losses. Ten Ferdinande were not operational.

21   Awakened at 0400 hours. Got ready. Took the commander's staff car to the bridgehead as a radio relay station to the corps. Very cold. Both sides exchanged artillery fire. Returned through Nikopol at 1400 hours. Took a wounded soldier from the main aid station to Nikopol. Radio traffic until 0100 hours.

22   Somewhat milder weather. Still more radio traffic. Receive felt boots. The 1st Battalion [schwere Panzerjäger-Abteilung 653] conducted a counterattack against Scheftschenko. The 3rd Battalion [Sturmpanzer-Abteilung 216] destroyed 3 tanks yesterday and 2 today. The 1st Battalion reported 9 enemy tanks destroyed.

23   Black ice and rain; overcast, misty. RN 2, a Panzer IV, was not operational due to engine damage. Radio traffic died down.

24   Weather has improved. Normal radio traffic. We were still in Prokoskoye.

25   Mild weather. Many comrades departed on leave. The Russians attacked again with strong armored forces. Three Ferdinand from the 1st Battalion destroyed 44 enemy tanks and 10 antitank guns. Leutnant Kretschmer alone destroyed 21 of them. The commander departed by plane for leave. Feldwebel Eichhorn returned from leave. The 1st Battalion just scored its 600th "kill" since 5 July 1943.

26   Stormy, but mild, weather. Heavy radio traffic again. Stuka attack by the Luftwaffe. Radio traffic until midnight.

27   Clear, cold weather. The Luftwaffe attacked again.

28   It was cold. Less radio traffic. The Luftwaffe attacked the front in waves throughout the day. Russian air activity during the night. Bombs landed nearby.

29   Hoarfrost in the morning. German air attacks again today. Radio duty.

30   Mild weather. Radio duty.

December 1943

1   Heavy fog in the morning. Almost spring-like weather in the afternoon.

2   Nice weather. Radio duty. Comrade Lietz returns from the 3rd Battalion [Sturmpanzer-Abteilung 216]. Visited a music hall at 1500 hours, a small diversion.

3   It has become colder. Advance party let for Germany today. The regiment will probably pull out. We provide home addresses for possible leave. Wrote my last letter from Russia. Radio duty.

4   Misty and rainy. Seelinger returned with halftrack RN 6. Medium radio traffic.

5   Snow fell for a second time today, the Second Advent. This time it remained on the ground. The countryside has changed.

6   Heavy frost. Cleaned weapons.

7   Frost and very cold. We picked up 4 wagon loads of wood from the island on the Dnepr by 1500 hours. Took it across by ferry. Mud was forming on the roads again; the weather was becoming milder.

8   Mild weather. Snow has thawed. Heavy rain towards evening. We were expecting a large Russian attack soon.

9   Cold again today. It snowed the entire day. Constructed positions around Prokoskoye. Five transports have already departed for Germany.

10   Very cold; it was snowing. We were still in Prokoskoye. Unfortunately, it would be some time before we loaded aboard the train. Departure date still unknown. I was too hasty with my last letter from Russia. Sent Christmas greetings home as a precautionary measure.

11   Very cold, frost. Otherwise nothing out of the ordinary.

12   Radio duty. Comrades had to perform calisthenics from 0600 to 0700 hours. We heard that the dam at Saporoshye had been blown up yet again. We feared flooding along the Dnepr.

13   Took a truck to the island again to pick up wood. My vehicle became stuck. Returned around 1530 hours.

14   Very cold. Radio duty. Loading date still unknown.

15   Cold and windy. Calisthenics from 0700 to 0815 hours. Radio duty.

16   Very cold. It snowed again. Weapons inspection at 1400 hours. Four of the Ferdinande of the Kampfgruppe departed for rail loading. We were to turn over the vehicles to another unit. Our loading date was still unknown.

17   Very cold, frost. One of the four Ferdinande burned out completely on the way to the rail station. The remaining five Ferdinande departed for the rail station today. All support elements were withdrawn from the bridgehead. Radio duty.

18   Cloudy, very cold. Most of the vehicles were turned over to another unit. Baggage was loaded onto rail cars. Medium radio traffic. By this point, we have been in Prokoskoye for six weeks.

19   Still cold. Turned over the rest of our vehicles. The Russians attacked again. Several Ferdinande unloaded and moved to the front for combat.

20   Guard duty during the night. Cold weather. Partisan fighting in the area. Sixty-seven enemy tanks were destroyed in the Nikopol Bridgehead yesterday. Heavy radio traffic until 2400 hours.

21   Freezing cold. Had a mild cold. Radio duty. Ferdinande in combat today. The Russians attacked again. Air activity on both sides. We will depart for the Nikopol train station tomorrow.

22   Awakened at 0400 hours. Dismantled everything. Departed at 0600 hours for the Nikopol train station. We moved to a neighboring village in halftrack RN 5. Feldwebel Eichhorn's brother was there and he will go with us. Very cold during the move. The road was slick. We were at the loading ramp at 0800 hours. Everything was loaded by noon. We remained at the ramp overnight. I slept in the halftrack. Very cold.

23   The train pulled into the station at 0900 hours. We built a stove in our rail car and made ourselves comfortable. We ran a 150 meter cable from our rail car to the halftrack's radio receiver. This would allow us to hear the radio during the trip. We departed Nikopol at 1300 hours. Arrived at Apostolovo at 1500 hours. Long delay. Receive 150 cigarettes.

24   Christmas Eve. We were in the train station from 0300–1100 hours. Our Leutnant delivered a Christmas speech, presented awards and announced promotions at 0945 hours. Received Christmas donations. Weather: Foggy, misty, very cold. Continue moving at 1100 hours. Another delay from 1400–2100 hours. Christmas music on the radio. We erected a small Christmas tree in our rail car and celebrate our Christmas there with thoughts of home. Continued moving until 2200 hours. At 2200 hours we were in a train station 35 kilometers from Rumanian controlled territory.

25   Waited for a locomotive. Very cold. We continued at 1130 hours, but not through Nikolayev. We reached the Bug River at 1400 hours. We left Russia and traveled through Rumanian territory. The train crossed the 2-kilometer-long Bug Bridge. Barrage balloons were attached to the bridge support. A delay after crossing the bridge. The locomotive seemed to be damaged. Continued moving at 1600 hours.

26   It was raining. We passed Nikolayev to the north and moved northwest to Novossensk. Arrived at 1145. Departed again at 1400 hours. It snowed during the night.

27   Very cold. 500–600 kilometers to the border. We arrived in Balta during the evening. Remained there until the next day.

28   Departed for Przemysl at 1000 hours. Many delays along the way.

29   Arrived in Schmerinka at 0730 hours. Move through Kirany and Tarnopol towards Lemberg on this day, with many delays.

30   Arrived in Lemberg. Continued moving at 1130 hours to Przemysl, arriving there at 1500 hours. Received a sundry packet and one bottle of champagne. We were deloused immediately after our arrival.

31   New Year's Eve. Departed Lemberg at 0100 hours towards Reichshof. Locomotive was damaged. We continued moving at 0900 hours through Tarnov and Krakow. Switched locomotives. Continued throughout the Protectorate at 1600 hours. Midnight, change of year. A festive noise making begins with submachine guns, carbines, pistols and flare guns. Continued moving throughout the night.

January 1944

1   We traveled through Bohemia-Moravia, to Ludenburg. Short delay. Continued at 1030 hours towards Vienna. Halt at a train station 24 kilometers outside of Vienna. We received a second delousing.

2   The train station was called Straßhof. We departed for Vienna at 0600 hours. Reached the west train station at 0900 hours and continued towards St. Pölten at 1015 hours, arriving there at 1200 hours. Unloaded everything. We occupied an army barracks.

3   Awakened at 0600 hours. Formation at 0700 hours. Health and welfare examination at 1000 hours. I will go on leave tomorrow.

On leave from 4–25 January 1944. Barracks duty at the St. Pölten army barracks from 26 January 1944 to 10 March 1944. I was then transferred to Panzer-Regiment 35. This ended my stay with schweres Panzerjäger-Regiment 656.

Wehrpaß entries from the 1./schwere Panzerjäger-Abteilung 653 from June 1943 to December 1943:

13 June 1943–4 July 1943	Duties in the Operational Area
5–25 July 1943	Defensive Fighting in the East 1943
5–12 July 1943	Offensive Fighting in the Kursk Area
13 July 1943–25 August 1943	Defensive Fighting in the Orel-Briansk Area
26 August 1943–10 September 1943	Duties in the Operational Area
11–27 September 1943	Defensive Fighting in Southern Russia and Withdrawal to the Dnepr
28 September 1943–25 December 1943	Defensive Fighting Along the Dnepr
28 September 1943–14 October 1943	Defensive Fighting in the Saporoshye Bridgehead
15 October 1943–9 December 1943	Defensive Fighting in the Dnepropetrovsk / Krivoi Rog Area
20–29 November 1943	First Phase of Defensive Fighting in the Nikopol Bridgehead
9–25 December 1943	Second Phase of Defensive Fighting in the Nikopol Bridgehead and northwest of Saporoshye

In April 1942, Adolf Hitler viewed both types of Tiger prototypes, one from Henschel and the other from Porsche. Hitler decided to accept delivery of both vehicles without prior testing. Production progressed at full speed in the Nibelungen Works, so that 10 Tiger VK4501(P)'s were available in June 1942. The photo shows Professor Porsche inspecting one of these vehicles at the Nibelungen Works in St. Valentin (Austria). SCHNEIDER

The engine and drive-train problems with the Porsche Tiger could not be solved in a timely manner. In August 1942, the Nibelungen Works of the Steyr-Daimler-Puch Corporation. Thereafter, individual Porsche Tiger VK4501(P)'s were tested and used for training at the Döllersheim Training area in the Austrian forest. SCHNEIDER

Both schwere Panzerjäger-Abteilung 653 and schwere Panzer-Jäger-Abteilung 654 were activated at Enns (Austria) in 1943. Personnel were provided through personnel levies from other formations and new recruits from replacement battalions, army transportation depots, training units and labor units. The soldiers were assembled into units and participated in some portions of converting the Tiger VK4501(P)'s into Ferdinande. SABROWSKY

This photograph shows the Porsche Tiger chassis assembly line at the Nibelungen Works on 23 April 1943. Chassis number 150091 was the last one completed. Behind the Ferdinand chassis are a row of Panzer IV chassis, the primary product of the Nibelungen Works.
SPIELBERGER

A view of Ferdinande in the production hall at the Nibelungen Works at St. Valentin. The chassis are in various states of completion. Two vehicles already have the Alkett superstructure and main guns installed.
SPIELBERGER

Installation of the main guns and superstructures proceeded without problems, since all the necessary equipment was available. Under field conditions, any work on the superstructure was virtually impossible without a 16-ton portal crane.
SPIELBERGER

The 100-ton cranes at the Nibelungen works easily carried the enormous weight of the Ferdinand through the production hall and placed the vehicle within centimeters of where it needed to be. This is a Ferdinand with chassis number 150064.

Ferdinande in a row at the Nibelungen Works production hall. The vehicles are almost completed. Only the engine cover plates (gratings) still need to be attached. It is of interest that the Ferdinand on the far right—chassis number 150027—has reinforced towing eyes, while the other vehicles are still in their original form. SPIELBERGER

There were constant orientation briefings on the factory grounds at the Nibelungen Works, as well as test drives with the Ferdinand tank destroyer. The vehicle in the photograph—chassis number 150096—is a training and testing vehicle. SPIELBERGER

A three-part regulation was released for the Panzerjäger Tiger (P) on 1 May 1943. These instructions served as a technical manual and service guidelines for the vehicle drivers and maintenance personnel. The three regulations contained the following materials:

- D-656/1: Panzerjäger Tiger (P)
  A. Description of Chassis.
  B. Instructions for Drive Train.
  C. Maintenance Instructions.
  D. Lubrication Instructions.
- D-656/2: Panzerjäger Tiger (P): Maintenance Instructions for the Chassis (minus electrical portions)
- D-656/3: Panzerjäger Tiger (P): Maintenance Instructions for Electrical Portions of the Chassis.

The following are excerpts from D-656/1:
    The armored hull is illustrated in its function as a chassis. The gasoline engines with their generators, the electric motors, the suspension and the 88-mm main gun and superstructure are all installed onto the chassis.
    Two engine assemblies, each consisting of one gasoline engine and one attached generator, are housed in the engine compartment in the center of the hull. Fuel tanks are installed in the compartments on both sides of the engines. Two radiators and two ventilators are installed on both sidewalls above the generators.
    A firewall separates the engine compartment from the forward driver/radio operator compartment while another separates it from the rear fighting compartment.
    The electricity supplied by the two generators flows to two electric motors at the rear of the vehicle. These power the drive sprockets through a cutch, connecting shaft and final drives. The final drives hold both drive sprockets and are bolted to the side of the hull. The parking brake is applied to the clutch.

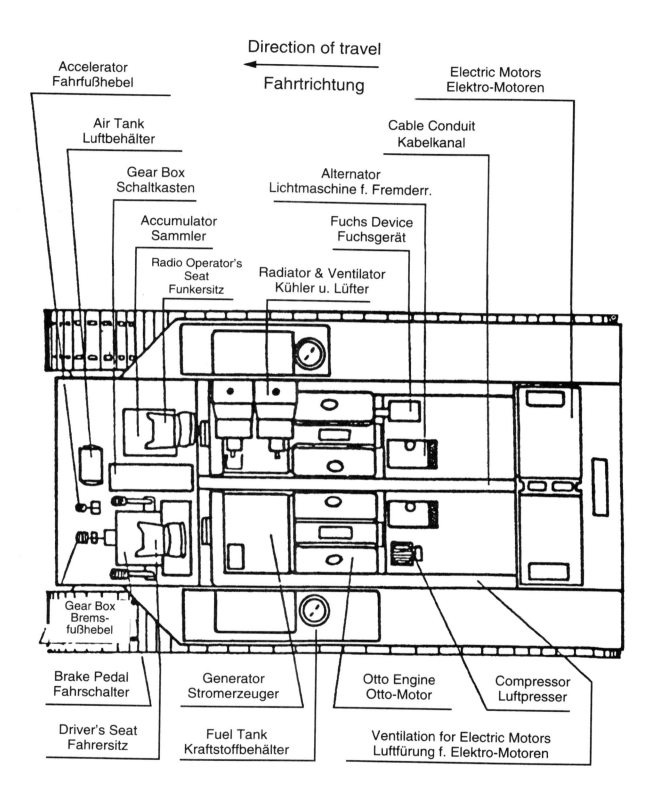

Direction of travel

Fahrtrichtung

Accelerator
Fahrfußhebel

Air Tank
Luftbehälter

Gear Box
Schaltkasten

Accumulator
Sammler

Radio Operator's
Seat
Funkersitz

Electric Motors
Elektro-Motoren

Cable Conduit
Kabelkanal

Alternator
Lichtmaschine f. Fremderr.

Fuchs Device
Fuchsgerät

Radiator & Ventilator
Kühler u. Lüfter

Gear Box
Brems-
fußhebel

Brake Pedal
Fahrschalter

Driver's Seat
Fahrersitz

Generator
Stromerzeuger

Fuel Tank
Kraftstoffbehälter

Otto Engine
Otto-Motor

Ventilation for Electric Motors
Luftfürung f. Elektro-Motoren

Compressor
Luftpresser

Superstructure of the Panzerjäger Tiger (p) in cross-section. Regulation D-656/1.

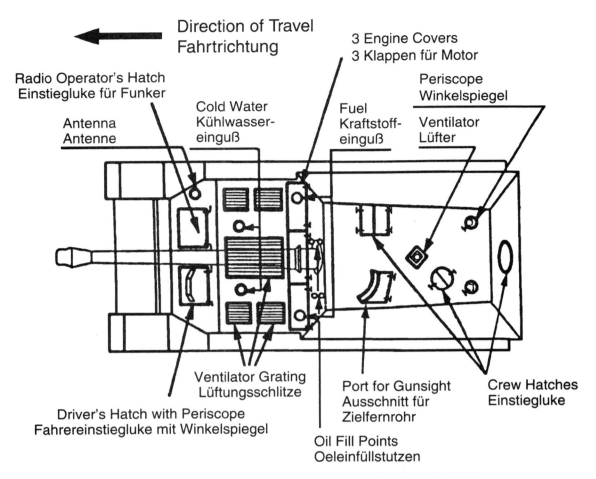

Direction of Travel
Fahrtrichtung

3 Engine Covers
3 Klappen für Motor

Radio Operator's Hatch
Einstiegluke für Funker

Periscope
Winkelspiegel

Cold Water
Kühlwasser-
einguß

Fuel
Kraftstoff-
einguß

Antenna
Antenne

Ventilator
Lüfter

Ventilator Grating
Lüftungsschlitze

Port for Gunsight
Ausschnitt für
Zielfernrohr

Crew Hatches
Einstiegluke

Driver's Hatch with Periscope
Fahrereinstiegluke mit Winkelspiegel

Oil Fill Points
Oeleinfüllstutzen

Layout of hatches on the deck and superstructure. Regulation D-656/1.

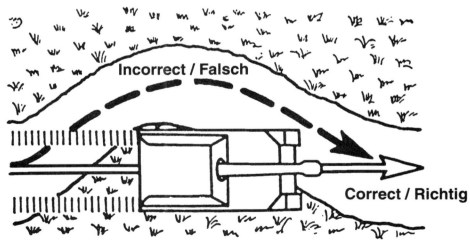

Incorrect / Falsch

Correct / Richtig

Cross Country Driving / Fahren im Gelände

Steering movements will be made only when they are unavoidable. The driver will select an orientation point on the horizon that is in his general direction of travel and move directly towards it. Bends in the road will not be followed. Regulation D-656/1.

**Long load-bearing surface
causes great steering resistance in a depression.**

**Short load-bearing surfaces
cause little steering resistance on a rise.**

CROSS-COUNTRY STEERING

Steer only in areas where there is little resistance to the steering movement. The driver must plan ahead when he moves, searching for small rises and solid ground upon which to make steering movements. Regulation D-656/1.

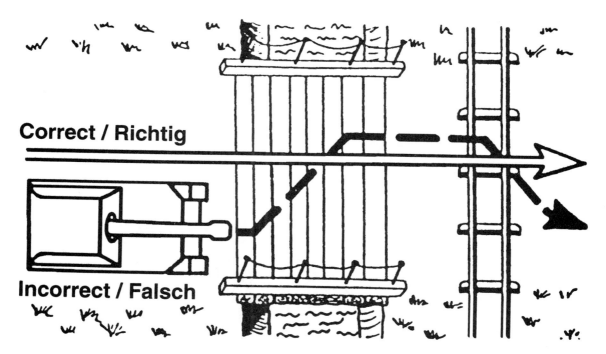

DRIVING ACROSS BRIDGES AND TRACKS

Do not make steering movements on bridges or tracks, since this may destroy them and damage the suspension when making such movements on tracks. Regulation D-656/1.

Correct / Richtig   **Incorrect / Falsch**   **Correct / Richtig**

Driving Over Tree Stumps
Überfahren von Baumstümpfen

Incorrect / Falsch

Climbing Over Obstacles
Erklettern von Hindernissen

DRIVING IN A RUT

Do not move in deep, well-worn ruts. The hull of the tank destroyer will get stuck easily and place excessive demands upon the suspension and engines when attempting to move out of them again. Regulation D-656/1.

Move slowly over large tree stumps with one of the tracks, or the hull will become stuck. Negotiate vertical obstacles (walls, barricades, etc.) with the help of logs placed under the tracks. Regulation D-656/1.

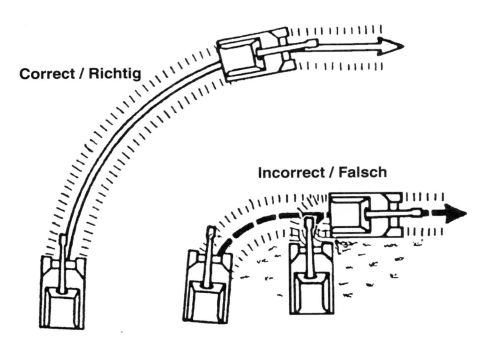

Correct / Richtig

Incorrect / Falsch

NEGOTIATING CURVES

Make all directional changes with as wide a turn as possible. Make tight turns or pivot steer only when absolutely necessary. Regulation D-656/1.

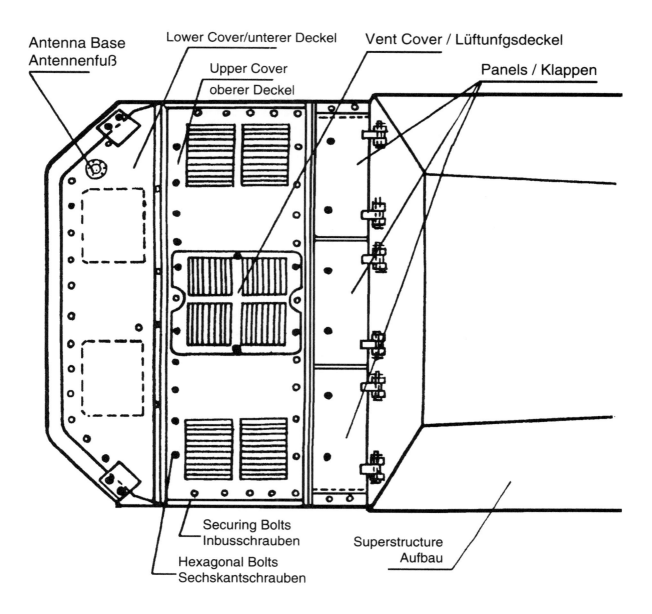

Antenna Base
Antennenfuß

Lower Cover/unterer Deckel

Upper Cover
oberer Deckel

Vent Cover / Lüftunfgsdeckel

Panels / Klappen

Securing Bolts
Inbusschrauben

Hexagonal Bolts
Sechskantschrauben

Superstructure
Aufbau

Instructions for removing the covers (gratings) and panels for the fuel points and central vent cover. Regulation D-656/1.

On 8 May 1943, the final Ferdinand—chassis number 150100—left the Nibelungen Works. The workers bestowed their best wishes and a few comments reflective of the times upon the vehicle.

SCHNEIDER

SCHNEIDER

SCHNEIDER

Tied down and covered with tarps, the first five Ferdinande are ready for transport from the Nibelungen Works. Additional Ferdinande can be seen on the Ssyms Special rail cars behind them. Due to weight considerations, each transport train could only move five Ferdinande at a time. SPIELBERGER

Schwere Panzerjäger-Abteilung 653 provided the transport personnel. The vehicles departed the Nibelungen Works without the protective shield in front of the gun mantle. These shields were delivered later.

The Ferdinande arriving in Rouen (France) were sent to Pelessier Barracks on the left bank of the Seine and turned over to the crews of schwere Panzer-Jäger-Abteilung 654. This Ferdinand is chassis number 150047. The transport detail from schwere Panzerjäger-Abteilung 653 then returned to its home station at Neusiedl. APPEL

Factory-fresh trucks (MAN MK 4500's) await issuance to the battalion in the battalion square. RIECKER

The complement of vehicle issued to the redesignated and reorganized battalion must be considered quite lavish. This image show newly issued Kübelwagen (Kfz. 1) and Büssing NAG 4500's. Some of the truck feature a built-up superstructure, which were used as maintenance vehicles. HENNING

The battalion's Recovery Platoon takes delivery of its new FAMO 18-ton halftracks (Sd.Kfz. 9). The battalion received a total of 15 of these outstanding vehicles. Despite their enormous towing capacity, they were still underpowered for attempting to tow a Ferdinand. In such cases, at least three of them had to be used in tandem. ROTH

The Ferdinand crews of the battalion receive their first tactical training at the Leitha Training Area (Austria). All of the 8.8-centimeter main guns still lack the spalling shield at the base of the gun mantlet.
JAUGITZ

The Ferdinande trained together with elements of the radio-controlled battalion, as well as conducted crew- and battle drills. No tactical numbering system can be seen on the vehicles at this point.

Trials conducted at the Putlos Gunnery Range on the Baltic in May 1943. The Inspector general of the Armored Forces, Generaloberst Guderian, attended the trials which were designed to test the effect of adding a spalling shield in front of the gun mantlet. The Ferdinand in the foreground is a test vehicle from Kummersdorf (Chassis No. 150011). SCHNEIDER

The 2./schwere Panzerjäger-Abteilung 653 was the first unit to receive the Ferdinand (eight vehicles initially) at Neusiedl am See. These vehicles were also missing the protective shield on front of the gun mantlet. The significance of the white rectangle on the vehicle hull remains unknown to this day. HABECK

Tarpaulins protect the sensitive vehicles from dust and the rain, particularly around the gratings on the upper deck. KUBROW

The new Ferdinand tank destroyers were under constant guard, since they were still considered a secret weapon. Despite the strict security, the Soviets forces in the affected sectors of the Kursk front were well informed about the vehicles. BECK

The arrangement of basic-issue items can be seen within the sponson box on the right side of the vehicle. It was quickly discovered during the fighting at Kursk that this storage container was positioned poorly. Any nearby battle damage frequently damaged this box or even tore it completely off. It was subsequently moved to the rear of the vehicle. SCHLENZKA

Rear view of a Ferdinand. This photograph was taken during the issuance of the first vehicles to the battalion at Neusiedl am See. The round rear hatch is clearly visible. This hatch was fastened inside by large wing nuts. After making an emergency exit, the crew was usually unable to reinstall the hatch without outside assistance. This proved to be a serious disadvantage in the construction of the vehicle. LUDWIG

Tank destroyer 322 (chassis number 150013) is finished being "tied down" on a German rail system Ssyms flat car, specially designed for transporting German heavy tanks. The Ferdinand fit on the rail car almost perfectly, thus sparing the crew the considerable time and effort of putting on transport tracks, as required by crews of the Tiger series of tanks. Note the wooden blocks used to keep the vehicle from shifting during the long travel time. NERGER

Elements of the battalion's Headquarters Company during the rail movement to the Soviet Union. The quad 20-millimeter Flak has been removed from the rear deck of its prime mover, an Sd.Kfz. 7/1, and placed on the platform of a rail car to avoid having it strike any electrical lines during movement along electrified stretches. PETERS

The 1./schwere Panzerjäger-Abteilung 653 unloads at Smiyevka (30 kilometers south of Orel). The unit insignia of the 1./schwere Panzerjäger-Abteilung 653—the black "cannon eagle" on a white base—can be seen on the front hull of the Ferdinand next to the right-hand tow pintle. The officer with the visor cap is Oberleutnant Karl Seitz, the commander of the Headquarters Company. HENNING

Ferdinand 124 (chassis number 150012) of Feldwebel Rolf Schleicher in the Kuliki assembly area. Note the semi-circular mounting plate for the lifting jack on the front hull. Attaching equipment such as track blocks or lifting jacks to the front of the vehicle proved unsuccessful, since the items were often damaged or destroyed in the course of fighting. PETERS

After maneuver training by the 3./schwere Panzerjäger-Abteilung 653 around Davidova in June 1943. The men are covered in dust. The driver is Schütze Emanuel Zentgraf. Sitting on the front slope is the vehicle commander, Oberfeldwebel Emil Issler. ZENTGRAF

Attempts were made to rehearse the upcoming operations in the Orel area during an exercise in late June 1943. BIERMANN

Final preparations in the second assembly area. A crew of the 1./schwere Panzerjäger-Abteilung 653 cleans the main gun of its Ferdinand. The "cannon eagle", the unit insignia of Sturmgeschütz-Abteilung 197, is barely visible next to the right-hand too hook and pintle. MUSCHICK

Borgward IV demolition carriers of Panzer-Kompanie 314 (Fkl) move past vehicles and personnel of schwere Panzerjäger-Abteilung 653. The Ferdinande are in the process of having camouflage paint applied. HENNING

At the end of the exercise, the vehicles and crews are covered with a layer of dust. BIERMANN

A Büssing-NAG Type 4500 truck form the battalion ammunition section supplies this Ferdinand from the 1./schwere Panzerjäger-Abteilung 653 with antitank and high-explosive rounds. HENNING

Ferdinand 134 of Unteroffizier Reinhold Schlabs. The vehicle has not received a camouflage finish, but wires have been mounted to the sides for affixing vegetation. The Borgward IV has also not received a camouflage finish. MUSCHICK

Schwere Panzer-Abteilung 505 was also in the attack sector of the XXXXVI. Panzer-Korps. This photograph shows a Tiger of the battalion during an exercise in front of the assembly area of the Ferdinande. MUSCHICK

Together with the Ferdinande of schwere Panzerjäger-Abteilung 653 and schwere Panzer-Jäger-Abteilung 654, assault guns of Sturmgeschütz-Abteilung 177 and Sturmgeschütz-Abteilung 244 occupied attack positions within the sector of the XXXXI. Panzer-Korps. Elements of the ammunition section of schwere Panzer-jäger-Abteilung 653 can be seen in the background.

An extensively camouflaged Ferdinand moves into position on the day of the attack, 4 July 1943. Ferdinand 124 (chassis number 150012) was commanded by Feldwebel Hans Huber on this day. He relieved Feldwebel Rolf Schleicher, who was sent to a training course. The radio operator, Georg Lösch, sits outside the vehicle. SCHLEICHER

Well camouflaged, the crews of the battalion await the order to attack. This photograph shows Ferdinand 302 (chassis number 150098) of Wachtmeister Czichochewski. APPEL

Another heavily camouflaged Ferdinand—322 of the 3./schwere Panzerjäger-Abteilung 653—before the attack. SABROWSKY

The German attack for Operation "Citadel" started at 0330 hours on 5 July 1943. In this image, a Ferdinand moves out of its attack position. The muzzle cover was simply fired through, if there was an engagement. GAUL

A tank destroyer from the 1./schwere Panzerjäger-Abteilung 653 screens along the Orel - Kursk rail line. It was immobilized in Soviet minefield right at the beginning of the attack, since the lanes that had been cleared through the minefields were rendered virtually unrecognizable after the heavy artillery barrages. Most of the combat engineers who accompanied the attack were wounded by the murderous defensive fire. SCHÄFER

Two variations of the unit insignia.

The Sturmpanzer IV's of Sturmpanzer-Abteilung 216 also accompanied the Ferdinande and the Borgward IV's in the attack. They formed a second wave and fired directly over the Ferdinande. STERRENBERGER

The attack rolls forward. A Ferdinand from the 2./schwere Panzerjäger-Abteilung 653 passes a Borgward IV from Panzer-Kompanie 314 (Fkl) that has wound up in a ditch. The unit insignia of the company has been painted over. Only the abbreviation—BR for Hauptmann Braam, the company commander—can still be seen clearly. JAUGITZ

Steered by radio control, this Borgward IV approaches its target. It was intended to detonate the vehicles in the minefields to clear lanes. This goal only met with partial success.

Ferdinand 113 shortly after breaking into the first Soviet defensive belt. The driver, Fritz Poischen, sits on top. A few hours after this photograph was taken, the tank destroyer became immobilized in a minefield and had to be abandoned by the crew. POISCHEN

Ferdinand 124 of the
1./schwere Panzerjäger-
Abteilung 653 moving in the
vicinity of a command and
control assault gun from the
radio-control battalion. The
recognition panel for the 2nd
Platoon of the company is
clearly visible on the rear of
the Ferdinand. Of interest is
the large storage box above
the emergency escape hatch.
JAUGITZ

Soviet antitank-gun positions
in the first defensive belt
destroyed by Ferdinande on
the first day of the offensive.

HENNING

HENNING

Gunner Henning of the 1./schwere Panzerjäger-Abteilung 653 with a captured Soviet antitank rifle. This weapon was also potentially dangerous to the Ferdinand, since it was often fired at the tracks in an effort to immobilize it. HENNING

Ferdinand 101 (chassis number 150014) during a maintenance halt in July 1943. The vehicle was originally commanded by Hauptmann Spielmann, who was badly wounded by an antipersonnel mine on 6 July. The driver of the vehicle was Unteroffizier Karl Gresch. Clearly visible is the stenciled vehicle numeral, which was done in outline form. The recognition panel of the 1./schwere Panzerjäger-Abteilung 653—a white rectangle—is on the right side and partially hidden by crew items. Despite the enormous superstructure, there was little room for personal equipment inside, as evidenced by these cooking and eating utensils.
SCHLABS

A knocked-out T 34/76 (F), photographed on 6 July 1943.

The platoon leader's tank destroyer—Ferdinand 121 (chassis number 150080)—returns to the combat trains after an operation. The vehicle commander is Leutnant Hermann Lock and the gunner is Unteroffizier Kurt Titus. The men's faces are blackened and show the strain of a day of heavy fighting CANTZ

The acting commander of the 3./schwere Panzerjäger-Abteilung 653, Oberleutnant Hanns Weglin, commanded his company from this Steyr 1500 A/01 during the fighting. Notice the abundance of radio equipment and the KF marking (= Kompanie-Führer = acting company commander) on the vehicle's front door. BIERMANN

The destruction of a T 34 as photographed through the Sfl.Zf. 1a aiming scope. The average number of enemy armored vehicles knocked out by each Ferdinand from 5-20 July 1943 was 15.

A Soviet KV 1 in flames after a direct hit. The accuracy of the 8.8-centimeter Pak 43/1 L/71 was exceptional out to 3,000 meters. This photograph was taken through the gunner's Sfl.Zf. 1a.

The ammunition for the 8.8-centimeter main gun took on enormous proportions. The ammunition racks in the Ferdinand could only hold 42 of them. This basic load was not considered enough for an engagement; consequently, the crews carried considerably more rounds on board. BUSCH

A Ferdinand of the 2./schwere Panzerjäger-Abteilung 653 and its entire crew. This photograph was taken during the first phase of the attack. The unit marking of the former Sturmgeschütz-Abteilung 197, covered by a coat of paint, is faintly visible on the front slope. Muzzle covers were frequently left on the main guns, since they would not affect the accuracy of the gun if it had to fire through it in an emergency situation. POISCHEN

Sturmgeschütz-Abteilung 177 and Sturmgeschütz-Abteilung 244 also had their operations severely hampered by the heavily mined terrain. These two battalions supported the 86. Infanterie-Division and the 292. Infanterie-Division, and both lost numerous vehicles to mines. This assault gun from Sturmgeschütz-Abteilung 197 was lucky, inasmuch as the force of the mine explosion only blew it off of the road. ENGELBRECHT

Both of these ex-Soviet photographs show Ferdinande from schwere Panzerjäger-Abteilung 653 that were lost during enemy counterattacks. The top vehicle lost its forward set of roadwheels to a mine and had to be abandoned by its crew. The bottom vehicle was completely destroyed by its crew prior to it being abandoned.

Personnel of Panzer-Kompanie 314 (Fkl) observe the Ferdinande as they advance. A halftrack (Sd.Kfz. 9/1) from the battalion's Maintenance Company can be seen in the background. JAUGITZ

The results of a direct hit by an artillery shell on a Panzer III and a Borgward IV of Panzer-Kompanie 314 (Fkl). The sympathetic explosion of the 350-kilogram charge on the Borgward IV was what actually caused the complete destruction of both vehicles. The upper hull of the Panzer III was hurled onto the main gun of a Ferdinand by the force of the explosion. Two damaged Ferdinande are being recovered in the background. JAUGITZ

This Ferdinand of the 1./schwere Panzerjäger-Abteilung 653 suffered heavy damage. The right-hand track was damaged and several roadwheels were torn off by the force of the explosions of the mines. The right-hand tow hook and pintle were also shot off. The tow pintle is seen on the bow plate of the vehicle. Several hits by antitank-rifle rounds can also be seen on the vehicle. HENNING

Another view of the same vehicle seen in the previous photograph. The Ferdinand was moved to a wooded area to afford it some concealment from aerial observation. HENNING

Leutnant Henning von Zitzewitz from the headquarters staff of schweres Panzerjäger-Regiment 656 orients a Ferdinand gun commander from schwere Panzerjäger-Abteilung 653. This vehicle was probably one of the two held back as an equipment reserve for the battalion. The battalion headquarters did not receive its complement of Ferdinande until after it took over the remaining vehicles of schwere Panzer-Jäger-Abteilung 654 after the fighting in the Orel area. TAMS

The regimental staff of schweres Panzerjäger-Regiment 656 used several Sd.Kfz. 250/3's as command and control vehicles. The vehicles were all numbered; in this instance, it is RN 4 (= regiments-Nachrichtenzug = regimental signals platoon). IRMSCHER

The regimental commander, Oberstleutnant Ernst baron von Jungenfeld, flanked by two staff officers. The officer in the Panzer uniform is Leutnant Erich Irmscher, the headquarters staff commandant. IRMSCHER

Ferdinand 231 (chassis number 150094) with a three-color camouflage scheme. The gun commander was Oberfeldwebel Otto Hecker, one of the most successful commander in the 2./schwere Panzerjäger-Abteilung 653. LOHRMANN

Feldwebel Schwarz, a gun commander in the 3./schwere Panzerjäger-Abteilung 653, next to his Ferdinand. The vehicle was no longer operational by the afternoon of 8 July 1943 and shows signs of the heavy fighting that took place. Note the bent deck plates from the impact of an artillery shell. Note also the missing mud guards and bent track blocks from a mine explosion. TILLWICK

Ferdinand 333 of Wachtmeister Bruno Schardin of the 3./schwere Panzerjäger-Abteilung 653 was surprised and captured by Soviet infantry in the vicinity of Alexandrovka. The Ferdinand had been screening German infantry forces there. In addition to the tank destroyer, the entire crew was captured. This ex-Soviet photograph shows the vehicle after the Battle of Orel with a painted inscription: German self-propelled Ferdinand gun, whose entire crew was captured by soldiers of the 129th Rifle Division."

A maintenance section effects repairs on a damaged Ferdinand (chassis number 150073) of the 3./schwere Panzerjäger-Abteilung 653 during a pause in the fighting. The gun commander was Unteroffizier Willi Petry. PETRY

Rear view of the same vehicle. The tool chest had been affixed to the rear of the vehicle right after the first day of fighting. The vehicle number—324—can clearly be seen as can the recognition panel for the 3./schwere Panzerjäger-Abteilung 653.

Unteroffizier Willi Petry of the 3./schwere Panzerjäger-Abteilung 653 at the vehicle commander's scope. The Sturmgeschütz III version of the commander's cupola that started to be mounted on the vehicles in 1944 considerably improved the ability of the commander to acquire targets in a close-hatch combat environment. PETRY

Ferdinand 332 and its crew: Gun commander Feldwebel Albin Heinickel (M 43 cap); to his left is the gunner, Unteroffizier Fridolin Weber. HEINICKEL

Using an Sd.Kfz. 9/1, the maintenance personnel remove one of the grating plates from the deck of Ferdinand 332. All of the access plates had to be removed before work could be performed on the two Maybach HL 120 TRM power plants.

The crew of Ferdinand 332 cleans the main gun. WEBER

Ferdinand 302 (chassis number 150098) during a pause in the fighting. The driver was wounded by shrapnel that came in through the open driver's hatch. In the background is a Marder II tank destroyer, which was armed with a 7.5-centimeter main gun. TILLWICK

**Feldwebel Albin Heinickel of the
3./schwere Panzerjäger-Abteilung 653.**
HEINICKEL

**Generaloberst Lothar Rendulic, Commanding General of the XXX. Armee-Korps, during a visit to the 3./schwere
Panzerjäger-Abteilung 653. Leutnant Franz Kretschmer, who has just returned from the fight, reports to the general.**
KRETSCHMER

Two Panther chassis were delivered to the battalion during Operation "Citadel". They were early D versions of the vehicle, and they did not have some of the features associated with the later Bergepanther (Recovery "Panther"), such as a spade and winch. Two bars were used to facilitate recoveries, although the Ferdinand also proved too heavy for just one of these vehicles as well.

A Ferdinand from the 1./schwere Panzerjäger-Abteilung 653 moves past a cameraman from the weekly newsreel. Unfortunately, very few professionally done photographic material depicting the Ferdinande at Orel have survived.

Soldiers of the 1./schwere Panzerjäger-Abteilung 653 are decorated in front of their comrades. From left to right: Unteroffizier Werner Kühl, Iron Cross, First Class (KIA in Italy in 1944); Unteroffizier Kurt Titus, Unteroffizier Barz, Iron Cross, Second Class; Gefreiter Georg Lösch, Iron Cross, Second Class; Gefreiter Garnier, Iron Cross, Second Class. PETERS

Unteroffizier Kurt Titus, the gunner in Ferdinand 121, received the Iron Cross, First Class, from his battalion commander, Major Steinwachs. TITUS

Generalmajor Heinz Traut awards the Knight's Cross to the Iron Cross to Leutnant Heinrich Teriete on 22 July 1943. Leutnant Teriete received this award for his crew's destruction of 22 Soviet tanks during the fighting at Shelyabug on 14 July 1943. In addition to commanding his vehicle, Teriete commanded a Kampfgruppe during the fighting. REIßNER

Leutnant Heinrich Teriete in front of his Ferdinand. NERGER

Following the fighting at Kursk and Orel, the battalion was divided into several small Kampfgruppen. On 31 July 1943, the last of these ad hoc Kampfgruppen was loaded aboard a train at the rail yards in Orel, bound for Karatchev. Following its departure, the rail installations were destroyed. SCHADE

This photograph shows a Ferdinand from the 3rd Platoon of the 1./schwere Panzer-Jäger-Abteilung 653 during the withdrawal to Karatchev. A rolled-up tarpaulin lies on the roof of the vehicle. The storage boxes that were originally placed on the right side of the vehicles were damaged on many of the Ferdinande during the fighting and were consequently moved to the rear of the vehicles by the battalion Maintenance Company. This proved to be a successful modification. HERTEL

VORLÄUFIGES BESITZZEUGNIS

DER FÜHRER
HAT DEM

Leutnant T e r i e t e ,
Zgfhr.s.Pz.Jäg.Abt.653

DAS RITTERKREUZ
DES EISERNEN KREUZES
AM 22.7.1943   VERLIEHEN

HQu OKH, DEN 24. Juli 1943

OBERKOMMANDO DES HEERES
I.A.

Generalmajor

Preliminary award document for the Knight's cross to the Iron Cross to Leutnant Teriete.

Besitzzeugnis

Dem

...........Unteroffizier Schmitt Andreas...........
[Name, Dienstgrad]

..........1./schw. Panzerjäger-Abt. 653..........
[Truppenteil, Dienststelle]

ist auf Grund

seiner am ...9..Juli..43...................... erlittenen

..ein.maligen Verwundung — ~~Beschädigung~~

das

Verwundetenabzeichen

in ...S..c.h..w..ar.z...........

verliehen worden.

Abt.Gef.Std.., den 24..Juli....19.43.

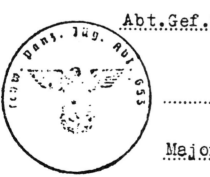

....
[Unterschrift]

Major u. Abteilungskommandeur.
[Dienstgrad und Dienststelle]

Award document for the Wound Badge in Black (for up to two wounds) to Unteroffizier Andreas Schmidt.

"The Withdrawal": Due to a shortage of heavy recovery vehicles, two Ferdinande tow a damaged one. The small, 24-ton bridge in the center of the photograph had to be bypassed in order to keep it intact for regular traffic. The Ferdinande generally inflicted quite a bit of damage to the infrastructure of the time, since it was not designed for anything remotely approaching such a heavy vehicle weight. THEIS

Recovering damaged Ferdinande was usually very difficult. A minimum of three 18-ton prime movers—the Sd.Kfz. 9—were needed to tow one Ferdinand along a level road! Depending on the terrain, up to five prime movers were needed. BIERMANN

Enormous demands were placed on the maintenance personnel. Suspension damage to the Ferdinande due to Soviet mines was a particular problem. This Ferdinand lost a complete set of roadwheels on its left side. PITZ

This photograph clearly shows the enormous efforts needed to recover a damaged or immobilized Ferdinand. Five 18-ton prime movers strain to pull a Ferdinand from the 1./schwere Panzerjäger-Abteilung 653 through the morass: A masterful achievement for the recovery section. HENNING

The battalion's Maintenance Company had two 16-ton portal cranes, which were used to remove the fighting compartment from the vehicles. Without these cranes, it would have been virtually impossible to work on the superstructures. These photographs were taken in the rear area, since such involved work could not be undertaken close to the front.

Removing the fighting compartment from Ferdinand 102 (chassis number 150024). The gun commander of this vehicle was Hauptfeldwebel Fritz Madaus. NITBAUER

In order to keep enough Ferdinande operational, parts were often taken from tank destroyers that had suffered so much damage that they could no longer be repaired. All functional parts were removed from such vehicles. This Ferdinand from schwere Panzer-Jäger-Abteilung 654 sits along the withdrawal route to Briansk. SCHULER

Ferdinand 612 (Chassis number 150022) at Briansk. This vehicle had belonged to the 2./schwere Panzer-Jäger-Abteilung 654, before it was transferred to schwere Panzerjäger-Abteilung 653. The vehicle displays the so-called "net" camouflage pattern typical of schwere Panzer-Jäger-Abteilung 654. DISTLER

To cover personnel losses within schwere Panzerjäger-Abteilung 653, individual soldiers and entire gun crews were transferred into the battalion from schwere Panzer-Jäger-Abteilung 654. A portion of the crew of Ferdinand 513—formerly of the 1./schwere Panzer-Jäger-Abteilung 654—pose for a commemorative photograph. The gun commander, Unteroffizier Peter Kohns, is wearing the M 43 field cap. To his right is the driver, Felix Hoffmann. KOHNS

Ferdinand 513 (Chassis number 150036) waits to be turned over to the sister battalion at Briansk. Note the tarpaulin over the engine intake grills. KOHNS

Ferdinand 133 of the 1./schwere Panzerjäger-Abteilung 653 (chassis number 150019) undergoes maintenance at Briansk. The right-hand drive sprocket has been removed from the vehicle. This was labor-intensive work that could not be performed in the vicinity of the front. HENNING

Formation and Employment of schwere Panzerjäger-Abteilung 653

Two tank destroyers from the 3./schwere Panzerjäger-Abteilung 653 have been loaded aboard the special Ssyms rail cars for transportation to Dnjepropetrovsk. The crew has set up housekeeping on the rail car—a possible inspiration for a model builder. TAMS

This photograph of Ferdinand 511 (chassis number 150040) was also taken at Briansk. This vehicle was originally commanded by Leutnant Hermann Feldheim of the 1./schwere Panzer-Jäger-Abteilung 654. Leutnant Feldheim was one of the most successful commanders of schwere Panzer-Jäger-Abteilung 654. Despite the prohibition of schweres Panzerjäger-Regiment 656 against the painting of "kill" rings on gun barrels, this vehicle displays 16 of them! TILLWICK

The rail movement to Dnjepropetrovsk as begun. Unteroffizier Wilhelm Flintrop sits at the front of the vehicle. The vehicle's driver, Unteroffizier Gärtner, stands next to the main gun. Both soldiers were assigned to the 1./schwere Panzerjäger-Abteilung 653. PETERS

The crew has made itself comfortable on top of the engine compartment, setting up a table and chairs. This is Ferdi-nand 621, formerly of the 2./schwere Panzerjäger-Abteilung 654. After the Ferdinande were transferred in from the sister battalion, Feldwebel Müller, of the battalion's Headquarters Company, took command of the vehicle.

The first transports of schweres Panzerjäger-Regiment 656 arrived at Dnjepropetrovsk between 26 August and 1 September 1943. This photograph shows vehicles from the Maintenance Company and one of the line companies of schwere Panzerjäger-Abteilung 653 just prior to unloading. The Bergepanther is one of the early models without a stabilization blade; it also demonstrates an unusually high silhouette by virtue of the object covered up by the tarpaulin. CARPENTIER

Regimental staff officers and a detail of officers from the staff sections of the Inspector General of the Armored Forces view one of the first overhauled Ferdinande at Dnjepropetrovsk. Based on the camouflage pattern, this vehicle must have been one of those transferred into the battalion from schwere Panzer-Jäger-Abteilung 654. The vehicle number, original painted as a white numeral, was removed and replaced with a numeral in black-outline form. The toolbox originally located on the right-front side of the vehicle has been relocated to the vehicle's rear. IRMSCHER

The urgently needed depot-level maintenance of the Ferdinande and the Sturmpanzer commenced in the "K Works" at Dnjepropetrovsk in September 1943. The Ferdinande were overhauled as much as the spare-parts situation allowed. They also received new engines. A removed hull roof with both engine-access grills and crew compartment section can be seen in the foreground. The two fighting compartments in the background have already had the modified protective shield placed on the main- gun barrel. WEIß

This photograph shows a fighting compartment being removed from a vehicle's hull by a 16-ton crane. The detached fighting compartment in the middle of the image has the newer version of the gun-mantlet protective shield. The two fighting compartments on the right still have the original shields in place. SCHULER

Rail transport of elements of schwere Panzerjäger-Abteilung 653 across the large bridge over the Dnjepr at Saporoshye. Of interest in this photograph is the presence of an additional armor plate above the gunner's sight to prevent shrapnel damage to it.
FEDERER

This photograph clearly shows vehicle numbering within the battalion. Ferdinand 112 was commanded by Stabsfeldwebel Slanarz; the driver was Hermann Looft. The Ferdinand in the middle of the image is Major Baumunk's command and control vehicle and has the markings IN1. The operational Ferdinande were ordered to form two Kampfgruppen: Gruppe Nord and Gruppe Süd. Major Georg Baumunk was the commander of Gruppe Nord. Gruppe Süd was under the command of Major Bruno Kahl, the commander of Sturmpanzer-Abteilung 216.
LOOFT

A Kampfgruppe composed of vehicles from all three line companies awaits the orders to begin rail loading at Dnjepropetrovsk. FEDERER

A gemischte ("mixed") Kampfgruppe composed of elements from all of the line companies moves out for commitment in the fighting at Saporoshye. An armed force propaganda company filmed the event for the weekly newsreel in Germany. PETERS

The dam at Saporoshye. At the time, it was the largest hydroelectric plant in the world. SABROWSKY

This photograph clearly shows the enormous dimensions of the dam. German forces blew it up on 15 October 1943.
IRMSCHER

A Ferdinand from the 1./schwere Panzerjäger-Abteilung 653 slowly approaches the dam. Despite the gigantic dimensions of the dam, the drivers were ordered to use the utmost caution when traversing it and completely avoid any sudden steering changes. IRMSCHER

Sturmpanzer IV's from the 3./schweres Panzerjäger-Regiment 656 (Sturmpanzer-Abteilung 216) were also rushed to the bridgehead to provide support to the grenadiers there. In this image, a section is preparing for combat operations. The lead vehicle is a command and control vehicle, identifiable by its two antennae. Note the rain cover over the driver's vision port. MAY

This "J" Model Panzer III—identifiable through its sideskirts an appliqué armor—accompanied the Ferdinande and Sturmpanzer into combat. It is a command and control vehicle from the regimental staff of schweres Panzerjäger-Regiment 656. Of interest is the Pampas recognition panel on the gun mantlet as well as the lettering on the turret sideskirt: RNZ (= Regiments-Nachrichten-Zug = regimental signals platoon). The latter was probably painted in yellow. IRMSCHER

Another Sturmpanzer IV from Sturmpanzer-Abteilung 216. Its vehicular number is 50, and it belongs to the 3./Sturmpanzer-Abteilung 216. The nickname Elly appears on the driver's vision port. CARPENTIER

The tracks provided by the Skoda Company proved to be too weak for the vehicle and suffered many problems. New track blocks had to be ordered constantly. This crew has covered the vehicle with replacement track blocks. A horseshow has been attached to the right-hand forward mud guard to usher in good luck. PAULUS

This photograph of members of the 2./schwere Panzerjäger-Abteilung 653 in the Saporoshye Bridgehead in September 1943 shows that the exception proves the rule! The Pampas crest appears to the left of the main gun, whereas the main-gun protective shield is still of the old type with a smooth exterior surface. PAULUS

The commander of this Ferdinand was a replacement from the Panzertruppe. That is why he wears the black Panzer uniform.
PAULUS

Two Ferdinande from schwere Panzerjäger-Abteilung 653 occupy screening positions within the bridgehead. The flat, treeless terrain was ideal for the long-ranging main gun, which could hit and kill targets out to 3,000 meters. Several assault guns can be seen moving in the background. PETERS

An oversized skull and crossbones adorns the front armor plate of this Ferdinand of the 3./schwere Panzerjäger-Abteilung 653. The vehicle was alternately commanded by Leutnant Göttelmann and Hauptfeldwebel Kürschner. Of interest is the fact that the driver is wearing a Soviet combat-vehicle helmet. PETERS

After rearming, this crew from the 1./schwere Panzerjäger-Abteilung 653 poses for a photograph with two 8.8-centimeter rounds. The gun commander is Unteroffizier Reinhold Schlabs, and the photograph was taken near Saporoshye in September 1943. SCHLABS

Despite the enormous armor protection the Ferdinand provided the crew, there were still frequent personnel losses among the companies. The cause of most of these losses was shrapnel entering the crew compartment. This Ferdinand from the 1./schwere Panzerjäger-Abteilung 653 received a bad hit. The driver, a heavily bandaged Unteroffizier Edgar Scheeler, stands in the driver's hatch. The body of one of the loaders is positioned on the right mudguard for the movement back to friendly lines. SCHLABS

This crew from the 1./schwere Panzerjäger-Abteilung 653 digs a protective dugout against shrapnel. After digging, the Ferdinand would then move over the dugout and any openings filled in with dirt. This allowed the crews to spend some time outside of the vehicle, while still remaining relatively protected against enemy fires. BÜRGIN

A tense situation during an attack against Soviet armor. The Ferdinand of Leutnant Helmut Ulbricht overheats and has an engine fire. The crew manages to extinguish the fire, and the recovery platoon brings the vehicle back to friendly lines. HENNING

A gemischte ("mixed") Kampfgruppe of 12 Ferdinande and 13 Sturmpanzer loads in Dnjepropetrovsk on 11 September 1943 for operations to hold the Ssinelnikovo-Pavlograd rail line. The battle group was commanded by Major Baumunk. Panthers also took part in the operation. THEIS

Leutnant Erich Irmscher, the commandant of the head-quarters of schweres Panzerjäger-Regiment 656 in Saporoshye in September 1943. As with much of the headquarters personnel, he had previously been assigned to Panzer-Regiment 35. IRMSCHER

The regimental Commander, Oberstleutnant Ernst Baron von Jungenfeld, received the German cross in Gold on 1 November 1943. The photograph shows him with Leutnant Erich Irmscher after having received the award. IRMSCHER

Bridges continued to be the biggest obstacles facing the Ferdinande. The enormous 72-ton combat weight of the vehicle made it necessary for combat engineers to exert labor-intensive efforts to reinforce and secure most bridges. When there was not enough time for such measures, problems such as those in this photograph arose. A Ferdinand from the 3./schwere Panzerjäger-Abteilung 653 broke through this bridge while withdrawing from the Saporoshye Bridgehead. The crew anxiously awaits the arrival of the recovery platoon. SABROWSKY

On 13 October 1943, the last Ferdinande of the battalion cross the dam back to the west side of the Dnjepr. This image shows Ferdinand 123 of the 1./schwere Panzerjäger-Abteilung 653.

After moving from Saporoshye to Nikopol, the battalion Maintenance Company set to work to overhauling the completely overworked vehicles. Fighting compartments are removed and stacked in this image.

In September 1943, the recovery version of the Ferdinand was put on display at the Nibelungen Works at St. Valentin. Schwere Panzerjäger-Abteilung 653 received three of these vehicles.

Maintenance personnel sit atop the main gun of a Ferdinand at Nikopol. Of interest is the fact that the Pampas crest has been painted on the front slope of the vehicle.

The Sturmpanzer IV's of Sturmpanzer-Abteilung 216 were also ordered to the Nikopol Bridgehead along with the Ferdinande of schwere Panzerjäger-Abteilung 653. The movement across the Dnjepr took place on a 1,000-ton ferry. The first Ferdinand carefully moves onto the ferry. STEINMÜLLER

Four Ferdinande are ready to cross on the ferry. SCHLEICHER

A Sturmpanzer IV moves across a wooden ramp to board the ferry. Notice the camouflage pattern on this vehicle. Tarpaulins protect the mantlet of the 15-centimeter main gun and the roof of the vehicle from the rain. The Sturmpanzer were not known for being watertight!
DR. RENOTIÉRE

The vehicles are fastened down for the crossing. Ferdinand 302 in the right-hand corner of this image, is the vehicle of the First Sergeant of the company. In the left-hand corn of the photograph, a Pampas crest is clearly visible.
WILHELM

The ferry moves across the river. A Sturmpanzer IV of the Headquarters Company of Sturmpanzer-Abteilung 216 is in the foreground. It can be identified by its roman numeral II. WILHELM

Ferdinand 121 (chassis number 150080), the 2nd Platoon leader's vehicle, after refueling at Nikopol. The small cross above the fighting compartment roof indicates where an artillery shell hit several days after this photograph was taken, partially penetrating the armor and wounding the crew. NEUNERT

Left to right: Radio Operator, Ruppert Weiß; Vehicle Commander, Hauptfeldwebel Horst Kürschner; Gunner, Unteroffizier Alois Moosdiele. KÜRSCHNER

Soviet T 34's knocked out by Ferdinande. Entire formations of Soviet tanks were often knocked out by just two or three Ferdinande of schwere Panzerjäger-Abteilung 653.

Leutnant Franz Kretschmer, a Platoon leader in the 3./schwere Panzerjäger-Abteilung 653, received the Knight's Cross on 17 December 1943 for his actions in the Nikopol Bridgehead.

Weather conditions grew dramatically worse in December 1943, and the heavy Ferdinande began sinking in the mire and the mud. This rare photograph shows a Ferdinand and its recovery-vehicle counterpart straining to pull a second Ferdinand from the morass. The recovery vehicle appears to have already bottomed out itself. Note the rear crew hatch on the recovery vehicle, which is actually a Panzer IV turret side hatch. SCHLENSKA

Ferdinand 234
(chassis number 150100)
was photographed from all
sides by its crew. The Pampas
crest is visible to the left
of the main gun.

BECK

BECK

The Pampas crest is also visible on the left rear of the fighting compartment. The recognition panel from Operation "Citadel" is also still present on the right-hand side, although it has lost any significance. BECK

Due to a shortage of protective shields for the gun mantlet, this platoon leader's vehicle—Ferdinand 211 of the 2./schwere Panzerjäger-Abteilung 653 (chassis number 150028)—moves into combat without one.

The tracks of the Ferdinand still leave massive ruts in the not-quite-frozen ground. The vehicle in the photograph above is almost touching the ground with the bottom of its hull. THEIS

A tracked crane vehicle—Sd.Kfz. 9/1—of the battalion maintenance elements tows a battle-damage signals half-track of the regimental headquarters. A Soviet antitank gun shot away its front axle. Unfortunately, the unit insignia of the Maintenance Company is only barely visible on the Sd.Kfz. 9/1: A Ferdinand with an eye patch!

In late December 1943, only two Sturmpanzer IV's were available for operations with the Ferdinande against Soviet armor. All of the other Sturmpanzer IV's had been transported to the Vienna Army Arsenal on 10 December 1943. THEIS

The battalion captured this Soviet KV 85 completely intact. The Maintenance Company removed its turret, and the vehicle entered German service as a recovery and transport vehicle.

The maintenance collection point for the regiment at Nikopol in December 1943 resembled a giant junkyard. Hardly any Ferdinand or Sturmpanzer IV was fully operational. All elements of the regiment await the order to rail load for Vienna.

Two soldiers of Sturmpanzer-Abteilung 216 pose on a Ferdinand in Nikopol for a commemorative photograph. The attached camouflage net is a bit unusual.

A Ferdinand from the 3./schwere Panzerjäger-Abteilung 653 has boarded the Ssyms car from an end ramp. The vehicle features a very washed-out coat of whitewash. THEIS

An Sd.Kfz. 250/3 from the regimental signals platoon. The same two soldiers who posed on the Ferdinand are seen here again.

A Ferdinand from the 3./schwere Panzerjäger-Abteilung 653 aboard a Ssyms car.

Feldwebel Schiestel's Ferdinand 334; he can be seen in front of his vehicle, wearing the sheepskin coat and camouflage trousers. SCHIESTEL

Overhaul of the Ferdinande at St. Valentin, Austria
(JANUARY TO MARCH 1944)

The desperately needed maintenance for the Ferdinande brought back from Russia began with great difficulties. The Nibelungen Works in St. Valentin initially declined to accept the vehicles, because it would seriously disrupt the continuous production of Panzer IV's. On orders from the Army High Command, however, a warehouse at the Nibelungen Works was cleared for a general overhaul. The first 8 Ferdinande began undergoing repairs on 19 January 1944. An order arrived from Berlin on the same day outlining the high priority for refitting schweres Panzerjäger-Regiment 656.

The following excerpts are from original documents in the Federal Archives and Freiburg Military Archives. They provide a summary of the difficulties associated with the general overhaul of the Ferdinande and Sturmpanzer.

19 January 1944: Orders for accelerated reconstitution of schweres Panzerjäger-Regiment 656.

19 January 1944: Eight Ferdinande have been disassembled at the Nibelungen Works. Their reconstruction has just begun. Repair parts from Schutno have not arrived yet.

19 January 1944:

TO: Nibelungen Works

FROM: Army High Command

SUBJECT: 15-Centimeter Sturmpanzer IV, Ferdinand Maintenance.

As agreed between HDL Saur and Certified Engineer of Austria, it is directed that responsibility for the completion of the 15-centimeter Sturmpanzer IV will be transferred from Vienna to the Nibelungen Works and, in exchange, repairing the Ferdinande will become the responsibility of the Vienna Main Vehicle Maintenance Facility.

21 January 1944:

TO: Army High Command

FROM: Vienna Main Vehicle Maintenance Facility 77, Arsenal.

SUBJECT: 15-centimeter Sturmpanzer IV and Ferdinand Maintenance.

Due to the transfer of Ferdinande already underway to the Nibelungen Works and the availability of repair parts in the Linz Army Material Depot, the Ferdinand repair site will remain in St. Valentin (except for those vehicles, about 6 total, which suffered serious damage from fire and explosions and therefore require a longer repair time). The Vienna Main Vehicle Maintenance Facility will assume responsibility for these 6 vehicles.

25 January 1944:

SUBJECT: Reconstitution of schweres Panzerjäger-Regiment 656

All field transports leaving Russia since 14 December 1943 have arrived at the Straßhof auxiliary rail station. A total of 16 transports from the regiment arrived between 16 December 1943 and 10 January 1944.

Ferdinande are at the Nibelungen Works in St. Valentin. Sturmpanzer IV, Command Panzer III, Panzer III (chassis), Panzer IV and Panzer V (chassis) [ammunition carriers] are at the Main Vehicle Maintenance Facility at the Vienna arsenal. Eighteen Ferdinande have been disassembled and are undergoing repairs at the Nibelungen Works. The entire Ferdinand repair effort depends upon the timely arrival of repair parts that are allegedly on a rail transport from Schutno and on the timely delivery of HL 120 replacement engines. Under these assumptions, an estimated maximum of 43 Ferdinande can be completed by 15 March 1944.

1 February 1944:

FROM: Armored Forces Inspector (In6)

TO: Oberst Mildebrath

Prepare one Ferdinand company immediately.

1 February 1944: Schweres Panzerjäger-Regiment 656 will prepare one Ferdinand company, consisting of 10–12 vehicles, for movement and operational commitment.

2 February 1944: 24 Ferdinande have been disassembled at the Nibelungen Works. Repair of the first series (8 vehicles) can be completed by approximately 10 February 1944. The order dated 1 February 1944 to prepare a company of 10–12 Ferdinande for operational commitment has slowed down the progress of the standard overhaul. Additionally, the departure of a Ferdinand company requires the detachment of a maintenance platoon. This will delay the rest of the repairs at least 3 weeks. Adhering to the completion deadline of 1 March 1944 is therefore impossible.

9 February 1944: The repair of the first series of 8 Ferdinande is almost complete. They will be ready by 11 February 1944. An additional 3 Ferdinande to complete the Ferdinand company will be provided by interrupting the planned overhauls and initiating accelerated maintenance.

11 February 1944: Only 2 companies from the regiment arriving on 21 January 1944 will deploy by the 15 February 1944 deadline [One Ferdinand company and one Sturmpanzer company]. The rest of the regiment [1,800 officers and men] will remain in St. Pölten until 1 March 1944.

1 March 1944:

I./schweres Panzerjäger-Regiment 656 [schwere Panzerjäger-Abteilung 653]

8 Ferdinande were completed on 26 February 1944 and deployed to St. Pölten. They were assigned to the 2./schwere Panzerjäger-Abteilung 653 for activation and training. The 25 remaining Ferdinande and 2 recovery Ferdinande have all been disassembled, except for the last 4, and currently occupy Dock 2, Warehouse 8 of the Nibelungen Works . . .

An estimated completion date for 8 Ferdinande (under favorable conditions) is 8 March 1944. Since completion of the remaining 19 Ferdinande is contingent upon the delivery of suspension systems and engine gratings, these tanks must remain disassembled . . . until these parts arrive. 2 Bergepanther and 3 Panzer III ammunition carriers have been completed. The remaining 2 Panzer III's and 2 ammunition carriers will be completed at the Vienna arsenal by 10 March 1944.

The 4 burned-out Ferdinand chassis were disassembled at the Nibelungen Works, and the hulls were sent to Vienna, in the most rapid manner possible, for repair at the arsenal.

The battalion requests that the 2 Ferdinande in Kummersdorf be released so that they also can be overhauled at the Nibelungen Works or Vienna Arsenal and have the necessary modifications made. The battalion requests the hydraulic tank provided by the regiment for use as a recovery vehicle.

[Author's Note: The Ferdinande in Kummersdorf were the two vehicles used for testing by the Motor Vehicle Research Station of the Army Evaluation Office. They were chassis numbers 150010 and 150011.]

1944 FERDINAND MAINTENANCE STATUS

1 January 1944:	0 Ferdinande in maintenance; 0 completed in December 1943
1 February 1944:	? Ferdinande in maintenance; ? completed in January 1944
1 March 1944:	32 Ferdinande in maintenance; 20 completed in February 1944
1 April 1944:	5 Ferdinande in maintenance; 27 completed in March 1944

Many modifications were made to the Ferdinande. The vehicles received the long-recommended hull machine gun, manned by the radio operator, for close-in defense. The easily damaged gratings were also replaced and a commander's cupola with periscopes—identical to that used in the Sturmgeschütz III—was also installed also. The vehicles also received new HL 120 engines and the Zimmerit anti-mine coating, obligatory after 1944, as well as the sand-yellow primer. Vehicle numbers had not been assigned to the vehicles yet.

Operations in Italy by the 1./schwere Panzerjäger-Abteilung 653

(FEBRUARY TO AUGUST 1944)

During the gray of dawn on 22 January 1944, the US VI Corps began landing at Anzio and Nettuno in the Italian Theater (Operation "Shingle"). Few German combat forces with suitable combat power were available to conduct an effective counterattack against the beachhead. The German leadership (14. Armee) managed to quickly piece together elements, however, with which it was able to form a reasonably stable containment ring around the beachhead.

Schweres Panzerjäger-Regiment 656 received an order on 1 February 1944 to immediately prepare a Ferdinand company for movement and operational commitment and rapidly deploy Sturmpanzer-Abteilung 216 to Italy. The Flak Platoon from the Headquarters Company of schwere Panzerjäger-Abteilung 653 was attached to Sturmpanzer-Abteilung 216 effective 6 February 1944. Under the leadership of Oberfeldwebel Herbert Weller, it remained with this battalion until the end of the war.

The 1./schwere Panzerjäger-Abteilung 653, under the command of Oberleutnant Helmut Ulbricht, received 11 completely overhauled and rebuilt Ferdinande on 15 February 1944. The authorized strength of 14 guns could not be achieved due to the repair situation. The company also received a complete maintenance platoon with a portal crane, an 18-ton prime mover (Sd.Kfz. 9/1) and a recovery Ferdinand. The rail loading began on 16 February 1944 at the Nibelungen Works at St. Valentin. The train halted at Pöchlarn, Parndorf and Neusiedl, before the final transport to Italy began.

The journey to Italy progressed through Salzburg, Innsbruck, the Brenner Pass, Bozen, Trento, Bologna and Florence. It arrived in Rome on 24 February 1944. The tanks and wheeled vehicles unloaded at the Ostiense Rail Station in the center of the Eternal City.

DUTY POSITIONS, 1./SCHWERE PANZERJÄGER-ABTEILUNG 653

Company Commander:	Oberleutnant/Hauptmann Helmut Ulbricht
Platoon Leader/Executive Officer:	Leutnant Werner Haberland
Platoon Leader:	Leutnant Hermann Löck
Assigned while in Italy:	Leutnant Willi Grupe (killed 7 June 1944)
First Sergeant:	Hauptfeldwebel Erich Kochan
Combat Trains Sergeant:	Stabsfeldwebel Willi Slanarz
Supply Column Sergeant:	Oberfeldwebel Karl Wedler
Pay Sergeant:	Feldwebel Otto Peters

Supply Sergeant: Stabsfeldwebel Rudolf Junker
Assistant Supply Sergeant: Unteroffizier Heinz Henning
Maintenance Sergeant: Werkmeister Hans Adam

The first assembly area for the Ferdinande was in the town of Genzano (di Roma) on Lake Nemi, not far from the summer residence of the Pope, Castell Gandolfo. The company combat trains remained in Tor Sapienza, a suburb of Rome. The maintenance platoon also remained in Rome.

The 1./schwere Panzerjäger-Abteilung 653 was attached to schwere Panzer-Abteilung 508 (Tiger I), under the command of Major Hudel. (Source: Federal Archives / Freiburg Military Archives).

Orders dated 24 February 1944:

One company from schwere Panzerjäger-Abteilung 653 (Ferdinand) will be allocated to the Headquarters of the 14. Armee. The company will be attached to schwere Panzer-Abteilung 508 (LXXVI. Panzer-Korps/Headquarters 14. Armee), both tactically and administratively.

Orders dated 27 February 1944:

Schwere Panzer-Abteilung 508 and one company of Ferdinande attached to Fallschirm-Panzer-Division "Hermann Göring" ["Herman Göring" Armored Division].

The Ferdinande, along with the Tigers and other quickly assembled armored formations, were to conduct operations against the beachhead. Toward this end, all armored elements were attached to the LXXVI. Panzer-Korps under General der Panzertruppen Herr (commander of the 13. Panzer-Division on the Eastern Front). An armored attack force was created under an ad hoc armor headquarters commanded by Oberst Schmidt. This force consisted of the 1./Panzer-Regiment 4, schwere Panzer-Abteilung 508, 1./schwere Panzerjäger-Abteilung 653, II./Panzer-Regiment 26, Sturmpanzer-Abteilung 216 and Panzer-Abteilung (Fkl) 301. This formation worked together with the Fallschirm-Panzer-Division "Hermann Göring", the 363. Infanterie-Division, and the two Panzergrenadier-Regimenter of the 26. Panzer-Division—Panzergrenadier-Regiment 9 and Panzergrenadier-Regiment 67.

The Allied air supremacy and incredible effect of the American naval artillery forced all vehicles to constantly camouflage themselves and be careful while moving in the assembly area. The second German attack against the beachhead began at 0400 hours on 28 February 1944. The first attack, conducted from 16 February 1944 to 18 February 1944, failed despite many sacrifices and heavy losses.

The terrain in the area of the former Pontino Marshes was not well suited for an attack by heavy tracked vehicles. Due to the continuous rainfall and flooding of the dams, only the paved roads were trafficable. Diverting to the marshy terrain resulted in the heavy tanks becoming stuck immediately. A Ferdinand deployed as part of Kampfgruppe Stein (schwere Panzer-Abteilung 508) was lost in this manner on 1 March 1944. Along the Cisterna–Nettuno road, near the town of Isola Bella, the lead Ferdinand under the command of Unteroffizier Werner Kühl went off the road while trying to turn around at a destroyed bridge. An idler arm from the suspension was bent on the road embankment, and the vehicle was immobilized. Recovery attempts by a Tiger I from schwere Panzer-Abteilung 508 failed in the face of heavy enemy fire. The Tiger I also had to be abandoned. Unteroffizier Kühl was killed by artillery shrapnel during a second recovery attempt, so further attempts were not undertaken. The company lost another Ferdinand to a mine a short time later. This vehicle also could not be recovered in the face of enemy fire and had to be destroyed by Oberleutnant Ulbricht.

Unteroffizier Heinz Henning, in conjunction with former gunner, Heinrich Schäfer, described the loss of these two Ferdinande in a letter to the author:

Heinrich Schäfer was the gunner in the Ferdinand commanded by Unteroffizier Werner Kühl. Oberleutnant Stein [schwere Panzer-Abteilung 508], as was customary in our unit, moved along the road at the head of our attacking tanks. Due to their heavy weights, the Tigers and Ferdinande had to remain on solid roads. Open terrain was too soft.

Oberleutnant Stein had Unteroffizier Kühl to take over the lead position because of the heavy frontal armor on his Ferdinand. Oberleutnant Stein would screen the flanks with his turret. A destroyed bridge in front of the town of Isola Bella ended the advance. Unteroffizier Kühl turned the tank destroyer around on the road. The Ferdinand went off the road and into a ditch with one of its tracks and became stuck. Oberleutnant Stein wanted to recover the Ferdinand with his Tiger. Both loaders refused to exit their vehicles because of the enemy mortar and artillery barrages. Heinrich Schäfer therefore voluntarily left his vehicle and attached the Ferdinand to the Tiger. The roadwheel on the second roadwheel arm was already shot up.

Two S hooks broke during the recovery attempt. All subsequent recovery attempts were in vain, because the non-functional idler arm was bent diagonally between the lower track and entire upper track . . . It made no difference whether the vehicle attempted to move forwards or backwards. A typical Porsche Tiger ailment.

Completely out of breath, Heinrich Schäfer reached the crew compartment again and, fortunately for him, collapsed, exhausted, at the rear of the compartment. A kinetic energy round penetrated the armor on the side of the crew compartment. Unteroffizier Kühl and one of the loaders suffered minor shrapnel wounds. Unteroffizier Kühl gave the order to abandon the vehicle and all of us hastened back to our front line.

This was the first Ferdinand destroyed in Italy. Unteroffizier Reinhold Schlabs was also a member of Kampfgruppe Stein and his Ferdinand was positioned on the macadam-reinforced road. Another ridiculous recovery attempt had to be made that evening.

Werner Kühl suffered a serious injury to his shoulder during the attempt and died from his wound on the following day. He was posthumously promoted to Feldwebel.

At this point, I had to create a skid-like roadwheel replacement out of a large wooden log. We tried and practiced this in Velletri. The defective roadwheel had to be removed and the freed hub inserted into a groove carved into the log. About 30 combat engineers were to provide infantry support for us during a night operation. The destroyed bridge at Isola Bella was

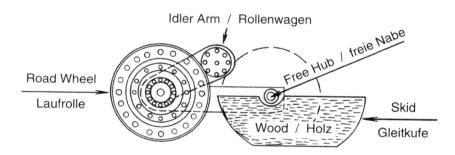

Diagram by Karlheinz Münch, based on a sketch by Heinz Henning.

to be captured in a raid beforehand. This failed in a rain of steel and phosphorus. We were not able to get near the Ferdinand. The operation had to be scrapped. In the end, schwere Panzer-Abteilung 508 suffered many killed and missing. The Ferdinand was located between the two fronts and, as a result, was not reported as a total loss at first.

The same thing occurred with Feldwebel Gustav Koss' Ferdinand. Feldwebel Koss was on an unimproved road about 200 meters parallel to the notorious macadam road. He was a bit farther back when he ran over a mine. Unteroffizier Golinski and I were present when an armored recovery vehicle, driven by Willi Löffler, attempted to tow the vehicle. I sat forward in the radio operator's position, next to the driver. It was hell, with shells bursting all around us. A dead comrade from the maintenance platoon was laid next to the driver on the track-guard cover. This recovery attempt also had to be abandoned. The commander, Oberleutnant Helmut Ulbricht, accompanied by his wheeled-vehicle driver, Otto Weller, personally blew up the Ferdinand during a dark night. I was the third man on this mission.

The gun crews and members of the 1./schwere Panzerjäger-Abteilung 653 remained in their relatively quiet assembly areas and quarters near Cisterna and Velletri until mid-May 1944. An order from the Führer Headquarters on 1 May 1944 directed that the name Ferdinand for the Porsche tank destroyer (Sd.Kfz. 184) be removed from all records and replaced with the designation Elefant ["Elephant"]. Increased enemy artillery fire on 19 May 1944 indicated an impending attempt by the Allies to break out of the beachhead. The Americans mounted a huge attack, with an incredible amount of materiel, against German positions on 24 May 1944. The 9 Elefanten of the 1./schwere Panzerjäger-Abteilung 653 waited for the attack 2 kilometers behind the front line in prepared positions along National Highway No. 7, the Via Appia.

Several letters and notes from former radio operator, Oberschütze Herbert Ströll, described the quiet days before the Allied attack:

Italy, 26 April 1944: Yesterday, on 25 April, I was ordered forward from our supply detachment in Tor Sapienza. My former tank driver, best friend and comrade, who was from Luxembourg, unfortunately had to remain with the supply detachment and, as a result, we were separated. I went with our First Sergeant to our supply point at the estate of Count Ciano, where two tank crews were resting. They greeted me with a friendly hello and their first question to me was: "Well, Herbert, are you staying with us to play some music?"

I replied: "Unfortunately, only until tomorrow. I'm going forward as a radioman for a tank crew that is occupying a position there."

On the next afternoon, I went forward from the supply point with the mess truck. We drove through Velletri, a nice little city at the foot of the Albano Mountains. Then we drove through Cisterna, which had been reduced to its foundation walls. Just as we passed the first buildings, a sentry called to us: "Stop, the Americans are shelling the road intersection!" We continued moving anyway. Our driver accelerated 20 meters before the intersection and we were barely past it when a heavy shell exploded there. Another 900–1000 meters, and we were there. I immediately reported to my vehicle commander, an Oberfeldwebel. He said: "Well, I hope everything will work out. We should get along just fine."

Degenhardt and Ceczane are also members of this crew. It was a happy reunion. Our Ferdinand is in a draw, so well camouflaged that the best aerial observer cannot see it. Two meters next to the tank destroyer is the bunker we live in. I was amazed at how wonderfully everything was arranged. The room is big enough to stand and walk comfortably. The walls are covered with bright blankets and cloth; there is a table in the middle, three chairs, an upholstered chair and two benches. There is a full bottle of wine on the table at all hours of the day. Everyone can take as much of it as often as he wants. There is a wooden cabinet in the right corner that contains rations, six dishes, tableware and bottles of wine. Pictures of beautiful women peer out at us from the walls. The bunker looks like a small bar in the truest sense of the word.

An infantry howitzer occupies a position 50 meters from us and fires many times during the day. Unfortunately, we cannot be out in the open very much, because the enemy can see us and fire upon us every time we move. Sometimes the enemy fires a barrage, and his shells land all around the howitzer position and damned close to our bunker. During one such unexpected barrage, such as the one that occurred the previous evening, we raced to the cellar and threw ourselves in with such speed that the table, glasses and everything else scattered. Thank the Lord that we were then there in our "bar". Even as I write this now, light and heavy shells land in the area. This does not bother us, however, since we are already used to the howling and crashing.

Today I tested the radio equipment and radio operator's machine gun, so that they will all be functional in case of an alert. The front line is only 900 meters away, then 1,000–1,200 meters of no-man's-land, and then enemy positions. Our heavy and light guns are firing again, and the enemy does not refrain from answering. The commander, gunner and both loaders are engaged in checkers. They are having a championship tournament. There is such incoming fire that the entire table wobbles. Whenever the enemy is quiet for an hour, we sit in front of the bunker and sun ourselves. Our bunker is called the "Villa of Fine Drops". This is because we always have wine. We have placed a sign with this inscription in front of the bunker so that every infantryman on the way to the front can see it. Many soldiers passing by have received a glass of wine from the "Villa of Fine Drops". I will take pictures of the bunker and camouflaged vehicle in the next few days so that you at home can see how a soldier lives at the front.

27 April 1944: It is 10 o'clock in the morning and the sun is shining magnificently. Leutnant Haberland and Feldwebel Roos visited us 10 minutes ago. Roos is the commander of a Ferdinand about 1,500 meters from us. He was amazed by our bunker. We told all manner of jokes, causing great peals of laughter. A glass of wine made the retelling of the tales that much better. Leutnant Haberland informed us that a half bag of mail is en route for our company. Everyone is happy and says: "I hope there is some for me." Our battalion's 2nd and 3rd Companies are in the Lemberg area. Our mail always goes to Lemberg first and then to our company. Therefore we seldom receive mail.

28 April 1944: Nothing new today, except for artillery fire!! We were playing checkers at 9 in the morning when an enemy barrage suddenly started. Shells fell all around our bunker with ear-splitting explosions. The shells landed right next to our "bar". The candle blew out and smoke poured in through the door. We all frantically sought cover under the table. Everything turned out fine, however. Pale and shaking, we pulled ourselves to our feet. "Lucky again," our commander said. Right after that we piled more beams, rocks and dirt onto the bunker, so that it is even more solid. We can do nothing but listen and quickly seek cover when one of those things comes whistling in. People at home have no idea what it is like when one of those heavy shells lands next to you. Your entire body starts trembling. I hope tonight will stay quieter!

1 May 1944: We woke up at 8 in the morning, gathered flowers and shined our shoes in preparation for the day's festivities. We poured the wine, and made a toast to the 1st of May. Then we had breakfast. For lunch, we had goulash and pudding with marmalade sauce. We were able to sun ourselves during the afternoon. Afterwards, the gunner, one loader and I went to Cisterna to forage. The Americans suddenly shelled the city and we had to depart. It is 2100 hours now and the "Tommies" have sent a couple of heavy packages in our direction again. On the whole, however, the day was relatively quiet. We are drinking wine again and playing checkers, along with wrestling and some acrobatics.

5 May 1944: This was a very sad day for our crew. At noon, the driver, gunner and one loader went off in search of cauliflower. They had to go through the town of Cisterna. They entered a completely demolished building to see if they could find anything useful. Three shells soared by, the third one landing right in front of the house. The driver was seriously wounded on the back of his head, so that the gunner believed he had been killed. The loader was wounded in the foot. The gunner came running back and exclaimed, "Fritz has been hit . . . he's dead!" It was a terrible blow to us, since Fritz had always been so full of life.

When we recovered Fritz, we discovered that he was still alive. He even opened his eyes at the main aid station, but he could not speak. We were beside ourselves with joy. The loader will probably return to us in several weeks. Our only hope for Fritz is that he is well again soon. Our new driver and loader have already arrived.

7 May 1944: Today we received the sad news that our Fritz has died. He was buried in the Military Cemetery at Velletri. Our commander is very distraught by this event. It is very difficult to write of this to Fritz' wife. Yes, the greatest sacrifice for the Fatherland.

9 May 1944: At exactly 1600 hours my crew called for me to come eat inside the bunker. We barely sat down to eat when a shell landed directly in front of the bunker. Luckily, the stone wall blocked all the shrapnel. After this explosion, somebody yelled, "Get out!" In a matter of seconds, we all jumped out of the bunker and into the hole under our Ferdinand. Immediately thereafter, shells crashed all around the tank for 15 minutes. Those were difficult minutes. My pack lay in front of the vehicle. It was ripped to pieces by the shrapnel. Towel and tie completely torn up; sunglasses broken. Another comrade's blanket and coveralls were shredded. Our coffee container was hit by two large pieces of shrapnel and the coffee poured out. Our driver also had all the articles in his pack ripped to pieces.

10 May 1944: We have expanded the hole under the vehicle into a nice bunker. Dirt has been piled up along the outside to protect against shrapnel. This makes us feel secure. Terrible fireworks broke out at 2200 hours. We had just lain down to sleep at 2300 hours when the order came: "Alert!" We jumped out of the hole, cleared all of our belongings from the bunker in great haste and stowed them in the vehicle. I immediately prepared my radio operator's machine gun and activated all earphones and microphones in the crew compartment. We were ready in 10 minutes. Then we lay down under the Ferdinand again and awaited our marching orders. Prisoners were brought in who stated that the "Tommies" would attack tomorrow. The artillery also fired all calibers, but the enemy did not attack.

11 May 1944: It is 6 in the evening. The day was somewhat quieter. I went with both loaders to look for peas at 1500 hours. We went about 1,500 meters from our vehicle, in the direction of Cisterna. We had just started picking, when we heard a very loud whistle. I was just able to yell, "Look out!" At that moment, a shell landed 25 meters behind us. To our great fortune, it was a smoke shell that produced very little shrapnel. I yelled: "Let's get out of here . . . now!" We ran about 60 meters to a small ditch. Two more shells landed on the same spot we had been standing. We pressed ourselves tighter into the ditch and the shrapnel flew over us.

Our four crews will be relieved tomorrow and return to the Ciano Estate. Our comrades from the four incoming crews celebrated their departure at Count Ciano's estate yesterday. I hope everything will go well tonight and we will celebrate tomorrow.

13 May 1943: We were finally relieved today. We arranged for a wonderful room in the Ciano Estate. The radio we brought from Cisterna is hooked up. The armed forces station in Italy brings us the most beautiful music.

19 May 1943: Yesterday's Wehrmacht Daily Report stated: "Increased enemy artillery fire indicates that a large offensive is not far away." As we listened to the radio, we knew that we would not be fortunate enough to remain at the estate for much longer. Shortly after 2400 hours, as we slept like babies, the order to move came. We shot out of bed, hastily packing and loading our equipment. At 0300 hours we moved our vehicles through Velletri in march formation. The "Tommies" did not fire a single round from 2000 hours until 0700 hours the next morning: The quiet before the storm indicating that their offensive would begin soon. However, the enemy did not attack.

We are now four kilometers behind the front line, ready to move to the road and join the fighting at any moment. We have dug a sleeping hole under the Ferdinand again. Our vehicle is next to an old house. Acquired two boxes and placed a door across them, providing a surface upon which to write and eat. It rained an hour ago, after many hot, long days. The rain lasts for a while longer. We have received tropical uniforms, but only the combat crews.

22 May 1944: Last night at 2100 hours we moved to our battle position, from where we would open fire in the event of an attack. We have dug a hole under our Ferdinand once again, for sleeping and protection from shrapnel.

25 May 1944: The enemy offensive began at 0900 hours yesterday. We were ready with our vehicle at 1000 hours and watched for the enemy. We could see nothing, however. Heavy enemy artillery fire landed all around us continuously. Feldwebel Roos suddenly sent a radio message: "Track shot up; Loader Tobias killed!" Enemy infantry had already passed us on the right. Despite this, we remained in our battle position until 2230 hours. Then we moved back 1.5 kilometers, rearmed and refueled. I climbed into my cramped radio compartment at 0100 hours and slept until 10 after 3 in the morning. We moved forward again at 0330 hours. We had barely pulled into our battle position when the enemy spotted us and the shells crashed into the ground about 25 meters in front of the tank destroyer. Czecane, who was camouflaging the gun tube, just had time to jump into the driver's hatch. Fireworks such as we had never seen before erupted around us. The commander and gunner had just climbed out of the vehicle and could not make it back in this fire. We thought they would not escape with their lives. The loader screamed over the intercom: "Back up, back up!" I screamed to the driver: "Hurry, step on it and back up." We moved in reverse about one kilometer without the gun commander and gunner. We were all alone in the middle of the fireworks in this small sector of the front. The German infantry had withdrawn. Fortunately, our commander and gunner made it through on foot.

After a while, we moved forward again without infantry support. We had a building on one side as cover. A sudden explosion 20 meters to our front. I saw and recognized enemy tanks through my optics. They were 1,200 meters away from us in the woods. I saw one fire. I called to the driver: "Enemy round . . . watch out!" Three seconds later, we were hit between the driver and radio operator stations, but our sloped frontal armor deflected the shell downwards. We fired back at him, but he was able to escape. We moved back at 2200 hours.

26 May 1944: Four o'clock in the morning; a new operation. We were positioned in the middle of the main road to Cisterna. A sudden radio message: "Enemy tanks!" I loaded my machine gun and peered continuously through the optics. Sweat dripped from my face in the heat. We still did not see any tanks. They moved around us to the left and attempted to surround us. Suddenly, the gun commander screamed: "Tank, hurry . . . fire, fire!" An American tank emerged onto our road from a defile on the left. We decided his fate in a matter of seconds. The first hit blew him sky high. Three men jumped out as the first flames erupted from the tank. I wanted to shoot but, damn it, my machine gun jammed. A Tiger tank half a gun tube in front of us also fired at the tank, but we were faster! Two men from the American crew came forward and surrendered. They approached our tank with raised hands, constantly looking at the machine gun I had aimed at them. I let them live.

We had a small problem with the engine shortly thereafter and moved back through enemy fire to the maintenance section. We remained there for two days. We moved forward again today. We are now occupying a position 5 kilometers behind the front and waiting for orders. The enemy is still attacking and is just outside of Velletri.

This concludes the notes from Herbert Ströll.

The crew of Leutnant Grupe (gunner: Albert Riecker) succeed in knocking out 4 Shermans, but friendly losses occurred immediately. Feldwebel Edmund Roos' tank destroyer was hit in the track and had to be abandoned. The loader, the aforementioned Tobias, was killed while evacuating the vehicle. An Elefant burned out from an engine fire between Cisterna and Cori and was abandoned. Allied pressure on the German positions grew stronger, and the front was withdrawn on 25 May 1944. Fighting continuous defensive engagements, the Elefanten of the 1./schwere Panzerjäger-Abteilung 653 withdrew through Velletri, La Nuvio and Checchina towards Rome.

An aerial attack by bombers on the motor pool in the unit area in Rome on 2 June 1944 completely destroyed several of the company's wheeled vehicles. Unfortunately, a Panzer III that had been converted to an ammunition carrier was hit, killing the driver, Hermann Mörke, and the radio operator, Felix Pawlowski.

The company's supply and maintenance detachments left Rome on 3–4 June 1944, two days before its occupation by the Allies. The American dive bombers began a merciless pursuit of the Elefanten, which were too slow and completely unsuited for withdrawal actions. The company lost a gun to an American dive bomber along the Via Aurelia on 5 June 1944. Obergefreiter Lässig was killed during the attack. On 10 June 1944, dive bombers attacked Feldwebel Schlab's Elefant during a halt near Orvieto. It was hit inside numerous times through the open side hatch and burned out completely. The mountainous, curving and tortuous withdrawal routes also took their toll on the enormous vehicles. A tragic accident occurred on 7 June 1944 along the withdrawal route between Monte Fiascone and Orvieto. An old Roman bridge collapsed under the weight of the very heavy tank destroyer and the Elefant plummeted into the depths. The commander, Leutnant Willi Grupe, was crushed by the main gun when it broke loose from its mountings. The driver, Gefreiter Hermann Looft, was miraculously unharmed. Hermann Looft described the accident as follows in a letter to the author:

Early June 1944: We had engine problems and I moved at half-power with one engine. On the way to the maintenance section, we encountered a bridge. It was not a steel bridge, but a stream crossing made of sand and stones, with embankments on both sides (about 8–10 meters high). I stopped in front of the bridge. A sign indicated a capacity of 12 tons . . . or more? I said to Leutnant Grupe, who was standing in the commander's station: "What now?" He replied: "I can see tracks from one of our guns, we'll make it across too." (The tracks, as we found out later, were from the lighter armored recovery version of the Ferdinand.)

"Move out."

I moved forward, but half way onto the bridge it collapsed and our Ferdinand tumbled to the right along with the embankment and gravel. We landed almost upside down on the bottom. I immediately turned off the engine and waited. I had lowered my seat as we fell, but the hatch remained open. I was rescued through this hatch.

Leutnant Grupe had ducked back into the fighting compartment and was crushed by the main gun. All our shouts did not help; he gave no sign of life. Three crew members sitting on top of the vehicle during the movement were able to jump left onto what remained of the bridge. They were not injured. One of the loaders jumped to the right, in front of the tank, and was slightly injured. On orders from Hauptmann Ulbricht, Leutnant Grupe's body was later recovered and the Ferdinand was blown up. I was wounded on the same day and taken to the aid station and later back to Oberammergau in Germany. That was the end of Italy for me.

Another Elefant had to remain behind in Ficulle due to mechanical problems, and the crew destroyed it. The company had only 3 guns remaining at that point. Since excessive demands had been placed upon the tracks and engines, which had to constantly be repaired, these vehicles were barely operational. Repair parts seldom arrived, since they had to be transported by truck from motor parks in the

Reich. After 13 June 1944, the company was only considered a Kampfgruppe. Despite urgent requests by Hauptmann Ulbricht to withdraw his Company from the Italian Theater—a request supported by his chain-of-command—the Army High Command declined.

The daily logs of the 14. Armee contained the following information about the vehicle status and operations of the company from 1 April to 25 June 1944 (excerpted information from the Federal Archives / Freiburg Military Archives: RH 20-14/36):

1./SCHWERE PANZERJÄGER-ABTEILUNG 653

Date	Operational	In Maintenance
24 February 1944	2	—
25 February 1944	2	—
26 February 1944	2	—
27 February 1944	8	—
28 February 1944	8	—
29 February 1944	—	11
1 March 1944	—	10
5 March 1944	6	4
7 March 1944	6	4
10 March 1944	6	—
15 March 1944	6	—
20 March 1944	6	—
25 March 1944	8	—
31 March 1944	9	2 total losses in March
1 April to 18 May 1944	9	—
19–23 May 1944	9*	—
24–27 May 1944	No reports **	—
28–30 May 1944	5	—
31 May 1944	3	—
1 June 1944	2	—
2 June 1944	3	—
3–13 June 1944	No reports	—
14 June 1944	—	3
18 June 1944	1	—
19–20 June 1944	No reports	—
21 June 1944	3	—

* The Ferdinande started being reported as Elefanten from this date forward.
** The Allies commenced their breakout offensive from the Anzio and Nettuno Bridgeheads during this period.

continued

1./SCHWERE PANZERJÄGER-ABTEILUNG 653

Date	Operational	In Maintenance
22 June 1944	No report	—
23 June 1944	2	—
24 June 1944	No report	—
25 June 1944	2	—
29 June 1944***	No report	—
1 July 1944	1	—

*** Four total losses in June.

An order issued on 26 June 1944 stated that all Elefanten still available in Italy would remain there for use in operations. Crews from the 1./schwere Panzerjäger-Abteilung 653 without vehicles would be sent to the army replacement detachment in St. Pölten. This did not occur, however.

Excerpt from the daily logs of the 14. Armee (Federal Archives / Freiburg Military Archives RH 20-14/35):

FROM: Field Army Headquarters, 13 June 1944
TO: schwere Panzer-Abteilung 508 with attached 1./schwere Panzerjäger-Abteilung 653 (Elefant)
    On 14 June 1944, in the area south of Rapolano (25 kilometers east/southeast of Sienna), there are
    12 non-operational Tigers and
    3 non-operational Elefanten
    assembled along with a maintenance platoon. Of these, there will probably be
    5 Tigers and 2 Elefanten
    operational by 16 June 1944, which can be deployed as a consolidated tank platoon. Repair to the rest of the vehicles will require an additional 10 days.

Another excerpt from the daily logs of the 14. Armee (Federal Archives / Freiburg Military Archives RH 20-14/35):

FROM: Headquarters, 14. Armee
TO: Inspector General of the Armored Forces/Operations

No. 4570/44 SECRET
16 June 1944

I. Fallschirmjäger-Korps

The I. Fallschirmjäger-Korps will have Panzer-Kompanie Hintz attached to it on the night of 17 June 1944. This company will consist of a platoon from schwere Panzer-Abteilung 508 (6 Tigers), a platoon of Panthers from the I./Panzer-Regiment 4 (5 Panthers) and an Elefant from the 1./schwere Panzerjäger-Abteilung 653.

The tank company will deploy to the northern edge of the town 4 kilometers southeast of 48/101. The commander will report to the command post of the I. Fallschirmjäger-Korps on the afternoon of 16 June 1944. If the tactical situation permits, the Panther platoon must be given the opportunity to conduct an oil change before departure.

After the company's arrival, the 3 Panthers presently assigned to the 4. Fallschirmjäger-Division will be withdrawn, if possible, and sent to the I./Panzer-Regiment 4 for maintenance.

The 1./schwere Panzerjäger-Abteilung 653 continued to withdraw through Sienna, San Casciano (26 June 1944) and Impruneta (I July 1944), through Florence (9 July 1944) and Bologna/Modena (18 July 1944). It reached Mantua on 22 July 1944 and then Piadena on 2 August 1944, where the remainder of the company was finally loaded aboard special rail cars. The company arrived in Vienna on 6 August 1944. The remaining three Elefanten and the recovery Elefant were turned over to the Army Arsenal in Vienna for repairs. The soldiers of the company occupied billets in a brewery in Leising from 7-10 August 1944. The movement order for the company arrived on 11 August 1944. On 13 August 1944, the 1./schwere Panzerjäger-Abteilung 653 arrived at the Mielau Training Area in Poland. From there, the members of the company departed on leave on 18 August 1944.

ITALIAN CAMPAIGN: OPERATIONAL STATUS OF VEHICLES OF 1./SCHWERE PANZERJÄGER-ABTEILUNG 653 (BY MONTH)

Vehicle Type	FEB	MAR	MAY	APR	JUN	JUL	AUG
Ferdinande/Elefanten	11	9	9	—	3	—	—
Recovery Vehicles	1	1	1	—	1	—	—
Ammunition Carriers	2	2	2	—	1	—	—
Prime Movers	—	—	—	—	5	—	—
1–3 ton halftracks	2	2	2	—	—	—	—
8–18 ton halftracks	4	4	4	—	—	—	—
Motorcycles with Sidecars	5	5	5	—	5	—	—
Other vehicles	8	8	8	—	8	—	—
Cross-country staff cars	2	2	2	—	1	—	—

continued

ITALIAN CAMPAIGN: OPERATIONAL STATUS OF VEHICLES OF 1./SCHWERE PANZERJÄGER-ABTEILUNG 653 (BY MONTH)

Vehicle Type	FEB	MAR	MAY	APR	JUN	JUL	AUG
Support vehicles	11	11	11	—	8	—	—
Cross-country trucks	11	12	12	—	3	—	—
Support vehicles	37	37	37	—	26	—	—
Maultier halftracks	—	—	—	—	7	—	—
TOTALS	94	93	93	—	63	—	—

PERSONNEL STATUS OF THE 1./SCHWERE PANZERJÄGER-ABTEILUNG 653 IN ITALY: ASSIGNED STRENGTHS

Month	Officer	NCO	Enlisted	Totals
February	4	67	130	201
March	4	67	137	208
April	4	67	137	208
May*	?	?	?	?
June	3	49	152	206 **
July***	?	?	?	?
August****				

* No report available for May 1944.
** Included are 2 Hilfsfreiwillige (Soviet POW's who volunteered to work for the German Armed Forces). In addition there are figures reported for an attached Maintenance Company and supply element: No officers/1 civilian official/10 noncommissioned officers/76 enlister personnel/4 Hiwis for a total of 91 personnel. When added to the company strength figures, this brings the total number of personnel to 297.
*** No report available for July 1944.
**** No report available for August 1944.

PERSONNEL STATUS OF THE 1./SCHWERE PANZERJÄGER-ABTEILUNG 653 IN ITALY: LOSSES

Month*	Officer KIA/WIA/MIA/Ill/Other	NCO/Enlisted KIA/WIA/MIA/Ill/Other
February	0 / 0 / 0 / 0 / 0	0 / 7 / 0 / 3 / 1
March	0 / 0 / 0 / 0 / 0	3 / 4 / 0 / 3 / 0
April	0 / 0 / 0 / 0 / 0	0 / 2 / 0 / 1 / 0
June	1 / 0 / 0 / 0 / 0	3 / 9 / 3 / 5 / 2

* Only months were reports are available are reported.

Obergefreiter Emil Bürgin's pocket diary provides information about the assembly areas, operational routes and individual vehicle losses in Italy. Bürgin was a Elefant driver in the company. (Author's Note: Individual dates are only from operations and rest periods of Obergefreiter Emil Bürgin. They are not identical to all situations in the company.)

Date	Activity
1 January 1944 (Saturday)	In Lemberg and across the border at Przemysl
5 January 1944 (Wednesday)	Arrive at Nibelungen Works
6 January 1944	Turn in vehicle and go to St. Pölten
7 January 1944	Leave
28 January 1944	End of leave
29 January 1944	Arrive in St. Pölten at 0600 hours
1 February 1944	Leave in Ennsdorf
5 February 1944	Return from leave at 0700 hours and go to Nibelungen Works at 1400 hours. Quarters at an inn in Strengdorf.
6 February 1944	Duty at the Nibelungen Works
9 February 1944 (Wednesday)	Rail load the vehicle at the Nibelungen Works, depart at 0030 hours
11 February 1944 (Friday)	In Pöchlarn (Lower Austria); remain there until Sunday
13 February 1944 (Sunday)	Depart Pöchlarn at 2000 hours
16 February 1944 (Wednesday)	Rail load vehicles again at Nibelungen Works
17 February 1944 (Thursday)	Depart the Works at 0020 hours
18 February 1944 (Friday)	Delay at Pöchlarn
19 February 1944 (Saturday)	Arrive at Bruck and Parndorf; move to Neusiedl (road march)
21 February 1944 (Monday)	Rail load again in Parndorf, depart at 2000 hours; Cross the Brenner Pass during the night
24 February 1944 (Thursday)	Unload in Rome at 1000 hours, move to royal riding hall
25 February 1944	Move to assembly area
27 February 1944	Assembly area
28 February 1944	Velletri
29 February 1944 (Tuesday)	Arrive at Hill F at ? hours
1 March 1944 (Wednesday)	A gun breaks down
2 March 1944	No further advance during operations, we are 15 kilometers from the Mediterranean coast at Nettuno
3 March 1944	Nothing new during operations, first air attack
4 March 1944	Screening in Cisterna
5 March 1944	Back to rest in a village near Velletri
6 March 1944	Repair vehicle, class with the commander
7 March 1944	Repair vehicle, guard duty at night
8 March 1944	Work on the vehicle
11 March 1944	Go to Rome, tour the city
12 March 1944 (Sunday)	At the Ciano Estate

Date	Activity
13 March 1944	At the Ciano Estate
14 March 1944	At the Ciano Estate
15 March 1944	At the Ciano Estate
16 March 1944	Move to assembly area at 2000 hours
17 March 1944 (Friday)	Went to the maintenance section in Rome
18 March 1944	With field trains (Tor Sapienza)
19 March 1944	With field trains
20 March 1944	Move to assembly area near Genzano di Roma again at 1400 hours
21 March 1944	Quarters in the Ciano Estate, work on the tank destroyer
22 March 1944	At the estate of the former Italian Secretary of State, Count Ciano
23 March 1944	Maintenance
24 March 1944	Maintenance and guard duty
25 March 1944	Guard duty
26 March 1944	Take a walk to Genzano di Roma
27 March 1944	Maintenance
28 March 1944	Maintenance and guard duty
29 March 1944	Guard duty
30 March 1944	Maintenance
31 March 1944	Maintenance
1 April 1944	Construct position near Cisterna, commander promoted to Hauptmann. Mail arrives; receive 19 letters
6 April 1944	Guard duty
7 April 1944	Guard duty
8 April 1944	Bake a cake: 1 kilogram flour, 4 eggs, 2 lemons, 1 pound of sugar, some salt and a few drops of whiskey
9 April 1944	An hour of celebration between 1000-1100 hours. Formation in front of commander at 1700 hours; receive the tank assault badge
10 April 1944	Guard duty
11 April 1944	Guard duty
12 April 1944	Mortar fire in our assembly area
14 April 1944	Off duty; wonderful sun bathing
18 April 1944	To the front at Cisterna; relieve a wounded driver there
19 April 1944	Artillery attack
25 April 1944	Receive six 100-gram packages
26 April 1944	Return from Cisterna to the Ciano Estate near Genzano
28 April 1944	Take a walk through Nemi (on the ocean) to Genzano and back to the estate
29 April 1944	Receive a 100-gram package
30 April 1944	Take a walk to Genzano

Date	Activity
1 May 1944 (Monday)	Promoted to Obergefreiter
4 May 1944	Transfer gasoline
5 May 1944	Receive a new field post office number: 07965
9 May 1944	Visit the variety show in Rome
11 May 1944	Receive mail and sundries; 4 packages
12 May 1944	Relief; go to Cisterna, 2 kilometers behind the front
24 May 1944 (Wednesday)	"Tommy" attacks; withdraw behind Cisterna
25 May 1944 (Thursday)	Our vehicle burned between Cisterna and Cori and we had to leave it for "Tommy"
26 May 1944	Back to the combat trains in Velletri
27 May 1944	Back to the support detachment in Tor Sapienza (Stabsfeldwebel Slanarz)
2 June 1944 (Friday)	Take over my old gun near Marino
3 June 1944 (Saturday)	Move back to the maintenance section
4 June 1944 (Sunday)	Hastily depart from Tor Sapienza at 2200 hours; "Tommy" is 2 kilometers behind us
5 June 1944 (Monday)	One Ferdinand destroyed by aircraft during the movement
6 June 1944 (Tuesday)	Move through Rome
7 June 1944 (Wednesday)	Rome occupied by the Americans
8 June 1944 (Thursday)	Through Orvieto
10 June 1944 (Saturday)	One gun destroyed by fighter-bombers
11 June 1944 (Sunday)	Near Ficulle, our gun will not move; company has a total of 3 tank destroyers
13 June 1944	Assemble at a farm as a Kampfgruppe
16 June 1944	Depart for the front at 1000 hours
17 June 1944	Repairs in Montepulciano
18 June 1944	Move to assembly area; roast two geese
20 June 1944	Slaughter a pig; receive mail
21 June 1944	Into combat. Artillery attack while roasting food
22 June 1944 (Thursday)	Remain in the vehicle the entire day
23 June 1944 (Friday)	Remain in the vehicle; write, sleep and eat
24 June 1944	In the vehicle
25 June 1944	In the vehicle
26 June 1944	Withdraw to S. Casciano
27 June 1944	Repair vehicle in S. Casciano
28 June 1944	Return to assembly area in Cerbaia at 2400 hours
30 June 1944	Track broken; 2 bottles of beer
1 July 1944 (Saturday)	In Impruneta, receive 3 liters of beer
2 July 1944 (Sunday)	Occupy new positions along the highway, our tank destroyer is the only one remaining one in operation

Date	Activity
3 July 1944 (Monday)	Move back to the suburbs of Florence
5 July 1944 (Wednesday)	In the outskirts of Florence
6 July 1944	Quarters in a mill
8 July 1944	Move off again towards Florence
9 July 1944 (Sunday)	Through Florence to Pistoia, on the pass to Poretta at 0700 hours
17 July 1944 (Monday)	Depart Poretta at 2000 hours
18 July 1944	In Bologna at 0700 hours; in Modena at 1200 hours
19 July 1944	At the Po River in Borgoforte at 1900 hours
20 July 1944	We cannot cross the river because of a water shortage
21 July 1944 (Friday)	Cross the Po at 2200 hours
22 July 1944	In a village on the Minicio River near Mantua
23 July 1944	In the village
28 July 1944 (Friday)	Move to the rail station at 2200 hours
29 July 1944	[Elefant] breaks down on the road between Marcaria and St. Marino
30 July 1944	At a farm
1 August 1944 (Tuesday)	At the farm
2 August 1944	Continue moving through Bozzolo to Piadena
3 August 1944 (Thursday)	Rail load at Piadena; depart at 2400 hours
4 August 1944 (Friday)	From Piadena through Brescia
5 August 1944 (Saturday)	In Verona
6 August 1944 (Sunday)	In Simmering at 1100 hours and in Vienna at 1500 hours
7 August 1944	In Liesing; billets in a brewery
8 August 1944	In Liesing
10 August 1944	Prepare to rail load
11 August 1944	Rail load at 1400 hours and depart Vienna (arsenal) at 1800 hours
13 August 1944 (Sunday)	Arrive in Mielau; move to the training area
15 August 1944	Receive the Iron Cross, Second Class
17 August 1944	Receive leave authorization
18 August 1944 (Friday)	Depart Mielau at 0500 hours; depart Eylau at 1330 hours
19 August 1944	Home at 2000 hours

This concludes calendar entries from Obergefreiter Bürgin

Schwere Panzerjäger-Abteilung 653
1. Kompanie – Italy, February 1944

Members of the 1./schwere Panzerjäger-Abteilung 653 during their rail movement to Italy. Standing, from left to right: Unteroffizier Höppner, Feldwebel Kurt Albinius, Feldwebel Gottschalk, Stabsfeldwebel Junker, Unteroffizier Heinz Henning. Sitting, from left to right: Unteroffizier Molkenthin, Unteroffizier Albert Riecker, Leutnant Werner Haberland and Rechnungsführer (Pay Sergeant) Otto Peters. PETERS

Oberleutnant Hellmut Ulbricht, Company Commander of the 1./schwere Panzerjäger-Abteilung 653. He commanded this company throughout its employment in Italy and was promoted to Hauptmann on 1 April 1944. He assumed command of the battalion's new Support Company after receipt of the Jagdtiger tank destroyer. He received the iron cross, Second Class on 13 July 1941, the Iron cross, First Class on 26 September 1941 and the German cross in Gold on 3 December 1944. PETERS

The transport halts at the Brenner Pass on 25 February 1944. Remnants of snow can be seen on the rail car. Two crew members stand in front of an Elefant, as the vehicle was officially redesignated after February 1944. Hermann Cantz is on the right. CANTZ

An Elefant photographed during the move to Italy. The Zimmerit, the name given to the anti-magnetic-charge paste applied to the vehicle at the Nibelungen Works, is clearly visible. In front of the enormous vehicle are (left to right): Unteroffizier Molkenthin, Unteroffizier Riecker, Stabsfeldwebel Junker and Unteroffizier Peters. PETERS

The Elefanten refuel after unloading and then move to the designated assembly area in the vicinity of Cisterna and Velletri. This photograph was also taken near the old city wall and shows radio operator Hans Distler. DISTLER

A heavy Büssing-NAG 4500-series truck of the company's attached maintenance platoon. The crew has mounted snow chains to assist in negotiating the soft, wet ground. PITZ

The Elefanten were attached to the schwere Panzer-Abteilung 508 for operations. The Tiger battalion, in turn, was attached to Fallschirm-Panzer-Division "Hermann Göring". The crews make final preparations for the attack on 29 February 1944.

Heavy recovery equipment of the Allies pushed the Elefant off the road after the successful breakout from the beach-heads on 25 May 1944. This photograph also shows an immobilized and abandoned Tiger I from Kampfgruppe Ober-leutnant Stein (primarily schwere Panzer-Abteilung 508), which also could not be recovered.

Feldwebel Reinhold Schlabs, a vehicle commander in the 1./schwere Panzerjäger-Abteilung 653. Members of the battalion did not receive the black panzer uniform until after it had been reequipped with the Jagdtiger tank destroyer. SCHLABS

The same vehicle photographed during a test drive, which was also used to bring back a cask of wine. An explosion from a mine tore off the right-hand mudguard. GRESCH

Front and rear views of an Elefant that was photographed I march 1944 in the vicinity of Cisterna. The driver of the vehicle was Feldwebel Karl Gresch. The Elefant displays all of the modifications undertaken at the Nibelungen Works. Note the storage box at the rear of the vehicle with Zimmerit coating.

This Elefant is parked in front of the maintenance facility in Rome in march 1944. The gunner, Albert Riecker, sits on top of the main gun. The vehicle clearly shows the three-color camouflage pattern used by the German Armed Forces at this stage of the war: sand yellow, reddish brown and green. RIECKER

The maintenance company of Sturmpanzer-Abteilung 216 occupies a warehouse immediately adjacent to the maintenance platoon attached to the 1./schwere Panzerjäger-Abteilung 653. Notice the different versions of the Sturmpanzer IV and Panzer II on the left-hand side of the photograph.

Three 18-ton prime movers tow a disabled Elefant. The Elefant is being towed backwards. Synchronizing the movement of such a recovery column required constant coordination and adjustment. Failure to do so could result in damage to one or more of the prime movers. BÖSMÜLLER

A perfectly camouflaged Elefant in the Velletri area. The main gun is draped with straw mats and other material. The crew pays cards to pass the time until the next operation. RIECKER

Two Elefanten had to be abandoned due to maintenance problems during the retrograde operations at the end of May 1944. Elefant 102 (chassis number 150071) was captured by US forces and sent to the Aberdeen Proving Grounds for further examination. It can still be seen on display there today.

German forces withdraw from Rome on 6 June 1944. An Elefant prepares to pass several stationary Sd.Kfz. 250's, which are overflowing with soldiers from the 3. Panzergrenadier-Division. Allied forces occupied Rome the same day. BUSCH

Side views of the same vehicle at a captured-vehicle collection point in Italy. The large U seen at the top of the rear of the fighting compartment stands for Ulbricht, the company commander. The crew booby trapped the vehicle with grenades and mines prior to its abandonment. Appropriate warnings have been written on the sides of the vehicle by US soldiers.

Leutnant Werner Haberland, Platoon Leader in the 1./schwere Panzerjäger-Abteilung 653 in June 1944. He took command of the company when the battalion was reequipped with the Jagdtiger tank destroyer BUSCH

Feldwebel Andreas Schmitt, Gun Commander in the 1./schwere Panzerjäger-Abteilung 653. BUSCH

Schmitt's entire crew pose with their platoon leader for a commemorative photograph. Standing, from left to right: Gerhard Busch (Gunner), Leutnant Haberland, Feldwebel Andreas Schmidt and Unteroffizier Poischen (Driver). BUSCH

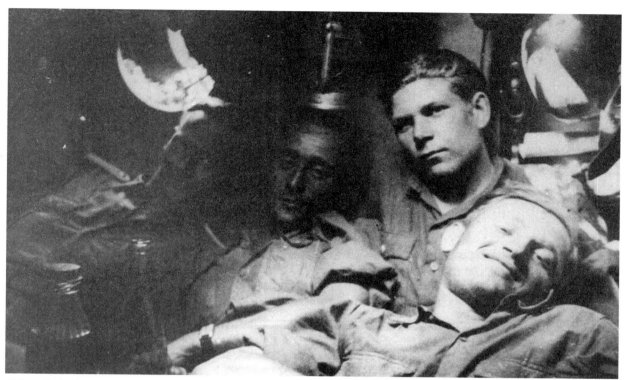

Although the interior had very large dimensions, there was not much room left over for the crew inside the fighting compartment when completely filled with equipment and ammunition. BUSCH

The Elefant became a home for the crews during the continuous withdrawals. The soldiers rarely had time to rest. Even meals were cooked underneath the vehicle as a precaution against being hit by shrapnel. BUSCH

BESITZZEUGNIS

DEM

Rainer Statz, Gefreiter
(NAME, DIENSTGRAD)

1./Schw. Panzer-Jäger-Abteilung 653
(TRUPPENTEIL, DIENSTSTELLE)

IST AUF GRUND

SEINER AM 31.5.1944 ERLITTENEN

1 MALIGEN VERWUNDUNG – BESCHÄDIGUNG

DAS

VERWUNDETENABZEICHEN

IN *Schwarz*

VERLIEHEN WORDEN.

Abt.Gef.Std. DEN 19.7. 1944

(UNTERSCHRIFT)

Major u. Abt. Kommandeur.
(DIENSTGRAD UND DIENSTSTELLE)

Certificate awarding the Wound Badge in Black to Gefreiter Rainer Statz.

1./schw.Panzerjäger-Abteilung 653   O.U.,den 7.4.1944

B e s c h e i n i g u n g .
==

(Nur gültig in Verbindung mit dem Soldbuch)

Der..... Obschtze. L o o f t , Hermann

wurde auf gepanzerten Vollkettenfahrzeugen über 30 t mit elek-
trischem Antrieb praktisch und theoretisch ausgebildet. Die
Ausbildung wurde abgeschlossen. Der Genannte ist berechtigt,
Fahrzeuge dieser Klasse zu führen.

Hermann Looft   Hauptmann und Kompanie-Chef

Eigenhändige Unterschrift

Certificate authorizing Oberschütze Hermann Looft to drive a fully tracked vehicle weighing more than 30 tons and powered electrically. The certificate states that he has received both theoretical and hand-on training.

Soldbucheinlage

Fw. Schmitt

Eins.-Tage	Tag	Ort nach Rgt.-Bef.	Bescheinig. d. Kp.-Fü.
1.	18. 9.	Leonovo-Gromosdowo	
2.	5. 7.	Durchbr.Bahn Orel-Kursk	
3.	8. 7.	Abw.i.Polewaja-Bachbogen	
4.	9. 7.	Angr. " "	
5.	18.11.	Angr.nördl.Nesabudina	
6	19.11.	Kampf um Höhe 195,1	
7.	20.11.	Verteidig.d.Dorf Marjewka	
8.	21.11.	Angr.auf Höhe 185,1	
9.	22.11.	Angr.auf Höhe 185,8	
10.	23.11.	Verteidig. d.Dorf Katerinowka	
11.	27.11.	Pz.-Schlacht b.Koschasowka	
12.	28.11.	Abw.eines Pz.-Angr. bei Miropol	
1944 13.	23. 5.	Abw.südl.Cisterna	
14.	24. 5.	Abw.zw.Velletri-Cisterna	
15.	28. 5.	Abw.südwestl. La Nuvio	
16.	29. 5.	" " " "	
17.	3. 6.	Abw.ostw.T.chintschina	
18.	5. 6.	Abw.Via Aurelia,nördl.Rom	

Eins.-Tage	Tag	Ort nach Rgt.-Bef.	Bescheinig. d. Kp.-Fü.
19.	6. 6.	Abw.südostw.Brecciano-see	
20.	7. 6.	Abw.im Raum Monterosi	

Uptlieutnant u. Komp.Chef

Soldbuch entries for Feldwebel Schmitt certifying what engagements he participated in.

Feldwebel Reinhold Schlab's Elefant burns on the withdrawal route to Orvieto. American fighter-bombers spotted the vehicle and immediately attacked it. Direct hits on the engine and crew compartments set the vehicle ablaze. MÜNCH

Penetrations to the storage container are clearly visible in this photograph. An Oberleutnant of the 715. Infanterie-Division took these images as he passed the burning Elefant with his company of Italian assault guns. MÜNCH

Elefant 124 was abandoned at Soriano in the vicinity of Viterbo. It appears as though attempts were made to repair the track, as indicated by the detached roadwheel arm on the front glacis. The shortage of heavy recovery assets made the abandonment of the vehicle inevitable, however.

A pause during the withdrawal to Modena. Unteroffizier Fritz Klein leans against the front glacis. Unteroffizier Klein was killed in Schwetzingen (Germany) on 30 March 1945, while serving as the gunner on a Jagdtiger. BÜRGIN

The same vehicle from a different angle. Notice the U on the front armor as well as the 653. BÜRGIN

The Elefant tracks proved to be too weak for the demands placed on them by the heavy vehicle. Repairs were no longer arriving for the unit, and the crews and maintenance personnel had to resort to improvised methods to keep the vehicles running. This photograph shows a crew hammering in track pins, a tiresome and physically demanding job. BÜRGIN

The crew of the recovery Elefant takes a break during the withdrawal to Modena. A damaged Elefant is in tow. The recovery Elefant used in Italy had the chassis number of 150005. BÜRGIN

This photograph clearly shows the tremendous width of the tracks of the Elefant. The recovery Elefant was especially well liked by its crew, since it was relatively light and more maneuverable than its fully armed counterpart. The vehicle was used not only for recovery operations, but also for the transportation of supplies and evacuation of the wounded. As indicated by the shredded mudguards, this vehicle has seen a lot of action. The commander of this vehicle in Italy was Unteroffizier Edgar Scheeler (with cigarette). BÜRGIN

At the end of their rope in terms of mechanical condition, the remaining vehicles of the company boarded trains on 2 August 1944 at Piadena. The recovery Elefant only has half of its track, since the remainder had been used up. BÜRGIN

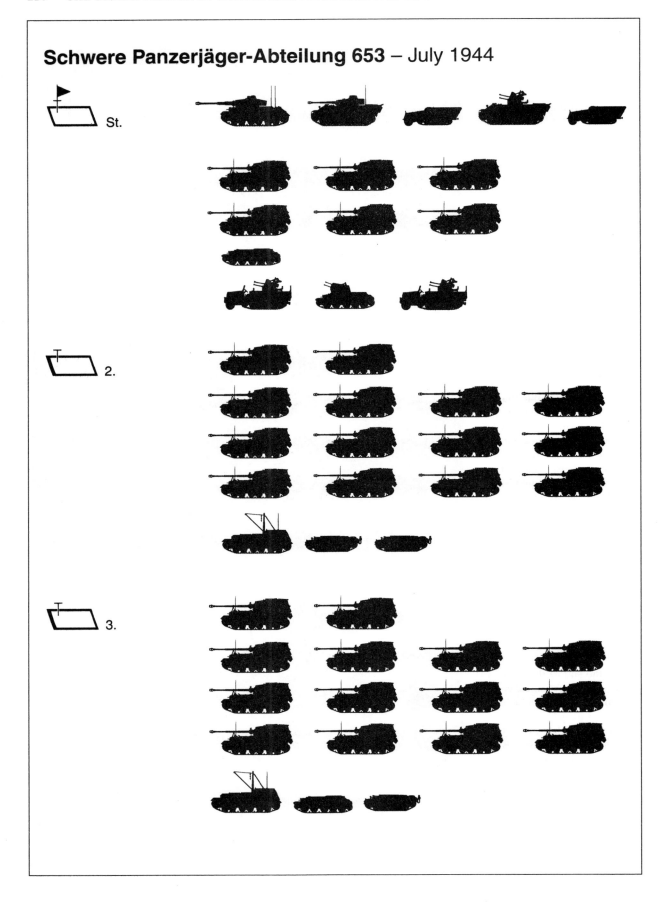

Schwere Panzerjäger-Abteilung 653 – July 1944

Operations in the Soviet Union, 2. and 3./schwere Panzerjäger-Abteilung 653

(APRIL TO OCTOBER 1944)

The accelerated equipping of the 1./schwere Panzerjäger-Abteilung 653 with overhauled and rebuilt Ferdinande made it impossible to meet the repair completion deadline of 15 March 1944. The remaining vehicle overhauls were delayed considerably. By 28 February 1944, the 2./schwere Panzerjäger-Abteilung 653 had received only 8 Ferdinande at St. Pölten for equipping and training. On 1 March 1944, there were still 21 Ferdinande and 2 recovery Ferdinande undergoing repairs at the Nibelungen Works. Four Ferdinande that burned out in Russia were turned over to the Vienna Army Arsenal, because repairing them at the Nibelungen Works was too costly.

On 31 March 1944, the general overhaul of the Ferdinande had progressed to the point where the battalion was only one Ferdinand short of its combat strength. The 2. and 3./schwere Panzerjäger-Abteilung 653 began rail loading in St. Pölten (Austria) for Russia on 2 April 1944,.

The new commander of the battalion was Hauptmann Rudolf Grillenberger.

BATTALION LEADERSHIP POSITIONS (AS OF: 1 APRIL 1944)

Commander:	Hauptmann Rudolf Grillenberger
Adjutant:	Oberleutnant Kurt Scherer
Battalion Surgeon:	Dr. Wolfgang Prellwitz
Paymaster:	Oberzahlmeister Karl Koch
Headquarters Company:	Leutnant Fritz Klos
1./schwere Panzerjäger-Abteilung 653:	Oberleutnant Werner Salamon
1./schwere Panzerjäger-Abteilung 653:	Oberleutnant Bernhard Konnak
Maintenance Company:	Leutnant Büttner

BATTALION PERSONNEL STATUS (AS OF: 1 APRIL 1944)
(MINUS THE 1./SCHWERE PANZERJÄGER-ABTEILUNG 653 AND THE
1ST MAINTENANCE PLATOON OF THE MAINTENANCE COMPANY [IN ITALY])

Personnel	Authorized	Actual	Shortage
Officers	23	23	—
Civilian Officials	8	6	2
Noncommissioned Officers	235	201	34
Enlisted Personnel	731	776	—
Hiwis	—	20	—

BATTALION WEAPON STATUS (AS OF: 1 APRIL 1944)
(MINUS THE 1./SCHWERE PANZERJÄGER-ABTEILUNG 653 AND THE
1ST MAINTENANCE PLATOON OF THE MAINTENANCE COMPANY [IN ITALY])

Weapon	Authorized	Actual	Shortage
Rifles	639	620	19
Handguns (Pistols)	375	354	21
Submachine Guns	128	118	10
Flare Guns	54	37	17
MG 34	60	51	9
Quad 2-centimeter Flak	4	4	—
8.8-centimeter Pak 43/2 L71	31	30	1

BATTALION VEHICLE STATUS (AS OF: 1 APRIL 1944)
(MINUS THE 1./SCHWERE PANZERJÄGER-ABTEILUNG 653 AND THE
1ST MAINTENANCE PLATOON OF THE MAINTENANCE COMPANY [IN ITALY])

Vehicle	Authorized	Actual	Shortage
Motorcycle	24	23	1
Motorcycle with Sidecar	6	6	—
Staff Car	41	38	3
Truck	71	56	15
Maultier Halftrack	11	25	—
Prime Mover	29	22	7
Trailers	11	9	2
Ferdinand	31	30	1
Recovery Ferdinand	2	2	—
Bergepanther	2	1	1
Panzer III Ammunition Carrier	4	2	2
Armored Ambulance	1	1	—

The Red Army offensive began west of Kiev during the last days of December 1943. The 1st Ukrainian Front advanced continuously against the Heeresgruppe Süd (Army Group South), reaching Schepetovka, Rovno and Lutzk by early February 1944. The Soviet forces thus succeeded in driving a wedge, several hundred kilometers wide and deep, between the Heeresgruppe Süd and Heeresgruppe Mitte (Army Group Center). The last remaining rail line north of the Carpathians—from Odessa to Lemberg—was vitally important to the German military leaders. In turn, it was a lucrative short-range objective between Proskurov and Tarnopol for the Soviet divisions.

On 25 March 1944, Soviet troops surrounded the important road junction of Tarnopol. Hitler then declared it a "fortified area." On 30 March 1944, Generalfeldmarschall Model relieved Generalfeldmarschall von Manstein, and Heeresgruppe Süd was redesignated as Heeresgruppe Nordukraine (Army Group Northern Ukraine.)

The Germans moved forces into the threatened area as quickly as possible. Among them: 100. Jäger-Division (light infantry), 349. Infanterie-Division, 367. Infanterie-Division, 9. SS-Panzer-Division "Hohenstaufen", 10. SS-Panzer-Division "Frundsberg" and schwere Panzerjäger-Abteilung 653 (minus its 1st Company, which had been sent to Italy).

Schwere Panzerjäger-Abteilung 653 arrived at Brzezany on 6 April 944 and was attached to the XXIV. Panzer-Korps. The battalion occupied an assembly area in Kozova on 7 April 1944. The battalion staff, maintenance company, combat engineer platoon and Flak platoon were in Podhayce. Together with elements of the 9. SS-Panzer-Division "Hohenstaufen", to which the two available Ferdinand companies of schwere Panzerjäger-Abteilung 653 were attached, the advance began on 8 April 1944 to relieve encircled Tarnopol. The formations advanced to the southeast, through Uvsye, to Zlotniki, where they were to force a crossing of the Strypa and expand the bridgehead already forged by the 100. Jäger-Division on 6 April 1944.

Muddy and mired roads made it impossible to move in an speedy fashion. The SS grenadiers who dismounted their vehicles in Uvsye could no longer keep up with the Ferdinande. The knee-deep mud even hindered the enormous Ferdinande. Some of the vehicles dug themselves into the mire up to their hulls and required incredible efforts for recovery. Most of the tank destroyers were out of action due to overheated engines. The Ferdinande still remaining operational took part in capturing Malovody and Chatki (on 8 April 944). On the afternoon of 8 April 1944, the 4 remaining Ferdinande of the 2./schwere Panzerjäger-Abteilung 653 reached the western bank of the Strypa, north of Zlotniki. They fired upon the eastern bank, destroying 1 antitank gun and 2 tanks.

On 9 April 1944, the remaining operational elements from both of the battalion's companies crossed the ford through the Strypa at Zlotniki. The heavy tanks could barely deploy in the marshy area and occupied defensive positions between Burkanov (11 April 1944) and Havoranka (16 April 1944). After the Germans evacuated their bridgehead on the afternoon of 16 April 1944, powerful Soviet forces pursued the battalion and also crossed the Strypa at Zlotniki. These forces were thrown back to the eastern bank in heavy fighting. The 2./schwere Panzerjäger-Abteilung 653 lost 2 Ferdinande during this operation. (One tank destroyer was destroyed by a round in the flank; the other received a serious hit in the rear. Both Ferdinande were recovered, but the maintenance company could not repair them.)

The front stabilized and short-term improvements in the weather provided more solid ground conditions. The 100. Jäger-Division, supported by the 2./schwere Panzerjäger-Abteilung 653, forced Soviet forces out of their positions along a stream flowing into the Strypa from south of Plotycza, between Chatki and Sokolov. This hard fighting pushed the Soviets back onto the eastern bank of the Strypa, so that the entire divisional front again ran along the western bank. The Soviets deployed very few tanks during the fighting, since they could not stand up to the Ferdinande. In their place, they used heavy antitank guns—8.5 and 12.2 centimeter—as well as the difficult-to-locate wooden mines. These inflicted much damage upon the Ferdinande, particularly to the suspension and tracks.

The muzzle brake on one main gun was so badly damaged that the gun tube broke loose from its mount when the next round was fired. The vehicle's gunner was killed and the gun commander, Leutnant

Grunder, was wounded on his arm. On 18 April 1944, the relief attempt on Tarnopol—Operation "Index Finger"—was finally called off.

A relatively quiet time began for the battalion, which occupied the greater Brzezany area. All elements of the battalion attended training courses to improve the soldiers' proficiency and orient the arriving replacements. Officers, officer candidates and other leaders conducted planning exercises and sand-table demonstrations. The fuel situation usually prevented actual training on the vehicles. In early May 1944, the Führer Headquarters ordered the Ferdinand renamed as the Elefant.

Under Major Grillenberger—promoted on 1 July 1944—the battalion constructed, tested and deployed a number of "special vehicles." The battalion received a Porsche Tiger VK 4501 (8.8-centimeter KwK 36 L/56) with hydraulic power towards the end of May. The maintenance company also fabricated many noteworthy vehicles:

- 1 Bergepanther with a non-moving Panzer IV turret (75 mm KwK)
- 1 Bergepanther mounting a quad 2-centimeter Flak
- 1 T 34 mounting a quad 2-centimeter Flak
- 2 Soviet T 34's as ammunition carriers

These modifications were carried out by the battalion's master armorer, Stabsfeldwebel Anton Brunnthaler. In June 1944, the battalion also received 4 additional Elefanten, upon which the Nibelungen Works in St. Valentin had installed modified rear hatches. These vehicles had the detachable, round hatch replaced with a hinged rear door, making installation and removal of the main gun during repairs considerably easier.

ORGANIZATION OF SCHWERE PANZERJÄGER-ABTEILUNG 653
(MINUS THE 1./SCHWERE PANZERJÄGER-ABTEILUNG 653 AND THE
1ST MAINTENANCE PLATOON) (AS OF: 1 JULY 1944)

Headquarters and Headquarters Company
- Commander: Major Rudolf Grillenberger
- Adjutant: Oberleutnant Kurt Scherer
- Field Trains: 1 armored ambulance; 1 Bergepanther mounting a quad 2-centimeter Flak; 1 radio station in a halftrack; 1 command and control Tiger (VK 4501)
- Headquarters Company (Commander: Leutnant Fritz Klos): Signal Platoon; Combat-Engineer Platoon
- Flak Platoon (Platoon Leader: Stabsfeldwebel Voigt): 1 quad 2-centimeter Flak; 1 T 34 mounting a quad 2-centimeter Flak; 1 quad 2-centimeter Flak mounted on a prime mover
- Reconnaissance and Tank Destroyer Platoon (Platoon Leader: Leutnant Robert Wiesenfarth): 1 halftrack car; 6 Elefanten; 1 T 34 (modified to serve as an armored ammunition carrier)
- Supply Section
- Rations Section
- Administrative and Support Section
- Medical Section
- Combat Trains
- Maintenance Section

2./schwere Panzerjäger-Abteilung 653

- Commander: Oberleutnant Werner Salamon
- Headquarters Section: 2 Elefanten
- 1st Platoon: 4 Elefanten
- 2nd Platoon: 4 Elefanten
- 3rd Platoon: 4 Elefanten
- Combat Trains I: 2 Panzer III (modified to serve as armored ammunition carriers); 1 recovery Elefant
- Combat Trains II
- Field Trains
- Maintenance Section

3./schwere Panzerjäger-Abteilung 653

- Commander: Oberleutnant Franz Kretschmer
- Headquarters Section: 2 Elefanten
- 1st Platoon: 4 Elefanten
- 2nd Platoon: 4 Elefanten
- 3rd Platoon: 4 Elefanten
- Combat Trains I: 1 Panzer III (modified to serve as an armored ammunition carrier); 1 recovery Elefant
- Combat Trains II
- Field Trains
- Maintenance Section

Maintenance Company

- Commander: Leutnant Hans Demleitner
- Signal Maintenance Section
- Weapons Maintenance Section
- 2nd Maintenance Platoon
- 3rd Platoon (Recovery)
- Field Trains

Both Soviet field-army groups, the 1st Ukrainian Front and the 4th Ukrainian Front, began their offensive against Heeresgruppe Nordukraine on 13 July 1944. After splitting the 1. Panzer-Armee and the 4. Panzer-Armee, they surrounded the LIX. Armee-Korps in Brody. The 1. Panzer-Armee had to pull back south, through Lemberg, to the Beskids. The 4. Panzer-Armee withdrew to the Vistula, but it could not eliminate the enemy bridgehead at Baranov.

Schwere Panzerjäger-Abteilung 653 was caught in the maelstrom of attacking Soviet divisions at Pomeryany and Rohatyn on 14 August 1944, and it had to fight a continuous rearguard action while withdrawing towards Lemberg. Kurowice and Yeziezanka were contested stations along this withdrawal. The weaknesses of the Elefanten were shamelessly exposed during this round of fighting. The smallest problems took these very heavy, technically complex vehicles out of action, and they could not be recovered during the withdrawal. The fuel shortage also forced the destruction of many vehicles. Bridges of insufficient capacity were often an insurmountable obstacle for the Elefanten and the tank destroyers simply had to be left behind. By the end of July 1944, the battalion had lost 22 Elefanten, a total of 60% of its complement!

BATTALION PERSONNEL LOSSES (1–31 JULY 1944)

Personnel	KIA	WIA	Ill	Transferred	MIA
Officers	—	1	1	1	—
Noncommissioned officers and enlisted personnel	5	19	2	—	11
Totals	5	20	3	1	11

BATTALION VEHICLE LOSSES (1–31 JULY 1944)

Recovery Elefant	2
Panzer III / T 34 Ammunition Carrier	4
Elefanten	19
Porsche Tiger VK 4501	1
Prime Movers	6

Former gun commander, Oberfeldwebel Albin Heinickel of the 3./ schwere Panzerjäger-Abteilung 653, describes his experiences during the withdrawal:

It was 21 July 1944, near Zloby-Uharla.

I was with my Elefant in defilade (half concealed) on high ground overlooking a Soviet village. My orders were to protect the German forces withdrawing along the main road from a flank attack. Unbeknownst to us, a heavy Soviet antitank gun had occupied a position inside the village. I observed the village through my periscope and barely saw the flash, when the antitank round struck the commander' s cupola of the Elefant.

The periscope, vision blocks and metal hatch ring were literally blown into my face. The fingers of my right hand resting on the telescope optics were torn off. I also suffered severe head and eye injuries, a broken nose and shrapnel wounds to my chest and upper thigh. I was unconscious for 1 1/2 days. My comrades evacuated me and loaded me onto another unit's truck as a seriously wounded casualty. My comrades later told me that our Elefant was blown up on the same day by our forces. It had become stuck in a streambed while trying to detour around a weak bridge and could not be recovered.

The battalion continued to withdraw through Przemysl and Tarnov to Bad Rabka (near Krakow). The battalion rested there for several days, attached to the Northern Ukraine Armored Training Command. After losing a large portion of its heavy armored vehicles, the battalion was recommended for outfitting with the Jagdtiger tank destroyer. After a battlefield reconstitution, the majority of the battalion returned to the Reich (Vienna and Döllersheim). The remaining Elefanten were consolidated under the command of Oberleutnant Werner Salamon. They initially remained with the 17. Armee of Armeegruppe A, and were later attached to the XXXXVIII. Panzer-Korps of the 4. Armee.

FERDINAND (ELEFANT) VEHICLE STATUS
2. AND 3./SCHWERE PANZERJÄGER-ABTEILUNG 653

Date	Operational	Under Repair	Comments
8 April 1944	31		Transport to Heeresgruppe Nordukraine
10 April 1944			Behind the front in an assembly area
12 April 1944			Penetrated enemy positions
13 April 1944			Attached to 9. SS-Panzer-Division "Hohen-staufen" (1. Panzer-Armee)
17 April 1944	12		
18 April 1944	18		Received 1 Elefant in April
21 April 1944	20		
30 April 1944	13		Reported 3 total losses
1 May 1944	16	14	With the XXIV. Panzer-Korps
10 May 1944	21		
11 May 1944	21		
20 May 1944	27		
21 May 1944	27		
30 May 1944	25		
31 May 1944	25		
1 June 1944	28	2	30 Elefanten available at XXIV. Panzer-Korps
1 June 1944	25		
10 June 1944	27		
11 June 1944	28		
20 June 1944	23		
21 June 1944	23		
30 June 1944	29		Received 4 Elefanten in June
1 July 1944	28	6	With XXIV. Panzer-Korps
1 July 1944	29		
10 July 1944	29		
11 July 1944	33		
18 July 1944	33		Soviet penetration behind the front
20 July 1944	14		
21 July 1944	14		
22 July 1944	12		
23–24 July 1944			No report
25 July–2 August 1944		0	Total losses reported for July: 23
1 August 1944	0	12	With Armor Instruction Command (Heeresgruppe Nordukraine)
3–5 August 1944			Battlefield reconstitution
4–6 August 1944			In Krakow
7–31 August 1944			No report. Total losses reported for August: 2

The diary of Unteroffizier Peter Kohns (Headquarters Company and 2./schwere Panzerjäger-Abteilung 653) describes the locations and operations of a Ferdinand crew in the battalion from 4 April 1944 to 1 September 1944:

4 April 1944: We departed the Nibelungen Works on 4 April for St. Pölten to rail load the tank destroyers. Departed St. Pölten at 1700 hours, moving through Pottenbrunn to Vienna.

5 April 1944: Moravian Weißenkirchen, Stauding, Schönnbrunn, Witkowitz (Oder), Marienburg, Moravian Ostrau Train Station, Oderberg, Leibersdorf, Waldsee, Pruchna, Ausschwitz, Krakow, Tarnov.

6 April 1944: Reichshof, Frycztak, Moderovka, Yasslo, Sanok (city).

7 April 1944: Sisko, Chyrov, Sambor, Lemberg.

8 April 1944: Sichov, Ziduczov, Rohatin, Potutory, Brzezany. Unloaded, during which the recovery Ferdinand bogged down next to the ramp. The same with another Ferdinand in the [3./schwere Panzerjäger-Abteilung 653].

9 April 1944: Freed the recovery Ferdinand and the other Ferdinand. Departed for Tarnopol at 1700 hours. Spent the night outside of Kozova (20 kilometers).

10 April 1944: Stuck in the mud outside of Uvsye (5 kilometers). Recovered by a halftrack during the evening.

11 April 1944: Continued through Uvsye-Chatki and along the front line in the morning. Remained at the Vaga Collective (10 kilometers).

12 April 1944: Halted during the march to Zlotniki (5 kilometers).

13 April 1944: In firing position forward of Zlotniki. Changed positions to the hill forward of Hayvoronka toward evening (3 kilometers,   attached to [the 3./schwere Panzerjäger-Abteilung 653]). Wounded in the right hand.

14 April 1944: In old firing position. Damage on T 34. Relieved during the evening. Halted in the wood in front of Zlotniki.

15 April 1944: Continued to the Vaga Collective in the morning. Occupied a dairy farm (8 kilometers).

19 April 1944: To the [2./schwere Panzerjäger-Abteilung 653] in Chatki in the evening (2 kilometers). Engine problems.

24 April 1944: Continued to Kampfgruppe Salamon in Malovady during the afternoon.

25 April 1944: In front of Siemikovcze (4 kilometers). Artillery attack.

26 April 1944: Attacked Siemikovcze. Tan over amine. Disarmed 46 mines. Back to the collective farm.

27 April 1944: Back to Malovody for repairs (5 kilometers).

3 May 1944: Through Uvsye to Sloboda-Zlota (10 kilometers).

15 May 1944: Gun transferred to [the 2./schwere Panzerjäger-Abteilung 653] (Vehicle 234).

21 May 1944: Received Silver Wound Badge

28 May 1944: Transferred with crew to [the 2./schwere Panzerjäger-Abteilung 653] (Field Post Office No. 25056D). Crew:
Commander: Unteroffizier Peter Kohns
Gunner: Unteroffizier Leo Koch
Loader: Gefreiter Bernhard Grethen
Loader: Obergefreiter Wolfgang Haupt
Radio operator: ?
Driver: Gefreiter Felix Hoffmann

7 June 1944: Test fire along the rail line ([. . .] 4 tanks, 7 kilometers).

18 June 1944: Concert by our battalion band (3 hours).

27 June 1944: Corps training exercise (8 kilometers).

9 July 1944: Changed position during the evening, across the Ploska Collective rail line to Chatki (8 kilometers).

14 July 1944: Changed position to the Denysov Collective (3 kilometers).

15 July 1944: Departed through Teofipolka.

16 July 1944: Attacked in the morning at Kabarovce with Leutnant Grunter's platoon and Oberst Kobold's Kampfgruppe. Destroyed one KV I tank, two ammunition trucks and three horse-drawn ammunition carriers.

18 July 1944: Wounded while recovering Grunter's gun: Unteroffizier Koch, Gefreiter Hoffmann, Gefreiter Grethen and I (shrapnel in my back and deaf in my right ear). Grunter's gun burns out after artillery hits it in an open hatch and engine grating. Ewers seriously wounded while recovering an ammunition carrier. Commander's gun destroyed. Leutnant Teriete, Unteroffizier Habeck, Unteroffizier Heinrich, Gefreiter Müller and Gefreiter Kleinig wounded. Unteroffizier Soft killed. Feldwebel Hansen wounded. Back to the maintenance section on the rail line to Presovce. Hoffmann and Bauer at the aid station.

19 July 1944: Moved by truck through Pomorzany to the combat trains in Verbov. Continued to Brzezany. Unteroffizier Jauch seriously injured in the head as the result of an accident. Gefreiter Jäger missing.

20 July 1944: Loaded aboard trains in Brzezany. Continued to Potutory in the evening.

21 July 1944: In Rohatin at 0200 hours. Continued to Chodorov in the evening.

22 July 1944: At Chodorov in the morning, then to the dispensary 4.5 kilometers south of Chodorov.

24 July 1944: Continued through Chodorov-Stryj. Occupied a forest between Stryj and Drohobyze. Back to my company. Announcement that reconstitution will take place in Hungary.

25 July 1944: Received movement orders.

26 July 1944: Departed through Drohobyze at 0200 hours. Trailer tore loose after leaving the city. Repaired it quickly. Trailer had turned over. Continued through Boyslav. Spent the night in Czorna.

27 July 1944: Continued at 0300 hours through Sisko, Zarcsov, Yanok, Zarczin and Krosna. Broke down in the city. Spent the night.

28 July 1944: Departed at 1000 hours. Moved back 7 kilometers, then continued through Zmigrod to Gorlice. Occupied a forest several kilometers south.

1 August 1944: Departed at 1400 hours through Gorlice, Ropaka, Grybov, New Sandez (Dunayev), Simanovo and Bad Rabka. Arrived towards 2400 hours. Occupied quarters in a school with a dormitory.

5 August 1944: My first NCO social with [the 2./schwere Panzerjäger-Abteilung 653] in a cellar. Excellent at first, then nasty fights.

6 August 1944: Took Unteroffizier Koch to Vienna.

9 August 1944: Unteroffizier Faltus shot in leg while cleaning his pistol (right leg fractured).

18 August 1944: Went through Chabovka-Sucha to Krakow with Petersen and Kleining for a medical examination. Diagnosis: Deaf in right ear due to explosion. Eardrum destroyed. No chance of recovery.

19 August 1944: Returned to Bad Rabka.

22 August 1944: Transferred to the Headquarters Company in Bergen, near Celle. Departed Chabovka at 1921 hours for Krakow. Unteroffizier Schmelzer was with me. Also transferred.

23 August 1944: Departed Krakow at 2200 hours. Moved through Kattowitz, Oppeln, Glogau, Breslau and Berlin. Continue to Magdeburg in the afternoon. Arrived there at 1800 hours.

25 August 1944: Continued at 0541 hours through Braunschweig, Hanover and Celle to Bergen. Took the truck to the Fallingbostel camp: Block 65, Room 26. Headquarters Company has not arrived yet.

26 August 1944: Company finally arrived this afternoon.

1 September 1944: Combat leave, 16 days.

17 September 1944: Returned to the company 6 hours late.

18 September 1944: Special leave for 12 days.

29 September 1944: Receive a telegram that the company had moved to Döllersheim.

1 October 1944: Arrive in St. Pölten at 1430 hours. Continued to Radlberg at 1500 hours. On foot to Pottenbrunn and spent the night in my old quarters.

2 October 1944: Continued at 0511 hours through Tulln, Göpfritz and Döllersheim. On foot through Markebrechts to the new portion of Camp Neunzen (5 kilometers). Arrived in the camp at 1130 hours.

5 October 1944: Transferred to the reconstituted [2./schwere Panzerjäger-Abteilung 653] (Jagdtiger).

The notes of Franz Kurrer of the 3./schwere Panzerjäger-Abteilung 653, a radioman on a Panzer III ammunition carrier, provide further information concerning this period. In this case, from 2 February to 19 September 1944.

2 February 1944:	St. Pölten
3–24 February 1944:	Leave
25 February 1944:	Returned from leave; in St. Pölten until 30 March 1944
2 April 1944:	Rail loading in St. Pölten
5 April 1944:	Unloaded in Brzecany
6 April 1944:	Brzecany-Kozova
7 April 1944:	Kozova-Solonik; combat operations
14 April 1944:	Brzecany-Podheize
15 April 1944:	Podheize-Kat
18–21 April 1944:	Gnilovodi
22–25 April 1944:	Pelovka; combat operations
26 April 1944:	Pelovka-Gnilovodi

Movements and Combat Operations of the 2./schwere Panzerjäger-Abteilung 653 and schwere Panzerjäger-Kompanie 614

(SEPTEMBER 1944 TO MAY 1945)

Due to the large number of vehicles lost by schwere Panzerjäger-Abteilung 653 during its withdrawal through Galicia in July 1944, the battalion could report only 12 Elefanten operational on 1 August 1944. These vehicles were combined into a single company: 2./schwere Panzerjäger-Abteilung 653. Oberleutnant Werner Salamon was the commander.

After a battlefield reconstitution in Krakow, where the company received an additional 2 Elefanten from St. Pölten—the 2./schwere Panzerjäger-Abteilung 653 was allocated to the 17. Armee (Heeresgruppe A) on 19 September 1944. While the 1./schwere Panzerjäger-Abteilung 653 was returning from Italy and the 3./schwere Panzerjäger-Abteilung 653 was moving to the Fallingbostel Training Area (and, later, to the Döllersheim Training Area), the 2./schwere Panzerjäger-Abteilung 653 remained in the Krakow/Tarnov area. According to official records for the November and December period, the 2./schwere Panzerjäger-Abteilung 653 was also known as the Elefant-Kompanie. Oberleutnant Werner Salamon relinquished command of the company on 24 November 1944 and Hauptmann Bernhard Konnak commanded it until mid-December 1944. On 15 December 1944, the company was redesignated as schwere Panzerjäger-Kompanie 614.

Schwere Panzerjäger-Kompanie 614 was allocated to the 4. Panzer-Armee December 1944. It occupied positions in the Kielce area. Soviet forces of the 1st Ukrainian Front attacked out of the Baranov Bridgehead on 12 January 1945, and the general offensive along the White Soviet Front began. The German forces barely had anything to counter the mighty onslaught. Emanuel Schlenzka, gun commander of an Elefant in the company, described his final combat operation in a letter to the author dated 26 July 1989:

Since I had been assigned to the 2./schwere Panzerjäger-Abteilung 653, I remained in the east with the rest of the Elefanten. From then on, we were constantly employed wherever situations were untenable. We were always rescuing green, inexperienced forces fresh from the Reich that had been formed from the Hitlerjugend ("Hitler Youth") and similar elements.

The Elefant was invulnerable in the front. Even the heavy Soviet "Josef Stalin" tank hit us many times on our frontal armor without any effect. On 12 January 1945, the Soviets began their big offensive and pincer movement. We had the mission of protecting the flanks of the vehicles breaking out of the Kielce pocket. My commander ordered me to screen the withdrawal. The terrain favored the Soviets, and they had constructed a trap to pick off each Elefant. It was 15 January 1945 when the Elefant moving in front of me, under Unteroffizier Karl Baasch, was knocked out. We picked up Unteroffizier Baasch and some of his crew, Unteroffizier Leo Koch and Unteroffizier Horst Peters. All three were wounded. Our Elefant suffered the same fate around noon on 15 January 1945. The vehicle had just received a full load of ammunition and had refueled, so it immediately burned out. Only three of us managed to escape from the vehicle. Our other comrades all perished in the vehicle.

I was captured by the Soviets three days later. I was able to escape in June 1945 and, after many unspeakable hardships, arrived in Bavaria in August 1945.

Schwere Panzerjäger-Kompanie 614 lost all of its Elefanten during the defensive fighting and withdrawal actions. Reports to the Inspector General of Armored Forces on 30 January 1945, 6 February 1945, 15 February 1945, 20 February 1945 and 24 February 1945 indicated that there were no operational Elefanten. At the end of January 1945, Hauptmann Ritter, who had meanwhile assumed command of the company, reported the company's status in a handwritten report (source: Federal Archives / Freiburg Military Archives):

Personnel: 1 officer; 12 noncommissioned officers; 39 enlisted personnel (5 crews on rail transport)

Equipment: 4 Elefanten; 1 Bergepanther; 1 DKW courier motorcycle; 1 light staff car; 2 medium Steyr staff cars; 1 medium Opel fuel truck; 1 medium Opel mess truck; 1 medium Opel Maultier (ammunition hauler); 2 heavy Büssing trucks; and 3 trailers.

The remainder of schwere Panzerjäger-Kompanie 614 withdrew through Oppeln, Breslau, Sorau (30 January 1945), the Sprottau area (15 February 1945) and through Frankfurt an der Oder to the greater Berlin area.

Telegram to the Inspector General of Armored Forces, dated 31 January 1945 (source: Federal Archives / Freiburg Military Archives):

TO: Inspector General of the Armored Forces (Berlin)

— SECRET —

Status of schwere Panzerjäger-Kompanie 614: Location: Sorau. Effective 28 January 1945: 20 noncommissioned officers; 75 enlisted personnel, including 5 crews and 6 Hiwis. 4 motorcycles; 6 staff cars; 9 trucks; 5 Maultiere; 2 18-ton prime movers.

Center staff liaison / Graf Strachwitz, Major
1/45, dated 30 January 1945

Telegram to the Inspector General of Armored Forces, dated 6 February 1945 (source: Federal Archives / Freiburg Military Archives):

TO: Inspector General of the Armored Forces (Berlin)

— SECRET —

TO: Heeresgruppe Mitte; Staff of the replacement Army; (INFO) In 6 of the Replacement Army; Wehrkreis III; Heeresgruppe Weichsel (Reichsführer-SS); Liaison Office, Inspector general of Armored forces at Heeresgruppe Mitte; WTL

Schwere Panzerjäger-Kompanie 614 (formerly the 2./schwere Panzerjäger-Abteilung 653) has been transferred from the sector of Heeresgruppe Mitte (Sprottau area) to the Replacement Army at Stahnsdorf for transport by express trains for reconstitution. The company is transferred with its current personnel and equipment, minus its heavy antitank guns.

Army High Command, Army Gen. Staff, Operations Section (Room 3)

2126/45 SECRET 6 February

OFFICIAL:

/signed/ Hessel

Oberstleutnant, Section Chief

Telegram from the Inspector General of Armored Forces, dated 15 February 1945 (source: Federal Archives / Freiburg Military Archives):

FROM: Inspector General of the Armored Forces (Berlin)

— SECRET —

Acknowledgment: In accordance with orders from the Inspector General of Armored Forces, Hauptmann Ritter will collect the remaining personnel and material in the Sorau area from

schwere Panzerjäger-Kompanie 614 (Elefant)

and move them immediately to Panzer-Aufklärungs-Ersatz und Ausbildungs-Abteilung 4 in Stahnsdorf for reconstitution.

All command members, fortress commanders and headquarters will immediately return all personnel and materiel belonging to schwere Panzerjäger-Kompanie 614 to Hauptmann Ritter.

Hauptmann Ritter will be supported by any means to accomplish his mission.

/signed/ Chief-of-Staff

DISTRIBUTION:

Hauptmann Ritter (3 x)

Copy: Daily Logs

Telegram from the Inspector General of Armored Forces, dated 20 February 1945 (source: Federal Archives / Freiburg Military Archives):

FROM: Inspector General of the Armored Forces (Berlin)
SUBJECT: [Battlefield] Reconstitution of schwere Panzerjäger-Kompanie 614

1) The Replacement Army is requested to conduct a battlefield reconstitution of schwere Panzerjäger-Kompanie 614 at the location of Panzer-Aufklärungs-Ersatz und Ausbildungs-Abteilung 4 in Stahnsdorf.

2) Organization: Heavy Tank Destroyer Company with 10 Elefanten, possibly Jagdtiger (Porsche Chassis), using Table of organization and Equipment 1148 c, dated 31 March 1943, as modified by AHM No. 488 (as support) with additional 16-ton Stabo portal crane.

3) Officer positions as ordered by Army Headquarters, Personnel Office. The Replacement Army will provide missing personnel.

4) The Inspector General of the Armored Forces provide armored vehicles. Motorized vehicles will not be provided. Additional materiel will be provided by the Replacement Army.

5) Efforts to make the Elefanten for the company operational will be accelerated by every means possible.

6) Provide reports on operational status to
Army General Staff / Operations
Army General Staff / Force Structure
Inspector General of the Armored Forces
Army Headquarters / Army General Staff / Force Structure
Inspector General of the Armored Forces, Force Structure II
No. 2454/45 (SECRET), dated 19 March 1945
Chief-of-Staff (Freyer)

Telegram from the Inspector General of Armored Forces, dated 22 February 1945 (source: Federal Archives / Freiburg Military Archives):

FROM: Inspector General of the Armored Forces (Berlin)
24 February 1945
SECRET
No. 11459/45 (SECRET)
22 February 1945
TO: Wehrkreis III
COPY FURNISHED: Army Headquarters, Personnel Office, P1; Inspector General of the Armored Forces; Army General Staff / Force Structure
REFERENCES: Army Headquarters / Army General Staff / Force Structure; Inspector General of the Armored Forces, Force Structure II, No. 2454/45 (SECRET) dated 19 February 1945
SUBJECT: [Battlefield] Reconstitution of schwere Panzerjäger-Kompanie 614

1) Wehrkreis III will work closely with AHA/In 6 at the location of Panzer-Aufklärungs-Ersatz und Ausbildungs-Abteilung 4 in Stahnsdorf to conduct a battlefield reconstitution of schwere Panzerjäger-Kompanie 614

2) Organization and Strength: Heavy Tank Destroyer Company in accordance with Tables of Organization and Equipment 1148 c (with 10 Elefanten, possibly Jagdtiger Porsche

Chassis), dated 31 March 1943, as modified by AHM 44, No. 488, and additional 16-ton Stabo portal crane.

3) Wheeled vehicles will not be provided.

4) Efforts to make the company's Elefanten operational will be accelerated by any means possible.

5) Other directives will be implemented in accordance with AHA Staff, Operations, No. 1/45 (SECRET COMMAND MATTER), dated 1 January 1945.

Army Headquarters / Replacement Army / AHA / Staff Operations (1)

No. 11459/45 (SECRET), dated 22 February 1945

OFFICIAL:

Littau, Major

Section Chief

On 25 February 1945, schwere Panzerjäger-Kompanie 614 occupied the Stahnsdorf area (Klein Stahnsdorf) west of Wünsdorf. There were only 4 Elefanten remaining, all of which were in need of major repairs.

Excerpt from a telegram to the Inspector General of Armored Forces, dated 3 March 1945 (Source: Federal Archives / Freiburg Military Archives):

6.) schwere Panzerjäger-Kompanie 614 (Inspector general of Armored Forces)

Personnel: 74 noncommissioned officers and enlisted

Combat equipment: Small arms; signals equipment; optics; range-finding equipment; 6 Jagdtiger; 9 motorcycles; 6 staff cars; 21 trucks; ammunition supply; maintenance equipment; Stabo portal crane with prime mover.

Spare parts en route from Linz for 4 Elefanten in need of repair.

Wehrkreis III, Logistics, No. 01369/45 (SECRET)

Dated 3 March 1945

/signed/ Vetter

Oberstleutnant

The following documents illuminate the company's final combat operations. Excerpt from a commander's report dated 20 April 1945 (source: Federal Archives / Freiburg Military Archives):

Inspector General of Armored Forces Army Headquarters

20 April 1945

Force Structure, No. F 640/45 (SECRET COMMAND MATTER)

Notes to Commander's Report on 20 April 45

II. Combat Forces in the Wünsdorf Area

1. . . .

2. . . .

3. schwere Panzerjäger-Kompanie 614 (4 Elefanten) in an assembly area west of Zehrensdorf.

SECRET COMMAND MATTER
Force Structure / Command Section
21 April 1945
No. F 619/45 (SECRET COMMAND MATTER)
                                            Daily Log
8 Copies 1st Copy
                                  I.

1) The following will be made available to create Kampfgruppe Möws:

Headquarters of the II./Panzer-Regiment 36 with all elements

4./Panzer-Regiment 11 (special equipment)

Panzergrenadier-Kompanie Ülzen (special equipment)

Panzer-Kompanie Kummersdorf (1st Escort Company)

Panzerjäger-Kompanie (mot.) Dresden

schwere Panzerjäger-Kompanie 614

The Kampfgruppe is attached to Oberst Kaether's Kampfgruppe south of Zossen. Combat elements of the II./Panzer-Regiment 36 will be transferred to Wittstock and reorganized into a tank-destroyer element.

2) The II./Panzer-Regiment 33 is redesignated a tank destroyer formation. Surplus vehicles and maintenance elements will be reassigned to the 7. Panzer-Division.

3) The II./Panzer-Regiment 2 has received the following tanks:

1)   2 Panthers and 2 Bergepanthers from Panzer-Bataillon 2108.

2)   1 Panzer V from the firm of Krupp and Druckenmüller.

3)   11 Panthers from Daimler and Benz, Marienfelde. Most of the Panthers [reported as] operational on the evening of 22 April 1945

4) Due to the production situation, 6 additional Panthers will be operational on 23 April 1945.

The Army Auxiliary Equipment Section in Spandau will form a special armored halftrack company:

Organization:

Commander: 1 Sd.Kfz. 251/3; 1 Sd.Kfz. 251/9; 1 Sd.Kfz. 251/1

1st Platoon: 4 Sd.Kfz. 251/1

2nd Platoon: 1 Sd.Kfz. 251/1; 3 Sd.Kfz. 251/16

3rd Platoon: 3 Sd.Kfz. 251/16

22 April 1945, 0600 hours.

Excerpt from the daily logs of the Inspector General of Armored Forces concerning the status of armored vehicles (source: Federal Archives / Freiburg Military Archives):

22 April 1945:
> 1. Kampfgruppe Ritter will be formed from armored force elements in the Zossen area.
> Organization: Headquarters, II./Panzer-Regiment 36
>> 4./Panzer-Regiment 11
>> Panzerspähwagen-Kompanie (Armored Car Company) (Biwa-Uelzen)
>> schwere Panzerjäger-Kompanie 614

Two of the Elefanten had to be left behind due to mechanical problems as the Soviets advanced.

Mr. Wolfgang Fleischer from the Dresden Museum of Military History wrote about this in a letter to the author on 21 April 1995:

I can now give you some more precise facts about the final combat operations of the Elefant tank destroyer. An eyewitness from Teupitz described the following scene: One Elefant remained on the main ramp at Mittenwalde and was scrapped 2 years later. There are distinct recollections of the gasoline-electric drive train with Maybach engines. The second Elefant occupied a firing position in Klein Köris, at the road fork to Löpten, and ended the war there.

Both of these vehicles made it to the Berlin inner-city area and took part in the fighting at the Karl-August-Platz and Trinity Church. Polish and Soviet troops captured them there on 1 May 1945. Most of the trains of schwere Panzerjäger-Kompanie 614 escaped the encirclement of Berlin and were captured by the British in Kiel.

This correspondence also contained the following attachments:

VEHICLE STATUS OF ELEFANT TANK DESTROYERS OF THE 2./SCHWERE PANZERJÄGER-ABTEILUNG 653 AND SCHWERE PANZERJÄGER-KOMPANIE 614

Date	Assigned	Operational	Comments
20 September 1944	14	14	17. Armee (Heeresgruppe A)
25 September 1944	14	14	
5 October 1944	14	14	
15 October 1944	14	14	Headquarters, 4. Panzer-Armee
25 October 1944	14	14	
31 October 1944	14	14	
25 November 1944	14	14	
5 December 1944	14	13	Designated as the Combat Company of schwere Panzerjäger-Abteilung 653. With the XXXXVIII. Panzer-Korps of the 4. Panzer-Armee
10 December 1944	14	13	
30 December 1944	14	14	With Heeresgruppe A (4. Panzer-Armee)

continued

VEHICLE STATUS OF ELEFANT TANK DESTROYERS OF THE
2./SCHWERE PANZERJÄGER-ABTEILUNG 653 AND SCHWERE PANZERJÄGER-KOMPANIE 614

Date	Assigned	Operational	Comments
15 January 1945	14	14	With Heeresgruppe A
25 January 1945			With Heeresgruppe Mitte
25 February 1945			at Stahnsdorf (near Wünsdorf)
1 April 1945			schwere Panzerjäger-Kompanie 614 undergoing battlefield reconstitution at Stahnsdorf
20 April 1945			schwere Panzerjäger-Kompanie 614 in assembly area west of Zehrensdorf in the Wünsdorf area (Headquarters of the Inspector General of Armored Forces

The former deputy commander of schwere Panzerjäger-Kompanie 614, Leutnant Heinrich Teriete, wrote the following about his time in combat with the company in a letter dated 22 February 1988:

. . . after a long stay in a field hospital, I was transferred to the 2./schwere Panzerjäger-Abteilung 653 under Oberleutnant Salamon, whose company I later took over. I was wounded again in the Galicia area. Hauptmann Konnak then took over the [company]. After my convalescence, I returned again to the [company].

We took over the last remaining Ferdinande / Elefanten in the Berlin area. We were a separate company. We never had the Königstiger or the Jagdtiger. We only received a tank with five turrets. The crew abandoned the vehicle during the final fighting for the Zossen Training Area near Berlin. My vehicle was knocked out and I was captured along with Hauptmann Ritter and returned home on 2 November 1949 . . .

The Federal Archives / Freiburg Military Archives provided a document outlining the operations of two vehicles closely connected with schwere Panzerjäger-Abteilung 653:

Inspector General of Armored Forces, Army Headquarters
31 March 1945
Force Structure, No. F 440/45 SECRET COMMAND MATTER
Commander's Report: 31 March 1945

A) Establishment of armored and mechanized infantry forces . . .
    5) Panzer-Kompanie Kummersdorf . . .
        a) Organization:
            3 tank platoons (partially mobile)
            1 armored reconnaissance platoon
            1 grenadier escort platoon
            1 tank platoon (non-mobile)

b)   Composition:
   3 Tank Platoons (partially mobile)
          1 Tiger II
          1 Jagdtiger
          4 Panther
          2 Panzer IV (long barrel)
          1 Panzer III (5-centimeter L/60)
          1 Nashorn
          1 Hummel (with 3-barreled Flak machine gun)
          2 Sherman
   1 Armored Reconnaissance Platoon
          1 4-wheeled armored car (7.5-centimeter L/24)
          1 4-wheeled armored car (2-centimeter rapid-fire cannon)
          1 captured armored car (twin)
          1 B IV C (2-centimeter rapid-fire cannon)
          2 B IV C (with machine gun)
   1 Tank Platoon (non-mobile)
          1 Tiger Porsche (8.8-centimeter L/70)
          1 Steyer 8.8 L/70 weapons carrier
          1 P 40 (I)

A general overhaul of all Ferdinande began in mid-January 1944 at the Nibelungen Works at St. Valentin (Austria). All of the tank destroyers were completely disassembled, overhauled and reassembled, with modifications applied, as necessary. SPIELBERGER

Feldwebel Fritz Schwarz holds a model of a Ferdinand that was painstakingly created in miniature by members of the 3./schwere Panzerjäger-Abteilung 653. This photograph was taken at St. Pölten (Austria) in February 1944. FEDERER

The rebuilt Elefanten stand ready for issue on the factory grounds. TILLWICK

The mess truck of the 2./schwere Panzerjäger-Abteilung 653 at St. Pölten in March 1944. The Pampas crest is still visible on the left-hand fender of the vehicle. The "Nibelungen Sword" was introduced shortly thereafter as the crest for the battalion. HOLZAPFEL

The modified version of the recovery vehicle was put on display at St. Pölten in late March 1944. The recovery Elefant shows the obligatory Zimmerit coating. The vehicles were equipped with MG 34's that could be fired from inside, thus providing a better defensive posture for the crews. The machine-gun mounts were those used on the Hetzer tank destroyers as well as the Sturmgeschütz III and Sturmgeschütz IV. TILLWICK

This recovery Elefant was sprayed with a sand-yellow primer and then given a camouflage coat of red brown and green. The interior seems to have been painted with a brighter color, as evidenced by the underside of the opened hatch. CARPENTIER

Front and rear views of an Elefant, as the vehicle was designated after February 1944. The redesigned battalion crest—the "Nibelungen Sword"—can be seen to the left of the main gun and on the upper left rear of the fighting compartment.

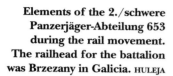

Elements of the 2./schwere Panzerjäger-Abteilung 653 during the rail movement. The railhead for the battalion was Brzezany in Galicia. HULEJA

The first train arrived at Brzezany on 8 April 1944. This Elefant was from the battalion headquarters and is seen shortly after detraining. WULFF

Terrain orientation for the crew of Elefant 323.

The gun commander's final briefing before the attack.
BIERMANN

Elefanten from the 3./schwere Panzerjäger-Abteilung 653 became mired up to their hulls in the soft ground. Recovery takes place after refueling. ZENTGRAF

An Elefant from the 3./schwere Panzerjäger-Abteilung 653 even managed to bog down on the main street of a village! The crew works tirelessly to free its vehicle, pausing only to have some commemorative photographs taken. WEBER

The tank destroyers cross the ford over the Strypa at Zlotniki on 9 April 1944 and roll onto the east bank of the river. ZENTGRAF

The driver of this Elefant, Emanuel Zentgraf, is seen here atop the engine compartment. A Schwimmwagen (amphibious staff car) of the 9. SS-Panzer-Division "Hohenstaufen" is in front of the massive tank destroyer.
ZENTGRAF

Maintenance personnel remove damaged running gear from an Elefant. An anti-tank round tore apart the track of the Elefant and damaged the right-hand drive sprocket beyond repair.

Members of the recovery platoon bring an intact T 34 back to the battalion's Maintenance Company. Many modified T 34 chassis were used within the battalion. They were employed as ammunition carriers, tow vehicles and Flak carriages.

"Punching" the gun tube on an Elefant was no easy task. Members of the crew of Elefant 332 are seen hard at work. ZENTGRAF

Soldiers of the 2./schwere Panzerjäger-Abteilung 653 have managed to procure additional rations. HOLZAPFEL

The drive sprocket has been removed from this Elefant. STEIGER

An Elefant from the Head-
quarters Company is prepared
for evacuation to a maintenance collection point. Elefanten assigned to the battalion
headquarters displayed no
vehicle numerals; only the battalion crest was visible. STEIGER

Installing a replacement HL
120 Maybach engine at the
field maintenance site. The
protective shield in front of
the gun mantlet has been
removed to allow better access
to the engine compartment.
JANOSKE

A frontal view of an Elefant
from the 3./schwere Panzerjäger-Abteilung 653. The Zimmerit coating applied at the
Nibelungen Works is clearly
visible. Helmut Kreyenhagen
stands in the radio operator's
station. KREYENHAGEN

Field maintenance on Elefant 334. The crane—an Sd.Kfz. 100—from the maintenance section lifts the engine-compartment deck with a 3-ton boom. SABROWSKY

This Elefant from the 3./schwere Panzerjäger-Abteilung 653 has been completely camouflaged with straw. Loader Matthias Carpentier stands in front of it. CARPENTIER

Also camouflaged with straw, this Elefant from the 3./schwere Panzerjäger-Abteilung 653 has been positioned between the small farmhouses characteristic of Galicia. WEBER

After a difficult operation, the Elefant also needs to have its "snout" cleaned.

Both loaders were responsible for reloading the vehicle. WEBER

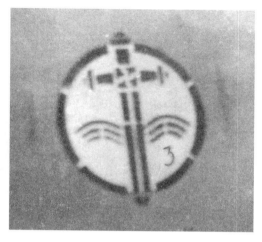

The unit insignia of schwere Panzerjäger-Abteilung 653. It depicts the Nibelungen sword and the waves of the Danube River, all symbolic of the German medieval epic, Song of the Nibelungen. The small 3 denotes the 3./schwere Panzerjäger-Abteilung 653. The entry penetration from a Soviet antitank rifle can be seen just below the insignia. Penetrations of up to 4-centimeters deep were discovered from the feared antitank rifles. ZENTGRAF

Maintenance is being performed on Elefant 334. The engine compartment has been opened up, as indicated by the raised engine grating and the removed driver and radio operator panels.

Elefant 332 receiving ammunition. One of the loaders pulls the 8.8-centimeter rounds through the small ammunition port in the emergency escape hatch. The commander of this Elefant at the time of this photograph was Oberfeldwebel Emil Issler. The driver was Emanuel Zentgraf. ZENTGRAF

This Elefant receives a new coat of camouflage paint at the assembly area at Brzezany. The air compressor is mounted on the Maultier truck. All Elefanten in the Tarnopol area of operations had a three-color camouflage scheme: sand, green and red-brown. SABROWSKY

Crewmembers of Elefant 334 constructed a rock mosaic of their battalion insignia and vehicle number in the garden of their quarters. SABROWSKY

Upon request of the battalion, it received a Porsche Tiger VK 4501 (P) command and control tank in the spring of 1944. Behind the vehicle on the Ssyms rail car is a Bergepanther, which has had a Panzer IV turret mounted upon it. WEIß

This photograph was taken during a halt in Lemberg (Lvov): Unteroffizier Hagelstein (Gun Commander), Gefreiter Gebele (Driver), Gefreiter Steinmüller (Loader), unidentified (Radio Operator) and unidentified (Gunner). STEINMÜLLER

A rear view shows details of the engine-compartment cover, over which an additional protective wire screen has been fastened. The lifting jack is attached to a fixture on the engine compartment. HAGELSTEIN

The Maintenance Company added several modifications to the before it was released for operations. An additional armor plate was welded in front of the round opening for the MG 34 in the front glacis. A deflector was also welded over the top of the driver's vision port to protect him against direct fire or shrapnel.

The Porsche Tiger VK 4501 (P) received the necessary equipment and modifications to make it a command and control vehicle. It was given the vehicle number of 003 and assigned to the headquarters.

JACOB

The command and control tank was intended for the Battalion Commander, Hauptmann Wegelin. Unteroffizier Hagelstein took over the vehicle, when the commander was reassigned. Both photographs show the Porsche Tiger VK 4501 (P) during combat operations. The turret is turned to 6 o'clock and the entire crew is positioned on top of it. The vehicle was reported as a total loss during the withdrawals of July and August 1944.

HAGELSTEIN

This rare photograph depicts the field-modified Bergepanther in operation. The Panzer IV turret was fixed in placed and could not traverse. The driver had to point the entire vehicle in the direction of fire.

The soldiers of the tank-destroyer and assault-gun forces were well trained in this, however. Portions of the crew have already been issued the black Panzer uniform. The battalion crest is faintly visible on the front slope.

For his actions contributing to the overhaul of the Ferdinande and the Sturmpanzer, Oberleutnant Wolfgang Römer was awarded the Knight's Cross of the War Service Cross with Swords on 4 June 1944 at St. Pölten. RÖMER

Collection point for the damaged vehicles of schwere Panzerjäger-Abteilung 653. A Bergepanther is positioned directly upon the loading ramp. It is a very early version without the stabilization spade. The Maintenance Company mounted a quad 2-centimeter Flak on this vehicles in June 1944. WEIß

VORLÄUFIGES BESITZZEUGNIS

IM NAMEN
DES DEUTSCHEN VOLKES

HABE ICH

DEM

OBERLEUTNANT

WOLFGANG RÖMER

DAS RITTERKREUZ
DES KRIEGSVERDIENSTKREUZES
MIT SCHWERTERN

VERLIEHEN.

DIE BESITZURKUNDE FOLGT NACH.

FÜHRER-HAUPTQUARTIER, DEN 4. JUNI 1944

DER FÜHRER

The award certificate for Römer's Knight's Cross of the War Service Cross with Swords, a very rare award.

A damaged Elefant of the 2./schwere Panzerjäger-Abteilung 653 that had to be returned to the Vienna Army Arsenal for repairs. A direct hit by a Soviet 15.2-centimeter artillery shell is visible to the right of the main gun. The fighting compartment was not penetrated, however. BECK

In order to train replacement drivers, the battalion conducted a driver-training course during the quiet period from May to June 1944. First attempts at driving were conducted with the lighter recovery Elefant. GAUL

The recovery Elefant was very maneuverable in difficult terrain. This rare photograph shows the top of the vehicle.
GAUL

Two Elefanten protect a wheeled vehicle column from marauding Soviet armor. The infantry to the side of the road take in the sight of the colossal vehicle. NERGER

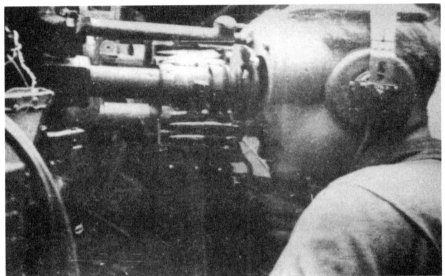

A view from the driver's station towards the radio operator, who also served as the hull machine-gun operator. The MG 34 was housed in a ball mount and aimed by the radio operated through movements of his head.
DR. RENOTIÉRE

Heavy rainfall has softened the ground. Even the normally very maneuverable T 34 has become stuck. A sledge hammer is employed to try to get the vehicle moving again.
BAYERLE

This photograph, taken in the summer of 1944, shows the same modified T 34. The vehicle number—305—indicates it was assigned to the 3./schwere Panzerjäger-Abteilung 653. BAYERLE

Gefreiter Franz Kurrer, the radio operator in the Panzer III ammunition carrier for the 3./schwere Panzerjäger-Abteilung 653.
KURRER

A Panzer III ammunition carrier from the 3./schwere Panzerjäger-Abteilung 653. It has chassis number 70208. KURRER

A Kübelwagen staff car from the Maintenance Company. The battalion insignia is visible on the left-hand front fender. KÜRSCHNER

Gefreiter Matthias Carpentier of the 3./schwere Panzer-jäger-Abteilung 653 in the Soviet Union in the summer of 1944. Note the wear of shoulder-strap slides that indicate his battalion. These could be removed for operational security reasons. CARPENTIER

A knocked-out SU 152 assault gun is inspected. An 8.8-centimeter round penetrated the fighting compartment next to the main gun. CARPENTIER

A Schwimmwagen from the battalion's Headquarters Company. The battalion insignia is clearly visible on the side of the vehicle.
STEINMÜLLER

BRÜNNTHALER

BRÜNNTHALER

During the quiet period from may to mid-July 1944, the battalion's Maintenance Company modified many captured vehicles. These photographs show a Soviet T 34 chassis that has had a German quad 2-centimeter Flak added in a mobile turret. The vehicle had a four-man crew and, according to the battalion armorer, performed well in combat. The Sturmgeschütz III seen below belonged to Sturmgeschütz-Brigade 322, which fought in the same sector of the front.

The turret walls were fabricated from a knocked-out Sd.Kfz. 251. Attachments for holding the ammunition containers were welded onto the hull. The vehicle seems to be the usual camouflage scheme of sand, green and reddish brown. CARPENTIER

The vehicle was assigned to the Headquarters Company of the battalion. It performed as well as any of the proven series of Flak vehicles. Unfortunately, the author was unable to determine its fate. TILLWICK

Elefant 301 of the Company Commander of the 3./schwere Panzerjäger-Abteilung 653, Oberleutnant Franz Kretschmer. The vehicle's driver was Unteroffizier Heinrich Appel. DR. RENOTIÉRE

An Elefant of the 3./schwere Panzerjäger-Abteilung 653 during the demonstrations. TILLWICK

Operational capabilities of the recovery Elefant are also demonstrated to the personnel from the 100. Jäger-Division. BIERMANN

The entire Panzerjäger Platoon of the Headquarters Company is assembled for the purposes of the demonstration exercise. DEMLEITNER

The vehicles returned to their assembly area after the exercise. DEMLEITNER

Maintenance and repair work on an 18-ton prime mover of the Recovery Platoon. DEMLEITNER

New tracks arrive for the Elefanten. DEMLEITNER

The 16-ton portal crane of the Maintenance Company. DEMLEITNER

This Elefant of the headquarters Company was photographed in July 1944 near Brzezany. The vehicle has the two-part hatch modification that was added at the Nibelungen Works to only four Elefanten. TAMS

This Elefant occupies an ambush position at the edge of a woodline and waits for Soviet armor. The interplay of light and shadow caused by the filtering of sunlight through the tree branches helps provide outstanding camouflage for the vehicle. SABROWSKY

This photograph of an Elefant was taken in July 1944 at St. Pölten. It is one of the four vehicles that received the two-part rear-hatch modification at the Nibelungen Works.
BRAUN

Elefant 224 of the 2./schwere Panzerjäger-Abteilung 653 broke through a bridge during the withdrawal towards Lemberg (Lvov). DEMLEITNER

The caved-in portion was secured against further collapse. DEMLEITNER

The tow cables are attached. DEMLEITNER

The recovery maintenance personnel work feverishly to recover the stricken vehicle. DEMLEITNER

The vehicle has rolled halfway onto its side. DEMLEITNER

The next Elefant in the column passed the accident area cautiously. DEMLEITNER

Prime movers support other Elefanten of the 2./schwere Panzerjäger-Abteilung 653. Some of them are approaching the accident site in reverse. DEMLEITNER

Elefant 232 hooks up to retrieve the stuck vehicle. DEMLEITNER

The recovery attempt was successful and Elefant 224 moves out to catch up with its column. DEMLEITNER

Another of the battalion's Elefanten at the location of the Maintenance Company at Bad Rabka. Note the two pennants on the antenna mast.

Schwere Panzerjäger-Abteilung 653 lost 60% of its combat strength during the withdrawal of August 1944! Only a few of the vehicles were actually lost in combat operations, however. Most of them had to be abandoned at water obstacles or ran out of fuel and had to be blown up by their crews. DEMLEITNER

Elefant 332 was one of the few tank destroyers to withstand the grueling withdrawal from Galicia relatively unscathed. Only a total of 12 Elefanten made it all the way back to Bad Rabka. WULFF

Leutnant Heinrich Teriete, the executive officer of the 2./schwere Panzerjäger-Abteilung 653 and its successor unit, schwere Panzerjäger-Kompanie 614. TERIETE

Besitzeugnis

Dem .... Leutnant ....
(Dienstgrad)

.... Heinrich T e r i e t e ....
(Vor- und Zuname)

.... s. Pz.Jg.Abt. 653 ....
(Truppenteil)

wurde das

Panzerkampfabzeichen

— Silber —
III. Stufe

verliehen.

O.U., den 21. Sept. 1944
(Ort und Datum)

(signature)
(Unterschrift)
Major und
Abteilungs-Kommandeur.

....
(Dienstgrad und Dienststellung)

Award certificate for the Third Level of the Tank Assault Badge in Silver to Leutnant Heinrich Teriete, denoting participation in a minimum of 75 separate armored engagements.

Besitzeugnis

Dem .... **Unteroffizier** ....
— Dienstgrad —

Heinrich Appel
Vor- und Zuname

3. Komp. /schw.Panzerjäger Abt. 653
Truppenteil

wurde das

Kraftfahrbewährungsabzeichen

in .... **Silber** .... verliehen.

Abt.Gef.St., d. 1.9.44
Ort und Tag

Unterschrift

Hauptmann u. stellv.Abt.Kdr.
Dienstgrad und Dienststellung

Award certificate for the Driver's badge in Silver to Unteroffizier Heinrich Appel.

Besitzeugnis

Dem .... **Obergefreiten** ....
(Dienstgrad)

.... Peter S c h a d e ....
(Vor- und Zuname)

.... 3. Komp./schw.Panzerjäger Abt. 653 ....
(Truppenteil)

für tapfere Teilnahme an 5o Einsatztagen

wurde das

Panzerkampfabzeichen

— Silber — III.Stufe —

verliehen.

Abt.Gef.St., den 6.1o.44
(Ort und Datum)

(Unterschrift)

Stempel

Major u.Abteilungskommandeur
(Dienstgrad und Dienststellung)

Award certificate for the Third Level of the Tank Assault Badge in Silver to Obergefreiter Peter Schade.

Since there were only 12 Elefanten left in the battalion at the end of August 1944, they were all consolidated into one company: 2./schwere Panzerjäger-Abteilung 653. After a battlefield reconstitution in the vicinity of Krakow, the company was sent to the Baranov Bridgehead. NONSEN

The 2./schwere Panzerjäger-Abteilung 653 was redesignated as schwere Panzerjäger-Kompanie 614 at the end of December 1944. During the grand offensive launched by the Soviets on 12 January 1945, which caused the entire Eastern front to collapse for the Germans, almost all of the Elefanten were either destroyed or lost due to mechanical failure. WILHELM

The last four Elefanten operated in the Königswusterhausen, Zossen and Berlin areas. Most of the support elements of schwere Panzerjäger-Kompanie 614 managed to break out of the Berlin encirclement. WILHELM

Schwere Panzerjäger-Abteilung 653 – March 1945

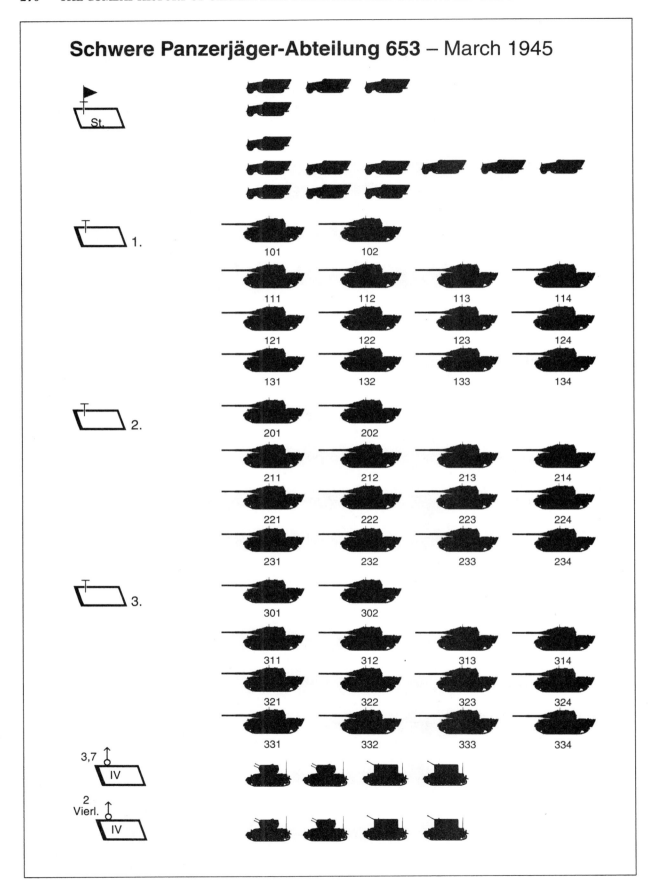

Training, Reorganization and Operations of schwere Panzerjäger-Abteilung 653 with the Jagdtiger Tank Destroyer

1944–1945

On 20 April 1944, Adolf Hitler viewed the first production model of the Jagdtiger tank destroyer. Hitler was so impressed with the vehicle that he ordered production to begin as soon as possible and continuously displayed a personal interest in the Jagdtiger, intervening on its behalf often.

The completion of individual Jagdtiger vehicles began in early June 1944 at the Nibelungen Works at St. Valentin (Austria). The first nine vehicles—chassis numbers 305001–305010, except for chassis 305002—were equipped with the so-called Porsche suspension, consisting of 4 sets of dual, overlapping roadwheels on each side. All the Jagdtiger tank destroyers that followed in this series—chassis 305002 and from chassis number 305011 forward—received the compartmented suspension with individually sprung roadwheels developed by the Henschel. They also received the Zimmerit coating.

TECHNICAL SPECIFICATIONS FOR THE JAGDTIGER TANK DESTROYER (SD.KFZ 186)

Builder:	Nibelungen Works
Combat Weight:	75 tons
Engine:	Maybach HL 230 P30
Maximum Speed:	41.5 kilometers per hour
Range (Road/CC):	170/120 kilometers
Fuel Consumption (Road/CC):	800 liters/100 liters
Crew:	6
Armament	
Main gun:	1 12.8-centimeter Pak 80 L/55
Secondary:	1 MG 34 (600); 1 MG 42

Effective 20 June 1944, a Jagdtiger training company was created at Panzerjäger-Ersatz- und Ausbildungs-Abteilung 7 in Munich (Freimarn). The commander was Hauptmann Konrad Rehnitz, who had received the Knight's Cross on 12 August 1942. The majority of the training company formed the cadre for the reconstituted 2./schwere Panzerjäger-Abteilung 653 in October 1944. The remainder of the per-

sonnel formed the separate Jagdtiger Replacement and Training Company based in Freistadt (Austria) (Panzerjäger-Ersatz- und Ausbildungs-Abteilung 17). The Company Commander was Oberleutnant Karl Seitz.

Members of the 1. and 3./schwere Panzerjäger-Abteilung 653 began test driving the Jagdtiger on 3 September 1944 with the Panzer-Ersatz- und Ausbildungs-Abteilung 500 in Fallingbostel. This initial orientation ended on 20 September 1944. Both companies moved to Linz (Austria) on 21 September 1944. They occupied quarters in Haag. From there, the soldiers went to the Nibelungen Works at St. Valentin on a daily basis to help work on the Jagdtiger series production. A heavy American air attack on 16 October 1944, however, brought the production at the Nibelungen Works almost to a halt. The 1. and 3./schwere Panzerjäger-Abteilung 653 were not able to attain their combat strength (14 vehicles each) by the end of December 1944. Both of these companies were transferred to the Döllersheim Training Area in Austria on 1 November 1944. Gunnery practice with the 12.8-centimeter main gun and driver's training and certification were conducted there until 17 November 1944.

DUTY POSITIONS IN SCHWERE PANZERJÄGER-ABTEILUNG 653 (AS OF: 1 DECEMBER 1944)

Commander:	Major Rudolf Grillenberger
Adjutant:	Oberleutnant Kurt Scherer
Liaison Officer:	Leutnant Hermann Knack
Headquarters Company Commander:	Hauptmann Bernhard Konnak
Signals Officer:	Leutnant Martens
Reconnaissance Platoon Leader:	Leutnant Kämmerer
Armored Flak Platoon Leader:	Leutnant Arthur Allspach
1./schwere Panzerjäger-Abteilung 653:	Oberleutnant Werner Haberland
2./schwere Panzerjäger-Abteilung 653:	Oberleutnant Robert Wiesenfarth
3./schwere Panzerjäger-Abteilung 653:	Oberleutnant Franz Kretschmer
Support Company:	Hauptmann Helmut Ulbricht
Maintenance Company:	Oberleutnant Karl Schulte
Battalion Engineer:	Regierungsbaurat Rudolf Schaffranek
Assistant Battalion Engineer:	Regierungsbaurat Erhard Jörger
Recovery Platoon Leader:	Leutnant Rolf Schleicher

With 7 Jagdtiger, the 1./schwere Panzerjäger-Abteilung 653 departed from the Döllersheim Training Area on 7 December 1944 to take part in the upcoming Ardennes Offensive (Battle of the Bulge). The departure railhead was at Göpfritz an der Wild. The initial transport of the battalion to the designated operational area Gemünd-Kall-Schleiden was unsuccessful. All of the battalion's transport trains were blocked by the completely bombed out rail lines. All the forces and supplies intended for the offensive had to remain in the Mosel Valley or in the Eifel Mountain Range. Only a handful of soldiers from the support company, under the command of Hauptmann Ulbricht, reached the assigned operational area at the beginning of the Ardennes Offensive on 15 December 1944.

The rail transport reports of Heeresgruppe B clearly describe the transportation problems the battalion faced from 12 to 31 December 1944:

12 December 1944: schwere Panzerjäger-Abteilung 653. Three trains from Döllersheim, near Cochem (objective: area around Gemünd). 2 trains unloaded in Wengerohr. One train en route to the detraining area.

14 December 1944: Movement ceased in the afternoon. All elements in Wengerohr area.

19 December 1944: Before noon: Three trains in the area around Kali (destination). One train departed Wittlich/Wengerohr area. One train en route to Koblenz.

21 December 1944: One train unloaded in Blankenheim (Eifel). [Elements of the 3./schwere Panzerjäger-Abteilung 653]

23 December 1944: New destination: Heeresgruppe G. Destination area: Zweibrücken.

25 December 1944: Heavy air attack on Wengerohr. [schwere Panzerjäger-Abteilung 653 lost some vehicles: halftracks and wheeled vehicles]

26 December 1944: One train scheduled to depart Weilerswist in the evening of 27 December 1944. Elements of schwere Panzerjäger-Abteilung 653 in the Wittlich/Wengerohr area scheduled to rail load in Ürzig (Mosel). Of the three trains en route, 2 are halted in the Wittlich/Wengerohr area and one is located in the Blankenheim (Eifel) area. Moving the special cars [Ssyms] forward has been impossible due to breaks in the rail line.

28 December 1944: The personnel have not arrived to load aboard the trains waiting in Duisdorf (near Bonn) and Ürzig.

29 December 1944: Personnel [elements of schwere Panzerjäger-Abteilung 653] have orders to move cross country from the Wittlich/Wengerohr area to Boppard.

30 December 1944: One train loaded for Bonn; one train currently loading in Bonn; one train arrived in the Zweibrücken area; two train equivalents marching cross country from the Wittlich area to the Boppard area [elements of the 1. and 3./schwere Panzerjäger-Abteilung 653]; one train halted in Bengel (Mosel); one train trapped near Trier/Ehrang (blocked in a tunnel).

31 December 1944: One element from the Jagdtiger[formation] departed Blankenheim (Eifel) at 0800 hours. 4 Jagdtiger loaded aboard trains in Reisdorf, near Bonn. Jagdtiger headquarters in Bad Münstereifel at 1230 hours. Remaining elements in Blankenheim (2 Jagdtiger, 2 armored recovery vehicles, 1 armored Flak vehicle) are not operational). Earliest rail load date is the evening of 2 January 1945. Evening: One train arrived in Zweibrücken; two train equivalents marching cross country from Wittlich to Boppard [elements of the 3./schwere Panzerjäger-Abteilung 653]; one train halted in Bengel (Mosel); one train still trapped in Trier/Ehrang.

Fragmented transports and road marches to the area of operations—some more than 130 kilometers—were inflicted upon these gigantic, accident-prone vehicles. This, together with the absence of all combat-support elements, was the reason for the battalion's ineffectiveness during the Ardennes Offensive.

25 December 1944

TO: Headquarters, 1. Armee
SUBJECT: schwere Panzerjäger-Abteilung 653

The following memorandum about Jagdtiger operations contains critical information:

Armament and mobility of the Jagdtiger favor solid, level, open terrain. The Jagdtiger is dependent upon bridges, because steep ditches and stream beds make considerable demands upon the chassis and drive train (combat weight: 80 tons).

There are still considerable problems with the Porsche suspension (the battalion still has 7 Porsche Jagdtiger, the rest have Henschel suspensions).

1) Strong jolts from the two-piece track, causing the main gun to go out of adjustment. The suspension springs are too tight.

2) Load bearing surface of compartmented suspension, with simple roadwheels, causes lateral stress on the tracks in poor terrain (rocky, depressions, curving roads), leading to bent tracks or broken track pins.

3) Special suspension parts, such as separate operational and rail transportation tracks, make resupply and maintenance more difficult.

Combat: Slow rate of fire (separate projectile and propellant casing. It is necessary to return to zero degree elevation after each round fired to unload the spent casing). This makes it necessary to employ a large number of Jagdtiger in an attack.

Strengths: Main gun has penetration power at 3,500 meters. Attacks dependent upon solid terrain and good visibility. Mechanical losses at about 40%, therefore deploy only in a consolidated unit or defensive power will be too weak during enemy counterattacks.

Headquarters, Heeresgruppe G
Chief-of-Staff
/signed/ Staedke
Generalmajor

The extremely difficult road marches caused a large number of breakdowns for the Jagdtiger. Engines and final drives proved to have defects and were too weak in construction. Sabotage by foreign workers in the factories was also suspected, since metal shavings were found in many engine oil filters.

The maintenance services had very few spare parts on hand and half of the Maintenance Company had already been moved to Zweibrücken. This caused unusually long repair times for the Jagdtiger, leading to complaints by the Army High Command. The Inspector General of Armored Forces therefore investigated all non-operational vehicles. The following documents provide information about the damage, as well as the inspection. (Federal Archives/Freiburg Military Archives):

General der Panzertruppen West   Location Classified, 9 January 1945
— Operations Directorate No. 371 (SECRET) —
SUBJECT: schwere Panzerjäger-Abteilung 653 (Jagdtiger)
TO: Commander-in-Chief in the West; Inspector general of Armored Forces

There are 2 operational Jagdtiger in the Boppard area. Per conversation with General der Panzertruppen West, rail loading has been ordered for the evening of 9 January 1945.

Two Jagdtiger in Emmelshausen, 12 kilometers west of St. Goar; both have damaged engines, [and the] oil pressure too low.

Two Jagdtiger in Gödenroth, 15 kilometers southwest of St. Goar, of which one has a damaged drive sprocket and one has broken cooling shaft.

Three Jagdtiger in Briedel an der Mosel, of which one has a damaged engine and oil pressure too low; one is losing radiator water and has electrical problems; [and] one has a damaged engine, defective valves and connecting rod.

Three Jagdtiger in Wengerohr, of which two have damaged engines and oil pressure too low; one has a damaged drive train.

Half of the Maintenance Company of schwere Panzerjäger-Abteilung 653 is currently working on the three Jagdtiger in Wengerohr. The work there is made more difficult by the fact that the Maintenance Company does not have a crane available. The Maintenance Company must use a railroad crane in Wengerohr. The two Jagdtiger repaired in Boppard are expected to arrive on the evening of 12 January 1945.

FOR THE GENERAL DER PANZERTRUPPEN WEST:

/signed/ Deputy Chief of Staff for Operations

SECRET

Army High Command, 16 January 1945

Johannis

Oberstleutnant

Chief Mechanized Vehicle Officer with

The Inspector General of Armored Forces

Bb. No. 1. 290/45 (SECRET)

Inspection Report

SUBJECT: Jagdtiger of schwere Panzerjäger-Abteilung 653

On orders from General Thomale, two specialists from the firms of Henschel and Maybach and I visited non-operational Jagdtiger from schwere Panzerjäger-Abteilung 653 on 13 and 14 January 1945 to determine the extent of their non-operational status.

Findings: 10 of 16 Jagdtiger had broken down in the Wittlich (Mosel) area during a movement to Boppard am Rhine (90 kilometer road march). These included:

6 with serious problems

4 x engine driveshaft damage

2 x engine damage

4 with moderate problems

1 x electrical short circuit causing an engine fire

1 x damage to the engine ventilator

1 x broken ventilator shaft

1 x leaking engine oil after a ruptured paper filter

See table for specific information about the problems.

Repairs

The parts necessary for repairs were ordered immediately and are en route. General der Panzertruppen West has dispatched a crane and 3 tank mechanics to provide support. A drivetrain specialist has also been sent to the battalion. The 4 vehicles with moderate problems can be repaired within 1 to 2 days of the arrival of repair parts. The serious cases will require 1 to 2 weeks.

Reasons for the unusually high number of breakdowns:

1) The heavy weight of the Jagdtiger (10 tons heavier than the Tiger II) makes it considerably more susceptible to damage and more cumbersome than the Tiger II. The chassis is overloaded and therefore easily damaged.

2) The training received by the drivers and maintenance personnel was insufficient, even though it was conducted at the Nibelungen Works. The Nibelungen Works, openly critical of and unfamiliar with the Henschel chassis, for example, gave the drivers completely insufficient instruction on the Olvar drive, so that the smallest problems cause complete failure.

I therefore suggest:

a) Immediate dispatch of a specialist from the Henschel Company, with good knowledge of the entire chassis, including the engine and drive train, to teach the drivers and maintenance personnel of schwere Panzerjäger-Abteilung 653.
Duration of instruction: About 2 weeks.

b) Jagdtiger driver training at the Henschel Company; correspondingly, establish Jagdtiger formations only in the Kassel area.

3) Schwere Panzerjäger-Abteilung 653 did not possess any special tools and could therefore not help itself in many situations. In. 6 has begun an investigation into the whereabouts of tool sets.

4) There is an absence of the expected motivation by the leadership (Oberleutnant Haberland, Commander of the 1./schwere Panzerjäger-Abteilung 653, and Baurat Jörger, Assistant Battalion Engineer) and drivers to repair their vehicles as quickly as possible or at least make preparations for repairs. Most vehicles stood idle for 5 days without any determination of what caused the damages or making any preparations for repairs. The irresponsibility of such actions was made clear to the responsible parties. General der Panzertruppen West has also been asked to oversee the battalion.

5) The piecemeal deployment of the battalion—some vehicles in the Wittlich area, the other vehicles in the Zweibrücken area—made it impossible to repair all vehicles because of the shortage of maintenance equipment (only one crane available at this time). Correspondingly, the battalion must operate together.

6) All of the battalion's maintenance elements were in the Zweibrücken area;, none in the Wittlich area. The maintenance elements should not be loaded after, or separate from, the combat elements.

General Conclusions

1) The company commanders, battalion engineer, maintenance sergeant and drivers of the 1. and 3./schwere Panzerjäger-Abteilung 653 all indicated that a march distance of 30-40 kilometers a day was good progress. The battalion initially anticipated a 3-day march from Wengerohr to Boppard (approximately 90 kilometers). As a noticeable record, several Jagdtiger accomplished this march in 2 days!

This is apparently the influence of training at the Nibelungen Works, which emphasized extreme care for the equipment. Schwere Panzerjäger-Abteilung 653 did not understand that such march goals negated the entire purpose of motorization.

2) At the Henschel Company, General Director Dr. Eng. Stieler von Heydekampf, Director Pertus and others informed me that the Jagdtiger has performed well at the front and has had outstanding success. Therefore, there are demands to construct more than the originally planned 150 Jagdtiger.

I explained that the Inspector General of Armored Forces had not yet heard anything about good performance and successes of the Jagdtiger. According to Oberleutnant Haberland, Company Commander of the 1./schwere Panzerjäger-Abteilung 653, only a few Jagdtiger have been deployed in the Zweibrücken area—as artillery. One Sherman has been knocked out and one Jagdtiger completely destroyed by an explosion (cause unknown).

Attachment: 1 Table.
Attachment to Inspection Report
SUBJECT: Damaged Jagdtiger of schwere Panzerjäger-Abteilung 653
Oberstleutnant Johannis
Bb. No. 1. 290/45 (SECRET)

A. Serious Problems

No.	Vehicle No.	Kilometers	Engine No.	Problems	Repairs
1	305010	207	a a m 832 1373 (Auto-Union) w/8 crank shaft bearings	No oil pressure; shavings in oil filter; #6 and #12 shaft housings worn	Replacement engine has been delivered
2	305014	174	228 a a m 832 1728 (Auto-Union)	No oil pressure; shavings in oil filter; shaft housings worn	Replacement engine has been delivered
3	305031	210	292 ere 61 352 (Maybach?)	No oil pressure; shavings in oil filter; shaft housings worn	Replacement engine en route
4	305017	215	a a m 832 1774 (Auto-Union)	No oil pressure; shavings in oil filter; shaft housings worn	Replacement engine on order
5	305012	ca. 250		Planetary support shaft broken in steering drive	Replacement engine on order
6	305025	223		Transmission will not shift; metal fragments in engine oil filter	Replacement engine has been delivered

B. Moderate Problems

No.	Vehicle No.	Kilometers	Engine No.	Problems	Repairs
7	305022	175	p y e 8322585	Knocking in cylinders 7–12; rocker arm shaft probably damaged	Repair parts taken from damaged engines 1–4
8	305011	402 (Driver training vehicle)		Engine fire; electrical short circuit; electric starter broken	Repair parts available. Dependent upon arrival of hand winch and crane.
9	305009	329		Broken universal joint on left ventilator shaft	Replacement parts en route
10	305019	406		Drive and steering not working; high oil loss due to broken seal at oil filter	Reseal oil filter; refill with oil

On New Year's Eve 1944/1945, exactly one hour before midnight, Heeresgruppe G (General der Panzertruppen Hermann Balck) began Operation "Nordwind" ("North Wind") in the Saar-Pfalz area. Its mission was to halt the advance of American and French forces from Strasbourg and the northern Vosges Mountains at the German border. Elements of schwere Panzerjäger-Abteilung 653 that had been earmarked for this operation, however, were still stuck at the Mosel in the area of operations of Heeresgruppe B. Only two Jagdtiger from the 3./schwere Panzerjäger-Abteilung 653 were present in this sector of the front at the beginning of the operation. Both of these Jagdtiger were attached to the 17. SS-Panzer-Grenadier-Division "Götz von Berlichingen" and employed in the XIII. SS-Armee-Korps sector (SS-Gruppenführer Simon).

Both Jagdtiger crossed the German border at Medelsheim and were committed in an advance towards Rimling. Four additional tank destroyers from the 1./schwere Panzerjäger-Abteilung 653 followed in this sector of the front on 4 January 1945. These were unloaded in Bruchmühlbach, near Zweibrücken. Together with elements of the 17. SS-Panzer-Grenadier-Division "Götz von Berlichingen", 2 or 3 Jagdtiger—one under Feldwebel Schlabs and another under Unteroffizier Jaskiela—attacked American-occupied Rimling, near Bitche (France). Jagdtiger 134 (chassis number 305024) was a total loss. A bazooka hit caused the ammunition on the vehicle to explode. The entire crew—Unteroffizier Fritz Jaskiela, Gerhard Fischer, Werner Janson, Rudolf Gaube, Franz Schröder and Franz Boketta—was killed. A former Jagdtiger commander in the 1./schwere Panzerjäger-Abteilung 653, Feldwebel Reinhold Schlabs, wrote the following about the loss of Jagdtiger 134 in a letter to the author dated 22 January 1991:

> We arrived in Rimling around noon. The area was completely quiet. We positioned ourselves on a slope on the edge of town, about 250–300 meters apart, without making contact with our own forces, and waited there about 2 hours.
>
> Suddenly a round exploded a hair's breadth away from my vehicle. The driver, Bürgin, started the engine with lightning speed and pulled back a vehicle length. At that moment, a second round struck at the exact spot where we had just been. Both rounds were accompanied by a rattling sound I had never heard before. The origin of the rounds could not be determined. A short time later, there was a heavy detonation at Jaskiela's gun, which was positioned some 300 meters to my right. This direct hit delivered death to the entire crew.
>
> The more I think about Rimling, I think there must have been a third vehicle further to our left, perhaps west/northwest . . . We were to force our way into the American winter positions and make things hot for them.

On the second day of the operation, the German attack in the XIII. SS-Armee-Korps sector already began to bog down. The LXXXIX. Armee-Korps, operating on the left flank, succeeded in pushing forward to the Moder River at Wingen and was able to hold this terrain until mid-March 1945. After the failed attempt to secure ground at Bitche, the XXXIX. Panzer-Korps (21. Panzer-Division and 25. Panzer-grenadier-Division) began operations in the salient at Lauterburg (Lauterbourg) and south of Weißenburg (Wissembourg), while the 10. SS-Panzer-Division "Frundsberg" began operations at Hatten and Rittershoffen.

At 2045 hours on 10 January 1945, Heeresgruppe G received orders from the Commander-in-Chief in the West. These orders paraphrased a Führer order that mandated the two Jagdtiger be attached to the 10. SS-Panzer-Division "Frundsberg" since "they were especially well suited for engaging bunkers."

An hour later, Heeresgruppe G transmitted attachment orders for the two Jagdtiger to the XXXIX. Panzer-Korps and the commander of schwere Panzerjäger-Abteilung 653. It ordered both Jagdtiger move into the area southwest of Lauterburg as soon as possible, combat ready and with ammunition.

TO: General der Panzertruppen West   5 February 1945
SUBJECT: Report on the [10. SS-Panzer-Division "Frundsberg"]

The enemy has conducted a surprise attack, with armor support, in the Drusenheim Forest during the last few days. It is certain that the Americans have captured a Jagdtiger and several Panthers. (Source: Federal Archives/Freiburg Military Archives)

The various vehicle locations, combat experiences and serious issues were reported to the Inspector General of Armored Forces as follows on 22 January 1945:

SECRET COMMAND MATTER

Inspector General of Armored Forces
No. 335/45 (SECRET COMMAND MATTER)
SUBJECT: schwere Panzerjäger-Abteilung 653 (Jagdtiger).

A) Vehicle Status (22 January 1945)

1) 5 Jagdtiger in the XXXIX. Panzer-Korps bridgehead. 4 operational; 1 in long-term maintenance

2) 8 Jagdtiger in the Bühl area. 4 operational; 2 each in short- and long-term maintenance

3) 5 Jagdtiger in transit from Saarpfalz

4) 4 Jagdtiger not yet loaded in the Zweibrücken area. 3 operational; 1 in short-term maintenance

5) 10 Jagdtiger in the Mosel-Rhine area. All operational.

6) 8 Flakpanzer IV in the Bühl area; 3 Bergepanther in the Zweibrücken area; 2 Bergepanther in the Mosel area.

B) Combat Experiences:

2 Jagdtiger with the XIV. SS-Armee-Korps were committed against the bunker line at Auenheim on 17 January 1945 as fire support for the infantry.

Good target effect. 6 high-explosive rounds.

18 January 1945: Operations against 4 impregnable bunkers. Outstanding accuracy at 1,000 meters. Armored turret on one bunker burst into flames after two rounds. Firing at bunker firing ports had good results. A counterattack by Shermans was repulsed, setting them ablaze with high-explosive rounds.

Ammunition used: 46 high-explosive rounds and 10 antitank rounds. No losses.

C) Serious Issues:

Supply and maintenance services, including cranes and towing vehicles, are still missing in operational areas. An entire maintenance platoon is still working at the Mosel. Shortage of replacement parts, especially drive trains, delays repairs. Command vehicles (9 halftracks) en route from Spandau since 5 December 1944. Convoy No. 2.470.251 has not yet been located.

Still a shortage of ammunition in ammunition depots. The following vehicles [and equipment] still have not arrived:

7 Sd.Kfz. 100's
2 light trucks
3 medium trucks

1 recovery tank
22 heavy trucks
2 Sd.Kfz. 9/1's
1 arc welder

Bergepanther are insufficient, even with winches. One Bergepanther and two 18-ton prime movers (Sd.Kfz. 9's) can tow a single Jagdtiger on a wide road.

Chief-of-Staff
Commander-in-Chief in the West
/signed/ Westphal
Operations/Armor Liaison Officer
No. 167/45 (SECRET COMMAND MATTER)

PERSONNEL STATUS FOR SCHWERE PANZERJÄGER-ABTEILUNG 653 (FEBRUARY 1945) (REPORT DATE: 1 FEBRUARY 1945) (SOURCE: FEDERAL ARCHIVES/FREIBURG MILITARY ARCHIVES)

Officers: 29 and 1 civilian official
Noncommissioned officers: 271 and 4 civilian officials
Enlisted personnel: 682
Hiwis: 13
Total: 1,000 personnel

CASUALTIES AND OTHER LOSSES
(PERIOD: 1–3 JANUARY 1945)

Personnel	KIA	WIA	MIA	Sick	Other
Officers	—	—	—	1 (civilian official)	—
Noncommissioned officers and enlisted personnel	11	5	—	6	4
Total	11	5	—	7	4

VEHICLE STATUS FOR SCHWERE PANZERJÄGER-ABTEILUNG 653
(FEBRUARY 1945)

Status	Jagdtiger	Bergepanzer	Flakpanzer
Authorized	45	5	8
Operational	22	4	7
Maintenance	19	—	1

On 10 January 1945, in accordance with orders from Army Headquarters and the Replacement Army (AHA/In 6 (VIIIE), No. 17654/44 (SECRET) dated 28 November 1944), an armored Flak platoon arrived at the battalion. It had 1 officer, 10 noncommissioned officers and 64 enlisted personnel. Since the existing table of organization and equipment for the battalion did not cover an armored Flak platoon, the entire platoon was entered under the "required" column for personnel strength accountability purposes. One position was occupied by an officer candidate, and two other officers were attached to the battalion.

Four Jagdtiger from the 1./schwere Panzerjäger-Abteilung 653 were transported from the XXXIX. Panzer-Korps area to Bühl (Baden) on 23 January 1945. These arrived at the Bühl train station on 25 January 1945 and conducted a road march to the towns of Muckenschopf and Momprechtshofen am Rhine. There were other tank destroyers from the 1. and 2./schwere Panzerjäger-Abteilung 653 waiting there to cross the Rhine on an engineer ferry. The river crossing took place without incident, and the tank destroyers occupied positions in Offendorf. The companies conducted reconnaissance towards Herrlisheim, Drusenheim and Sessenheim, but there were no combat operations. On 29 January 1945, the Jagdtiger were brought back to the eastern side of the Rhine River.

During the withdrawal of the Jagdtiger to the ferry on 29 January 1945, American fighter-bombers attacked a Flakpanzer IV "Wirbelwind" ("Whirlwind") that had occupied a position in Ludwigsfelde (Fort Louis). The crew succeeded in shooting down one of the fighter-bombers, but the armored Flak vehicle was seriously hit and the four crewmen lost their lives. One of those killed was the commander of the Flakpanzer platoon, Leutnant Arthur Allspach, as well as soldiers Herbert Poppe, Hilmar Kühne and Felix Wolfersberger.

After the transport back by ferry, the tank destroyers assembled again in the Bühl area (Gamshurst, Hatzenweier, Breithurst). These elements began rail loading on 5 February 1945 to move by train to the new assembly area near Landau in the Pfalz region.

Telegram dated 5 February 1945 (Source: Federal Archives/Military Archives):

SECRET COMMAND MATTER

Reference: Telephone Conversation with Major Wehrmann, 2 February 1945
SUBJECT: Jagdtiger

1) Operations of schwere Panzerjäger-Abteilung 653: Battalion is deployed with Heeresgruppe G, behind the left flank of the 1. Armee (Weissenburger Depression), as a heavy, mobile armored reserve in the main battle area to prevent armor penetrations.

2) Arrival of 25 additional Jagdtiger: The Commander-in-Chief in the West, in concurrence with General der Panzertruppen West, recommends using 10 vehicles to bring schwere Panzerjäger-Abteilung 653 to full strength and 15 vehicles to form a 4th Company in the same battalion. Assigning the latter [4th Company] to schwere Panzer-Abteilung 506 is disapproved due to maintenance, supply and operational reasons.

Assigning a Jagdtiger company to a Tiger battalion will cause the battalion to lose its mobility. Assignment to schwere Panzerjäger-Abteilung 559 or Panzerjäger-Abteilung 741 is also disapproved due to maintenance and operational reasons.

Commander-in-Chief in the West
Operations/Armor Liaison Officer
No. 295/45 (SECRET COMMAND MATTER)
/signed/ Zimmermann
Generalmajor

Telegram dated 6.2.1945 (Source: Federal Archives/Freiburg Military Archives)

SECRET COMMAND MATTER

TO: Inspector General of Armored Forces

REFERENCE: Telephone Conversation with Major Friedel on 6 February 1945

SUBJECT: Vehicle Status of schwere Panzerjäger-Abteilung 653 (Jagdtiger) as of 5 February 1945

1) Battalion assembling in the Landau area. 11 Jagdtiger arrived at assembly area (10 operational; 1 short-term maintenance).

2) Between Boppard and Briedel in the Mosel Valley: 8 Jagdtiger (1 operational; 4 short-term maintenance; 3 long-term maintenance).

3) 1 Jagdtiger (operational) in the St. Ingbert area.

4) 19 Jagdtiger (9 operational, 4 short-term maintenance, 6 long-term maintenance) between Bühl and assembly area; en route to assembly area.

5) 2 Jagdtiger en route from Döllersheim.

Commander-in-Chief in the West

Operations/Armor Liaison Officer

No. 300/45 (SECRET COMMAND MATTER)

/signed/ Zimmermann

Generalmajor

The Commander of the battalion, Major Rudolf Grillenberger, gave his assessment of his formation in the monthly status report (February 1945) to the Inspector General of Armored Forces (Source: Federal Archives/Freiburg Military Archives):

Training Status:

Training status for the 1st and 3rd Companies can be considered very good. Both companies have combat experience from the Russian Campaign, and some from the Italian Campaign. Even though combat experience with the Jagdtiger is still very limited, both companies have complete trust in the new equipment.

The 2nd Company has been reconstituted and arrived here on 23 January 1945. The cadre also consists of older, experienced soldiers. Classroom and technical training has been completed and is considered good.

Unit Morale:

Fighting spirit and the desire to bring the new weapons into combat has suffered due to fragmentation of the battalion. It was not possible to foster leadership, training and trust for some elements in a matter of two months. Additionally, these elements were behind the front, completely cut off and attempting to repair tanks with only expedient measures (especially elements in the Mosel Valley).

The Maintenance Company, split apart from the beginning, has been in the Zweibrücken area for 3 weeks due to transport difficulties and without any major maintenance missions. It could not move forward to the battalion's elements in the combat area, where it was desperately needed. The company commander is constantly on the go between elements of his unit, which also leads to problems.

With the exception of elements that are in combat and have a great fighting spirit, I cannot give a clear assessment of the battalion's morale.

Exceptional Problems:

In addition to the battalion's fragmentation mentioned above - with particular emphasis upon the fact that communication with these elements sometimes takes up to a week - there is also the major problem of incredibly weak maintenance units.

In the combat areas we are lacking:

1) The entire Maintenance Company, including the necessary lifting and recovery equipment.

2) Supply elements.

Maintenance squads and expedient measures were used during recovery and supply operations. Since this is the first time in combat for the Jagdtigers, the recurring problems of damage in steering, transmission, final drives and main guns are even more disadvantageous because of the above situation. Repairs are delayed, which weakens the trust the soldiers have in the usually outstanding vehicles. Vehicle drivers become anxious at the slightest problem, because expedient measures and exchanging parts is only a temporary measure, but not the solution to the problem.

Excessive demands on energy, as well as materiel, is the result. All of this will cease immediately if the order from Heeresgruppe G directing the battalion to assemble in its entirety in the area south of Landau is implemented promptly.

Grillenberger

Major and Battalion Commander

The elements of the battalion that slowly arrived at the new assembly area dispersed among the towns of Hayna (1. and elements of 2./schwere Panzerjäger-Abteilung 653), Erlenbach (2./schwere Panzerjäger-Abteilung 653), Steinweiler and Rohrbach. The battalion assembled in its entirety for the first time in this area and this allowed the Jagdtiger to be brought up to a reasonably good mechanical condition. The final drives remained a constant weak area, however.

Telegram dated 17 February 1945 (Source: Federal Archives/Freiburg Military Archives):

SECRET COMMAND MATTER

TO: Inspector General of Armored Forces, Berlin

REFERENCE: Armed Forces High Command/Army Staff (Force Structure), No. 3432/45 (SECRET COMMAND MATTER) dated 15 February 1945

SUBJECT: Deployment Preparations for schwere Panzerjäger-Abteilung 512 (Jagdtiger).

1) A series of problems with the final drives in Jagdtiger surfaced during operations by schwere Panzerjäger-Abteilung 653 (flaws in construction).

2) Modifications are necessary for all Jagdtiger.

3) First modifications will be made to Jagdtiger in the rear areas that have been newly constructed.

   a) 5 Jagdtiger from schwere Panzerjäger-Abteilung 512 in Döllersheim.

   b) 6 Jagdtigers in the Army Vehicle Point at Linz

4) This will delay readiness of the 1./ schwere Panzerjäger-Abteilung 512. Readiness time will be announced when modification times are calculated.

Inspector General of Armored Forces/Chief Vehicle Officer
Force Structure II, No. 746/45 (SECRET COMMAND MATTER) dated 16 February 1945
Chief-of-Staff
/signed/ Thomale
Generalmajor

As American and French pressure from Strasbourg against the German border became stronger in February 1945, the battalion received orders to halt the enemy at the approaches to the Westwall (Siegfried Line). The battalion began moving to the Hagenau area on 17 February 1945 (Source: Federal Archives/Freiburg Military Archives). Telegram dated 28 February 1945:

SECRET COMMAND MATTER

SUBJECT: schwere Panzerjäger-Abteilung 653 (Jagdtiger)
Commander-in-Chief in the West reports:

1) Jagdtiger operations: Map with firing positions of individual vehicles sent directly to Armed Forces High Command by Major Grillenberger. Battalion has reconnoitered all terrain, routes and bridges; reinforcement of key bridges is underway.

2) Ammunition: Contrary to the commander's report, there are 1,500 high-explosive rounds in the Monika Depot; in addition to 250 rounds at the battalion. Exact breakdown according to type and total follows.

3) Local Area Commander for St. Ingbert did not retain 2 Jagdtiger. Rail loading will take place no later than 27 February 1945. Responsibility rests with the battalion, according to a report by the Heeresgruppe G Liaison Officer. Investigation initiated.

Commander-in-Chief in the West
Operations/Armor Liaison Officer
No. 505/45 (SECRET COMMAND MATTER)
/signed/ Zimmermann
Generalmajor

Personnel Status for schwere Panzerjäger-Abteilung 653 (4 March 1945)
(Effective date of report: 1 March 1945) (Source: Federal Archives/Freiburg Military Archives)

Officers: 29 and 1 civilian official
Noncommissioned officers: 272 and 4 civilian officials
Enlisted personnel: 681
Hiwis: 13
Total: 1,000 personnel

CASUALTIES AND OTHER LOSSES
(PERIOD: 1–28 FEBRUARY 1945)

Personnel	KIA	WIA	MIA	Sick	Other
Officers	1	—	—	—	(Transferred)
Noncommissioned officers and enlisted personnel	—	2	—	14	26
Total	1	2	—	14	26

VEHICLE STATUS FOR SCHWERE PANZERJÄGER-ABTEILUNG 653
(FEBRUARY 1945)

Status	Jagdtiger	Bergepanzer	Flakpanzer	
Authorized	45	5	8	
Operational	31	3	6	
Maintenance	8	1	2	

Status	Halftracks	Motorcycles	Staff Cars	Staff Cars
Authorized	10	8	39	2
Operational	14	15	32	2
Maintenance	—	1	5	—

Status	Maultiere	Prime Movers (1–5 ton)	Prime Movers (8–18 ton)	Medium Trucks	Heavy Trucks
Authorized	6	8	15	32	87
Operational	13	6	14	30	53
Maintenance	3	—	3	2	9

WEAPONS STATUS FOR SCHWERE PANZERJÄGER-ABTEILUNG 653
(FEBRUARY 1945)

Status	Main guns	Quad 2-centimeter Flak	3.7-centimeter Flak	Machine Guns
Authorized	45	7	4	126
Operational	31	7	3	119
Maintenance	8	—	1	—

The final elements of the battalion arrived at the new assembly area in the Hagenau Forest at the beginning of March 1945. The Jagdtiger occupied positions in Soultz, Surbourg, Gunstett and near Morsbronn (les Bains). The tank destroyers fired indirect artillery missions against Hagenau with their 12.8-centimeter main guns. A propaganda company filmed this operation for the newsreel.

Unteroffizier Willi Maxheim (2./schwere Panzerjäger-Abteilung 653) described this indirect fire mission in a letter to the author dated 1 March 1988:

We were in the woods outside of Hagenau. Hagenau was partly in American, partly in German hands. [17. SS-Panzergrenadier-Division "Götz von Berlichingen" and 10. SS-Panzer-Division "Frundsberg"] had just been relieved from the sector. We were completely outnumbered. We were strictly forbidden to fire, since the fighter-bombers and reconnaissance aircraft were constantly in the sky because of good weather. A Volks-Grenadier-Division occupied our area.

They only had 7.5-centimeter Pak as light artillery! The Americans had light and sound measurement devices, as well as snipers, in a high-rise building in Hagenau, controlling the entire area. The artillery available in our sector was ineffective due to lack of mobility.

Major Grillenberger remembered that the battalion had many individuals with artillery training. He suggested using indirect artillery fire from a nearby town to knock out the Americans in the high rise. One of our officers, I no longer remember who he was or from which company, made preparations for the indirect fire.

Our location was found on the map. A clearing in the forest. Then the firing position was laid in. Also the base direction. Firing quadrants were borrowed from a horse-drawn element that had 10.5-centimeter cannon. The base direction and anchor point were identical, since corrections had to be made with the aiming telescope. The high position was measured with the quadrants, directly back to the base position of our main guns: Maximum range - 18 kilometers.

The knowledgeable officer was at an observation post outside Hagenau and directed the fire, which began at the last light of dusk. The high rise was hit several times. Immediately after the firing began, our position was fired upon by the Americans. We received the order to "button up" and continued firing unmolested.

SECRET COMMAND MATTER

[SUBJECT: Status Report of] schwere Panzerjäger-Abteilung 653 (as of 10 March 1945)

a) Personnel: 23 officers, 7 civil servants, 217 noncommissioned officers and 798 enlisted personnel

b) Armored vehicle status (as of 11 March 1945):

41 Jagdtiger

4 Flakpanzer IV "Ostwind" (3.7-centimeter)

4 Flakpanzer IV (2-centimeter)

1 Flakpanzer IV "Wirbelwind" (quad 2-centimeter)

4 Bergepanzer

14 Medium Halftracks

(Source: Federal Archives/Freiburg Military Archives)

The battalion spent the first two weeks of March 1945 in relative quiet in the Hagenau Forest. Bunkers and vehicle positions were constructed. During this period, Major Grillenberger and the battalion liaison officer, Leutnant Knack, used a Jagdtiger with its main gun removed as an observation vehicle.

The penetration of American forces into the Hunsrück Range made the situation untenable for German forces in the Saar-Pfalz sector and the withdrawal of the front unavoidable. The battalion was ordered to cover the withdrawal of the German forces. It received this order on the evening of 14 March 1945. There was heavy fighting during the night of 14/15 March 1945 and there were combat operations in Forstheim and at Höllenhof during daylight. Around noon on 15 March 1945, the 3./schwere Panzerjäger-Abteilung 653 had to break off an attack from Morsbronn (les Bains) against the high ground at Höl-lenhof, after suffering heavy losses. The company lost 5 tank destroyers to American fighter-bombers.

Unteroffizier Willi Maxheim (2./schwere Panzerjäger-Abteilung 653) described the battalion's attempt to attack Morsbronn (les Bains) in a letter to the author dated 8 February 1988:

> The Americans had captured a nearby village. The general in charge of the sector ordered the Jagdtiger to attack the village or bring it under fire. Our commander wanted to begin the attack shortly before dusk, the last "shooting light", when the fighter-bombers could no longer take off. It was always done this way because of the American air supremacy. But the general knew better! The [3./schwere Panzerjäger-Abteilung 653] had to move out. It left the assembly area near Höllenhof and moved uphill. I remember it distinctly, because I was a forward observer with a radio operator in a vineyard. I was to keep Oberleutnant Wiesenfarth apprised of the situation, since the 2./schwere Panzerjäger-Abteilung 653 was in an ambush position and would eventually join the attack. What we feared would happen, happened. The [3./schwere Panzerjäger-Abteilung 653] was barely underway when a swarm of fighter-bombers and artillery spotter aircraft appeared. Our comrades were blanketed with fire. They streamed back, having fired only a few rounds into the high ground. Leutnant Knack's Jagdtiger was bombed by 4 fighter-bombers and only an enormous cloud of dust could be seen. I thought: "Good night, Knack!" The vehicle came moving out of the dust cloud. He later told me the tank destroyer had rocked like a ship on the high seas. I do not remember how many total losses we had, but I watched everything through my binoculars.

Oberleutnant Franz Kretschmer's Jagdtiger 301 received a direct hit in the radio operator's hatch near Höllenhof on 16 March 1945 and burnt out. The radio operator, Hans Sager, suffered serious burns. The driver, Unteroffizier Heinrich Appel, was wounded by shrapnel. Jagdtiger 314 (Porsche chassis) was abandoned due to a damaged final drive and destroyed by the crew after the optics were removed. Feldwebel Heinz Telgmann's Jagdtiger 332 also had to be abandoned.

On the afternoon of 16 March 1945, the 1./schwere Panzerjäger-Abteilung 653 occupied positions between Gunstett and Surbourg. Oberleutnant Haberland succeeded there in knocking out a Sherman and an American howitzer. Here is an excerpt from the citation for Oberleutnant Haberland's German Cross in Gold (Source: Federal Archives/ Freiburg Military Archives):

> . . . Oberleutnant Haberland, who has since been distinguished by a promotion to this rank and appointed company commander, received a mission while operating with the 47. Volks-Grenadier-Division on 16 March 1945, in the area between Hagenau and Weißenburg, to deploy his company's 7 Jagdtiger to prevent the enemy from crossing the Sauer River and screen an orderly withdrawal of friendly elements. The enemy attack, with exceptionally powerful armor and infantry forces along the Laubach-Gunstett road, halted when the tank destroyers immediately opened fire. During this operation, Oberleutnant Haberland knocked out a Sherman with his gun and destroyed an enemy howitzer as it was moving into position shortly thereafter with a direct hit. The enemy then pulled his tanks and infantry forces back over a hill to renew the attack on Kampfgruppe Haberland from the north and southeast. A timely warning by radio to the group's elements positioned on both those flanks prevented the enemy from crossing the Sauer there as well. This prevented the enemy from successfully advancing into withdrawing friendly forces from the south. Thanks to the unprecedented aggressiveness

and perseverance of Oberleutnant Haberland and his Kampfgruppe, the extremely dangerous enemy penetration was delayed, so that the friendly withdrawal was conducted according to plan and without enemy interference on the following night.

Only 13 Jagdtigers were capable of conducting a road march during the withdrawal from the forward areas of the Westwall (Siegfried Line). The remaining 21 Jagdtigers had to move by rail transport or by large-scale towing operations to the new maintenance area at Bellheim, near Germersheim. During this withdrawal, Loader Herbert Scholz 2./schwere Panzerjäger-Abteilung 653) was killed during an artillery barrage when a shell exploded in the tree branches. The same company also lost Jagdtiger. Unteroffizier Neidler's vehicle had to be destroyed just outside of Weißenburg.

There were many fighter-bomber attacks against the Jagdtiger between Queichheim, Offenbach (Pfalz) and Dreihof. Unteroffizier Karl Hermann and Gefreiter Leopold Kroker, both from the 2./schwere Panzerjäger-Abteilung 653, were killed. In Besigheim, Jagdtiger 213 was destroyed due to final-drive damage, after the radio and gun optics were removed. Jagdtiger 234 was abandoned in Zeiskam, outside of Germersheim, due to the same problem.

Telegram dated 23 March 1945 (Source: Federal Archives/Freiburg Military Archives):

SECRET COMMAND MATTER

TO: Inspector General of Armored Forces, Operations, Force Structure

SUBJECT: Movement of schwere Panzerjäger-Abteilung 653 from the Hagenau Area

The officer sent to schwere Panzerjäger-Abteilung 653 by Commander-in-Chief in the West, Oberstleutnant (Ing.) Meyer, reported the following about the movement of the battalion:

1) The battalion's operational strength prior to 18 March 1945 was 41 Jagdtiger. During withdrawal from the main battle area, 7 Jagdtiger had to be destroyed forward of the Westwall, since recovery was not possible. On 18 March 1945, the operational strength was 34 Jagdtiger. Of these (from 18–21 March 1945):

   a) 18 operational vehicles were sent to the new area of operations; 5 by rail and 13 by road march.

   b) 16 damaged tanks sent to the new maintenance area at Bellheim, near Germersheim, by expedited rail movement or by towing. (1 Jagdtiger destroyed at the last possible moment, after removal of optics and other valuable equipment, due to the approaching enemy).

2) The damaged tank destroyers and heavy vehicles transported to Bellheim, including 4 Flakpanzer IV's and 2 18-ton prime movers, were rail loaded in Bellheim and Rhinezabern during the night of 21/22 March for transport to Grabenneudorf. Rail loading material was available.

3) Fuel shortages did not occur during the entire transport operation; fuel requirements for the 18 combat operational Jagdtiger were not investigated during the presence of Oberstleutnant Mayer. With a fuel consumption of 1 cubic meter per Jagdtiger, the total consump-

tion of the combat operational Jagdtiger was only 18 cubic meters. Allocation of an initial 90 cubic meters of gasoline fuel for 4 consumption sets. Further allocation of 125 cubic meters will enable the battalion to perform its assigned missions.

Commander-in-Chief in the West

Chief-of-Staff

/signed/ Westphal

General der Kavallerie

Telegram dated 23 March 1945 (Source: Federal Archives/Freiburg Military Archives):

SECRET COMMAND MATTER

TO: Inspector General of Armored Forces, Command Section, Force Structure (Zeppelin)

REFERENCE: Report from the Stopa at Heeresgruppe G

SUBJECT: schwere Panzerjäger-Abteilung 653

Armored vehicle status (as of 2000 hours, 22 March 1945): Operational 31; completely combat ready 2–3; evacuated by expedited rail 9 (1 in long-term maintenance) remainder in short-term maintenance; some long-term maintenance. Operational status may have changed by 2 during the night of 22/23 March 1945 due to demolition. Report urgent: Two-week mechanical overhaul needed for all vehicles.

Commander-in-Chief in the West

Operations/Armor Liaison Officer

No. 726/45 (SECRET COMMAND MATTER)

/signed/ Zimmermann

Generalmajor

Those elements of the battalion moving through Weißenburg (Wissembourg) received orders at Bad Bergzabern to delay the pursuing American armored spearheads. This succeeded with a substantial number of American tanks knocked out. The battalion reported 25 enemy tanks destroyed between Neustadt an der Weinstraße and Ludwigshafen. A Kampfgruppe from the 3./schwere Panzerjäger-Abteilung 653, under the command of Leutnant Kaspar Göggerle, wreaked havoc on an American tank column at Neustadt an der Weinstraße on 22 March 1945. At the same time, however, Jagdtiger 331 (chassis number 305020) and Jagdtiger 323 had to be abandoned due to mechanical problems.

A Kampfgruppe from the 2./schwere Panzerjäger-Abteilung 653 occupied firing positions in the town of Böhl on 21 March 1945 and waited there for the advancing American forces. The American attack, supported by tanks, began at 0800 hours on the morning of 22 March 1945. Leutnant Feineisen knocked out 6 tanks with his Jagdtiger. Unteroffizier Hagelstein reported 3 tanks knocked out, and Unteroffizier Kohns destroyed 2 halftracks. Two halftracks were captured and 13 American soldiers taken prisoner.

Leutnant Feineisen's Jagdtiger was towed away because of engine damage, but it was repaired in the woods near Iggelheim and sent back into combat again. Heavy fighting took place in Böhl, including bitter close-in fighting directly involving the Jagdtiger. Leutnant Feineisen was wounded twice. Feldwebel Löh had to give up his Jagdtiger and blew it up in Böhl. Unteroffizier Hagelstein's Jagdtiger received a direct artillery hit in the engine compartment at Iggelheim and burned out.

A Kampfgruppe from the 1./schwere Panzerjäger-Abteilung 653 under Oberleutnant Werner Haberland had success at Schifferstadt. Two American halftracks were swept completely off the road with one

12.8-centimeter antitank round from the Jagdtiger of Oberfeldwebel Gustav Koss. Here is another excerpt from the award recommendation for Oberleutnant Haberland's German Cross in Gold:

> . . . On 22 March 1945, the 3 tank destroyers in Kampfgruppe Haberland received the mission of covering the area around the Speyer Bridgehead and Schifferstadt and preventing the enemy from penetrating at all costs. Oberleutnant Haberland positioned his Jagdtiger on the roads approaching Schifferstadt from the north, northeast and east in such a manner as to decisively interdict the anticipated enemy advance and halt it. Around 0200 hours in the morning, two enemy halftracks appeared at a distance of 50 to 100 meters. One round took care of both of them. During the period that followed, the enemy refrained from conducting another probe or attack. During the late afternoon, Oberleutnant Haberland observed American armored vehicles assembling for an attack in the woods between Dannstadt and Mutterstadt. He immediately opened fire with his main gun and seriously damaged 2 enemy tanks, which had to be towed back to the rear. The rest turned back as well. Thanks to his decisiveness, Oberleutnant Haberland also succeeded in holding this sector so that the main line of resistance could be withdrawn during the next night without any incidents. This success deserves even more recognition because Oberleutnant Haberland had only limited infantry support and, despite heavy artillery fire and enemy air attacks, held on persistently until the last German elements withdrew.

Oberleutnant Werner Haberland, Company Commander of the 1./schwere Panzerjäger-Abteilung 653, was wounded during a fighter-bomber attack on 23 March 1945 and taken to a field hospital. In his place, Hauptmann Maximilian Wirsching—formerly of schwere Panzer-Abteilung 507, where he had been awarded the Knight' s Cross on 7 February 1945—took command of the company several days later and remained there until mid-April 1945. After that, Oberleutnant Haberland resumed command of the company again. The Jagdtiger of Kampfgruppe Haberland crossed the Rhine at Speyer on 22 March 1945. These included several tank destroyers from the 1. and, presumably, the 2./schwere Panzerjäger-Abteilung 653.

The damaged tank destroyers from the battalion bought back to the Bellheim area were loaded aboard waiting rail cars during the night of 22–23 March 1945 and then transported across the Rhine Bridge at Germersheim. All the battalion's other vehicles crossed the Rhine by 24 March 1945. The bridge was then blown up.

The battalion assembled its operational vehicles in the woods at Graben-Neudorf. The damaged vehicles requiring long-term maintenance were transported to Leonberg, near Stuttgart, where the Maintenance Company had been moved. Elements of the 1. and 2./schwere Panzerjäger-Abteilung 653 occupied positions in the Wiesental/Kronau area. Individual vehicles from all three companies occupied the threshing-machine warehouse in Unteröwisheim, where the Maintenance Company repaired them. On 27 March 1945, the battalion received the following order (excerpted):

Corps Order No. 8
Headquarters, XIII. SS-Armee-Korps
Corps Headquarters, 27 March 1945
Operations, No. 43/45 (SECRET)
    1) . . .
    2) . . .
    3) Schwere Panzerjäger-Abteilung 653, assembled in the area east of Kirrlach, will remain there, in the sector of the 47. Volks-Grenadier-Division and the 2. Gebirgsjäger-Division [2nd Mountain Division], working closely with both divisions to destroy enemy tanks that might pen-

etrate the sector. Additionally, reconnoiter for possible operations in a northerly direction in the Rhine Plain or foothills up to the Neckar River.

(Source: Federal Archives/Freiburg Military Archives)

The American forces, which had created a strong bridgehead at Oppenheim on 22 March 1944, advanced continuously towards the Rhine-Neckar triangle at this point, containing the cities of Mannheim and Heidelberg. Mannheim was under heavy American artillery fire on 28 March 1945 and capitulated on 29 March 1945. The LXXX. Armee-Korps, under the command of General der Infanterie Beyer, contained the following information in its daily logs on 28 and 29 March 1945 (excerpted):

28 March 1945:

Headquarters 1. Armee has authorized a new front line, which will run as follows in the evening:

Contact point at intersection 1.5 kilometers east of Großsachsen-Schriesheim-Ladenburg-Neckar Canal to Seckenheim-Altrip-Rhine River. Due to the situation, [this headquarters] will receive the following attachments during the late afternoon of 28 March: schwere Panzerjäger-Abteilung 653 with 8 operational Jagdpanzer VI's (Jagdtiger). The battalion will be attached to the 559. Volks-Grenadier-Division, but it will deploy on the southern bank of the Neckar River.

On the morning of 28 March, [this headquarters] received operational remnants of Sturmgeschütz-Brigade 280 (3 operational assault guns) in the woods 1.5 km east of Schatthausen, but they could not be committed because of insufficient fuel.

Excerpt from 29 March 1945:

Attacking south through and east of Schriesheim, the enemy pushed to the east of Dossenheim and turned west there towards Dossenheim, which was able to repulse all attacks from the northwest, also those from Rosenhof, by evening.

Two enemy tanks advancing south-southeast from Ladenburg to Schabenheim were repulsed. Attacking out of his bridgehead southwest of Ladenburg before noon, the enemy advanced on Neckarhausen, which we had recaptured during the night, and retook it. Enemy forces entering Edingen were pushed out by a counterattack supported by our Jagdtiger. An attack on Friedrichsfeld, supported by 4 amphibious tanks, was blocked with high friendly losses. South of Feudenheim, the enemy has been crossing the Neckar continuously at the power plant since the early afternoon. He is advancing along the highway up to the intersection southwest of Seckenheim, where our artillery fires upon him constantly.

The development of the situation forces us to occupy a smaller position during the night. The 559. Volks-Grenadier-Division will leave combat outposts behind on the northern bank and withdraw to the southern bank of the Neckar. The 198. Infanterie-Division will fall back to the Wieblingen-Grenzhof-Rhineall line.

Three Jagdtiger under the command of Leutnant Hans Knippenberg (1./schwere Panzerjäger-Abteilung 653) were ordered into combat at Heidelberg (Schwetzingen) to delay the American advance from Mannheim. The tank destroyers arrived in Schwetzingen around noon on 30 March 1945. The American armored spearhead reached the city earlier than anticipated and immediately engaged the Jagdtiger in combat. Leutnant Knippenberg's Jagdtiger 115—an unusual vehicle number inasmuch as it was not part of the battalion's numbering system and no explanation can be found for its use—got stuck at the edge of a field in northern Schwetzingen and the vehicle was immobilized. The crew—Leutnant Hans Knippenberg, Driver Hermann Looft, Radioman Hans Distler, Gunner Heinrich Schäfer and the two loaders (unknown)—blow up the vehicle and fire a Panzerfaust at it. The crew escaped without any personnel losses and fought its way through to the German lines at Sandhausen.

The second tank destroyer—Jagdtiger 131—rolled in front of the gun barrels of the American armored spearhead in downtown Schwetzingen and was knocked out at extremely close range (about 200 meters). It caught fire immediately. The driver, Alfred Hertel, was thrown out of the driver's hatch and only slightly injured. The gunner, Fritz Klein, was killed by machine-gun fire while evacuating the tank. The radio operator (identity unknown) died later of serious burns in a British field hospital. The other crewmembers survived the explosion, some with burns (Commander, Oberfeldwebel Kinnberger; Loader 1, Hermann Vielberth; Loader 2, ?).

The third Jagdtiger succeeded in escaping Schwetzingen and moved to Eppelheim, just outside of Heidelberg. While attempting to occupy a position there along the Mannheim-Heidelberg main road, it was hit in the track. It proved impossible to repair the track while under enemy fire, so the crew abandoned the Jagdtiger after blowing it up. The crew succeeded in reaching German lines near Sandhausen without any loss. (Crew: Commander, Oberfeldwebel Gustav Koss; Driver, Unteroffizier Fritz Poischen; Radio operator, ?; Gunner, Unteroffizier Horst Molkenthin; Loader 1, Obergefreiter Kurt Meins; Loader 2, ?; and Gefreiter Hermann Looft, who was riding on top of the vehicle.)

Telegram dated 30 March 1945 (Source: Federal Archives/Freiburg Military Archives):

TO: Inspector General for Armored Forces

— SECRET —

Armored vehicle status of schwere Panzerjäger-Abteilung 653 is currently 28 Jagdtiger. Currently operational: 6 Jagdtiger. Currently in short-term maintenance: 12 Jagdtiger. Currently in long-term maintenance: 10 Jagdtiger.

New losses since 25 March 1945: 6 Jagdtiger.

1 tank destroyer operational at the maintenance facility. An additional Jagdtiger ready for issue. Early on 29 March 1945, 10 Jagdtiger with long-term mechanical problems departed by rail to the Maintenance Company in Stuttgart.

On 29 March 1945, 1 truck with 4 Porsche roadwheel arm sets arrived in Bretten from the Nibelungen Works.

1 truck with final drives broke down near [Bad] Cannstatt; search party underway.

Headquarters, Heeresgruppe G

Senior Quartermaster

V/Armor

Log Entry 221/45

30 March 1945

/signed/ Harder

Major

A Jagdtiger from the 3./schwere Panzerjäger-Abteilung 653 (Driver: Walter Alberts) suffered a total loss on 31 March 1945 in Unteröwisheim. While repairing the air pre-cleaner on a tank destroyer, oxygen was sprayed into the pipe fitting instead of the required compressed air. A tremendous explosion completely destroyed the vehicle. Soldiers Herbert Wirsing (Gunner), Günther Schröder (Loader) and Feldwebel Alexander Kurat were killed.

Two Jagdtiger from the 1./schwere Panzerjäger-Abteilung 653 were ordered to screen towards Neckar-Enz on 3 April 1945. Feldwebel Reinhold Schlabs, a tank-destroyer commander with the 1./schwere Panzerjäger-Abteilung 653 wrote the following about this mission:

Leutnant Knippenberg and I went through Eppingen to Kirchardt to conduct the screen. My tank destroyer broke down with steering problems at the entrance to Kirchardt. It remained well camouflaged on the street because of heavy air activity. Leutnant Knippenberg and Unteroffizier Kohns' vehicle towed it back to Eppingen during the evening. There, Leutnant Knippenberg's Jagdtiger broke down with the same problem. Both vehicles remained in Eppingen and were to be recovered by maintenance personnel or picked up by flatbed trucks. Night arrived, but neither of these two options occurred. Then loud track noises announced the arrival of tanks from the west. There was no remaining hope for repairing or recovering the Jagdtiger. The tank destroyers were blown up after all [sensitive items] had been removed.

Telegram dated 7 April 1945 (Source: Federal Archives/Freiburg Military Archives):

TO: Inspector general of Armored Forces
Army Headquarters/Headquarters (Zeppelin)
— SECRET —
[SUBJECT:] Jagdtiger situation of schwere Panzerjäger-Abteilung 653 on 3 April 1945
    23 operational; 1 short-term [repair; 11 long-term [repair]. 11 new losses since 1 April 1945. 5 total losses since 1 April 1945
    Repair times cannot be determined; maintenance elements relocating and recovery difficulties. Last repair parts arrived from Nibelungen Works on 30 March 1945 at 1800 hours.
    Commander-in-Chief in the West
    Quartermaster, V/IP
    11126/SECRET
    /signed/ Mayer
    Oberstleutnant

The remainder of the battalion's withdrawal did not take place as a consolidated unit. Individually, or in small groups, the commanders attempted to bring their Jagdtiger through Kraichgau towards the Neckar-Enz position (between Heilbronn and Ludwigsburg). On 3 April 1945, the battalion command post was in Cleebronn. From there, individual vehicles were ordered into combat at Nordheim/Klingenberg, to fight the advancing American and French forces. Particularly heavy fighting took place with elements of the French 5th Armored Division (Battle Group 5) for the small village of Klingenberg. One Jagdtiger was destroyed during the fighting on 5 April 1945, and another Jagdtiger was blown up due to mechanical problems on the afternoon of the same day.

A Jagdtiger from the 2./schwere Panzerjäger-Abteilung 653 under Unteroffizier Peter Kohns had to be blown up at Lauffen am Neckar, because the vehicle could not be recovered. The withdrawal continued through Besigheim, Bietigheim, Bissingen, Marbach am Neckar, Backnang and Welzheim, where the command post of the 2./schwere Panzerjäger-Abteilung 653 was located on 7 April 1945.

A Kampfgruppe from the battalion was committed near Crailsheim on 7 April 1945 and destroyed many enemy tanks there, succeeding in stabilizing that sector of the front. Elements of the battalion did not begin withdrawing from Schwäbisch Hall until 13 April 1945, moving through Gaildorf, Aalen and Nördlingen. On 20 April 1945, the battalion command post was in Schweindorf, near Nördlingen. Orders arrived there that directed all crews without tanks to immediately move to Linz to pick up new Jagdtiger from the Nibelungen Works.

Telegram dated 17 April 1945 (Source: Federal Archives/Freiburg Military Archives):

COPIES FORWARDED TO:
   1) Army Issue Point Linz
   2) Commander-in-Chief in the West (INFO)
   3) General der Panzertruppen West/Army Headquarters/Army General Staff (Force Structure)

. . .

The vehicles at the Army Issue Point Linz (Nibelungen Works)—3 Jagdtigers—are assigned to schwere Panzerjäger-Abteilung 653.

Commander-in-Chief in the West is requested to coordinate transfer and transport with Army Issue Point Linz. Transfer will be reported by vehicle number by telegram to In 6 (Army Headquarters) and the Inspector General of Armored Forces.

Inspector General of Armored Forces/Sec. Org. K Nr. F 2000/45 (SECRET)

Salzburg was simultaneously designated as the new assembly area, where initial staff elements arrived on 11 April 1945. All Jagdtiger with long- and short-term repair work were transported by rail to the Maintenance Company at Leonberg, near Stuttgart. The battalion assembled there, and the guns were repaired as completely as the replacement parts situation permitted. American fighter-bombers conducted a heavy attack against the maintenance company on 8 April 1945. Many of the Maintenance Company's personnel and crewmembers were seriously wounded. Feldwebel Max Müller, Gun Commander in the 2./schwere Panzerjäger-Abteilung 653, was killed.

The vehicle situation in the battalion on 15 April 1945 clearly indicated the condition of the guns. Telegram dated 15 April 1945 (Source: Federal Archives/Freiburg Military Archives):

TO: Inspector General of Armored Forces/Army Headquarters/Army General Staff

— SECRET —

1) Combat vehicle status in schwere Panzerjäger-Abteilung 653: Assigned 17; Operational 5; Short-term [repair] 6; Long-term [repair] 6.

2) Recovery equipment situation (armored): Assigned 4; Operational 1; Short-term [repair] 2; Long-term [repair] 1.

3) Due to fuel shortages, movement to assembly areas in Ziesar and Nibelungen Works was not possible until 15 March 1945.

4) Critical parts needed immediately: 3 sets of tracks for 5 tanks; 3 sets of tracks for Jagdtiger IIb (Henschel chassis); 2 sets of tracks for Jagdtiger IIb (Porsche chassis).

Headquarters, Heeresgruppe G

Senior Quartermaster

V/Armored Vehicle Report

253/45 (SECRET), dated 15 April 1945

Operations

Fischer

Major

On 15 April 1945, Major Rudolf Grillenberger relinquished command of the battalion. His successor was Knight's Cross recipient Major Rolf Fromme (schwere Panzer-Abteilung 503). Leutnant Eichhorn became the new adjutant.

Elements of the battalion withdrew towards the Alps through Ulm, Vöhringen, Illertissen, Fürstenfeldbruck, Munich and Rosenheim. Many Jagdtiger were blown up in the Rosenheim and Bad Aibling areas due to mechanical problems (mostly drive train damage). One Jagdtiger from the 2./schwere Panzerjäger-Abteilung 653—Gun Commander: Leutnant Rudolf Braun—collapsed the Mangfall Bridge at Kolbermoor while crossing it and had to be abandoned there. The crew was uninjured. Other elements of the battalion made it to Lake Amm and destroyed their vehicles there (exiting at Etterschlag). The remainder of the Flak Platoon and Headquarters Company made it to Trallenstein and Schneitzelreuth, where they destroyed their last Flakpanzer IV. The Motor Sergeant in the Maintenance Company, Wilhelm Bohlen, wrote about the end of this part of the maintenance unit in a letter to the author dated 4 August 1989:

We received new tank destroyers with 12.8-centimeter main guns in Döllersheim and went west with them in December 1944. The Maintenance Company unloaded in Zweibrücken. We arrived too late for the Ardennes Offensive and therefore were only involved in the fighting during the withdrawal in the Westwall area. We were in Herxheim, near Landau, for several weeks and then withdrew back across the Rhine at Germersheim.

The remainder of the withdrawal took place incrementally through April 1945, passing through Stuttgart and Munich to Chiemig on Lake Chiem, where the Maintenance Company was dissolved. In order to escape the [Soviets], we took so me vehicles west again to the Ebersberg Forest. Our company commander, Oberleutnant Schulte, was surprised there by the Americans and captured. I was just able to escape into the woods. Unteroffizier Schork and Unteroffizier Sälzer, as well as my driver, Obergefreiter Buss, were with me. After several days, we were already in civilian clothes and traveling west on bicycles. The Americans stopped us and took us prisoner. I was held in Guting and Fürstenfeldbruck until the end of July 1945, and then released as a "Bavarian farmhand".

The elements of the battalion that arrived in Salzburg were assigned to Heeresgruppe Süd on 2 May 1945. They were to transfer from Salzburg to Linz. The holding area was near Henndorf (battalion command post)/Neumarkt. Elements of the supply company were at St. Gilgen.

Battalion Order
Duplicate

PRIORITY   1st Copy
2 May 1945
TO:
Headquarters, 1. Armee
Heeresgruppe Süd (INFO)
schwere Panzerjäger-Abteilung 653 (INFO)

. . .

Schwere Panzerjäger-Abteilung 653 is immediately allocated to Heeresgruppe Süd. It will move by road march through Salzburg to Linz. Advance party [is to report to] the 487th Staff (Linz) to establish contact with Heeresgruppe Süd from there.

Fuel for the movement will be provided by the Inspector General of Armored forces in direct coordination with Heeresgruppe Süd.

Commander-in-Chief in the West
Operations/Armor Liaison Officer
No. 5483/45 (SECRET COMMAND MATTER), 2 May 1945
/signed/ Zimmermann
Generalmajor

schwere Panzerjäger-Abteilung 653   Battalion Command Post, 2 May 1945

2335 hours
Battalion Movement Order
New Operational Area

1) In accordance with Commander-in-Chief in the West, Operations No. 4583/45 (SECRET COMMAND MATTER), dated 2 May 1945, the battalion has been allocated to Heeresgruppe Süd effective immediately. It will move by road march through Salzburg to Linz. [It will i]nitially occupy a holding area in the Henndorf-Seckisches Land-Neumarkt area northeast of Salzburg.

Elements of the supply company in St. Gilgen will remain there for the time being.

2) Reconnaissance Platoon, together with advance parties from the Headquarters Company, Supply Company, Maintenance Company and Recovery Platoon will reconnoiter the assigned area on 3 May 1945 for the entire battalion in accordance with oral orders from the adjutant. Reconnaissance Platoon will prepare a diagram of the area assigning unit portions.

Advance parties will report to Leutnant Christern at 0545 hours on 3 May 1945. Departure at 0600 hours.

3) Battalion Command Post in Henndorf. Contact Point in the courthouse or mayor's office.

4) Jagdtiger 312 and 324, including Unteroffizier Reimann's recovery group, 3 maintenance groups and one Kfz. 100 from the Maintenance Company (with final drives) will move to the new area during the night. Group commander is Oberleutnant Kretschmer.

5) Remaining elements of the battalion will move to the assigned area starting at 0800 hours on 3 May 1945 in the following order of march:

Battle Staff—Platoon A—Headquarters Company—Supply Elements (including 1st and 2nd)—Maintenance Group—remainder of Recovery Platoon. Maintenance Company will also move at 0800 hours. March group commanders: Company Commanders, Werkmeister Adam for the Maintenance Company.

March security (and trail element): Baurat Schaffranek.

6) The crews designated to take over Jagdtiger at Linz will remain ready at all times.

. . .

The end of the war for the majority of the battalion came at Bad Ischl/Pötschenpaß. Elements of the Supply Company and the Maintenance Company and the two remaining Jagdtiger were in Lieaen (Steiermark region of Austria) and were captured there by the Americans. Schwere Panzerjäger-Abteilung 653 ceased to exist on 8 May 1945. Crews without tank destroyers, who had been ordered to the Nibelungen Works, ended the war at the works, which were officially closed on 4 May 1945. The 8 Jagdtiger there were blown up by Leutnant Hans Knippenberg.

Several crews from schwere Panzerjäger-Abteilung 653 were able to escape with new Jagdtiger and were employed with a Waffen-SS Kampfgruppe. The Kampfgruppe was loaded aboard six-axle, heavy-load flat cars on 30 April 1945 for transport from St. Valentin to St. Leonhard am Forst, reaching its destination at dawn on 1 May 1945. The 4 Jagdtiger were placed under the command of an SS-Hauptsturmführer (captain) from the 1. SS-Panzer-Division "Leibstandarte SS Adolf Hitler". A former Jagdtiger commander with the 1./schwere Panzerjäger-Abteilung 653, Feldwebel Reinhold Schlabs, provided the follow first-hand account about the final combat efforts with operational Jagdtiger in a letter to the author dated 22 January 1991:

Two crews that departed immediately arrived at the Nibelungen Works simultaneously with two other crews from an unknown unit, including two Leutnants. The four crews were assigned to a Kampfgruppe under the command of an SS-Hauptsturmführer from the [1. SS-Panzer-Division "Leibstandarte SS Adolf Hitler"].

The 4 Jagdtiger rail loaded on 30 April 1945. We were to move to St. Pölten. The six-axle, heavy-load flat cars had to be hydraulically lifted onto rail cars at Wieselburg, because of the narrow-gauge rail line to St. Leonhard. Then we continued to St. Leonhard am Forst, reaching it at the first light of dawn on 1 May 1945. After unloading, the group advanced along the St. Pölten-Linz road. The planned operation at St. Pölten did not take place, because the Russians had already broken through the front.

The Jagdtiger moved in staggered intervals along the St. Pölten-Linz road towards Amstetten. A Jagdtiger under Feldwebel Golinski broke down at the bridge crossing the Ybbs and had to remain behind. The crew climbed aboard the other tank destroyers. Despite a roadblock in Amstetten, we succeeded in bypassing the marketplace, which was already occupied by Americans and Russians. The march continued to Strengberg.

The road climbed around a curve there and was filled by buses from a field post office. Progress was very slow up the mountain. Then 2 Russian tanks positioned themselves directly across the road at the entrance to Strengberg. The war was over. I must remark however, that our vehicles picked up many civilians during the march, who saw us as an opportunity to escape to the west.

Entries in the personal diary of Unteroffizier Peter Kohns concerning the final chapter of the battalion's history. Kohns was a gun commander in the 2./schwere Panzerjäger-Abteilung 653. He describes the march routes, operations and losses of the battalion. (Individual dates are not identical to the battalion as a whole in all situations.)

12 October 1944: Detached to commander's course for the Königstiger in Paderborn. Depart at 1420 hours through Göpfritz-Gmünd-Budweis-Pilsen-Marienbad.

13 October 1944: Continued through Eger [Cheb]-Plauen-Leipzig-Halle-Hildesheim-Hanover-Hameln-Altenbeken-Paderborn. To the Panzer post: 1st Tiger Company—training courses.

27 October 1944: Training completed.

28 October 1944: Departed Paderborn to return to my company.

1 November 1944: Arrived at the company.

1 December 1944: On a detail to Grafenwöhr.

2 December 1944: Arrived at Grafenwöhr.

7 December 1944: With Feldwebel Müller; transporting 3 Jagdtiger back to the company.

11 December 1944: Returned to the company in Göpfritz during the evening. [3./schwere Panzerjäger-Abteilung 653] rail loading.

12 December 1944: To Zwettl to pick up Volkswagen [staff cars].

30 December 1944: 1st Platoon received movement orders.

31 December 1944: Departed with my crew at 1535 hours through Göpfritz-Sigmundsherberg-Krems-Herzogenburg to Pottenbrunn. Remained for the night in our old quarters. Celebrated New Year's Eve. Crew at St. Pölten. Commander, Unteroffizier Peter Kohns; Gunner, Obergefreiter Sepp Gschwendtner; Loader 1, Michael Fischhaber; Loader 2, Josef Menke; Driver, ?; Radio operator, ?

1 January 1945: Continued to Linz at 2200 hours.

2 January 1945: To Tank Issue Point. Picked up a tank destroyer at noon.

3 January 1945: Departed Linz for Wels at 0300 hours. Continued through Amstetten to St. Pölten. Arrived at 2100 hours.

4 January 1945: Continued at 0204 hours through Herzogenburg-Tulln. Continued at 0700 hours to Göpfritz. Arrived at 1200 hours.

5 January 1945: Picked up a tank destroyer. Chassis number 300037; vehicle number 214.

12 January 1945: Gunnery practice at the Groß Poppen Range. Canceled due to fog.

15 January 1945: The entire company received movement orders.

17 January 1945: 3rd Platoon and Group Commander rail load.

18 January 1945: Second transport ready to load. Unteroffizier Schelers' Jagdtiger (driver) went off the rail car. Pulled back up with 4 Jagdtiger.

19 January 1945: Complete loading the 2nd transport. Everything continued smoothly for us. Departed at 1500 hours through Sigmundsherberg-Tulln-Herzogenburg-St. Pölten.

20 January 1945: Linz-Wels-Hattnang. In Seekirchen-Mattsee (14 kilometers outside of Salzburg). Halted from 1200–2400 hours due to air raid alert.

21 January 1945: Continued at 0130 hours through Salzburg-Rosenheim-Munich-Augsburg. Unteroffizier Sprott's car delayed 30 minutes outside of Rosenheim due to overheating. Halted outside of and in Augsburg due to air raid alerts.

22 January 1945: Ulm-Sigmaringen-Immendingen-Donaueschingen-Villingen-Hallsach.

23 January 1945: Offenburg-Bühl (Baden). Unloaded and replaced tracks. Gunnery lever broke off. Remained there overnight.

24 January 1945: Replaced gunnery lever and left front shock absorber. Continued through Hatzenweier and Unzhurst to Muckenschopf. Private quarters.

25 January 1945: Company crossed the Rhine. My Jagdtiger was in good condition. Moved to the tank ferry at Momprechtshofen towards evening. Crossed the Rhine without incident. Defective final drives 1 kilometer farther. Unteroffizier Neidler towed us to Offendorf. Halted in front of the tank ford.

26 January 1945: Replaced bolts on final drives. Changed positions in the town.

27 January 1945: On reconnaissance mission with Leutnant Feineisen. Prepared to move.

28 January 1945: Depart at 0430 yours, moving through Herrlisheim and Drusenheim to Sessenheim.

29 January 1945: Together with Feldwebel Müller, towed Feldwebel Ernst Markmann's Jagdtiger [1./schwere Panzerjäger-Abteilung 653] through Dalhunden, past Drusenheim and across the Rhine Embankment at 0200 hours. A Jagdtiger from the 1./schwere Panzerjäger-Abteilung 653 ran off the embankment twice. Pulled up again. Returned with the Rhine ferry. Continued to Momprechtshofen. Artillery shell exploded next to the recovery platoon near the town outskirts at 1730 hours. Gefreiter Rudolf Blüher was killed. Continued through Gamshurst-Unzhurst and Hatzenweier to Bühl. One Jagdtiger from the 1./schwere Panzerjäger-Abteilung 653 remained in Gamshurst.

30 January 1945: Through Hatzenweier to Breithurst. Occupied positions in a forest.

31 January 1945: Obergefreiter Gschwendtner with advance party.

3 February 1945: Made preparations and ready to move. Delayed.

4 February 1945: Ready to move at 1800 hours. Departed at 2130 hours. Jagdtiger 211 ran out of fuel short of Hatzenweier.

5 February 1945: Arrived in Bühl at 0300 hours. Rail loaded at 0900 hours. Departed at 1000 hours. Rested in Karlsruhe. Three soldiers wounded in Karlsruhe-Hagersfeld while playing around with a Panzerfaust. Germersheim-Lustadt-Hochstadt (Pfalz)-Landau-Rohrbach-Kandel.

6 February 1945: Unloaded and moved to Erlenbach. Unteroffizier Paillard's Flak mount had to be towed.

17 February 1945: Ready to move. Departed at 2200 hours for Kandel.

18 February 1945: Weißenburg-Sulz [Soultz]-Surburg [Surbourg]-Kreuzeckwald.

19 February 1945: Continued at 0630 hours to Gunstett-Eberbach. Occupied positions 3 kilometers outside of Reichshofen (Shirlenhof). Constructed bunkers during the intervening time. Dismounted reconnaissance patrols. Unteroffizier Koch seriously wounded.

15 March 1945: Moved forward to the assault position. Unteroffizier Neidler slightly wounded. Unteroffizier Gebele and Unteroffizier Schwarz seriously wounded.

16 March 1945: Moved back to 1 kilometer outside of Eberbach under half power (broken spring). Feldwebel Wilhelm Löh and Feldwebel Brieller helped me cross a bomb crater. Brieller continued towing alone. Through Gunstett to Kreuzeckwald.

17 March 1945: Repaired vehicle and pulled it under cover. Artillery attacked towards evening. Scholz killed. Some seriously wounded. Changed positions through Surburg [Surbourg]-Sulz [Soultz]-Schöneburg [Schoenenbourg]. Problems with the small universal joint on the far side of town. Continued moving slowly. Unteroffizier Neidler blew up his Jagdtiger.

18 March 1945: Occupied firing position in Weißenburg in the military barracks at 0300 hours. Small universal joint repaired. Towed the commander's gun to Windhof during the evening. From there through Schweigen to Bad Bergzabern.

19 March 1945: Arrived during the morning. First occupied quarters at the train station, then at Hotel Westenhöfer.

20 March 1945: Impflingen-Landau-Queichheim. Attacked by fighter-bombers on the far side of town. A bomb landed directly beside Feldwebel Wilhelm Löh's tank destroyer. Offenbach (Pfalz). Occupied positions in a patch of woods between Offenbach and Dreihof.

Unteroffizier Hermann and Gefreiter Kroker killed by fighter-bombers at 1300 hours. Continued at 2000 hours through Dreihof, Essingen, Groß Fischlingen and Altdorf.

21 March 1945: Venningen-Lachen-Speyerdorf. Then occupied a patch of woods. Continued in the morning to Haßloch and Böhl. Occupy firing positions in Böhl.

22 March 1945: Still in the old position. Americans attacked at 0800 hours. Leutnant Feineisen knocked out 6 tanks. Unteroffizier Hagelstein knocked out 3 tanks. All Shermans. I knocked out 2 [armored cars], captured 2 [armored cars] and took 13 prisoners. Leutnant Feineisen towed away in the forest behind Iggelheim. Feldwebel Löh blew up his vehicle in Böhl. Leutnant Feineisen and I moved forward again. Leutnant Feineisen wounded twice. I received a slight wound on my left hand. Americans at our gun on two occasions. Saved gun and moved away. Unteroffizier Hagelstein's Jagdtiger burnt out outside Iggelheim. Continued to Speyer in the evening. Fischhaber smashed his finger in the hatch.

26 March 1945: Jagdtiger only capable of moving. Unteroffizier Norbert Schier joined the crew. Moved through Bruchsal to Ubstat in the evening.

27 March 1945: Occupied Unteröwisheim.

31 March 1945: March orders for Wiesloch. Still not finished. Worked throughout the entire night. A Jagdtiger in the [3./schwere Panzerjäger-Abteilung 653] blew sky high through self-combustion (oxygen in air pre-cleaner). 3 men burned.

1 April 1945: Repairs completed. Moved to Menzingen in the evening. Left brake overheated outside of Unteröwisheim and the radiator was not working properly.

2 April 1945: Made it to Rohrbach. Halted there and repaired the radiator. Continued through Eppingen, Rischen and Kirchardt during the afternoon.

3 April 1945: Towed Feldwebel Schalbs' Jagdtiger [1./schwere Panzerjäger-Abteilung 653] to Eppingen along with Leutnant Knippenberg. Dismal towing. Leutnant Knippenberg's Jagdtiger experienced problems at the town entrance. Engine damage. Continued alone through Kleingartach to Niederhofen. Broke down at the entrance to the town. Brake had to be repaired. Maintenance section from the [3./schwere Panzerjäger-Abteilung 653] repaired the damage. An example of negligence by the Maintenance Platoon of the [1./schwere Panzerjäger-Abteilung 653]. Continued in the dark. Dismounted 1 kilometer outside of Niederhofen. Had to give my Jagdtiger to Oberfeldwebel Fritz Schwarz, from the [3./schwere Panzerjäger-Abteilung 653]. Schwarz took the Jagdtiger on to Nordheim. I went with Leutnant Zimmeck to the battalion command post in Cleebronn.

4 April 1945: Message about brake damage on the Jagdtiger. Reported on the recovery of my Jagdtiger in Iggelheim. To Frauenzimmern with Nielsen. Then to the company at Freudenthal. Went to Bissingen as a messenger and then back again. Went with Oberleutnant Wiesenfarth to the Jagdtiger at Nordheim and then back again.

5 April 1945: Took the commander to Bissingen with a sidecar motorcycle. Continued through Besigheim and ran into the gun. My Jagdtiger with steering and brake problems. A Jagdtiger from the [1./schwere Panzerjäger-Abteilung 653] burnt out. Leutnant Feineisen and crew wounded with burns. West to Bissingen with the Motor Sergeant. Arranged for my Jagdtiger to be towed. Returned to Lauffen. Went with the commander, through Lauffen-Bönnigheim, to the battalion command post in Cleebronn. Continued to Freudenthal. Took the VW back to Lauffen. Recovering my Jagdtiger was impossible due to the premature demolition of the railroad underpass by the engineers. Blew up a Jagdtiger from the [1./schwere Panzerjäger-Abteilung 653]. Returned to Besigheim-Bissingen-Freudenthal. Took the mess-hall trailer with me from Walheim.

6 April 1945: Went with Nielsen on a sidecar motorcycle as the advance party, through Bissingen, Bietigheim, Marbach, Backnang, Obergründen, Untergründen, Ebnet and Kaisersbach, to Welzheim. Returned through Backnang, Marbach, Neckarweihingen, Bietigheim and Bissingen to Freudenthal. Obergefreiter [?] blew up my Jagdtiger at 0200 hours.

7 April 1945: Company moved through Bissingen, Marbach, Backnang and Welzheim to join us. Drove the commander and command group forward during the evening. Commander's vehicle, Feldwebel Löh and Breiller in combat near Crailsheim. Unteroffizier Erler's right foot pinched off between drive sprocket and track.

9 April 1945: Feldwebel Müller killed by fighter-bombers at the Maintenance Company.

13 April 1945: Ration run with Unteroffizier Hagelstein through Gaildorf to Schwäbisch Hall. Changed positions in the new area; [moved] through Gaildorf, Wasseraifingen, Aalen, Nördlingen, Wassertrüdingen, Ehingen, Beyerberg and Burk. Arrived at 0200 hours on 14 April 1945.

17 April 1945: By truck through Arberg (accident 10 kilometers past Arberg), Gunzenhausen, Schwabach, Nuremberg, Neumühle Training Area. Picked up 4 Panther hulls and a Tatra. Returned in the evening. Left one hull behind after 2 kilometers; defective steering. All tank barricades up to Schwabach were closed. Left second hull behind at Schwabach; defective steering. Forsthof. Hulls ran out of fuel outside of Gunzenhausen.

18 April 1945: By truck through Gunzenhausen and Arberg to pick up fuel in Burk. Back again 10 kilometers outside of Arberg. Refueled vehicle. Towed Guilleaume to Burk. Went with Hagelstein through Arberg and Gunzenhausen to Spalt. Returned through Fünfbronn, Gunzenhausen, Arberg and Burk. On foot to Schlierberg (2 kilometers).

19 April 1945: With Unteroffizier Hagelstein through Dinkelsbühl and Nördlingen to Schweindorf.

20 April 1945: Picked up rations with Unteroffizier Hagelstein, moving through Nördlingen, Öttingen, Gunzenhausen, Fünfbronn, Spalt and Fünfbronn again.

21 April 1945: Back through Gunzenhausen, Öttingen, Nördlingen and Schweindorf. Obtained a staff car in Nördlingen. Picked up rations again in the evening: From Schweindorf, through Nördlingen, Öttingen, Ostheim, Heidenheim, Öttingen, Harburg, Donauwörth, and Oppertshofen.

22 April 1945: Donauwörth, Druisheim, and Alsmanhofen. Ration run in the evening through Donauwörth, Monheim, Bittenbronn, Langenaltheim, Solnhofen, Bieswang, Solnhofen, Langenaltheim, Bittenbronn, Möhren, Treuchtlingen, Windischhausen, Rohrbach and Deckersheim.

23 April 1945: Back through Rohrbach, Treuchtlingen, Möhren, Bittenbronn, Langenaltheim, Solnhofen and Bieswang. Towed the VW through Solnhofen, Langenaltheim, Bittenbronn, Monheim, Donauwörth, Rain and Neukirchen. Continue by staff car through Rain, Donauwörth, Augsburg, Ulm, Vöhringen and Schnürpflingen.

24 April 1945: Illertissen, Landsberg am Lech, Weilheim, Murnau, Kohlgrub, Steingaden, Lauterbach and Steingaden again. Occupied quarters on the Jagdberg.

25 April 1945: On foot to Lauterbach. Still have not found the battalion.

26 April 1945: Continued during the afternoon through Schongau, Forst and St. Leonhard to the "Central" Armored Strongpoint in Haid. Continued through Weilheim to the Support Company in Seeshaupt. Continued during the evening through Wolfratshausen, Buttenbronn, Zorneding and Eglharting. Spent the night in Stadel.

27 April 1945: Continued in the morning through Kirchseeon, Jacobneuharting, Egernau and Frauenneuharting. Quarters.

1 May 1945: Frauenneuharting, Rott am Inn and Griestätt.

2 May 1945: Halfing, Trauenstein, Freilassing, Steinbrunning, Freilassing and Peiting.

3 May 1945: I decided to end the war here, took the youngest member of my crew, Michael Fischhaber, and went with him through Stein, Halfing, Griestätt and Freiham. Crossed the Inn River by boat, after putting on civilian clothing. Attel and Atteltal near Rammerberg.

4 May 1945: Rammerberg and Tegernau.

5 May 1945: Through Eichhofen, Unter Eichhofen, Klein Rohrsdorf, Gailling, Wetterling, Hasslach, Wattenhofen, Reisenthal and Münster.

5 May 1945: Neu Münster, Heimathofen, Göppingen, Klein, Karolinenfeld and Arget. I brought Michael happily home. I remained at his family's farm until 15 May 1945 and patched together a bicycle, upon which I embarked on my journey home. After many delays, caused by the French, I arrived home on 28 August 1945.

Leutnant Rudolf Braun, a Platoon Leader in the 2./schwere Panzerjäger-Abteilung 653 (Jagdtiger), provided the following first-hand account about his time in combat with the battalion:

Now I have turned myself completely inside out to produce an account of everything that occurred 47 years ago. If I had written everything down immediately that I had experienced in 1945, then I could remember it all.

I came to the unit from Panzerjäger-Ersatz- und Ausbildungs-Abteilung 7 in Munich (Freimarn). My father, Major Braun, was the commander of the [battalion]. Hauptmann Rehnitz was the company commander responsible for training.

I was also at the Nibelungen Works in St. Valentin for a while and trained Jagdtiger crews at the assembly line, so to speak. We went to a training area at Döllersheim (not far from Vienna) before our transfer to the Hagenau Forest. We completed gunnery training there with [the 12.8-centimeter main gun]. My unit [2./schwere Panzerjäger-Abteilung 653] was stationed in the Pfalz town of Erlenbach before the spring offensive near Hagenau. One can hardly speak of a focused operation. We could not show ourselves at all during the day, because the enemy aircraft attacked us uninterruptedly. We camouflaged ourselves and hid in woods or barns. We were even spotted there, since the enormous vehicles left noticeable tracks in the forests and fields. We usually moved during the night. I know nothing about detailed vehicle losses. I merely heard that a Jagdtiger was hit and destroyed by directed artillery fire. We also suffered complete losses due to engine and drive-train damage. Both systems were not broken in for our 75-ton vehicles.

Major Grillenberger was our commander until he was relieved. As far as I know, the Führer personally demoted him due to his unsuccessful operations with the [battalion].

I can say the following about the withdrawal: I have before me original documents from Generalmajor Büscher [Commander of Germersheim Regional Support Area] stating that I was permitted to cross the railroad bridge at Germersheim with my unit—9 guns—on 21 March 1945! Shortly before that, Generalfeldmarschall Kesselring specifically forbade me from doing so under the threat of execution, since chaos had erupted at the bridge. We then covered a large portion of the withdrawal by train. To accomplish this, we had to exchange our wide tracks with narrow ones. We left the railroad at Ulm and then moved to Illertissen in the Allgäu region, and then through Krumbach, Landsberg, Munich and Grünwald to Kolbermoor.

It must have been 30 April 1945 or 1 May 1945 when a bridge in Kolbermoor collapsed while we were crossing it with a Jagdtiger. Fortunately, nobody was injured, since all of us, except the driver, were sitting on top of the tank and jumped off at the right moment. That was the end of the war for us.

The author sent an inquiry to the city of Kolbermoor in June 1992, pertaining to the above incident, whereupon the Mayor, Herr Kloo, replied:

Your information regarding the tank destroyers involved in the withdrawal are correct insofar as 2 tank destroyers were moving from Rosenheim through Kolbermoor. The lead tank destroyer broke through while crossing the bridge over the Werks Canal and remained in the canal. The second tank destroyer turned around and continued towards Bad Aibling. We know nothing about what became of this tank destroyer.

The tank lying in the canal was partially dismantled by American occupation forces about 2–3 months later and moved to an area between the canal and Mangfall. After 1 to 1-1/2 years, a local company cut it apart with a welder and cleared it away.

The pocket calendar of Obergefreiter Emil Bürgin—tank-destroyer driver in the 1./schwere Panzerjäger-Abteilung 653—provides information about orientation, drivers training, transport routes and operations with his Jagdtiger from September 1944 to March 1945. (Individual dates apply only to operations and rest periods for Obergefreiter Bürgin. They are not identical to all situations for the remainder of the company.)

2 September 1944 (Saturday): Departed from home at 0600 hours, end of leave.
3 September 1944: Arrived in Fallingbostel at 0030 hours.
4 September 1944 (Monday): Took over training vehicle.
10 September 1944: In Bomlitz, near Fallingbostel.
21 September 1944 (Thursday): Departed Fallingbostel at 1400 hours.
22 September 1944: Arrived in Linz at 2200 hours.
23 September 1944: Occupied quarters in the Haag College-Prep School, near Linz
24 September 1944: Put the school in order.
26 September 1944: At Nibelungen Works.
27 September 1944: Reported sick.
28 September 1944: Sick.
29 September 1944: Sick.
1 October 1944 (Sunday): Thanksgiving celebration at the Adolf-Hitler-Platz in Haag.
16 October 1944 (Monday): Bombing attack on the Nibelungen Works.
1 November 1944 (Wednesday): Departed Haag at 1400 hours for St. Pölten.
2 November 1944 (Thursday): Departed St. Pölten at 0600 hours for Döllersheim. Arrived in Döllersheim at 1200 hours.
3 November 1944: Infantry training.
4 November 1944: Off duty.
6 November 1944: Began drivers training with the Jagdtiger.
15 November 1944 (Wednesday): Concluded drivers training.
17 November 1944 (Friday): Test.
18 November 1944: Official trip to Grafenwöhr.
19 November 1944: Nuremberg.
20 November 1944 (Monday): Departed Nuremberg at 0700 hours. Arrived in Grafenwöhr at 1400 hours.
5 December 1944 (Tuesday): Departed Grafenwöhr.

6 December 1944 (Wednesday): Arrived in Döllersheim at 2300 hours.

7 December 1944 (Thursday): Rail loaded guns at 0900 hours and departed from Göpfritz an der Wild at 2200 hours.

8 December 1944: Through Linz.

10 December 1944 (Sunday): Train halted in Ockenheim.

11 December 1944: One day delay in Kriftel.

15 December 1944 (Friday): Arrived at the railhead station at Wittlich. (Beginning of the Ardennes Offensive)

16 December 1944: In Lüxem.

18 December 1944: Wengerohr

25 December 1944 (Monday): Air attack on Wengerohr, dug out buried individuals.

30 December 1944 (Saturday): Departed Wengerohr; motor march.

1 January 1945 (Monday): At the highest point of the Hunsrück Range.

2 January 1945: In Boppard on the Rhine.

3 January 1945: Rail loaded at Boppard.

4 January 1945: Unloaded at Bruchmühlbach.

8 January 1945 (Monday): Moved to assembly area at Zweibrücken.

9 January 1945 (Tuesday): Operations near Rimling; direct hit on a gun.

14 January 1945 (Sunday): Returned from operations; moved to Saarbrücken.

15 January 1945 (Monday): Arrived at Hühnerfeld.

22 January 1945 (Monday): Departed from Hühnerfeld

23 January 1945: Rail loaded at St. Ingbert.

25 January 1945 (Thursday): Unloaded at Bühl on the Rhine; moved to Muckenschopf.

7 February 1945 (Wednesday): Rail loaded at Bühl; moved to the Pfalz.

8 February 1945: By rail from Karlsruhe to Landay. Arrived at Hayna.

10 February 1945 (Saturday): In Hayna.

13 February 1945: To the battalion dispensary at Herxheim.

23 February 1945 (Friday): To the dispensary in Rohrbach (sick).

4 March 1945: From Röhrbach, through Landau and Neustadt, to Alzey

5 March 1945: To the field hospital in Alzey

9 March 1945: To the field hospital in Alzey (Pfalz).

15 March 1945: Americans moved closer; evacuated the field hospital. Departed at 2300 hours.

18 March 1945: In Eich am Rhein.

19 March 1945: Departed from Eich.

20 March 1945: In Darmstadt.

23 March 1945: In Bruchsal.

24 March 1945: In Heidelberg, to Nußloch.

Another important and presumably unique document pertaining to the operations of a Jagdtiger is the driver's log maintained by Obergefreiter Rainer Statz of the 1./schwere Panzerjäger-Abteilung 653. This document provides routes, locations, kilometers driven and damage that occurred. All entries are for his Jagdtiger (Type Henschel, Chassis Number 305023, Vehicle Number 113). The log began on 29 November 1944:

Date	Odometer	Route	Maintenance	Kilometers
2 December 1944	165	Döllersheim Rail Station	None	10
4 January 1945	175	Unloading Zweibrücken	None	100
28 January 1945		Maintenance Company	New transmission	
31 January 1945		New engine		
13 February 1945	275	Zweibrücken-Oberauerbach	Adjusted engine; adjusted transmission	34
19 February 1945	309	Rohrbach to Hagenau Woods	400 liters of fuel; installed new odometer	62
17 March 1945	062	Combat: Gunstett		15
18 March 1945	077	Combat: Gunstett	300 liters of fuel; 3 liters of transmission oil; 2 liters of engine oil	12
19 March 1945	089	Gunstett-Rohrbach	250 liters of fuel; 4 liters of engine oil; 7 liters of transmission oil	50
20 March 1945	139	Rohrbach. Combat: Mutterstadt		48
21 March 1945	187	Combat: Mutterstadt. 1 gun destroyed	300 liters of fuel; 2 liters of engine oil; 5 liters of transmission oil	39
22 March 1945	226	Rehhütte: 3 guns destroyed. Combat: Speyer	200 liters of fuel; 4 liters of engine oil	18
23 March 1945	244	Combat: Speyer. Neudorf	250 liters of fuel; 5 liters of engine oil; 7 liters of transmission oil	30
26 March 1945	274	Neudorf-Wiesental	Transmission oil loss; replace engine oil (25 liters)	15
28 March 1945	289	Wiesental: Maintenance Section (Reich Highway)	200 liters of fuel; 3 liters of engine oil; 6 liters of transmission oil	18
29 March 1945	307	Maintenance Section (Reich Highway). Unterbüllingsheim		55
30 March 1945	362	Unterbüllingsheim-Bretten	600 liters of fuel; 5 liters of engine oil; 9 liters of transmission oil. Small U-joint defective.	19
2 April 1945	381	Bretten-Itzingen	100	
3 April 1945	391	Itzingen-Leonberg-Vöhringen	300 liters of fuel; 4 liters of engine oil; 3 liters of transmission oil. Defective transmission.	35

Date	Odometer	Route	Maintenance	Kilometers
25 April 1945	426	Illertissen-Krumbach	400 liters of fuel; 5 liters of engine oil; 9 liters of transmission oil.	45
27 April 1945	471	Augsburg-Fürstenfeldbruck	250 liters of fuel.	23
20 April 1945	494	Fürstenfeldbruck-Rosenheim		109
4 May 1945	603	Destroyed Jagdtiger near Rosenheim	Defective right steering brake; no longer steerable.	

Notes from the medic, Gefreiter Johann Schleiß, illustrate the locations of the battalion headquarters during the period from 26 August 1944 to 7 May 1945:

1944

26 August	Arrived at Fallingbostel
2 October	Moved to Döllersheim
7 December	Rail loaded in Göpfritz to Wengerohr/Flußbach
9 December	Delayed at St. Goar (tunnel)
11/12 December	Arrival (?)

1945

2 January	Mittelbach (below Zweibrücken)
4 January	Seyweiler
10 January	Niederaubach (above Zweibrücken)
11 January	Altenwald (?)
20 January	Bühl (Baden)
21 January	Neusatz near Bühl
23 January	Muckenschopf
25 January	Crossed the Rhine at 0100 hours; Offendorf
28 January	Auenheim-Röschwoog
29 January	Sessenheim-Bühl (Baden)
30 January	Kappelwindeck (near Bühl)
3 February	Rail loading
5 February	Rohrbach-Herxheim
19 February	Weißenburg, Soultz, Surbourg
21 February	Höllenhof (supporting 3 companies)
8 March	Schirlenhof
14 March	Surbourg
15 March	Gundershoffen
16 March	Morsbronn/Lampertsloch
17 March	Kreuzwald (?)/Drachenbronn
18 March	Weißenburg/Schweighofen, Rechtenbach, Herxheim
19 March	Haßloch; element crossed the Rhine at Speyer
21 March	Schifferstadt
22 March	Iggelheim, Dudenhofen, Hanhofen
23 March	Berghausen, Germersheim (Rhine crossing)
24 March	Neudorf
25 March	Neudorf
26 March	Kronau

1945	
27 March	Grenzhof
28 March	Eppelheim
29 March	Eppelheim (artillery attack)
30 March	Altwiesloch
1 April	Michelfeld
2 April	Ochsenburg
3 April	Cleebronn
5 April	Gemmrigheim (Neckar)
6 April	Besigheim
8 April	Ludwigsburg (rail loading)
?	Schwäbisch Hall
?	Crailsheim
?	Nuremberg
24 April	Steinhausen (am Rottum ?)
26 April	Walkertshofen (?)
27 April	Kissing (near Augsburg)
28 April	Schondorf am Ammersee/Weßling
29 April	Munich (Geiselgasteig)/Sauerlach
30 April	Bad Aibling
1 May	Rosenheim/Schloßberg
2 May	Erlstätt (Lake Chiem)
3 May	Henndorf
4 May	Weißenbach (Lake Att)
5 May	Bad Ischl
6 May	Unzenau (2 hours as a prisoner)
7 May	Pötschenpaß-Liezen (war ended at 1500 hours)

Unteroffizier Horst Theis, a member of the 3./schwere Panzerjäger-Abteilung 653, provided the following first-hand account concerning his experiences with the Jagdtiger:

On 16 September 1944, I received an emergency leave of eight days to go home. After completing a course on 1 October 1944, I was promoted to Unteroffizier and started a 14-day leave (transferring between units) on 4 October 1944. I was assigned to my former battalion, schwere Panzerjäger-Abteilung 653, on 23 October.

At this time, having no weapons, the battalion was stationed at the Döllersheim Training Area in Austria, directly on the border of what was then the Protectorate. This time, I was assigned to the 3./schwere Panzerjäger-Abteilung 653, which was still commanded by Oberleutnant Kretschmer. Major Grillenberger was the battalion commander. We were to receive the latest weapon, the Jagdtiger, with a combat weight of almost 80 tons—the heaviest armored vehicle in the world.

Difficult weeks of training followed, until the battalion rail loaded for the west in early December 1944. The farther west we went, the more difficult the transportations situation became. We spent the Christmas period at the Ockenheim Train Station (near Bingen), since the trains could move neither forward or backward due to the rails having been destroyed by bombing.

After almost three weeks of movement, our train, which had been the last to depart, was the first to unload at Zweibrücken. Our combat tracks—20 centimeters wider—had not yet arrived, however. (The tank destroyers could not be transported by rail with the wider tracks.) As a result, we had to make do with our transportation tracks. After a night in the bunkers of the Westwall, we moved out on the evening of 31 December 1944 with our transport tracks through the snow and heavy frost. We moved towards the Lorraine border with just two tank destroyers, crossing it at Medelsheim at the start of the New Year. The following 10 days brought us together with the [17. SS-Panzer-Grenadier-Division "Götz von Berlichingen"] in the Erching-Rimling area; [the area of] the most difficult operations against the Americans.

Almost impossible demands were made of and achieved by the crew in the deep snow an heavy frost. Good results were obtained, even if they were costly. It quickly became clear to us that all we had to fear from the enemy was is superior air force and artillery, which was primarily directed by spotter aircraft. As a practical matter, the Luftwaffe never appeared any more. Our large vehicles presented an outstanding target in the snow. Camouflage was almost impossible. The Jagdtiger were often employed at night in contravention of doctrine. The midnight engagement at the mill at Rimling is still indelibly etched upon my memory. Without infantry support from the Waffen-SS, we probably would not have made it out of there.

After these difficult operations, there were wonderful days of rest from 11–23 January in Hühnerfeld (Sulzbach), in the vicinity of Saarbrücken. On 23 January 1945, we loaded aboard trains at St. Ingbert and rolled towards Bühl in the Baden area. Our tank destroyer received a quick overhaul there. We occupied positions in Obersasbach without incident. At the same time, other elements of the company were engaged in combat operations in the Bischweiler-Hagenau area.

On 5 February 1945, we moved to Rohrbach in the Pfalz region (Landau area). The 3./schwere Panzerjäger-Abteilung 653 occupied quarters at Hayna, which were excellent, as always. The battalion assembled I this area for the first time since operations had begun in the west. After resting for 12 days, we departed on 18 February 1945. We moved through Weißenburg and Wörth to our assembly area at Höllenhof (near Griesbach). This prevented me from attending a weaponry course, which had been slated to begin on 19 February 1945.

The new area was the second line of resistance along the Moder between the Hagenau Forest and the Pfalz Forest. Firing positions and bunkers were constructed during the relatively quiet days that followed. We also familiarized ourselves with the terrain.

After an officer candidate's examination on 10 March 1945, which casts a light on the ancillary things we concerned ourselves with at the time, we departed [on 12 March 1945] to rail load at Walburg in the Hagenau Forest. This did not occur, however. [Employed as artillery in an indirect-fire mode] for the first time, we initially fired at the American observation post in the high-rise building in Hagenau. Then, on the evening of 14 March 1945, an operations order arrived.

The situation along the entire Saar-Pfalz sector had become untenable after the Americans had started pushing through the Hunsrück Range and up the Rhine. Our forces had to withdraw very quickly. In our sector, our battalion and a Hetzer [tank destroyer] unit were given the mission of screening the withdrawal of most of the artillery, the assault guns and the infantry.

The days that followed were very difficult and brought with them the night fighting at Griesbach (15 March 1945) and the operations near Forstheim, Höllenhof and Weißenburg. It is only thanks to the great experience of our gun commanders in withdrawal operations and the exemplary performance of the Recovery Platoons that we did not suffer even higher losses during this ridiculous operation.

Our tank destroyer—Jagdtiger 314—together with Feldwebel Telgmann's Jagdtiger 322 had to be blown up at 0430 hour on the morning of 17 March 1945. American infantry had approached to within 150 meters, and out own infantry was not available.

After crossing the Maginot Line at Weißenburg and the Westwall at Bad Bergzabern, we reached the Maintenance Company at Rohrbach on 20 March 1945. Then came the operations at Neustadt an der Weinstraße and at Speyer, as well as the Rhine crossing on 23 March at Germersheim. Before that, we had amassed many boxes of combat rations. I spent the next three days as a truck driver on a fueler from the Support Company at Graben-Neudorf. We then moved through Bruchsal to Lamboldshausen, and I departed from there on official duty to St. Valentin (Vienna) on 29 March 1945. During the movement through Augsburg and Munich, we also took along our former commander's personal belongings to Linz. He had been demoted to Leutnant due to the unnecessary losses and failed battalion operations. Major Fromme became our new battalion commander.

We experienced another bombing attack in Linz on 31 March 1945, during which we almost suffered the loss of our truck, and reached St. Pölten late in the afternoon. From there, we continued to Vienna, where I spent Easter. After "Ivan" had already begun firing upon Vienna on the Monday after Easter, I left the city aboard one of the last trains early on Tuesday and reached St. Valentin that night. On the next day at the Nibelungen Works, we discovered that the repair parts we were to pick up had been buried during an air attack and had to be dug out. We spent the delay from 5–8 April 1945 with a drive from the [Nibelungen] Works that took us to our vehicle assembly area at the front line near Neulengbach-Herzogenburg. We bought 120 liters of wine in Krems and, after an adventurous journey, succeeded in reaching Haag safe and sound.

On 10 April 1945, we moved through Meggenhofen, Passau, Regensburg and Regenstauf, where we occupied quarters for 2 days. From there, we carried out our mission at the Grafenwöhr Training Area (near Weiden). On 14 April 1945, we continued through Augsburg to Fischach and, on 17 April 1945, to Krumbach, where we were able to rest for 2 days. On 20 April 1945, we finally reached the [3./schwere Panzerjäger-Abteilung 653] and the battalion, which had already reported us missing, in Vöhringen an der Iller. We departed on 23 April 1945, moving with the Maintenance Company to Lake Wörth. The Americans pursued vigorously, however, and we continued through Munich to Eglharting on 25 April 1945. We arrived at the location of the Support Company in Erding on 27 April 1945.

Sixteen crews were assembled here and departed for the Nibelungen Works on 30 April 45 to pick up new Jagdtiger for "The Final Battle". During the night of 6 May 1945, the Americans reached the Enns, the demarcation line with the Soviets. Since the SS had snatched the new Jagdtiger out from under our noses, we moved to the Alps as a consolidated group on 6 May 1945, as we had no desire to be captured by the Russians. It was a wonderful journey: Initially through the Enns Valley, then through the Trauern Valley, until we crossed into the capitulation zone of Heeresgruppe G at Radstadt during the night of 8/9 May 1945.

In Radstadt, we helped "liquidate" a supply depot. German tanks had blocked the only road north due to surrender negotiations, and the endless column was therefore diverted to Yugoslavia. We were forced to maneuver our fully loaded truck across unimproved dirt trails to the road to Salzburg. We wanted to drive our truck—well stocked with fuel and food—directly through Germany and drop off everyone near his home. We thus found ourselves completely alone on 9 May 1945, driving through the American sector along the road to Salzburg. We had deposited our pistols in a stream as a precaution. American armored cars and military police stopped us short of Salzburg and delivered us to a barracks, below the castle, at a collection point that night. Fortunately, they let us keep our well-stocked backpacks.

We were driven to an area near Bad Aibling on 31 May 1945. The following persons from the [3./schwere Panzerjäger-Abteilung 653] were with us: Fritz Schwarz, Ernst Gautan, Günther Northoff, Helmut Kreyenhangen, Eugen Bott, Robert Kutscha, Rainer Flohrs and Karl Schötteldreier.

Adding to the first-hand accounts, former radio operator Franz Kurrer of the 3./schwere Panzer-jäger-Abteilung 653 wrote the following to the author in a letter dated 28 June 1992:

Early September 1944: Leave (about 2 weeks). After this leave, orders to the Döllersheim Training Area. Created new unit there [sic!]; equipped with Jagdtiger.

18 December 1944: Moved from the training area to the rail yard at Göpfritz. Engine trouble on the way there and return to Döllersheim. All other Jagdtiger are loaded aboard trains bound for the Mosel.

21 December 1944: 2 Jagdtiger loaded aboard trains in Göpfritz. Jagdtiger 314 [had the following crew]:

    Gun Commander: Feldwebel Erich Bönike,

    Gunner: Horst Theis,

    Driver: Hubert Ressmann,

    Radio operator: Franz Kurrer

    Loaders: Walther Moises and Robert Kutscha

    Gun commanded by Unteroffizier Riedel (Jagdtiger ?). Crew: Unknown

24 December 1944: Ockenheim (siding)

26 December 1944: Unloaded in Zweibrücken without combat tracks. Spent two nights in a Westwall bunker.

29 December 1944: Both tank destroyers moved towards Medelsheim.

1 January 1945: We were awakened by the battalion commander and a general. The general wished us a "Happy New Year" and brought us a bottle of champagne for toasts.

Moved towards Medelsheim during the afternoon. The vehicle threw its track on an icy and steep incline. The entire track had to be taken apart and carried forward so that the tank could drive onto it again. Some of the track pins were in pieces.

About 1-1/2 weeks later, both tanks destroyers moved back to Zweibrücken, where our combat tracks had arrived. Both Jagdtiger then moved through St. Ingbert and Sulzbach to Hühnerfeld (near Saarbrücken). Other elements of the company also arrived there. In February 1945, around the 20th, we rail loaded in St. Ingbert. We then arrived in the Pfalz and unloaded in Kandel. We occupied quarters in Hayna. From Hayna, we moved to the Hagenau Forest (to Höllenfhof and Forstheim).

We towed another Jagdtiger during the withdrawal. After negotiating a winding road up a mountain, our vehicle broke down with final-drive problems and had to be blown up. The withdrawal continued through Schweigen am Weintor and Bad Bergzabern to Hayna. Unteroffizier Anton Moosdiele was wounded during an air attack on the Maintenance Company, and Feldwebel Bönike and crew took over his tank destroyer. We then moved towards Neustadt (Weinstraße) with several Jagdtiger. We broke down between Speyerdorf and Neustadt [an der Weinstraße] due to a defective track tensioner. We moved to Lachen during the night. We moved through Speyer to the forest at Graben-Neudorf during the following night. Two days later, to Bruchsal and Unteröwisheim. The Maintenance Company occupied the harvest warehouse.

On Easter Sunday, after departing from the Maintenance Company, our Jagdtiger broke down again. We marched on foot to Bretten and waited for a tank destroyer to tow us. It arrived and towed us to a forest near Mühlacker. From there, we loaded aboard a halftrack and moved to Leonberg and, later, to Illertissen. The repairs finally could be made in a forest near Vöhringen. Then I was transferred to the Support Detachment in Illerrieden. From there, I began my useless journey in a truck, armed with a sewing machine. Through Ulm, Dinkelsbühl, Nördlingen, Donauwörth, Augsburg, Munich, Seeshaupt, Lake Starnberg, back to Munich,

Gräfing, Rott am Inn, Laufen, Salzburg, Seekirchen, Mondsee and finally Lake Att. On 6 May 1945, we were captured by the Americans in Nußdorf on Lake Att. Then we went to a camp in Mauerkirchen, from where I was released on 22 May 1945.

Former Oberleutnant Karl Seitz of the Headquarters Company of schwere Panzerjäger-Abteilung 653 wrote the following about Panzerjäger-Ersatz- und Ausbildungs-Abteilung 17 at Freistadt (Austria) in a letter to the author dated 30 August 1990:

Although not necessarily a part of the history, I will attempt to explain how I returned to the [battalion] again in the autumn of 1944.

I was trained on assault guns at Bergen. The same took place in Mielau. Since I had been in charge of assault guns in 1940 in Jüterbog, none of this was new to me. The student became a teacher. Major Grillenberger still had contacts in Mielau, so it came to pass that I was requested by him in the autumn of 1944. When I reported to him, he told me that I would take command of the [reconstituted 2./schwere Panzerjäger-Abteilung 653], but first I would create a replacement and training company. That is how it remained.

This training company was transferred to St. Valentin in April 1945 to assist the Nibelungen Works with completing Jagdtiger. On 1 May 1945, it was disbanded and sent to an infantry division. The train was shot up by fighter-bombers, however. As a result, we were at the Göpfritz Train Station on 8 May 1945.

The 4 Jagdtiger in the replacement battalion, which we used for training, were destroyed during an air attack in the Mauthausen area during rail transport.

ASSIGNMENT OF JAGDTIGER TANK DESTROYERS

Issued To	No.	Date	Comments
Army Weapons Department	2	February 1944	1 Henschel chassis and 1 Porsche chassis variant
Tank-Destroyer School (Mielau)	1	30 June 1944	Porsche chassis
Replacement Detachment (Mielau)	3	28 August 1944	Porsche chassis
schwere Panzerjäger-Abteilung 653	3	5 October 1944	
Replacement Army (Döllersheim)	1	6 October 1944	
schwere Panzerjäger-Abteilung 653	3	7 October 1944	Porsche chassis
Replacement Army (Döllersheim)	1	8 October 1944	
Putlos (Gunnery School)	1	14 October 1944	Porsche chassis
schwere Panzerjäger-Abteilung 653	1	23 October 1944	
schwere Panzerjäger-Abteilung 653	1	23 October 1944	Henschel chassis
Replacement Army	3	23 October 1944	
Replacement Army	3	23 October 1944	Henschel chassis
Replacement Army	1	8 November 1944	Porsche chassis
schwere Panzerjäger-Abteilung 653	1	18 November 1944	

continued

ASSIGNMENT OF JAGDTIGER TANK DESTROYERS

Issued To	No.	Date	Comments
schwere Panzerjäger-Abteilung 653	1	18 November 1944	Henschel chassis
schwere Panzerjäger-Abteilung 653	3	18 November 1944	
schwere Panzerjäger-Abteilung 653	3	24 November 1944	Henschel chassis
schwere Panzerjäger-Abteilung 653	4	24 November 1944	
schwere Panzerjäger-Abteilung 653	3	7 December 1944	
schwere Panzerjäger-Abteilung 653	1	7 December 1944	
schwere Panzerjäger-Abteilung 653	1	8 December 1944	
schwere Panzerjäger-Abteilung 653	1	8 December 1944	
schwere Panzerjäger-Abteilung 653	4	11 December 1944	Henschel chassis
schwere Panzerjäger-Abteilung 653	3	11 December 1944	Henschel chassis
schwere Panzerjäger-Abteilung 653	1	11 December 1944	
schwere Panzerjäger-Abteilung 653	1	11 December 1944	
schwere Panzerjäger-Abteilung 653	1	12 December 1944	
schwere Panzerjäger-Abteilung 653	1	29 December 1944	
schwere Panzerjäger-Abteilung 653	4	2 January 1945	
schwere Panzerjäger-Abteilung 653	1	3 January 1945	
schwere Panzerjäger-Abteilung 653	4	4 January 1945	
schwere Panzerjäger-Abteilung 653	1	6 January 1945	
schwere Panzerjäger-Abteilung 653	4	9 January 1945	
schwere Panzerjäger-Abteilung 653	1	13 January 1945	
schwere Panzerjäger-Abteilung 653	1	13 January 1945	
schwere Panzerjäger-Abteilung 653	1	13 January 1945	
schwere Panzerjäger-Abteilung 653	1	25 January 1945	
schwere Panzerjäger-Abteilung 653	4	17 April 1945	Telegram

VEHICLE STATUS: SCHWERE PANZERJÄGER-ABTEILUNG 653

Date	Jagdtiger Operational/In maintenance	Bergepanzer Operational/In maintenance	Flakpanzer Operational/In maintenance
30 December 1944	5/2	—/—	—/—
1 January 1945	6/1	0/0	0/0
1 February 1945	22/19	4/0	7/1
5 February 1945	25/12	?/?	?/?
1 March 1945	31/8	3/1	6/2
15 March 1945	38/3	3/1	6/2
25 March 1945	28/13	?/?	?/?

continued

VEHICLE STATUS: SCHWERE PANZERJÄGER-ABTEILUNG 653

Date	Jagdtiger Operational/In maintenance	Bergepanzer Operational/In maintenance	Flakpanzer Operational/In maintenance
26 March 1945	9/19 (Bretten area)	?/?	?/?
10 April 1945	10/7*	?/?	?/?
26 April 1945	1/13**	?/?	?/?

* 4 total losses since last report
** Of the 13 in maintenance: 7 short-term repair; 6 long-term repair

JAGDTIGER GUN COMMANDERS OF SCHWERE PANZERJÄGER-ABTEILUNG 653

1./schwere Panzerjäger-Abteilung 653

1. Oberleutnant Werner Haberland
2. Leutnant Hans Knippenberg
3. Oberfeldwebel Gustav Koss
4. Oberfeldwebel Ferdinand Kinnberger
5. Feldwebel Wilhelm Flintrop
6. Feldwebel Horst Golinski
7. Feldwebel Ernst Markmann
8. Feldwebel Erich Pretzler
9. Feldwebel Edmund Roos
10. Feldwebel Reinhold Schlabs
11. Feldwebel Andreas Schmitt
12. Unteroffizier Heinz Henning
13. Unteroffizier Fritz Jaskiela
14. Unteroffizier Fritz Weinberger (?)

2./schwere Panzerjäger-Abteilung 653

1. Oberleutnant Robert Wiesenfarth
2. Leutnant Feineisen
3. Leutnant Rudolf Braun
4. Leutnant Zwack/Stabsfeldwebel Ernst Geile
5. Oberfeldwebel Wilhelm Löh
6. Oberfeldwebel Steiner (?)
7. Feldwebel Johann Mühlhauser
8. Feldwebel Max Müller (killed 8 April 1945)
9. Unteroffizier Heinrich Brieller
10. Unteroffizier Ernst August Hagelstein
11. Unteroffizier Peter Kohns
12. Unteroffizier Willi Maxheim
13. Unteroffizier Neidler
14. Unteroffizier Karl Sprott

3./schwere Panzerjäger-Abteilung 653

 1. Oberleutnant Franz Kretschmer
 2. Leutnant Hermann Knack
 3. Leutnant Kaspar Göggerle
 4. Oberfeldwebel Emil Issler
 5. Oberfeldwebel Fritz Schwarz
 6. Feldwebel Otto Bott
 7. Feldwebel Alfred Schiestl
 8. Feldwebel Heinz Telgmann
 9. Feldwebel Heinz Tolgauer
10. Feldwebel Erich Bönicke
11. Unteroffizier Fritz Riedel
12. ?
13. ?
14. ?

HIGH AWARDS AND PRESENTED TO MEMBERS OF STURMGESCHÜTZ-ABTEILUNG 197/SCHWERE PANZERJÄGER-ABTEILUNG 653

Knight's Cross of the Iron Cross

Johann Spielmann
27 March 1942
Oberleutnant
Platoon Leader in the 1./Sturmgeschütz-Abteilung 197
804th recipient of the Oak Leaves to the Knight's Cross on 28 March 1945

Heinrich Teriete
22 July 1943
Leutnant
Platoon Leader
schwere Panzerjäger-Abteilung 653

Franz Kretschmer
17 December 1943
Leutnant (Reserve)
Platoon Leader
I./schweres Panzerjäger-Regiment 656 (schwere Panzerjäger-Abteilung 653)

Entered into the Army Honor Roll

Johann Spielmann
Platoon Leader
1./Sturmgeschütz-Abteilung 197
at Tulmchak
13–14 March 1942
Entered on 28 March 1942

German Cross in Gold

Oberleutnant Ulrich Brinke
8 January 1943
Battery Commander
1./Sturmgeschütz-Abteilung 197

Feldwebel (Reserve) Wilhelm Flintrop
27 April 1945
Gun Commander
1./schwere Panzerjäger-Abteilung 653

Oberleutnant Bernhard Konnak
26 December 1943
Company Commander
3./schwere Panzerjäger-Abteilung 653

Hauptmann Eberhard Kuntze
21 October 1943
Company Commander
2./schwere Panzerjäger-Abteilung 653

Oberfeldwebel Friedrich W. Meigen
6 September 1943
Platoon Leader
2./schwere Panzerjäger-Abteilung 653

Oberleutnant Gerald de la Renotiére
28 July 1942
Battery Commander
3./Sturmgeschütz-Abteilung 197

Oberwachtmeister Fritz Schrödel
11 April 1942
Gun Commander
1./Sturmgeschütz-Abteilung 197

Hauptmann Heinz Steinwachs
25 March 1942
Commander
Sturmgeschütz-Abteilung 197

Hauptmann Helmut Ulbricht
3 December 1944
Company Commander
1./schwere Panzerjäger-Abteilung 653

Recommended, but not awarded before the end of the war

Oberleutnant Werner Haberland
Company Commander
1./schwere Panzerjäger-Abteilung 653

After familiarization with the new Jagdtiger tank destroyer, personnel of the 1. and 3./schwere Panzerjäger-Abteilung 653 were issued their vehicles form Panzer-Ersatz- und Ausbildungs-Abteilung 500 at Fallingbostel on the Lüneburg Heath in early September 1944. TILLWICK

Three Porsche Jagdtiger were available to the battalion for training. All of the vehicles had received a coat of Zimmerit and show only national markings. They did not receive a camouflage scheme. CARPENTIER

The reconstituted 2./schwere Panzerjäger-Abteilung 653 received two Jagdtiger at Döllersheim for training purposes in late October 1944. These were the Porsche versions, with chassis numbers 305009 and 305010. One of the company platoon leaders, Leutnant Rudolf Braun, stands in front of a Jagdtiger. GÖGGERLE

This photograph clearly demonstrates the smaller width of the transport tracks for the Jagdtiger. BRAUN

A tarpaulin helps prevent water and moisture from entering the fighting compartment. Even the Jagdtiger proved not to be completely watertight! GÖGGERLE

A view of the enormous gun mantlet on these vehicles (here: 305010). A barrel cover has been placed over the radio operator's MG 34. BRAUN

BRAUN

Although Porsche Jagdtiger 305009 did not receive a camouflage finish, its sister vehicle, Porsche Jagdtiger 305010 (seen below), did. The latter vehicle received a three-color camouflage scheme with so-called "snake lines" on portions of it. Note also the slightly different gun travel locks on the vehicles.

BRAUN

Under very stringent operational security conditions, the Jagdtiger of the 1. and 3./schwere Panzerjäger-Abteilung 653 were loaded aboard trains at Göpfritz an dem Wild (near Döllersheim) I early December 1944. Despite photography being forbidden, Unteroffizier Theis was able to take this picture of Jagdtiger 314 (Porsche). THEIS

Gefreiter Matthias Carpentier of the 3./schwere Panzer-jäger-Abteilung 653 in the winter of 1944/45. CARPENTIER

Oberleutnant Kurt Scherer, the battalion adjutant until March 1945. SCHERER

Unteroffizier Heinrich Appel of the 3./schwere Panzer-jäger-Abteilung 653. Appel was the driver for Oberleutnant Franz Kretschmer on Jagdtiger 301. APPEL

Unteroffizier Helmut Kreyenhagen in the winter of 1944/45. KREYENHAGEN

This Sd.Kfz. 251/8 armored ambulance was assigned to the battalion headquarters in the winter of 1944/45. Gefreiter Schleiß, a medic, stands in front of it. SCHLEIß

Feldwebel Erich Bönike, the commander of Jagdtiger 314, brings a main-gun round to his vehicle. THEIS

Rearming near Seyeiler. Some of the large main-gun rounds for the vehicle can be seen on the engine deck. From left to right: Ressmann Moises and Theis. THEIS

The crew prepares to finish exchanging transport tracks for combat ones. THEIS

Despite the camouflage, the Jagdtiger were constantly being spotted and then attacked by Allied fighter-bombers. The tracks left by the heavy vehicles were easy to acquire from the air. This photograph was taken shortly after a fighter-bomber attack on Jagdtiger 314, which the vehicle barely survived. THEIS

Oberleutnant Kretschmer's Jagdtiger 301, damaged near Zweibrücken. The vehicle was finished in only a sand-colored primer. As a result, the field-expedient camouflage method of applying sheets to the superstructure, gun barrel and hull was used. THEIS

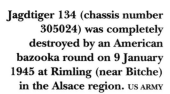

Jagdtiger 134 (chassis number 305024) was completely destroyed by an American bazooka round on 9 January 1945 at Rimling (near Bitche) in the Alsace region. US ARMY

The entire crew—Unteroffizier Fritz Jskiela, Gerhard Fischer, Werner Janson, Rudolf Gaube, Franz Schröder and Franz Boketta—was killed. American soldiers documented the "kill" on 28 January 1945. US ARMY

The driver's station in a Jagdtiger. Steering was accomplished with the half steering wheel. The driver's vision port for driving while "buttoned up" can be seen above the steering wheel. The instrument panel was positioned to the driver's right. JENTZ

Both of these photographs show the Jagdtiger production line at the Nibelungen Works at St. Valentin (Austria). They were taken on 16 January 1945 and show Jagdtiger from a later production series, recognizable by the additional spare-track hooks on their fighting compartment side panels.

A well-camouflaged Jagdtiger is ready to be picked up at St. Valentin. The vehicle has received a three-color camouflage scheme. The appellation "Sunny Boy" was painted on the gun mantlet. It is not known whether this vehicle was delivered to schwere Panzerjäger-Abteilung 653 or schwere Panzerjäger-Abteilung 512. SCHMIDT

Rail transport of Jagdtiger of the 2./schwere Panzerjäger-Abteilung 653 to assembly areas in the Palatinate region of Germany. The Jagdtiger have been camouflaged with vegetation. The danger of discovery and attack by Allied aircraft was particularly great during the day. Whenever possible, all transport movements were done at night. TUMBRINK

The completely bombed out rail installation at Karlsruhe was bypassed on 5 February 1945. WULFF

A Jagdtiger (chassis number 305032) of the 3./schwere Panzerjäger-Abteilung 653 during rail transport to the Palatinate region. Note that this vehicle was loaded aboard a Ssyms car with combat tracks. This was permitted only in the most critical situations, since this made adjoining traffic impossible. WULFF

Unteroffizier Tams of the Headquarters Company of schwere Panzerjäger-Abteilung 653 on guard duty at the edge of the Hagenau Forest. TAMS

A view inside an Sd.Kfz. 251/3 assigned to the battalion's Reconnaissance Platoon. Unteroffizier Hans Tams commanded this vehicle. TAMS

Oberleutnant Werner Haberland rolls into the new assembly area near Hagenau with Jagdtiger 101 at twilight. Moving the tank destroyers was only possible during the evening or night because of Allied air supremacy. KNIPPENBERG

At 0430 hours on 17 March 1945 both of these Jagdtiger of the 3./schwere Panzer-jäger-Abteilung 653—vehicles 314 (Porsche) and 332 (Henschel)—had to be abandoned by their crews and destroyed near Morsbronn les Bains. US ARMY

An abandoned American armored recovery vehicle is claimed by the battalion. Unfortunately, there is no information about the ultimate fate of this vehicle. WULFF

Jagdtiger 314 was abandoned due to final-drive damage. An American soldier examines the vehicle on 8 March 1945. This photograph clearly shows the vehicle's camouflage pattern and black vehicle numerals. Note that this vehicle, which has a Porsche chassis, does not have an application of Zimmerit anti-magnetic paste. US ARMY

One of the company headquarters Jagdtiger of the 1./schwere Panzerjäger-Abteilung 653—Jagdtiger 102 (Porsche)—had to be abandoned and destroyed near Rittershofen during the withdrawal fro the Hagenau Forest.

Jagdtiger 332 is examined by American soldiers. A mount for an MG 42 can be seen on the rear engine deck. The vehicle had been commanded by Feldwebel Telgmann. R.A.C.

Jagdtiger 234 of the 2./schwere Panzerjäger-Abteilung 653 was abandoned in the village of Zeiskam (Palatinate region). American tankers and infantrymen take in the spectacle of the gigantic vehicle. This is a mid-series Jagdtiger, as indicated by the track hooks in the middle of the fighting compartment. JENTZ

A Kampfgruppe from the 3./schwere Panzerjäger-Abteilung 653, under the command of Leutnant Kasper Göggerle, shot up an American armored column during a firefight just outside of Neustadt an der Weinstraße. The burned-out Sherman hulls still littered the roadside after the end of the war.

On 21 March 1945, the American armored spearhead reached Neustadt an der Weinstraße. The column passes two abandoned vehicles of Kampfgruppe Göggerle on the Landauer Straße. The armored jeep with the brigadier general probably contains one of the assistant division commanders.

American forces examine the two Jagdtiger more closely on 23 March 1945. These two vehicles are Jagdtiger 331 (chassis number 305020) and Jagdtiger 323. Both had to be destroyed by their crews due to final-drive damage. The vehicle in the background is now the restaurant Zur Bahnkurve. US ARMY

A close-up of the gun mantlet on Jagdtiger 331. The mantlet had been it on its collar, breaking off a piece of it. This vehicle was later shipped back to the Aberdeen Proving Grounds for a more thorough examination, where it remains on display today. US ARMY

ROHRBACH

ROHRBACH

French forces, which arrived at Neustadt an der Weinstraße as occupation forces after the Americans continued their advance, towed Jagdtiger 323 to the town square, where it remained until it was scrapped.

Heavy fighting took place in the Palatinate villages of Böhl and Iggelheim on 21 and 22 April 1945. Two Jagdtiger from the 2./schwere Panzerjäger-Abteilung 653 were lost during the fighting. This photograph shows the vehicle of Unteroffizier Hagelstein, which burnt out after its engine compartment received a direct hit from an artillery shell. BORTOLUZZI

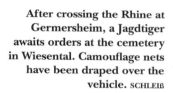

After crossing the Rhine at Germersheim, a Jagdtiger awaits orders at the cemetery in Wiesental. Camouflage nets have been draped over the vehicle. SCHLEIß

Unfortunately, this photograph of an abandoned Jagdtiger taken in Schwetzingen on 30 March 1945 is of poor quality. The vehicle number appears to be 115. The author could not determine whether this number was ever actually used. Some of the crew of this vehicle were Leutnant Hans Knippenberg (Gun Commander), Hermann Looft (Driver) Hans Distler (Radio Operator) and Heinrich Schäfer (Gunner). MÜNCH

The Jagdtiger remained at this location until the spring of 1947. Many occupation soldiers took advantage of this to have their photographs taken aboard the enormous vehicles. DE MEYER

Schwetzingen, 30 March 1945. Jagdtiger 131 is it by an American Sherman at 200 meters and bursts into flames. A photographer in Schwetzingen documented the event several days after the engagement. The vehicle's crew: Oberfeldwebel Ferdinand Kinnberger (Gun Commander), Unteroffizier Fritz Klein (Gunner), Alfred Hertel (Driver), unidentified (Radio Operator), Hermann Vielberth (Loader 1) and unidentified (Loader 2). DE MEYER

The explosion catapulted the driver, Alfred Hertel, out of the vehicle and the tank destroyer continued to rolled forward into the house owned by the Krebs family (corner of Heidelberger Straße and Mannheimer Straße). The impact caused the gun to shear loose from its mount and point skywards.
SCHWETZINGEN CITY ARCHIVES

Unteroffizier fritz Klein was killed by machine-gun fire while abandoning the vehicle. The radio operator dies of severe burns several months later in a British field hospital.
SCHWETZINGEN CITY ARCHIVES

American engineers attempted to recover the Jagdtiger in the spring of 1946. They abandoned their effort after the entire crane on one truck was torn loose from its mountings. MÜNCH

The vehicle remained as a reminder of the war at this location until the spring of 1947. It was then dismantled and taken away for scrap.
SCHWETZINGEN CITY ARCHIVES

Eppingen in the Kraichau area at the end of the war. These two Jagdtiger from the 1./schwere Panzerjäger-Abteilung 653 remained in the middle of the town. The vehicle with the missing main gun was Leutnant Hans Knippenberg's Jagdtiger 114. Behind it is Feldwebel Schlab's Jagdtiger. Both Jagdtiger had to be abandoned due to final-drive problems. STIEFEL

The vehicle number of Feldwebel Schlabs' Jagdtiger has not been determined to this day. Even the chassis number on the front slope cannot be read. An interesting note is that this Jagdtiger featured a spotted ambush pattern (see the right-hand fender). STIEFEL

An American soldier photographed Feldwebel Schlabs' Jagdtiger after the capture of Eppingen. Internal components and equipment litter the area around the vehicle, thrown there by the force of the demolition charges.

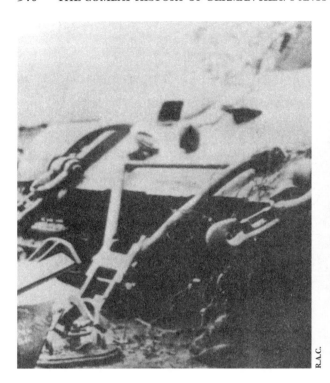
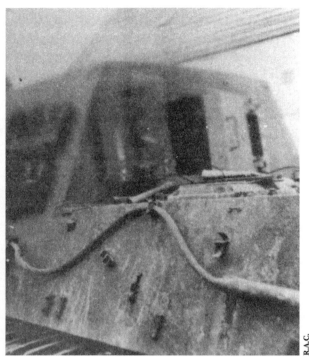

Three close-ups of Jagdtiger
114 in Eppingen in April 1945.

Rear view of Jagdtiger 114. This photograph was taken in the summer of 1945. STIEFEL

Due to a shortage of heavy recovery means, both of the Jagdtiger in Eppingen had to be dismantled on the spot by salvage teams with cutting torches. STIEFEL

This photograph, taken in the summer of 1945, clearly shows vehicle number 114 on the first vehicle. Only the hull of the second Jagdtiger remained by this time. The entire fighting compartment had already been removed for salvage. STIEFEL

Stabsfeldwebel Adolf Rohde, the leader of the battalion's platoon of armored Flak vehicles, in the spring of 1945. ROHDE

Oberleutnant Maximilian Wirsching took command of the 1./schwere Panzerjäger-Abteilung 653 in late March 1945, when Oberleutnant Haberland was wounded. Oberleutnant Wirsching was injured in a vehicle accident in mid-April 1945, and Oberleutnant Haberland resumed command of the company again. Note: Oberleutnant Wirsching received the Knight's Cross to the Iron cross on 7 February 1945, while assigned to schwere Panzer-Abteilung 507. REIßNER

Feldwebel Reinhold Schlabs (viewer's left) and Feldwebel Franz Gärtner of the 1./schwere Panzerjäger-Abteilung 653. This photograph was taken on 20 April 1945 at Schweindorf (near Nördlingen). While they were there, orders arrived from the German Army High Command that all crews without tank destroyers were to report to the Nibelungen Works immediately. SCHLABS

Members of the Armored Reconnaissance Platoon of the battalion at Illertissen at the end of April 1945. Sitting at the front of the hood of the halftrack are (left to right): Unteroffizier Hans Tams, Feldwebel Heinz Borngässer and Unteroffizier Rudolf Ludwig. TAMS

Jagdtiger 113 was abandoned and blown up by its crew in May 1945 in a patch of woods near Rosenheim. American soldiers photographed the vehicle after the end of the war. The explosion blew off the roof of the fighting compartment and split the welding seams. AUERBACH

The armored plates blown off the fighting compartment of this Jagdtiger indicate an internal explosion. When performed according "to the book", a self-demolition required the placement of two charges: One in the driver's compartment, to make the vehicle mechanically inoperable, and one in the breech of the main gun, to make it inoperable. DEVEY

This Jagdtiger is also missing its roof and the sides of its fighting compartment. Americans photographed the wreck somewhere in southern Germany at the end of the war.

This photograph of an Sd.Kfz. 251/8 armored ambulance was taken in Austria several days before the battalion capitulated. SCHLEIß

A combat group with three Jagdtiger, commanded by an SS-Hauptsturmführer from the 1. SS-Panzer-Division "Leibstandarte SS Adolf Hitler", at Strenberg (Austria) on 5 May 1945. The tank destroyers had to stop at a Soviet roadblock, and the crews became Soviet prisoners. The prisoners were eventually handed over to the advancing American forces, however. AUERBACH

Members from all of the battalion's companies assembled for a group photograph in early May 1945. Leutnant Rolf Schleicher, the leader of the battalion's Recovery Platoon, wears the second-pattern, mouse-gray Panzer tunic constructed out of denim material. THEIS

An American and Soviet soldier pose for a photograph on a Jagdtiger. A toy teddy bear has been painted on the front of the fighting compartment to the left of the main gun. AUERBACH

Thanks to the help of a former gun commander, Feldwebel Reinhold Schlabs, the author was able to identify the location of the estate where the Jagdtiger were halted by American and Soviet forces at the end of the war. This photograph shows the building shortly after the end of the war. SCHLABS

Tests with captured German vehicles were conducted at the Kubinka Proving Grounds outside of Moscow shortly after the end of the war. This is one of the Jagdtiger captured at Strengberg (Austria) on 5 May 1945. DUSKE

A rear view of this vehicle is of particular interest. since recovery/towing equipment has been attached between the exhausts. This was a modification that was probably only added to the very final group of Jagdtiger produced. NETREBENKO

This Jagdtiger had chassis number 305083. The vehicle's camouflage scheme has been applied in relatively large patches. The German national insignia have been applied on the sides above the replacement track blocks. A mount for an MG 42 is attached to the rear deck above the engine compartment. ANDERSON

The condition of the captured Jagdtiger is remarkably good. Almost all of the captured German vehicles have been stored in a warehouse at Kubinka.

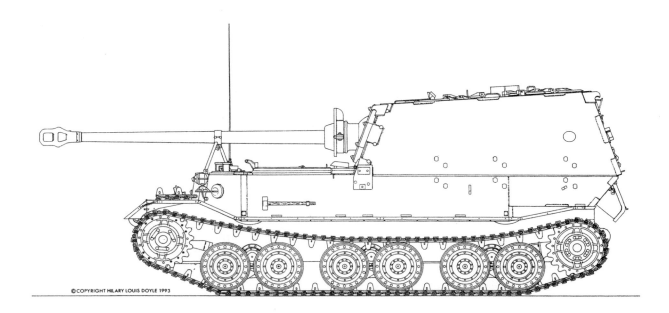

1.) Ferdinand tank destroyer (original design of May 1943): Left-side view.

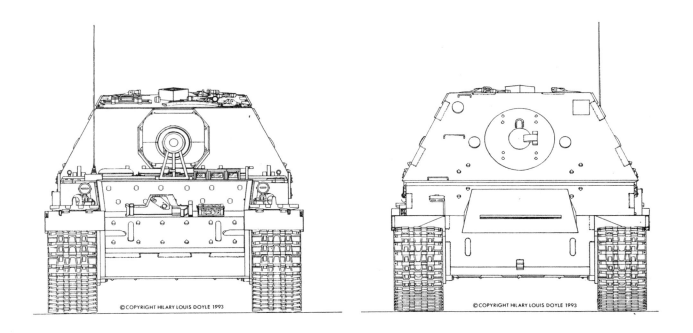

2.) Front view
(Vehicle without radio operator's machine gun).

3.) Rear view.

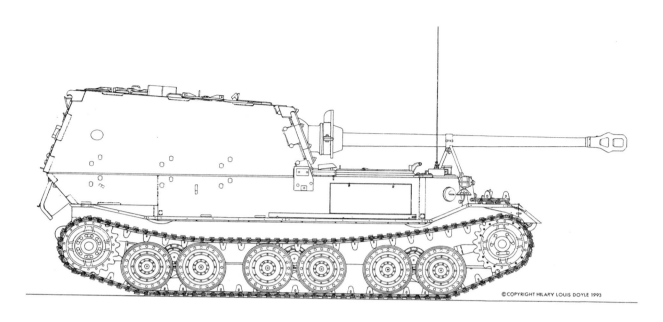

4.) Right-side view of the vehicle with tool box and compartment for spare antennae.

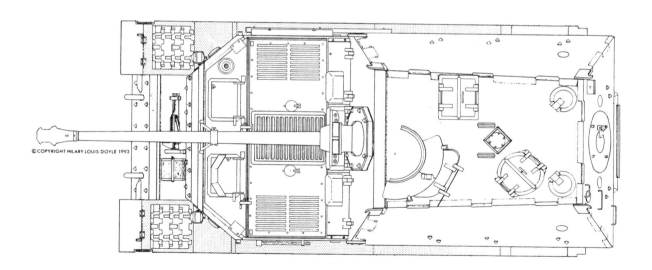

5.) Top view: Early version of the grating for the engine cover as well as the rectangular, split hatch for the vehicle commander. The two small, round covers on the roof of the fighting compartment are for periscope observation.

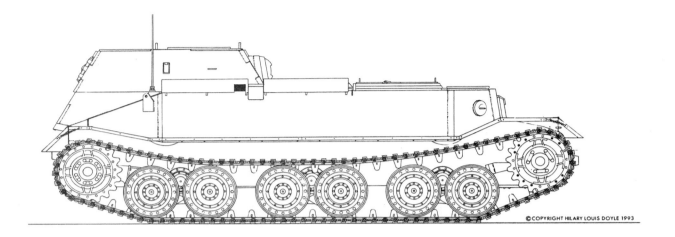

6.) Right-side view: Recovery Ferdinand (early model).

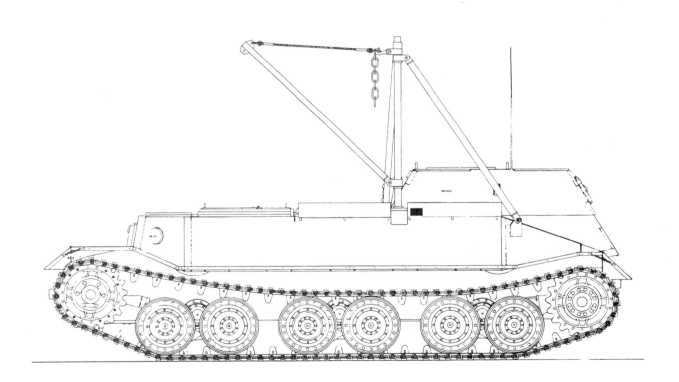

7.) Left-side view: 2-ton crane erected.

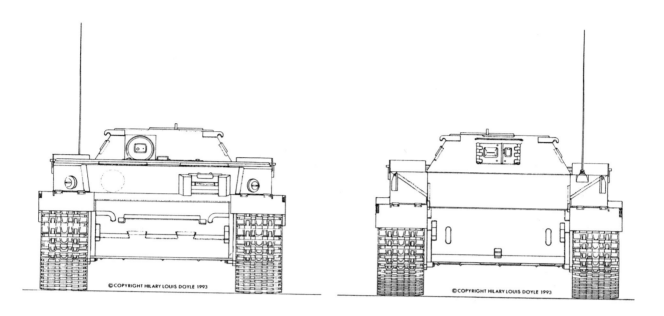

8.) Front view: Original Tiger (P) recovery-vehicle front hull. The mount for the radio-operation machine gun is missing. No supplemental armor.

9.) Rear view: Tool boxes are mounted on both sides of the crew compartment. The split rear hatch was adopted from the one found on a Panzer IV.

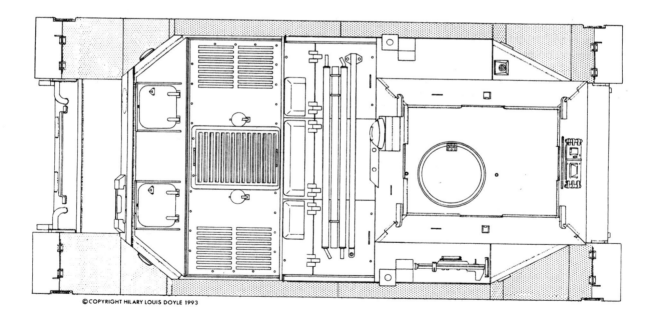

10.) Top view: The 2-ton crane has been broken down to its major sub-assemblies and stowed on the vehicle.

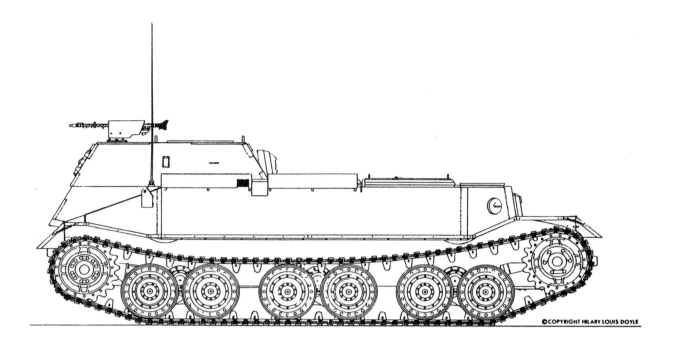

11.) Right-side view: Recovery Elefant (version modified in 1944). The MG 34 is mounted for all-round defense of the vehicle.

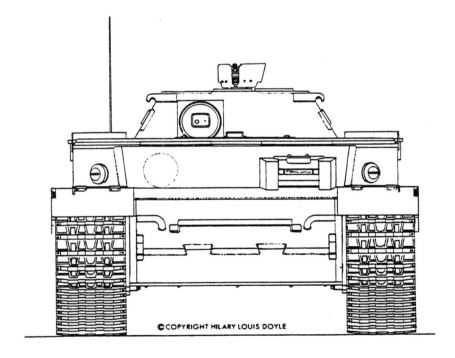

12.) Front view: Recovery Elefant.

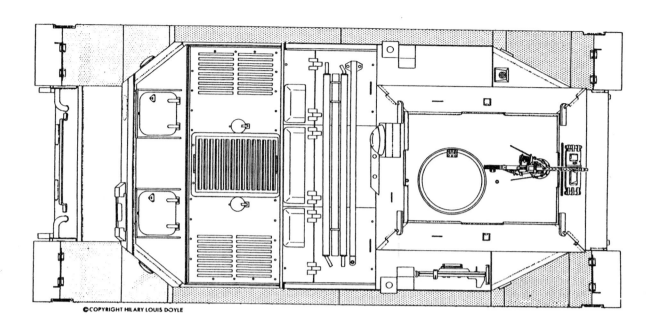

13.) Top view: recovery Elefant.

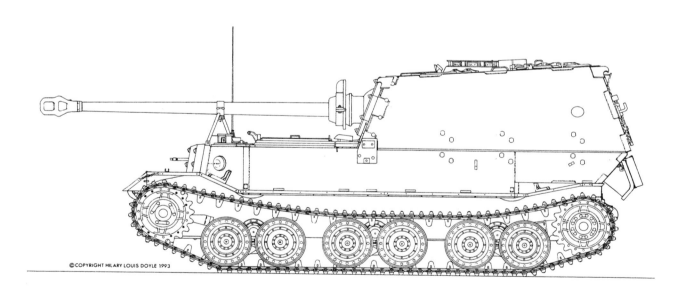

14.) Elefant (after the depot-level overhaul in 1944): New tracks (Kgs 64/640/130) mounted in the opposite direction of the original ones; radio operator's machine gun; additional armored gratings over the radiators; new commander's hatch (a la StuG III); reinforced track-guard covers; tools stowed at the rear; and shrapnel guard in front of the gun mantlet reversed.

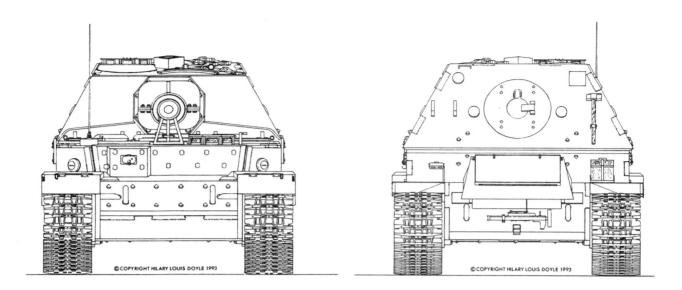

©COPYRIGHT HILARY LOUIS DOYLE 1993

©COPYRIGHT HILARY LOUIS DOYLE 1993

15.) Front view: Driving lights missing; rain gutters attached to the left.and right of the front of the fighting compartment.

16.) Rear view: Vehicle jack and tools stowed at the rear; mounting attachments for spare track blocks mounted on the left rear of the fighting compartment.

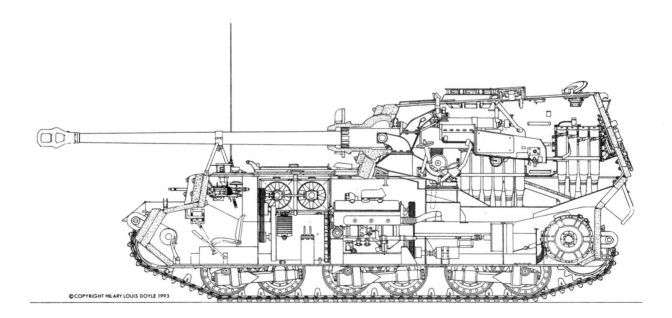

©COPYRIGHT HILARY LOUIS DOYLE 1993

17.) Elefant (cross-section): Driver and radio-operator compartments in the front, separated from the engine compartment by a firewall. Engine compartment, containing the cooling unit and the generator, two Maybach HL 120 engines, the electrical system, as well as generators and ventilators for cooling the transmission. Electric driving motors and hot air exhaust at the rear. Roadwheel torsion bars attached lengthwise. Main gun travel lock on the roof of the hull. Ammunition racks for six rounds each on the leaf and right sides of the fighting compartment. Improved ammunition storage for nine additional rounds in the rear corners of the fighting compartment.

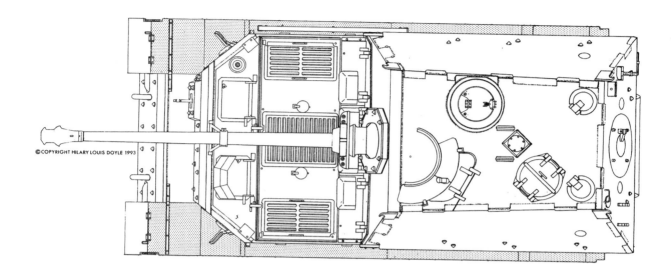

18.) Top view: Overhead view of the new armored cooling covers.

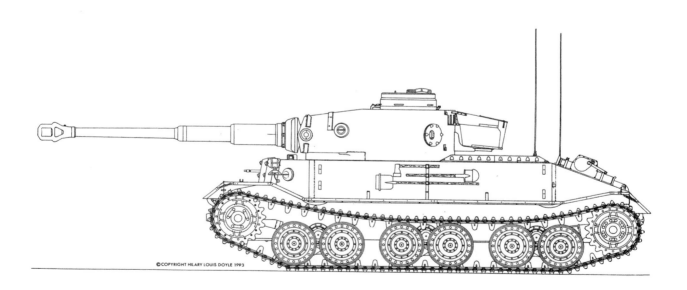

19.) Panzerkampfwagen Tiger (P) VK 4501: Command and control tank for schwere Panzerjäger-Abteilung 653.

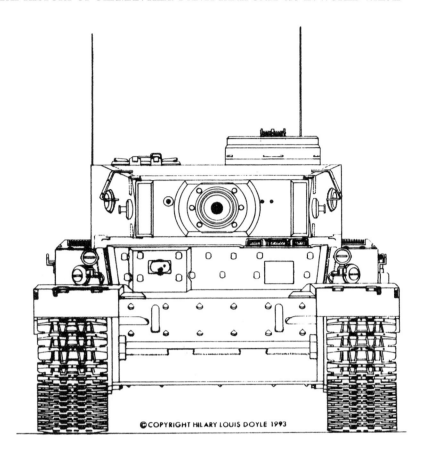

20.) Front view.

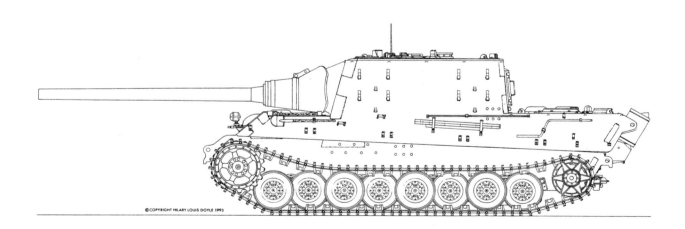

21.) Jagdtiger (Porsche suspension).

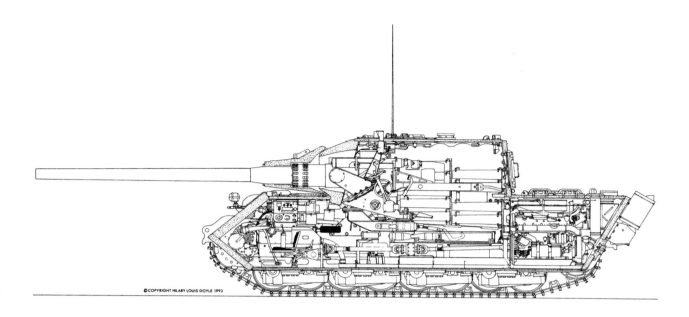

22.) Jagdtiger (Porsche engine): Cross section through the length of a combat-ready vehicle. Driver and radio operator compartments in front. Roadwheel torsion bars mounted lengthwise. Separated ammunition (shell and cartridge) on the walls of the fighting compartment, under the floor at the rear of the fighting compartment and underneath the main-gun mount. Engine compartment with Maybach HL 230 P 45 engine.

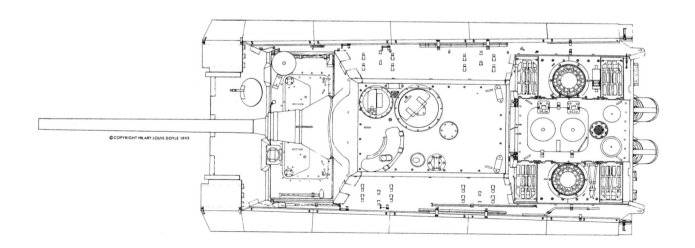

23.) Top view: Jagdtiger (Porsche).

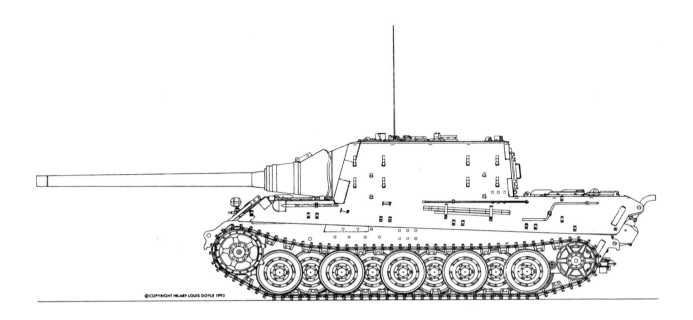

24.) Jagdtiger (Henschel suspension).

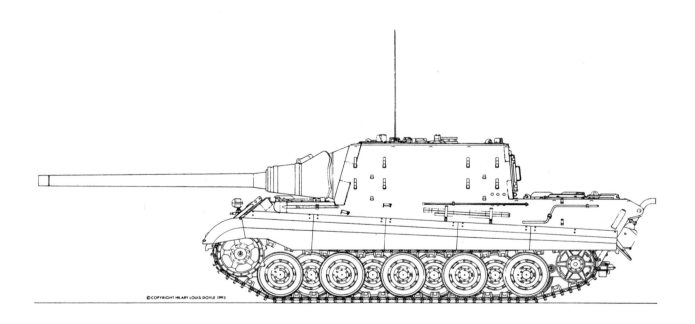

25.) Jagdtiger (Henschel suspension): Vehicle with track guards.

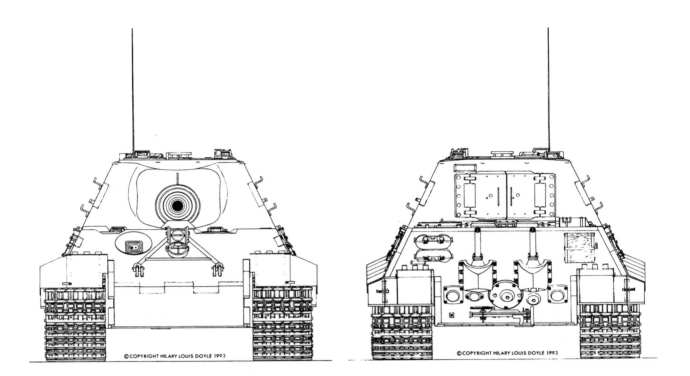

26.) Front view: Jagdtiger (Henschel suspension).   **27.) Rear view: Jagdtiger (Henschel suspension).**

APPENDIX

COMPARISON OF WWII GERMAN ARMY RANKS TO PRESENT-DAY US ARMY RANKS

ENLISTED

US Army	German Army	Waffen-SS
Private	*Schütze*	*SS-Schütze*
Private First Class	*Oberschütze*	*SS-Oberschütze*
Corporal	*Gefreiter*	*SS-Sturmmann*
(Senior Corporal)	*Obergefreiter*	*SS-Rottenführer*
(Staff Corporal)	*Stabsgefreiter*	(None)

NONCOMMISSIONED OFFICERS

US Army	German Army	Waffen-SS
Sergeant	*Unteroffizier*	*SS-Unterscharführer*
Staff Sergeant	*Feldwebel*	*SS-Oberscharführer*
Sergeant First Class	*Oberfeldwebel*	*SS-Hauptscharführer*
Master Sergeant	*Hauptfeldwebel*	*SS-Sturmscharführer*
Sergeant Major	*Stabsfeldwebel*	(None)

OFFICERS

US Army	German Army	Waffen-SS
Lieutenant	*Leutnant*	*SS-Untersturmführer*
First Lieutenant	*Oberleutnant*	*SS-Obersturmführer*
Captain	*Hauptmann*	*SS-Hauptsturmführer*
Major	*Major*	*SS-Sturmbannführer*
Lieutenant Colonel	*Oberstleutnant*	*SS-Obersturmbannführer*

OFFICERS

US Army	German Army	Waffen-SS
Colonel	*Oberst*	*SS-Oberführer* or
		SS-Standartenführer
Brigadier General	*Generalmajor*	*SS-Brigadeführer*
Major General	*Generalleutnant*	*SS-Gruppenführer*
Lieutenant General	*General der Panzertruppen* etc.	*SS-Obergruppenführer*
General	*Generaloberst*	*SS-Oberstgruppenführer*
General of the Army	*Feldmarschall*	*Reichsführer-SS*

GERMAN ARMY COMBAT AWARDS

Knight's Cross to the Iron Cross with
Oak Leaves, Swords and Diamonds
Knight's Cross to the Iron Cross with
Oak Leaves and Swords
Knight's Cross to the Iron Cross with
Oak Leaves
Knights Cross to the Iron Cross
German Cross in Gold
Iron Cross, First Class
Iron Cross, Second Class

It is very difficult to compare German decorations for valor with those of contemporary armies. An American soldier could receive a Distinguished Service Cross or Medal of Honor (the nation's second and first highest awards for valor, respectively) for an incredibly heroic deed, without having received any prior decorations for valor. It was not uncommon to see Medal of Honor winners with no other decorations for valor. German soldiers, on the other hand, received decorations for valor in succession, starting with the Iron Cross, Second Class. Individuals received a Knight's Cross as a first award for exceptional heroism on some rare occasions, but the Oak Leaves (or higher) were never awarded as a first decoration for valor. The award of the Knight's Cross generally followed awards of the Iron Crosses in almost all cases. The German Cross was an intermediate award that bridged the gap between the Iron Cross and Knight's Cross, but it was not a stepping stone to the Knight's Cross. The German Cross in Gold was given for heroism in combat.

Only a small handful of German soldiers received the Diamonds to the Knight's Cross during the entire six years of the Second World War. It is probably held in the highest esteem of any award that has ever been created. Oberst Hans Rudel, the famous Stuka pilot, was the only recipient of a special award of Gold Oak Leaves in addition to the Diamonds. This was for an incredible record of destroying more 500 enemy tanks and one battleship. Officers receive the lion's share of the higher decorations in most armies and this was even more prevalent in the German military. Although some enlisted soldiers received the Knight's Cross, the Oak Leaves and above were reserved almost exclusively for officers. It was not uncommon for a ground or naval commander to receive such a decoration for the performance of his entire unit. Indeed, general officers were awarded higher levels of the Knight's cross for having contributed significantly to the final outcome of a battle or campaign. Pilots more often received them for personal performance and valor, with a number of "kills" or similar verifiable achievement associated with each successive level of the award.

BIBLIOGRAPHY

PUBLISHED SOURCES

"Anzio—Then and Now" in *After the Battle*, Number 52, 1986.

Armored Fighting Vehicles of Germany in WWII. New York: Arco Publishing Company, 1978.

Auerbach, William. "Last of the Panzers" in *Tanks Illustrated No. 9*. London: Arms and Armour Press, 1984.

Buffetaut, Yves. *Au Coeur du Reich*. Paris: n.p., 1993

————. *La Campagne d'Allemagne Rhin et Danube*. Paris: n.p., 1992.

Chamberlain, Doyle, and Jentz. *Encyclopedia of German Tanks of WWII*. London: Arms and Armour Press, 1978.

Chamberlain and Milsom. *Self-Propelled Antitank and Antiaircraft Guns*. London: MacDonald and Janes, 1975.

Carell, Paul. *Verbrannte Erde*. Frankfurt am Main / Berlin: Ullstein-Verlag, 1978.

————. *Der Rußland-Feldzug fotografiert von Soldaten*. Frankfurt am Main and Berlin: Ullstein-Verlag, 1968.

Culver, Bruce. *Panzer Colours 3*. London: Arms and Armour Press, 1984.

Davies, W. J. K. *Panzerjäger*. London: Almark Publishing, 1979.

Die 29. Panzer-Grenadier-Division (Falke-Division) 1936–1945. Friedberg: Podzun-Pallas-Verlag, 1984.

Eiermann, Richard, and Patrick Remm. *Kraichgau 1945. Band: 1. Kriegsende und Neubeginn*. Ubstadt-Weiher: Heimatverein Kraichgau e.V., Sonderveröffentlichung Nr. 12, Verlag Regional Kultur, 1995.

Elfrath / Scheibert. *Panzer in Rußland*. Friedberg: Podzun-Verlag, 1971.

Engelmann, Joachim / Scheibert, Horst. *Deutsche Artillerie 1939–1945*. N.p.: C. A. Starke Verlag, 1974.

Engelmann, Joachim. *Zitadelle 1943*. Friedberg: Podzun-Verlag. 1979.

Euler, Helmuth. *ntscheidungsschlacht an Rhein und Ruhr*. Stuttgart: Motorbuch-Verlag, 1980.

Feist and Culver. *Tiger*. Bellingham, Washington: Ryton Publications, 1992.

Feist and Dario. *Panzerjäger*. Carrolton: Squadron Signal Publications, 1972.

Fellgiebel, Peer. *Die Ritterkreuzträger des Eisernen Kreuzes 1939–1945*. Friedberg: Podzun-Verlag, 1986.

Fricke, Gerd. "'Fester Platz' Tarnopol 1944" in *Einzelschriften zur militärischen Geschichte des Zweiten Weltkrieges*. Freiburg and Breisgau: Verlag Rombach, n.d.

Fürbringer, Herbert. *Die 9. SS Panzer-Division*. Paris: Edition Heimdal, 1984.

Nehring, Walter. *Die Geschichte der deutschen Panzerwaffe 1916–1945*. Berlin: Propyläen-Verlag, 1969.

German Tanks of World War Two. N.p. (Japan): Koku-Fan, 1976.

"German Heavy Tank Tiger in War" in *Tank Magazine*. N.p.: n.p., 1982.

"German Experimental Tanks and Heavy AFV's" in *Tank Magazine*. N.p. (Japan): Delta Publishing, 1988.

"German Army, Volume I" in *Tank Magazine*. N.p. (Japan): Delta Publishing, 1993.

"German Army, Volume II" in *Tank Magazine*. N.p. (Japan): Delta Publishing, 1994.

Guderian, Heinz. *Erinnerungen eines Soldaten*. Stuttgart: Motorbuch-Verlag, 1994.

Haupt, Werner. *Endkampf im Westen, 1945*. Friedberg: Podzun-Verlag, 1979.

Healy, Mark. *Kursk 1943* (Campaign Series No. 16). London: Osprey Military, 1992.

Jentz, Thomas L. et. al. *Tiger I* (New Vanguard No. 1). London: Osprey Military, 1993.

———. *Tiger II* (New Vanguard No. 1). London: Osprey Military, 1993.

John, Antonius, Prof. *Kursk 43—Szenen einer Entscheidungsschlacht*. N.p.: H+H Konzept Verlag, 1993.

Kleine and Kühn. *Tiger—Die Geschichte einer legendären Waffe 1942–1945*. Stuttgart: Motorbuch-Verlag, 1976.

Kurowski, Franz, and Gottfried Tornau. *Sturmartillerie 1939–1945*. Stuttgart: Motorbuch-Verlag, 1978.

Kurowski, Franz. *Von der Polizeigruppe z.b.V. "Wecke" zum Fallschirmpanzerkorps "Hermann Göring"*. Osnabrück: Biblio-Verlag, n.d.

Leiwig, Heinz. *Finale 1945 Rhein-Main*. N.p.: Droste Verlag, 1985.

Le Tissier, Tony. *Der Kampf um Berlin 1945*. N.p.: Ullstein-Verlag, 1994.

Von Manteuffel, Hasso. *Die 7. Panzer-Division*. Friedberg: Podzun-Verlag, 1965.

Naumann, Joachim. *Die 4. Panzer-Division*. Bonn: Selbstverlag, 1989.

Nosbüsch, Johannes Prof. "Damit es nicht vergessen wird". Landau: Pfälzische Verlagsanstalt GmbH, 1986.

Otte, Alfred. *Die weißen Spiegel*. Friedberg: Podzun-Verlag, n.d.

Oswald, Werner. Kraftfahrzeuge und Panzer. Stuttgart: Motorbuch-Verlag (11th edition), 1982.

Pallude, J.-P. *Battle of the Bulge—Then and Now*. London: After the Battle, 1984.

"Panzerkampfwagen VI Tiger" in *Koku-Fan Magazine*. N.p. (Japan): n.p., 1972.

Piekalkiewicz, Janusz. *Krieg der Panzer 1939–1945*. N.p.: Bertelsmann, n.d.

Piekalkiewicz, Janusz. *Unternehmen Zitadelle*. N.p.: Lübbe-Verlag, 1983.

Quarrie, Bruce. *Fallschirmpanzer-Division "Hermann Göring"* (Vanguard No. 4). London: Osprey, 1978.

Scheibert, Horst. *Die "Tiger"-Familie*. Friedberg: Podzun-Pallas-Verlag, 1979.

———. *Die Träger des Deutschen Kreuzes in Gold*. Friedberg: Podzun-Pallas-Verlag, 1992.

———. *Panzerjäger und Sturmgeschütze*. Friedberg: Podzun-Pallas-Verlag, n.d.

———. *Das war Guderian*. Friedberg: Podzun-Pallas-Verlag, n.d.

———. *Kampf und Untergang der deutschen Panzertruppe*. Friedberg: Podzun-Pallas-Verlag, n.d.

Schmitz and Thies. *Die Truppenkennzeichen, Band I: Heer*. Osnabrück: Biblio-Verlag, 1987.

Schmitz, G. *Die 16. Panzer-Grenadier-Division*. Friedberg: Podzun-Pallas-Verlag, n.d.

Schneider, Wolfgang. *Elefant—Jagdtiger—Sturmtiger* (Waffen Arsenal Band 99). Friedberg: Podzun-Pallas-Verlag, n.d.

Spielberger, Walter J. *Profile: Panzerjäger Tiger (P) Elefant*. N.p.: n.p., n.d.

———. *Der Panzerkampfwagen Tiger und seine Abarten*. Stuttgart: Motorbuch-Verlag, 1977.

———. *Spezial-Panzerfahrzeuge*. Stuttgart: Motorbuch-Verlag, 1987.

———. *Schwere Jagdpanzer*. Stuttgart: Motorbuch-Verlag, 1993.

———. *Sturmgeschütze*. Stuttgart: Motorbuch-Verlag, 1991.

Spielberger and Feist. *Panzerkampfwagen VI Tiger I and Tiger II "Königstiger"*. N.p.: Feist Publications, 1968.

Stöber, Hans. *Die Flugabwehrverbände der Waffen-SS*. N.p.: Schütz-Verlag, n.d.

Strauß, Franz-Josef. *Die 2. Panzer-Division*. Friedberg: Podzun-Verlag, n.d.

"Tank Destroyers" in *Koku-Fan Magazine*. N.p. (Japan): n.p., 1977.

Tieke, Wilhelm. *Das Ende zwischen Oder und Elbe, Der Kampf um Berlin 1945*. Stuttgart: Motorbuch-Verlag, 1992.

The Tiger Tanks. N.p.: Aero Publishers, Inc., 1966.

Time-Life. *Der Feldzug in Italien*. N.p.: n.p., n.d.

Time-Life. *Die Ardennenoffensive*. N.p.: n.p., n.d.

Time-Life. *Der Vormarsch der Roten Armee*. N.p.: n.p., n.d.

Time-Life. *Entscheidung im Westen.* N.p.: n.p., n.d.

Thomas, Franz et. al. *Sturmartillerie im Bild 1940–1945.* Osnabrück: Biblio-Verlag, 1986.

United States War Department Technical Manual. *Handbook on German Military Forces.* 15 March 1945

Waffen-Revue (Issues 65, 66 and 67). Schwäbisch Hall: Verlag Journal-Schwend GmbH.

Wise, Terence. *D-Day to Berlin.* London: Arms and Armour Press, 1979.

Wörn, Karl. *Schwetzingen, lebendige Stadt.* Schwetzingen: Schwetzinger Verlagsdruckerei GmbH, 1968

Zaloga, Steven J. *Battle of the Bulge* (Tanks Illustrated No. 2). London: Arms and Armour Press, 1983.

Zaloga / Grandsen. *The Eastern Front 1941–1945.* London: Arms and Armour Press, 1993.

UNPUBLISHED SOURCES

Daily Logs of the 1./Sturmgeschütz-Abteilung 197.

First-hand accounts of Johann Spielmann, Heinz Steinwachs and Horst Theis (3./schwere Panzer-jäger-Abteilung 653)

Diary notes from Peter Kohns (2./schwere Panzerjäger-Abteilung 653), Rolf Sabrowsky (3./schwere Panzerjäger-Abteilung 653), Heinrich Skodell (1./Sturmgeschütz-Abteilung 197)

Karlheinz Münch. *Synopsis of Operational Dates, schwere Panzerjäger-Abteilung 653.* Schwetzingen: self-published, 1991.

Calendar entries from Emil Bürgin (1./schwere Panzerjäger-Abteilung 653)

ABOUT THE AUTHOR AND ARTIST

Author Karlheinz Münch works as a mapmaker at the Surveyors Office of the city of Mannheim. After his service in the German Army, his hobby was modeling, but this soon evolved into a keen interest in the history of German armored formations. Since 1986 he has intensively researched the history of the German antitank forces of the World War II era. He has authored the history of this battalion's sister formation, schwere Panzer-Jäger-Abteilung 654 and is also busy at work on a number of other manuscripts on this thematic area.

He has written articles for several specialty magazines and has contributed photo material to other writers. He is married and has one son. Karlheinz lives in Schwetzingen, near Heidelberg. He would appreciate any new material that readers can contribute and may be contacted through the publisher.

Artist Jean Restayn was born in Paris. He is married and has one daughter. An artist with a special interest in military history, he has illustrated many articles and several books for various publishers. He is an author in his own right and has written or co-authored a number of titles for JJ Fedorowicz Publishing, Inc., including *The Battle for Kharkov* and *Operation Citadel*. He is currently finishing up several new photo albums for publication.

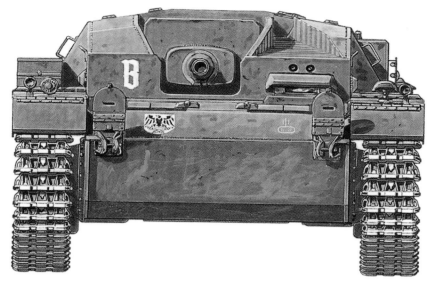

Assault Gun B of the 1./Sturmgeschütz-Abteilung 197, March 1941

1. Batterie

Z2, an Sd.Kfz. 250 Observation Halftrack of the 2./Sturmgeschütz-Abteilung 197 during the Balkans Campaign in April 1941.

Assault Gun Z1 of the 1./Sturmgeschütz-Abteilung 197. This vehicle was commanded by Leutnant Spielmann during the campaign on the Crimea in 1942.

Z3, an Sd.Kfz. 250 Observation Halftrack of the
1./Sturmgeschütz-Abteilung 197 during the
campaign on the Crimea in 1942.

The assault gun commanded by Wilhelm Biermann
of the 3./Sturmgeschütz-Abteilung 197 during the
winter of 1942/43 in the Soviet Union.

Ferdinand of the 3./schwere
Panzerjäger-Abteilung 653 at
Neusiedel (Austria) in May 1943.

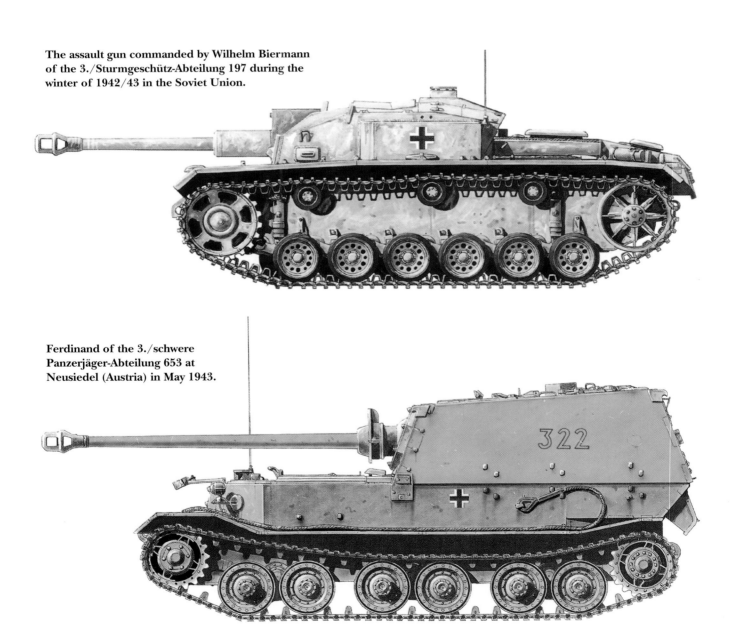

Top left: A white recognition panel of the 1./schwere Panzerjäger-Abteilung 653 during Operation "Zitadelle" in the Orel area on 5 July 1943. Ferdinand 101 was commanded by the company commander, Hauptmann Spielmann. *Top right:* A white recognition panel of the 1./schwere Panzerjäger-Abteilung 653 during Operation "Zitadelle" in the Orel area on 5 July 1943. Ferdinand 111 was commanded by Leutnant Ulbricht.

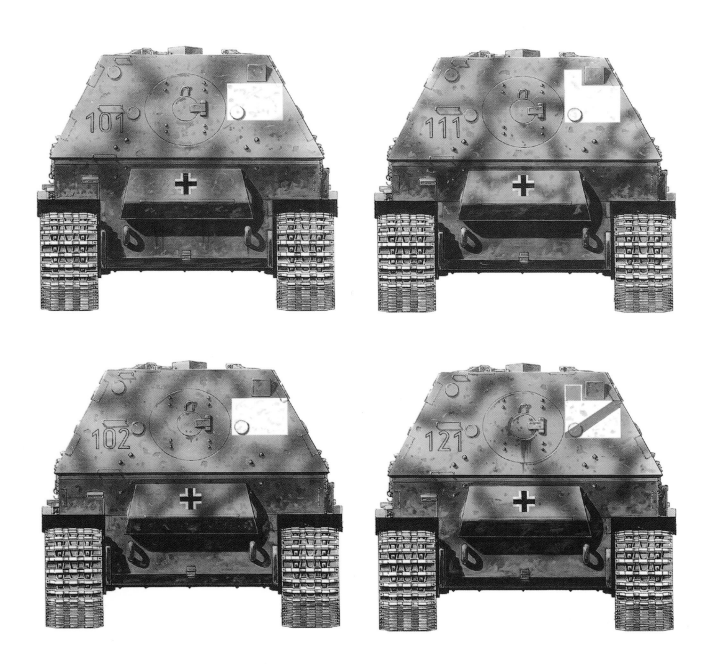

Bottom left: A white recognition panel of the 1./schwere Panzerjäger-Abteilung 653 during Operation "Zitadelle" in the Orel area on 5 July 1943. Ferdinand 102 was commanded by Hauptfeldwebel Madaus. *Bottom right:* A white recognition panel of the 1./schwere Panzerjäger-Abteilung 653 during Operation "Zitadelle" in the Orel area on 5 July 1943. Ferdinand 121 was commanded by Leutnant Löck.

Top left: A white recognition panel of the 1./schwere Panzerjäger-Abteilung 653 during Operation "Zitadelle" in the Orel area on 5 July 1943. Ferdinand 131 is believed to have been commanded by Oberfeldwebel Koss. *Top right:* A red recognition panel of the 2./schwere Panzerjäger-Abteilung 653 during Operation "Zitadelle" in the Orel area on 5 July 1943. Ferdinand 202 was commanded by Hauptfeldwebel Schmidt.

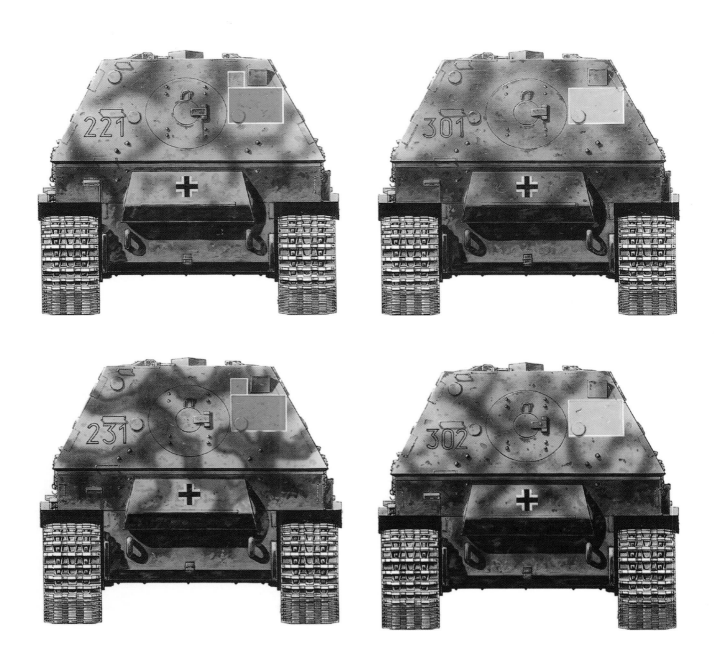

Bottom left: A red recognition panel of the 2./schwere Panzerjäger-Abteilung 653 during Operation "Zitadelle" in the Orel area on 5 July 1943. Ferdinand 201 was commanded by the company commander, Hauptmann Kuntze. *Bottom right:* A red recognition panel of the 2./schwere Panzerjäger-Abteilung 653 during Operation "Zitadelle" in the Orel area on 5 July 1943. Ferdinand 211 was commanded by Leutnant Schrader.

Top left: A red recognition panel of the 2./schwere Panzerjäger-Abteilung 653 during Operation "Zitadelle" in the Orel area on 5 July 1943. Ferdinand 221 was commanded by Leutnant Göttelmann. *Top right:* A yellow recognition panel of the 3./schwere Panzerjäger-Abteilung 653 during Operation "Zitadelle" in the Orel area on 5 July 1943. Ferdinand 301 was commanded by the acting company commander, Oberleutnant Salamon.

Unternehmen "Zitadelle" Orel, 5. Juli 1943
1.Kompanie s.Pz.Jg.Abt.653
(White recognition panel)
Ferdinand 131
Geschützführer: Ofw. Koss (?)

Unternehmen "Zitadelle" Orel, 5. Juli 1943
2.Kompanie s.Pz.Jg.Abt.653
(Red recognition panel)
Ferdinand 202
Geschützführer: Hauptfw. Schmidt

Unternehmen "Zitadelle" Orel, 5. Juli 1943
2.Kompanie s.Pz.Jg.Abt.653
(Red recognition panel)
Ferdinand 201
Geschützführer: Hauptmann Kuntze

Unternehmen "Zitadelle" Orel, 5. Juli 1943
2.Kompanie s.Pz.Jg.Abt.653
(Red recognition panel)
Ferdinand 211
Geschützführer: Leutnant Schrader

Bottom left: A red recognition panel of the 2./schwere Panzerjäger-Abteilung 653 during Operation "Zitadelle" in the Orel area on 5 July 1943. Ferdinand 231 was commanded by Oberfeldwebel Meigen. *Bottom right:* A yellow recognition panel of the 3./schwere Panzerjäger-Abteilung 653 during Operation "Zitadelle" in the Orel area on 5 July 1943. Ferdinand 302 was commanded by Wilhelm Czichochewski.

Top left: A yellow recognition panel of the 3./schwere Panzerjäger-Abteilung 653 during Operation "Zitadelle" in the Orel area on 5 July 1943. Ferdinand 311 was commanded by Oberleutnant Lange. *Top right:* A yellow recognition panel of the 3./schwere Panzerjäger-Abteilung 653 during Operation "Zitadelle" in the Orel area on 5 July 1943. Ferdinand 334 was commanded by Fahnenjunker (Officer Candidate) Opitz.

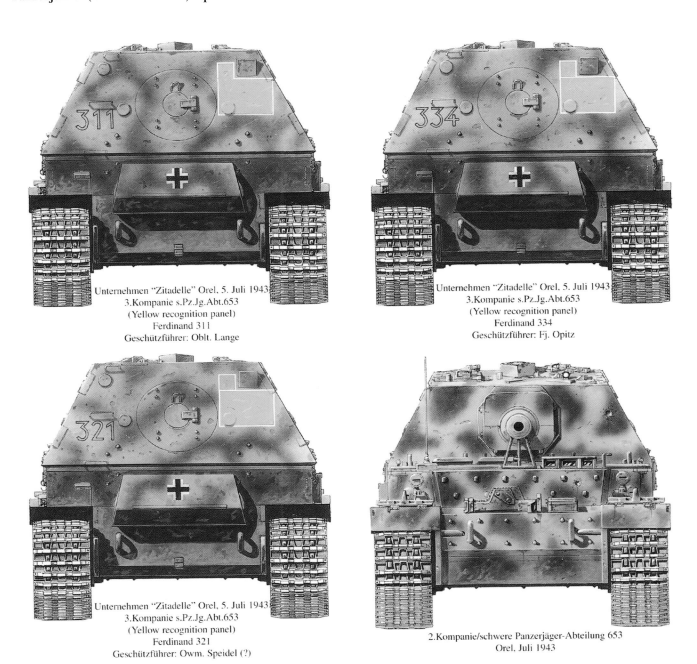

Unternehmen "Zitadelle" Orel, 5. Juli 1943
3.Kompanie s.Pz.Jg.Abt.653
(Yellow recognition panel)
Ferdinand 311
Geschützführer: Oblt. Lange

Unternehmen "Zitadelle" Orel, 5. Juli 1943
3.Kompanie s.Pz.Jg.Abt.653
(Yellow recognition panel)
Ferdinand 334
Geschützführer: Fj. Opitz

Unternehmen "Zitadelle" Orel, 5. Juli 1943
3.Kompanie s.Pz.Jg.Abt.653
(Yellow recognition panel)
Ferdinand 321
Geschützführer: Owm. Speidel (?)

2.Kompanie/schwere Panzerjäger-Abteilung 653
Orel, Juli 1943

Bottom left: A yellow recognition panel of the 3./schwere Panzerjäger-Abteilung 653 during Operation "Zitadelle" in the Orel area on 5 July 1943. Ferdinand 321 is believed to have been commanded by Oberwachtmeister Speidel. *Bottom right:* A Ferdinand of the 2./schwere Panzerjäger-Abteilung 653 during the fighting at Orel in July 1943.

The Ferdinand of Leutnant Löck of the 1./schwere Panzerjäger-Abteilung 653 during the fighting at Orel in July 1943.

A Sturmpanzer IV of the Headquarters Company of Sturmpanzer-Abteilung 216 during the fighting at Orel in July 1943.

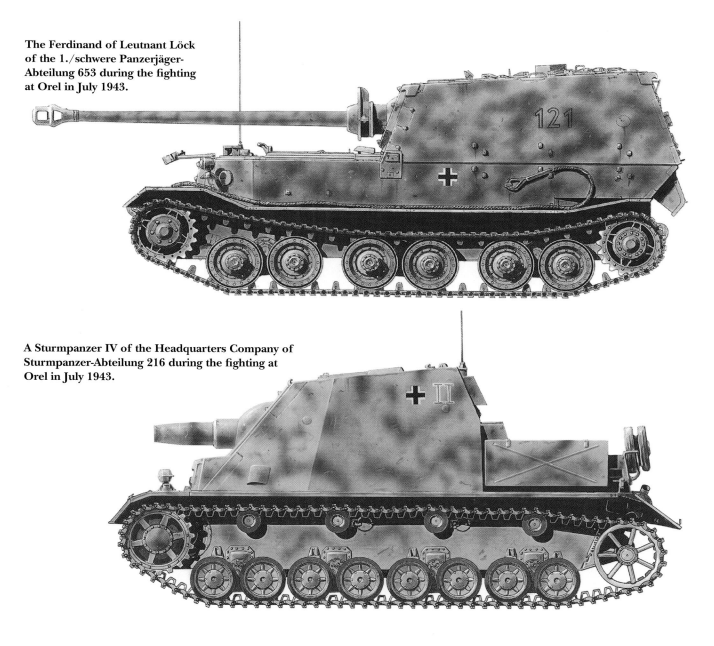
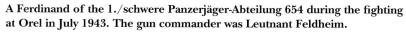

A Ferdinand of the 1./schwere Panzerjäger-Abteilung 654 during the fighting at Orel in July 1943. The gun commander was Leutnant Feldheim.

A Ferdinand of the 2./schwere Panzerjäger-Abteilung 653 during the fighting at Orel in July 1943.

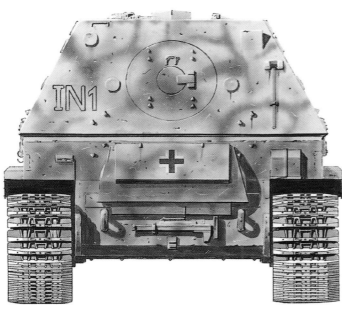

The Ferdinand of Major Baumunk, the commander of Kampfgruppe Nord, at the Saporoshje Bridgehead in September 1943.

A Ferdinand of the 2./schwere Panzerjäger-Abteilung 653 at the Saporoshje Bridgehead in September 1943.

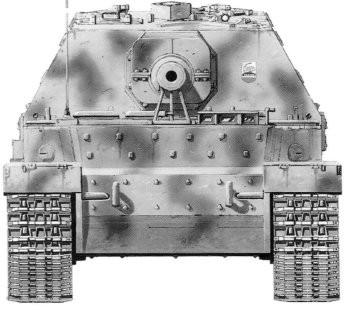

Stabs – Kompanie

Stabs – Kompanie

Stabs – Kompanie

1. Batterie

1. / 216

1. / 653

2. Batterie

3. Batterie

2. / 216

2. / 653

Werkstatt

Battery insignia of Sturmgeschütz-Abteilung 197, featuring the "Cannon Eagle".

3. / 216

3. / 653

Versorgung

Versorgung

Werkstatt

Werkstatt

Unit and formation insignia of schweres Panzerjäger-Regiment 656 during the period from September to December 1943. (Versorgung = Supply; Werkstatt = Maintenance)

The "death's head" featured on one of the Ferdinande of the 3./schwere Panzerjäger-Abteilung 653 at the Saporoshje Bridgehead in September 1943.

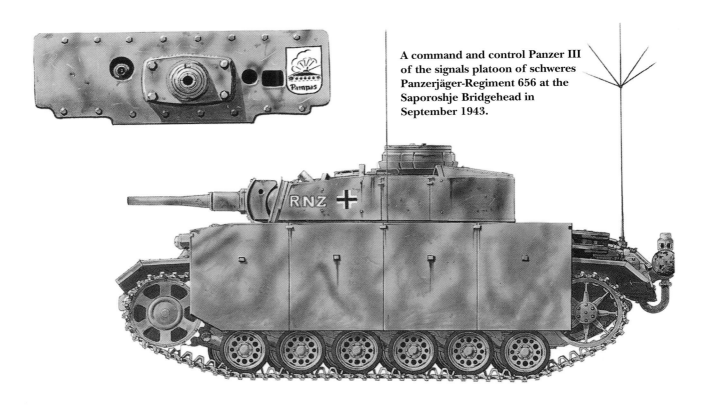

A command and control Panzer III of the signals platoon of schweres Panzerjäger-Regiment 656 at the Saporoshje Bridgehead in September 1943.

A Ferdinand of the 1./schwere Panzerjäger-Abteilung 653 at the Nikopol Bridgehead in November and December 1943.

New battalion insignia of the schwere Panzerjäger-Abteilung 653—the "Nibelungen Sword"—effective March 1944.

Front view of the same vehicle.

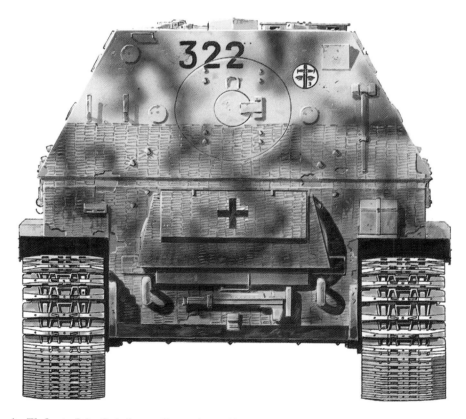

An Elefant of the 3./schwere Panzerjäger-Abteilung 653 during the fighting in the Galicia region of the Soviet Union in April 1944.

A Elefant of the 1./schwere
Panzerjäger-Abteilung 653
in Italy in May 1944.

Front and rear views of an Elefant of the
2./schwere Panzerjäger-Abteilung 653 during
the fighting in the Galicia region of the Soviet
Union in May 1944.

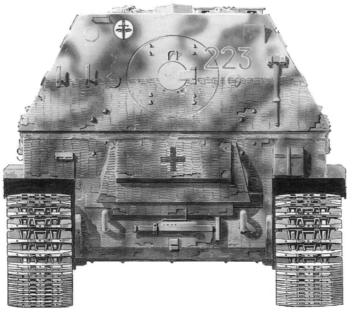

A recovery Panther modified by the addition of a fixed Panzer IV turret with operable main gun. This vehicle was assigned to the Recovery Platoon of the Headquarters Company of schwere Panzerjäger-Abteilung 653 and was used in Galicia in the Soviet Union in June 1944.

A field-made Flakpanzer of the Flak Platoon of the headquarters Company of schwere Panzerjäger-Abteilung 653. This vehicle was based on the chassis of a captured T 34 and employed in Galicia in the Soviet Union in June 1944.

A command and control Tiger VK 4501 (P) of the battalion headquarters in Galicia in the Soviet Union in June 1944.

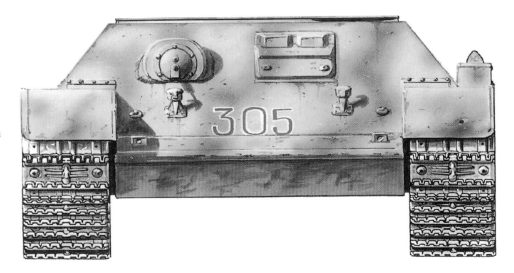

Field-made ammunition carrier of the 3./schwere Panzerjäger-Abteilung 653 in Galicia in the Soviet Union in July 1944. The vehicle was based on the chassis of a captured T 34.

Left: An Elefant with the improved rear hatch. Four of these vehicles were so modified and saw operations starting in June and July 1944.

Below: A Recovery Elefant of the 3./schwere Panzerjäger-Abteilung 653 in Galicia in the Soviet Union in July 1944.

An Elefant of the 2./schwere Panzerjäger-Abteilung 653 in Galicia in the Soviet Union in August 1944.

A Jagdtiger (Porsche) of the Driver Training Platoon of Panzerjäger-Ersatz- und Ausbildungs-Abteilung 17 at Freistadt (Austria) in February 1945.

A Jagdtiger of the 3./schwere Panzerjäger-Abteilung 653 at Neustadt an der Weinstraße in March 1945.

The Jagdtiger of Leutnant Knippenberg of the 1./schwere Panzerjäger-Abteilung 653 at Eppingen (Kraichgau) in April 1945.

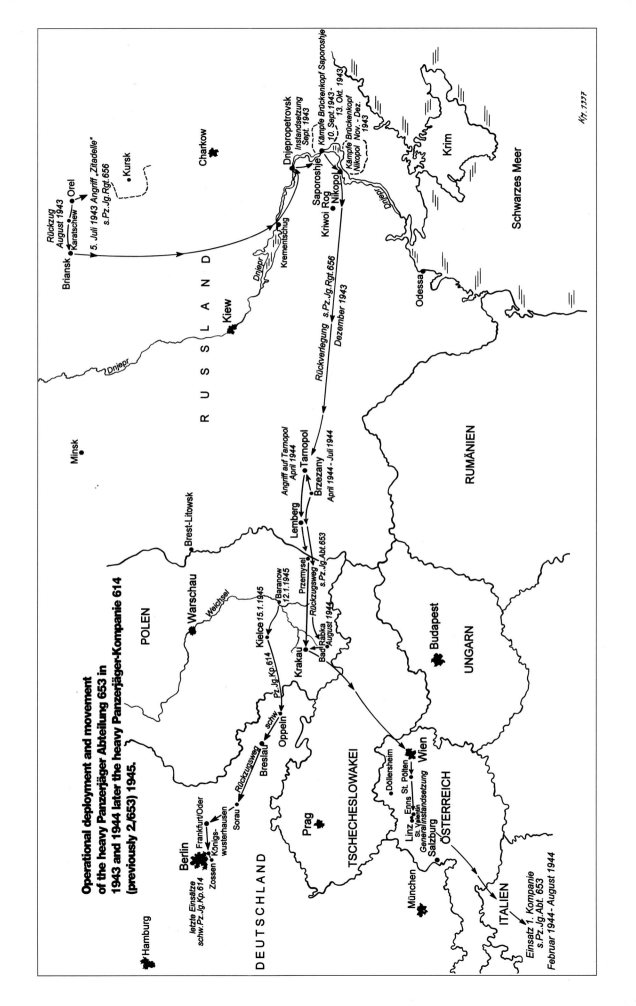

Operational deployment and movement of the heavy Panzerjäger Abteilung 653 in 1943 and 1944 later the heavy Panzerjäger-Kompanie 614 (previously 2./653) 1945.

Kt. 1337

Schwarzes Meer

Krim

RUMÄNIEN

UNGARN

Budapest

ITALIEN

ÖSTERREICH

Einsatz 1. Kompanie s.Pz.Jg.Abt. 653 Februar 1944 - August 1944

Wien

St. Pölten
Dollersheim
Linz Enns
St. Valentin *Generalinstandsetzung*
Salzburg

München

TSCHECHESLOWAKEI

Prag

DEUTSCHLAND

Hamburg

Berlin
Frankfurt/Oder
Königs-
wusterhausen
Zossen
Sorau
letzte Einsätze schw.Pz.Jg.Kp.614

Rückzugsweg
Breslau
Oppelin

schw.
Pz.Jg.Kp.614

Kielce 15.1.1945
Baranow 12.1.1945
Przemysel
s.Pz.Jg.Abt.653
Rückzugsweg

Krakau
Bad Rabka
August 1944

POLEN

Warschau

Weichsel

Brest-Litowsk

Minsk

Lemberg
Brzezany
April 1944 - Juli 1944

Tarnopol
Angriff auf Tarnopol April 1944

R U S S L A N D

Dnjepr

Kiew

Dnjepr

Krementschug

Charkow

Kursk

Briansk
Karatschew Orel
Rückzug August 1943

5. Juli 1943 Angriff „Zitadelle" s.Pz.Jg.Rgt. 656

Dnjepropetrovsk
Instandsetzung Sept. 1943

Saporoshje
Kriwoi Rog
Nikopol

Kämpfe Brückenkopf Saporoshje 10. Sept. 1943 - 13. Okt. 1943

Kämpfe Brückenkopf Nikopol Nov. - Dez. 1943

Rückverlegung s.Pz.Jg.Rgt.656 Dezember 1943

Odessa

Dnjepr